OTHER A TO Z GUIDES FROM
THE SCARECROW PRESS, INC.

The A to Z of Australian and New Zealand Cinema

Albert Moran
Errol Vieth

The A to Z Guide Series, No. 48

The Scarecrow Press, Inc.
Lanham • Toronto • Plymouth, UK
2009

Published by Scarecrow Press, Inc.
A wholly owned subsidary of
The Rowman & Littlefield Publishing Group, Inc.
4501 Forbes Boulevard, Suite 200, Lanham, Maryland 20706
http://www.scarecrowpress.com

Estover Road, Plymouth PL6 7PY, United Kingdom

British Library Cataloguing in Publication Information Available

Library of Congress Cataloging-in-Publication Data

The hardback version of this book was cataloged by the Library of Congress as
follows:

Moran, Albert.
  Historical dictionary of Australian and New Zealand cinema / Albert Moran,
Errol Vieth.
    p. cm. — (Historical dictionaries of literature and the arts ; 6)
  Includes bibliographical references.
  1. Motion pictures—Australia—Dictionaries. 2. Motion pictures—New
Zealand—Dictionaries. I. Title: Australian and New Zealand cinema. II. Vieth,
Errol, 1950– III. Title. IV. Series.
PN1993.5.A8M66 2005
791.43'0994'03—dc22   2005015419

ISBN 978-0-8108-6831-1 (pbk. : alk. paper)
ISBN 978-0-8108-6347-7 (ebook)

⊚™ The paper used in this publication meets the minimum requirements of
American National Standard for Information Sciences—Permanence of
Paper for Printed Library Materials, ANSI/NISO Z39.48-1992.

Printed in the United States of America

for our parents:

Marjorie Avery and the late Eric Vieth
and the late Albert and Susanna Moran.

Contents

Editor's Foreword

Not so very long ago, it might have seemed odd to start this subseries of volumes on national cinemas with Australia and New Zealand. They were rather dull, peripheral places that did not generate many films and whose topics were not necessarily of interest to outsiders. Although they did entertain the locals, and sometimes showed up in film festivals, that was about it.

Times have changed. In both countries, the film industry has matured impressively and they are now churning out first-rate films, conceived by excellent directors and producers and featuring casts that include local actors and actresses who are so well known abroad that many fans do not even realize where they come from. Some of the more recent films are about the region, but many more are "international," of interest to a very broad public. Even more extraordinary, films which, earlier, would certainly have been produced in Hollywood are now being filmed in Australia and New Zealand, and not only for cost reasons. This latter phenomenon, by the way, stems partly from the role played by government that, even in this highly entrepreneurial sector, has worked uncommonly well. Thus, in more ways than one, Australia and New Zealand have moved center stage.

The A to Z of Australian and New Zealand Cinema adopts the standard format of other books in the Literature and Arts series with one important variation. The national cinemas of Australia and New Zealand, although increasingly integrated with one another, still have many differences. Some are purely historical, others remain to the present day. Thus, there are two separate parts, although they are cross-referenced to one another. The two chronologies trace their evolution over time. The two dictionary sections include entries on significant actors, directors, producers, and others, as well as on the relevant companies and government or private sector bodies. There are also entries on major genres and themes and some of the outstanding films. The single bibliography, fairly extensive and broken down by key topics, offers further reading.

This volume was written by two leading scholars living in Australia but with substantial exposure to New Zealand. Dr. Moran is presently senior lecturer at the School of Film, Media and Cultural Studies of Griffith University in Queensland. During more than a quarter century in academia, most of this at Griffith University, he has taught and written about many aspects of the cinema and television. He has written numerous articles and authored, edited, or coedited nearly 20 books on cinema and television. Dr. Vieth is senior lecturer at the School of Contemporary Communication of Central Queensland University. He has also lectured and written widely, much of this related to cinema and in particular science fiction films. Their combined knowledge, and substantial experience in conveying it to others, has resulted in a handy guide that is not only informative but very readable.

Jon Woronoff
Series Editor

Preface

This book will assist researchers, students, teachers, and other readers to explore and understand the nature and achievements of the Australian and New Zealand film industries — especially if they have minimal prior knowledge. For that reason, the introduction and chronology sections are quite detailed. In themselves, they are sufficiently extensive to acquaint readers with the breadth of the industry, and provide specific information, which is more readily found in the dictionary section.

The historical dictionary serves as a comprehensive resource. It is not an exhaustive encyclopedia nor is it a record of all films. Rather it contains the films that fared well, both commercially and critically, in Australia or New Zealand, and in the international market. Similarly, we also include films that are otherwise significant as examples of a genre, style, or a particular theme. The general student at this point in time might not be interested in the vast numbers of missing films from the silent era, so those films are only touched on. Actors and actresses are reasonably well represented, but with the space constraints, many worthy players have been omitted. Similar restrictions apply to directors and other crew. Several texts provide exhaustive detail of the Australian and New Zealand industries, but some of those books are now quite old, and they do not offer the coherence of the present volume. This dictionary complements these, rather than replaces them. Readers will learn about the booms and busts of the two industries, as well as the relation of these infrastructures with the rest of the world.

Any reference work that seeks to be compact rather than exhaustive must always face the problem of selection. We are aware that our criteria of inclusion have been that of an informed subjectivity. With a great deal of experience as both teachers and researchers on the subject of this book, we have sought to include whatever we deem necessary to sustain the interest and needs of our students and other readers, but being careful not to overburden the user with material that is irrelevant or tangential.

The book is comprised of three sections: Australia, New Zealand, and the Bibliography. This sectioning has advantages and disadvantages. It allows a differentiated discussion of the two industries, given that both function in contexts that are different: for example, not only are the government mechanisms different, so too are the subjects of the films. The notion of national identity, for example, brings to mind different ideas and representations. The disadvantage is that the dividing line between the two industries is quite blurred. Cast and crew move freely between the countries, appearing in and making films in both places. Thus, people born in one country, retaining their nationality, work in the other. In this sense, the divide between them is artificial. However, the bibliography is not divided because this would be an artificial divide, given that many books deal with both the Australian and New Zealand industries and the films of both countries.

Many people made this book possible. First, those people who have worked in documenting the film industry; that is, the librarians, archivists and other analysts, critics, and writers in Australia and New Zealand. Second, the researchers associated with this book have contributed immensely. David Adair and Di Oliver assisted Albert Moran with his research, and Christina Hunt assisted Errol Vieth. Geraldine Connor assisted with formatting the bibliography. Third, our families provided the supporting infrastructure for this project and we are forever in their debt. Finally, we would like to thank Jon Woronoff at Scarecrow Press who first suggested the project and has been the soul of advice and patience.

Errol Vieth
Central Queensland University
Rockhampton, Queensland, Australia

Albert Moran
Griffith University
Brisbane, Queensland, Australia

Reader's Note

This book is divided into two sections, focusing on Australian and New Zealand cinema, respectively. In each section, references to another entry are indicated in boldface type. In addition, the entries in one section contain references to entries in the other section of the book. Thus, the entry for Jane Campion is in the New Zealand section, and this entry is cross-referenced in the Australian section by an asterisk before the name of Jane Campion. For example, in the Australian section is an entry for the Australian Film Television and Radio School, containing the text, "Directors include ***Jane Campion**, ..."

The term "Commonwealth" in the Australia section means the federation of Australian states and territories that exist within the geographical place called Australia. A "state" in Australia refers to the next political level under "Commonwealth." States include Queensland, New South Wales, Victoria, Tasmania, South Australia, and Western Australia.

The currency used in the Australia section is the Australian dollar, and that in the New Zealand section is the New Zealand dollar. Sometimes, other currencies are used and are indicated by the normal prefix, thus "US$."

AUSTRALIA

Acronyms and Abbreviations

ABC	Australian Broadcasting Corporation (formerly, Commission)
ACCC	Australian Competition and Consumer Commission
ACMI	Australian Centre for the Moving Image
ACTF	Australian Children's Television Foundation
AFC	Australian Film Commission
AFDC	Australian Film Development Corporation
AFI	Australian Film Institute
AFPA	Australian Film Producers Association
AFTRS	Australian Film Television and Radio School
AFTS	Australian Film and Television School
ALMA	American Latino Media Arts
ASCAP	American Society of Composers, Authors, and Publishers
AWU	Australian Workers Union
BAFTA	British Academy of Film and Television Arts
BCC	Birch, Carroll and Coyle
BIFF	Brisbane International Film Festival
BFI	British Film Institute
CFU	Commonwealth Film Unit (when it is used in a British context, however, it stands for Crown Film Unit)
DAT	Digital Audio Tape
FCCA	Film Critics Circle Australia
FFC	Film Finance Corporation Australia
FTPA	Film and Television Producers Association
GUO	Greater Union Organisation
HMAS	His (or Her) Majesty's Australian Ship
IFFPA	Independent Feature Film Producers Association
MGM	Metro Goldwyn Mayer

MP	Member of Parliament
NIDA	National Institute of Dramatic Art
NSWFTO	New South Wales Film and Television Office
OFLC	Office of Film and Literature Classification
POW	Prisoner of War
PFTC	Pacific Film and Television Commission
SAFC	South Australian Film Corporation
SAG	Screen Actors Guild (United States)
SP	Starting-price (bookmaker)
UNESCO	United Nations Educational, Scientific and Cultural Organization
WIFT	Women in Film and Television
WWF	Waterside Workers Federation

Chronology

1894 30 November: Five weeks after first being used in London to show films, Thomas Edison's "kinetoscope" 35mm film-viewers seduced Australian audiences into a love affair with cinema that has never paled. The kinetoscope allowed one viewer at a time to watch an endless loop of film, of about 15 minutes in length. Twenty-five thousand Australians saw this exhibition in the first month.

1895 March: Charles McMahon, perhaps Australia's first film entrepreneur and producer, opened the "Edison Electric Parlour," showcasing kinetoscopes and gramophones, in Pitt Street, Sydney. **September:** Audiences in the outback mining town of Charters Towers marveled at the Edison "kinetophone" viewers that brought the first sound film to Australia.

1896 August: Carl Hertz, an American magician, presented a theatrical screening of moving pictures as part of a variety program in Melbourne. **September:** Maurice Sestier, an employee of the Lumière brothers, arrived with the first motion picture camera to reach Australia and, in a private showing sponsored by Joseph McMahon and Walter Barnett, screened the first films made by the Lumière brothers. In late **September** or early **October**, Sestier made the first Australian film, copying the Lumière film *Photographers Debark at Lyon* (1895) in theme and title: *Passengers Alighting from the Paddle Steamer "Brighton" at Manly*. **5 November:** Sestier followed this with the *1896 Melbourne Cup* capturing on film the horse race that brings the country to a standstill every year.

1897 August: Under the direction of Major Joseph Perry, the Limelight Department of the Salvation Army, based in Melbourne, began shooting short (23-minute) motion picture films describing the Army's social and religious work. One of these was a dramatized version of its "prison-gate" brigade. By 1900, the department was the preeminent filmmaker in Australia. Over the next six years, it was responsible for 80 percent of all film shot in Australia, much of it nonreligious film made under contract to, or commissioned by, state governments and the New Zealand Government. **3 November:** The Sydney Polytechnic embarked on the exhibition of films until September 1898, beginning with the 1897 Melbourne Cup and including many local actuality films.

1898 Sponsored by Cambridge University, British zoologist Alfred Haddon shot the world's first film of an anthropological field trip in the Torres Strait Islands, just north of Cape York. **May:** In Melbourne, the Salvation Army premiered its first films, entitled *Our Social Triumphs*. The films toured throughout Australia and New Zealand.

1899   December: The Salvation Army's Limelight Department shot 13 short films (averaging three minutes) on the life and death of Jesus Christ. Called *The Passion Films*, they began touring in 1900.

1900   January: The Limelight Department joined with the photographic company Baker and Rouse to cover the inauguration ceremonies of the Commonwealth of Australia. **13 September:** Combining 13 film segments, 200 magic lantern slides, music, and lectures, *Soldier of the Cross* screened in Melbourne to an audience of 4,000. This was the Salvation Army's most ambitious project.

1901 University of Melbourne biology professor and ethnographer, Baldwin Spencer, filmed the Aboriginal tribes of the Central Desert in South Australia and the Northern Territory, using 3,000 feet of stock.

1904   March: The Tait brothers began exhibiting films with a program of newsreels and music at Melbourne Town Hall.

1905   1 July: Cozens Spencer commissioned locally shot actuality material and combined these for a season of films in Sydney.

1906   March Thomas J. West signed a long lease on the Palace Theatre, Sydney, showing mainly nonfiction film. He signed the first "city first-run" agreement with Pathé Frères. West owned theaters in the United Kingdom and New Zealand. **26 December:** The first fictional feature film in Australia—and arguably the world—*The Story of the Kelly Gang*, was released in Melbourne and was a huge commercial success. Australian filmmaking declined because of the monopoly practices of the exhibition conglomerate comprising West, Spencer, Pathé, Tait, Johnson and Gibson, and J.D. Williams. This group favored imported material over locally produced film based on cost criteria, effectively arresting Australian production temporarily.

1907 The Carroll brothers bought the exhibition rights to *The Story of the Kelly Gang* for Queensland, beginning the enterprises of the Birch, Carroll and Coyle exhibition chain. **December:** The development of permanent cinemas became a reality after T.J. West purchased more long leases for large exhibition theaters in Sydney and Melbourne. Other exhibitors followed.

1909 Dr. Arthur Russell began showing films every Saturday night in a leased hall in Melbourne, and shortly after founded Hoyts Pictures. Pathe Frères became the first overseas film company to set up a distribution network.

1910 Concerned by the apparent lack of moral standards in the industry and in films, the Salvation Army closed down its Limelight Department. **12 March:** The premiere of Cozen Spencer's debut production film, *The Life and Adventures of John Vane, the Notorious Australian Bushranger*, marked the start of a three-year "golden age" of Australian filmmaking. Between 1910 and 1912, almost 90 narrative films were made.

1911 **4 March:** Capitalizing on the growth in the industry, numerous filmmaking companies coalesced. Johnson and Gibson merged to form Amalgamated Pictures Ltd. **24 April:** Raymond Longford directed his first feature, *The Fatal Wedding*, for Cozens Spencer. Longford went on to make 30 features over the next 20 years, making him, arguably, the most prolific director in Australian film history. **September:** Spencer opened a glassed-roof film studio in Sydney, in an attempt to utilize natural light. **6 December:** The first official Commonwealth cinematographer, James Pinkerton Campbell, was appointed.

1912 Because bushranging films were now banned in New South Wales, production ceased as a large market segment was closed. This popular genre was banned because the films portrayed the police in an unsympathetic light. In a further rationalization of the industry, West's, Spencer's, and Amalgamated Pictures merged and became the General Film Co. The popularity of film promoted theater development, and new luxury cinema "palaces" opened: the Majestic Theatre belonged to

Amalgamated, while the Greater J.D. Williams Amusement Co. opened the Melba and Crystal Palace in Melbourne and Sydney respectively.

1913 American expansion into the Australian industry effectively strangled local production. **6 January:** The Greater J.D. Williams Amusement Co. combined with the General Film Co. to form Australasian Films Ltd. and Union Theatres, establishing an effective monopoly in the industry. They agreed to cease local production in order to focus on the distribution and exhibition of overseas films. **19 July:** Two significant films were released. The first was Frank Hurley's 1,200-m documentary *The Home of the Blizzard*, recording the Douglas Mawson expedition to Antarctica. The second was Raymond Longford's last film for Cozens Spencer, *Australia Calls*. Recycling and therefore strengthening a paranoia theme that was to be utilized by politicians through to the 1960s, the film prophesized an Asian invasion of Australia.

1914 Two local feature films were the first to dramatize World War I. *A Long, Long Way to Tipperary* was released on 16 November and *The Day* on 23 November. To spur local production, the federal government imposed a tax on imported film, which was reduced in 1918.

1915 Hoyts Pictures had expanded into Sydney, and Melbourne and its suburbs. World War I momentarily spurred film production focused on wartime exploits. Australasian Films made the recruiting films *Will They Never Come?* and *The Hero of the Dardenelles*. The theater company J.C. Williamson made films about the Dardenelles—signaling the effect that campaign was to have on Australian cultural history—and the naval battle between HMAS *Sydney* and the German cruiser *Emden*.

1916 State governments appointed censorship boards to classify and regulate films. New South Wales appointed its board in this year, South Australia followed in 1917 and Tasmania joined in 1920.

1917 **June:** Frank Hurley was appointed the first official war cinematographer, serving in France and the Middle East.

1918 George Birch joined the Carroll brothers, bringing the Earl Court Theatre in Rockhampton into the chain. **11 March:** Popular athlete Reg (Snowy) Baker starred in *The Enemy Within*, about fifth columnists within Australia.

1919   4 September: Snowy Baker and E.J. Carroll contracted American filmmakers Wilfred Lucas and Bess Meredyth to make three outback Westerns starring Baker, all in 1920: *The Man from Kangaroo, The Shadow of Lightning,* and *The Jackeroo of Coolabong.* **4 October:** Raymond Longford's *The Sentimental Bloke* was released. Based on the poetry of C.J. Dennis, this film was arguably the most important production of the silent period, earning better returns and critical reviews than any film to that date. The sequel, *Ginger Mick,* was released in 1920. Later in the year, New York–based Fox News appointed Claude Carter as their cameraman and reporter in Australia.

1920   21 February: Films about Ned Kelly, and bushrangers, have always fascinated Australians. Harry Southwell's version of *The Kelly Gang* was released and *Robbery under Arms* followed later in the year. **24 July:** Raymond Longford's first adaptation of the Steele Rudd stories was released as *On Our Selection.* The sequel, *Rudd's New Selection,* was released in 1921. **April:** Filmmaker Beaumont Smith returned to Australia to make *The Man from Snowy River.* He had tried to make the film in the United States, but high production costs thwarted him. **19 June:** *The Breaking of the Drought* was released in Australia, but was later banned for export because the realistic scenes of drought in rural areas were considered "harmful to the Commonwealth."

1920–1929   Union Theatres gradually formed a mutually beneficial relationship with the rapidly expanding Queensland exhibitor Birch, Carroll and Coyle.

1921   Ronald Davis and George Malcolm experimented with short films synchronized with sound-on-disc, while Sydney engineer Ray Allsop experimented with synchronized sound-on-cylinder. Managing director of Union Theatres, Stuart Doyle, modernized his theater chain in an attempt to attract audiences. **5 November:** Raymond Longford made the last of four films, *The Blue Mountains Mystery,* for the Southern Cross Feature Film Co. **3 December:** Frank Hurley's documentary of two journeys through New Guinea opened to critical and popular acclaim, which was repeated when he took the film to the United Kingdom, the United States, and Canada.

1922   Virgil Coyle added his two theaters in Townsville to the Birch and Carroll chain, forming Birch, Carroll and Coyle. **May:** Lottie

Lyell and Raymond Longford formed Longford-Lyell Australian Productions.

1922–23   Ninety-four percent of all films screened in Australia were made in the United States, after they achieved dominance during World War I.

1924   New picture palaces, offering unrivaled sumptuousness, opened in Brisbane (the Wintergarden), Sydney (the Prince Edward), and Melbourne (the Capitol).

1925   The Commonwealth Film Laboratories were established, later changing their name to Colorfilm. **24 October:** Australian expatriate actress in Hollywood, Louise Lovely, starred in *Jewelled Nights*, which was released in Australia. At the same time, *The Mystery of the Hansom Cab*—directed by and starring another expatriate, Arthur Shirley—was released. **21 December:** Lottie Lyell, business partner and friend of Raymond Longford, died of tuberculosis at the age of 35. She contributed a vast amount to the early Australian industry, as scriptwriter, actress, producer, director, and editor.

1926   Hoyts Pictures, Electric Theatres, and Associated Theatres merged to become Hoyts Theatres Ltd. with Frank Thring Sr. as managing director. There were now two cinema chains: Union Theatres and Hoyts Theatres. In Victoria, the Censorship of Films Act stipulated that theaters screen 2,000 feet of Australian film each session. Exhibitors addressed this requirement by screening locally made short films before the feature. **25 January:** Charles Chauvel's first feature, *The Moth of Moombi*, was released. His second feature, *Greenhide*, premiered later in the year. **22 November:** Paulette, Phyllis, and Isobel McDonagh began their career as filmmakers, releasing *Those Who Love*. They made three more films: *The Far Paradise* (1928), *The Cheaters* (1930), and *Two Minutes' Silence* (1934).

1927   **3 March:** A Parliamentary Select Committee was established, to "enquire into and report into the moving-picture industry in Australia." **May:** The Select Committee was converted into a Royal Commission, effectively enhancing its authority and scope. **9 May:** The American, Dr. Lee De Forest, who had perfected an amplification system for sound-on-film, filmed the visit by the Duke and Duchess of York to Canberra to open the first federal parliament to sit in the federal capital, Canberra. **20 June:** *For the Term of His Natural Life* premiered. Produced by Australasian films, its budget and production values were far ahead of any film produced to date, and made a substantial profit in Australia, but lost money overseas because it had to compete with sound productions.

1928   Union Theatres renovated the magnificent State Theatre in Sydney. **26 April:** The Royal Commission tabled its findings. It recommended cash prizes for best production, and revised censorship legislation. A Federal Board of Censors was established, along with a Censorship Board of Appeal, and a new ratings system was implemented. **March:** In his directorial debut, Ken G. Hall directed the sequences that were added to the film *Unsere Emden* (released as *The Exploits of the Emden*) for its release in Australia. **29 December:** The feature-length sound films, *The Jazz Singer* (1927) and *The Red Dance* (1928), opened in Sydney.

1929   Ray Allsop built a "Raycophone" sound projector, and filmed four sound-on-disc musical short films. Other inventors experimented with sound-on-film, in an attempt to produce a cheaper technology than that from overseas. **8 August:** Equipment for the local shooting of *Movietone News* arrived, and the first newsreel was shown on **2 November**.

1930   Radio engineer Arthur Smith and Clive Cross developed a viable optical sound system, used in the feature *On Our Selection* (1932) and, from 1931, the weekly newsreel *Cinesound Review*. **May:** Filming began on the first Australian all-talkie, *Showgirl's Luck*. It was finally released in **December 1931**. **1 September:** In an attempt to cash in on film exhibition in Australia, the Fox Film Corporation bought a controlling interest in Hoyts Theatres. The managing director of Hoyts, Frank. Thring Sr., resigned to form Eftee Film Productions.

1931   **May:** Efftee Productions, representing Frank Thring Sr.'s ambitious move into film production, released the two short features *A Co-Respondent's Course* and *The Haunted Barn*. **July:** Thring joined Noel Monkman to establish Australian Educational Films, producing five short films on the Great Barrier Reef—pioneering underwater photography—and other wildlife documentaries. These were released through Efftee. **26 September:** Director/producer A.R. Harwood formed A.R. Harwood Talkie Productions, with the aim of making the first Australian sound features. He released *Spur of the Moment* and *Isle of Intrigue*, which were the first Australian feature-length talkies.

15 October: Union Theatres, bankrupted during the Great Depression, sold its assets to the newly incorporated Greater Union Theatres. **7 November:** Cinesound began producing newsreels under the generic title *Cinesound Review*.

1932   The American-owned Fox Film Corporation increased its shareholding in Hoyts Theatres. **26 May:** Eftee released its most expensive feature *The Sentimental Bloke*. The next film, *His Royal Highness*, starred comedian George Wallace in his debut performance. **3 June:** Cinesound Productions was formed to take over filmmaking activities from the failed Australian Educational Films, while British Empire Films took over its distribution. **6 August:** A sound version of *On Our Selection* was released and was immediately successful. Made by Australasian Films under the direction of Ken G. Hall, the film used sound recording equipment developed locally for the company. Hall went on to make 16 profitable features for the production company Cinesound over the next eight years.

1933   15 March: Errol Flynn, in his debut role as mutiny leader Fletcher Christian, starred in *In the Wake of the Bounty*, Charles Chauvel's first sound film.

1934   February: Because it could not obtain equitable distribution in Australia, Efftee suspended production after making seven features and 80 short films. The founder, Frank Thring Sr. died in 1936, and the company folded. **June:** The question of protection of the local film industry, in the form of a quota system, was the subject of a New South Wales state government enquiry. It reported in this month, recommending a quota for Australian films for five years. **1 June:** Director Raymond Longford's final film, *The Man They Could Not Hang*, was released.

1935   The industry expressed optimism after the long Depression and because of government intervention. Hoyts and Greater Union expanded their distribution circuits and modernized their cinemas. New cinemas sprang up in the suburbs. **September:** National Studios completed a film complex in Sydney, and National Productions was formed to produce the films. **17 September:** The film industry was granted a lease of life through the passing of the *N.S.W. Cinematograph Films (Australian Quota) Act*. In the first year, at least 5 percent of all films distributed, and 4 percent of films screened, had to be of Australian origin.

1936   January: National Productions began shooting its only film, *The Flying Doctors*. **9 May:** The industry decided to be more aggressive in looking to markets outside Australia. Cinesound's Ken Hall attempted to break into the US market with films that dealt with international interests, played in an Australian context. American actress Helen Twelvetrees starred in the first film of this push, *Thoroughbred*.

1937   30 June: Norman B. Rydge assumed control of Greater Union Theatres. In one of the longest reigns in media history, he was managing director and chairman for 43 years, until 1980. **December:** Because it had difficulty enforcing the film quota system, New South Wales passed further legislation to scale down the quotas.

1938   *Dad and Dave Come to Town* was released. **December:** In a different method of support for the local industry, the New South Wales government guaranteed funding for the production of four films: *Dad Rudd* (1940), *Forty Thousand Horseman* (1940), *That Certain Something* (1941), and *The Power and the Glory* (1941).

1940   February: Damien Parer, Australia's second war cameraman, was sent to the Middle East, and later served in Papua New Guinea. The 1942 documentary about the war in Papua New Guinea, *Kokoda Front Line*, was edited from Parer's footage, and won an Academy Award for best documentary in 1942. **14 June:** After releasing *Dad Rudd M.P.*, Cinesound postponed features production for the duration of World War II. **26 December:** The first Australian film released on the global market was Charles Chauvel's *Forty Thousand Horsemen*. The film cemented Chauvel's reputation as well as that of actor Chips Rafferty.

1944   Damien Parer was killed in action.

1945   26 April: The Australian National Film Board was established to implement John Grierson's recommendations concerning Australian documentary production. The Board evolved later into the Commonwealth Film Unit and now Film Australia. The production arm was the Films Division, Department of Information.

1946   The Waterside Workers Federation financed the production of Joris Ivens' *Indonesia Calling*, denoting an emerging interest in the production of left-wing documentaries. Supported by various left-wing trade unions, the noted Dutch documentarist and (briefly) Dutch Film Commissioner made the polemical documentary under the nose of the Australian police. The film was a strong plea against the attempt to reimpose colonial rule on the Indonesian people. **March:** In an action that evinces the growing multinational nature of the industry, and an international interest in the Australian market, Greater Union Theatres sold a 50-percent interest to the British Rank Organisation. **27 June:** Greater Union Theatres, in partnership with Columbia Pictures and Cinesound, released Ken G. Hall's final feature, *Smithy*. Although it was successful, Greater Union decided not to resume film production in association with Cinesound. **27 September:** Made with the assistance of the wartime Federal Government, *The Overlanders* premiered to critical and audience acclaim in Australia and overseas, and persuaded Ealing, the British production company, to establish a production branch in Australia.

1947 19 December: Like Ealing, the overseas company Children's Entertainment Films set up a production unit in Australia that was to operate until 1960. They produced and released on this date the film *Bush Christmas*.

1949 16 December: *Sons of Matthew,* Charles Chauvel's pioneering melodrama—an epic in both its production and its story—was released. It was his best film and one of the most significant films in Australian film history.

1951 Through prohibiting the formation of film production companies with capital in excess of stg£10,000, the Capital Issues Board effectively stopped the work of filmmakers like Ken Hall and Ealing studios.

1952 The Waterside Worker's Federation Film Unit released the first of its documentaries arguing for social action, *Pensions for Veterans*. **January:** Ealing studios, partly as a result of the ruling of the Capital Issues Board in 1950, decided to end local production. The studio had invested in Australia, producing many films like *The Overlanders*, *Eureka Stockade* (1949), and *Bitter Springs* (1950). The docudrama *Mike and Stefani* was released by the Department of the Interior. The docudrama told of the difficulties faced by immigrants in settling in Australia, bringing to national attention a new dimension of social policy.

1953 This year marked the beginnings of annual film festivals in both Sydney and Melbourne. **January:** *Captain Thunderbolt* reinvigorated the market for films about bushrangers, and was Cecil Holmes' directorial debut in feature films. **4 June:** Lee Robinson and Chips Rafferty produced and directed the first of five genre films, *The Phantom Stockman*, based on the Western genre, and making a healthy profit in Australia and overseas.

1954   John Heyer's documentary depicting life along the Birdsville Track, *The Back of Beyond*, was released, later to win the Grand Prix at the Venice Film Festival. The Department of the Interior produced the first full-length color film of the monarch's visit, *The Queen in Australia*.

1955   3 January: Charles Chauvel's *Jedda*, the first Australian color feature, explored the issues of cultural contact between Aboriginal and other Australians, suggesting that such contact might contain the seeds of tragedy.

1956   The Commonwealth Film Unit (now Film Australia) was reformed out of the Department of the Interior's Film Division. **16 September:** Television broadcasting began, initially with a further depressing effect on the already-depressed feature film production and exhibition sectors.

1957   March: Cecil Holmes' *Three in One* was released for limited screenings in Australia. Adapted from Frank Hardy and Henry Lawson stories, the film explored mateship from a left-wing perspective. It won critical acclaim overseas.

1958   The Australian Film Institute (AFI) was formed to promote "an awareness and appreciation of film" and awarded its first prize to *Grampians Wonderland*.

1960   8 December: *The Sundowners* premiered in New York. This film represented a change in the nature of filmmaking, as it was the last of some 14 films since 1944 that were made by overseas corporations primarily for overseas audiences, that were made in Australia, and that capitalized on Australian locations.

1961   Birch, Carroll and Coyle opened their first drive-in, the Tropicaire, in Mt. Isa, Queensland. **1 January:** The Australian Film Producers Association lobbied the Liberal Government to declare, through the Postmaster-General—the office responsible for regulating the airwaves—

that television advertisements were to be produced in Australia. This was a form of protection of the industry.

1963   29 October: The Vincent Committee, set up the previous year as a Senate Select Committee, recommended government aid for the film industry. While these recommendations were not implemented, they highlighted the growing support for some form of government assistance to the industry.

1966   19 August: Significantly, a film about immigrant experiences was not only one of the few films made in the period but was also successful. *They're a Weird Mob* was an Anglo-Australian production that opened in Sydney to record box offices, indicating a demand for Australian product.

1968 Significant relaxation of film censorship occurred under the Minister for Customs, Don Chipp. **November:** The UNESCO committee for Mass Communication joined others in recommending Commonwealth support for the film industry, but went further in recommending the establishment of a film and television school.

1969   27 March: Tim Burstall's first feature, *Two Thousand Weeks*, opened in Melbourne. **May:** Another committee, the Film and Television Committee of the Australian Council for the Arts, mirrored the call of the 1968 UNESCO committee for a film and television school and government support for the industry. It also recommended the establishment of a film fund and the purchase of television time to show the films.

1970   5 March: Responding to the recommendations of various committees, the federal government established the Australian Film Development Corporation (AFDC) to promote the making of Australian films. **7 July:** The newly established Experimental Film and Television fund made its first loan to filmmakers. Surprisingly, in the light of current events, the first film that was completed was a documentary about the Vietnam moratorium movement, *Or Forever Hold Your Peace*.

1971   March: The Australian Film Development Corporation commenced operations. The Commonwealth Film Unit released *Three to Go* for commercial television. Peter Weir, Brian Hannant, and Oliver Howes directed the film, an innovative three-part feature on youth issues. **November:** The Commonwealth film censors introduced the "R" rating, indicating that entrance to the film was restricted to those over 18. **9 December:** The first feature funded by the AFDC, *Stockade*, was released. **27 December:** Tim Burstall's *Stork*, a sexual, lowbrow, anarchistic comedy, was the first of the "ocker" cycle. Its box office success encouraged wider investment in films.

1972 Written by Barry Humphries, Bruce Beresford's *The Adventures of Barry Mackenzie*, another in the "ocker" cycle, earned huge returns for its backers, engendering confidence in the industry and confirming the Australian feature film production revival was up and running. **23 March:** The first nondocumentary funded through the Experimental Film and Television Fund, *A City's Child*, was released.

1973 The Commonwealth Film Unit was renamed Film Australia. **January:** The Australian Film and Television School (later, The Australian Film, Television and Radio School—AFTRS) opened, with an initial intake of 12 students including Gillian Armstrong and Phillip Noyce. **1 February:** Filmmakers, concerned about American domination of the film market, demonstrated during Jack Valenti's visit to Sydney. He was president of the Motion Picture Producers' Association of America. **March:** Tim Burstall's second in the "ocker" cycle, *Alvin Purple*, was released, quickly becoming the most profitable film since *On Our Selection* (1932). **April:** The Labor government of Don Dunstan established the South Australian Film Corporation, the first state corporation of its kind, in an attempt to develop cultural industries, which, it was envisaged, would balance the decline in white goods manufacturing in that state. All other states established similar bodies over the next eight years. **30 June:** The Tariff Board concluded its enquiry into the film and television industry, recommending radical restructuring of the film industry: production, distribution, and exhibition. Apart from the recommendation to replace the Australian Film Development Corporation, the government ignored the report.

1974 *27A*, one of a series of low-budget, social realist films was released, examining urban alienation. Others included *The Office Picnic* (1973), *Pure S* (1975), and *Mouth to Mouth* (1978). **October:** Filmmaker Peter Weir released *The Cars That Ate Paris*, his first feature.

1975 Birch, Carroll and Coyle replaced the single screen cinema in Townsville with an air-conditioned, twin cinema complex. Hoyts opened the first multiplex in Sydney. **March:** The Australian Film Commission (AFC) Act was passed, and the AFC replaced the Australian Film Development Corporation. **May:** The first government-sponsored delegation went to Cannes to promote Australian films. Ken Hannam's *Sunday Too Far Away* received critical acclaim at the festival. **8 August:** Peter Weir's *Picnic at Hanging Rock* was critically and popularly acclaimed, making over four times its costs, a huge return in the industry. The film also indicated the emergence of the period/art film, with its focus on gentler, but not always less menacing times. Both this film and *Sunday Too Far Away* denoted a "new wave" in Australian filmmaking, turning away from the "ocker" films of earlier in the decade. **4 September:** The Greater Union Organisation had not invested in the production of film since *Sons of Matthew* in 1949. Recognizing the profit potential of local production, the company began to invest once again in film, beginning with *The Man from Hong Kong*.

1975–1977 Color television broadcasting began in Australia, coinciding with a period of unemployment, and inflation, correlating with a slump of 30 percent to 40 percent in cinema attendances.

1976 Donald Crombie's *Caddie* (**9 April**), Fred Schepisi's *The Devil's Playground* (**12 August**), and Henri Safran's *Storm Boy* (**19 November**)—the third film supported by The South Australian Film Corporation—opened to critical and audience acclaim. The first television presentation of the Australian Film Institute awards took place, and the best film of the year was *The Devil's Playground*.

1977 Bruce Beresford's *The Getting of Wisdom* and Peter Weir's *The Last Wave* were released. New directors like Gillian Armstrong, Phillip Noyce, and Ken Cameron—later to make their mark on the industry—released short films. Bruce Petty's *Leisure* won the American Academy Award for best animated short. **April:** The AFPA was superseded by the Independent Feature Film Producers Association (IFFPA).

1978 Recognizing that Australian films could be and had to be successful in a global market, both the Australian Film Corporation and the N.S.W. Film Corporation opened offices in the United States. **24 April:** In a blatant example of censorship in the film industry, Home Affairs Minister Robert Ellicott vetoed funding of *The Unknown Industrial Prisoner*, on the grounds that it was not a commercial venture. **May:**

Fred Schepisi's *The Chant of Jimmy Blacksmith* was critically acclaimed at the Cannes Film Festival. The film marked the entry into film production of the Hoyts exhibition chain. **28 July:** Phillip Noyce's *Newsfront* opened to critical and audience acclaim in Sydney. **28 November:** In another gesture of support for the industry, the government again liberalized tax laws allowing for a 100 percent tax write-off over two years—previously this was 15 years—for film investment.

1979 Hoyts entered the distribution sector. **February:** The Film and Television Producers Association (FTPA) superseded the IFFPA. **April:** George Miller's *Mad Max* earned $1 million in its first week of release in Australia and, after its international release, became the highest-grossing film up to that time. **17 August:** Gillian Armstrong's *My Brilliant Career* was released. This was one of the few Australian films of the art and period cycle to achieve success at the box office. **October:** The Australian Film Commission changed its focus to a more commercial operation, aiming for self-sufficiency by recovering costs on a global market, rather than funding the development of filmmakers and esoteric films. **November:** Actors Equity and the Film and Television Producers Association negotiated the Film Actors Award. The award was a form of protection for Australian actors, effectively preventing filmmakers hiring cast from overseas for local films and films that government funds supported.

1980 **May:** Bruce Beresford's *Breaker Morant* was acclaimed at Cannes, winning Jack Thompson a best supporting actor award. American critics applauded this film and *My Brilliant Career*. Rupert Murdoch and Robert Stigwood established R & R Films, which invested $2.6 million in *Gallipoli*, and planned to invest $10 million a year in local production. **June–September:** Investment in films slowed to a trickle when the government announced it would tighten the tax laws to prevent investors using film investment as a blatant tax avoidance measure.

1981 **24 June:** The industry was further promoted through new tax laws that increased the deduction to 150 percent for funds invested in film, but it could be claimed only when the film had earned income. In addition, 50 percent of revenue would be tax free. **7 August:** Peter Weir's *Gallipoli* was released and won immediate critical acclaim. Besides setting records in the Australian box office, it set house records in the United States as well. It was the first Australian film to be distributed by an American major; namely Paramount. **December:** Dr. George Miller's *Mad Max 2: The Road Warrior* created box office records in Australia and the United States for an Australian film, taking US$12 million in the first three weeks.

1982 *Far East*, an Australian remake of the Warner classic *Casablanca*, was released. **20 March:** *The Man from Snowy River* grossed $8 million in its first eight weeks, beating the record set by *Star Wars* as the quickest-earning film in Australia. **July:** Four Australians bought out the interests of the US company Twentieth Century Fox in the Hoyts conglomerate.

1983 Victoria introduced a new governing structure for the State Film Centre and recognized emergent new media forms based on digital technology. The tax concession on film production was reduced from 150 percent to 133 percent. Films shown at Australian Film Festivals no longer required clearance or a rating from the Film Censorship Board. American Linda Hunt won an Oscar for best supporting actress for her role in Peter Weir's *The Year of Living Dangerously* (1982). Film Australia released the feature-length spoof documentary *Cane Toads*. *Goodbye Paradise* transposed the conventions of the Hollywood *film noir* to the Gold Coast.

1984 Film Australia's first production of a feature film, *Annie's Coming Out*, was based on a true story concerning a disabled girl's struggle for recognition as a human being. The film achieved wide commercial release. The National Film and Sound Archive was established as an organization independent of the National Library. Victoria legislated for X-ratings for sexually explicit, nonviolent videos.

1985 Leon Fink bought out the other three owners of Hoyts, restructuring and renaming it Hoyts Corporation. Australian-born Rupert Murdoch bought Twentieth Century Fox and the Metromedia Broadcasting Stations. Tax concessions for film investors were reduced from 133 percent to 120 percent. Fifty percent of Australian households owned a videocassette recorder.

1986 *The Empty Beach* was the first feature based on the Cliff Hardy crime novels written by Peter Corris with actor Bryan Brown appearing as Hardy. Peter Faiman's *Crocodile Dundee* was released to audience acclaim in Australia and overseas. This film had the highest box office takings in Australia, and remains the most successful Australian film in the United States. At the other end of the spectrum, Jane Campion's *Peel* won the Palme d'Or for best short film at Cannes.

1987 Tim Burstall directed a remake of *Kangaroo* first made by Lewis Milestone in 1952 and based on the novel by D.H. Lawrence.

1988 The Film Finance Corporation Australia (FFC) was established to control Federal Government investment in film production and re-place the role of 10BA tax incentives, which were reduced to a 100-percent write-off. John Cornell's *Crocodile Dundee II* was the top Australian film by local gross box office ($24.9 million). The New South Wales government established the N.S.W. Film and Television Office to support local filmmakers with script development, production investment, skill enhancement, policy issues and expert location, and industry advice. The Australian Film Television and Radio School (AFTRS) opened its new facilities at North Ryde, NSW.

1989 In conjunction with Warners and Village Roadshow, Birch, Carroll and Coyle opened multiplexes in Queensland shopping centers. Yahoo Serious's *Young Einstein* (1988) was the highest ranking Australian film by gross box office ($10.1 million). Jane Campion made her first feature, *Sweetie*.

1990 *The Delinquents* was the top Australian film by local gross box office ($2.6 million). Dean Semler won best cinematography Oscar for *Dances with Wolves*.

1990–1991 Sound systems changed from analogue to digital, using digital audio tape (DAT) technology.

1991 Greater Union took over Birch, Carroll and Coyle. Peter Weir's *Green Card*—filmed in America and backed by the Film Finance Corporation—was the top Australian film by local gross box office ($10.6 million). Jocelyn Moorehouse's first feature *Proof* won a special mention for excellence—the Camera d'Or Jury—at Cannes. The Queensland government established the Pacific Film and Television Commission to work with the Warner Roadshow MovieWorld Studios in attracting film production to Queensland.

1992 Documentarist Dennis O'Rourke's *The Good Woman of Bangkok* was released. The film proved highly controversial with its depiction of not only a Thai prostitute, but also the involvement of the filmmaker with the woman. Baz Luhrman's first feature, *Strictly Ballroom*, was the top Australian film by local gross box office ($18.8 million). Australian Luciana Arrighi shared the best art direction Oscar for *Howard's End* with Ian Whittaker. The inaugural Brisbane International Film Festival (BIFF) was held under the auspices of the Pacific Film and Television Commission. Geoffrey Wright's first feature *Romper Stomper* was the subject of critical controversy for its depiction of racism and violence.

1993 The new MA film classification was created, requiring children under 15 to be accompanied by an adult. *The Piano* was the top Australian film by local gross box office ($9.2 million), and the film won prizes worldwide. Jane Campion won the Oscar for best original screenplay, American Holly Hunter won an Oscar for best actress, and New Zealander Anna Pacquin won an Oscar for best supporting actress. At Cannes, Campion shared the Palme d'Or and Holly Hunter won the award for best actress in a leading role. The Australian Film Commission had provided script development funding for this film. The Sydney Tropicana Short Film Festival was launched.

1994 Hoyts Cinemas, now an international company, with 47 percent of the shares held by the American company Hellman and Friedman, owned 1,500 screens in Australia, New Zealand, the United States, Europe, and Mexico. Stephan Elliott's *The Adventures of Priscilla, Queen of the Desert* was the top Australian film by local gross box office ($14.8 million). Lizzie Gardiner and Tim Chappel won the Oscar for best costume design for this film. P.J. Hogan's first feature, *Muriel's Wedding* had a local gross box office of $14.1 million. The South Australian Film Corporation ceased being a producer and became a film development agency, providing investment, development programs, and training support for film, television, and new media production in South Australia.

1995 Australian producer Bruce Davey shared the Academy Award for best picture of the year with Mel Gibson and Alan Ladd Jr. and Australians Peter Frampton and Paul Pattison shared the Oscar for best achievement in makeup with Lois Burwell, for *Braveheart*. **December:** Chris Noonan's *Babe* was the top Australian film by local gross box office, taking $10.9 million in two weeks. Australian John Cox shared the Oscar for best achievement in visual effects for this film.

1996   Scott Hicks' *Shine* was released to wide critical acclaim and commercial success at the Sundance Film Festival, and won Geoffrey Rush a best actor Academy Award in this year. *Shine* showed that Australian filmmakers could compete on an international market through drawing on global themes.

1997   Rob Sitch's *The Castle* was the top Australian film by local gross box office ($10.3 million).

1998   The rebanning of Pasolini's *Salo* indicated a new regime of repressive censorship regulation. The Seven television network sold its holdings in MGM for US$389 million. **May:** After many disputes over the site, Fox Studios opened in Sydney, on prime real estate previously used by the Agricultural Society.

1999   The Packer family, through its company Consolidated Press Holdings, purchased the last parcel of shares of Hoyts Cinemas from the American company Hellman and Friedman, effectively turning Hoyts Cinemas into a private company. The National Film and Sound Archive changed its name to ScreenSound Australia—the National Screen and Sound Archive. John Woo's *Mission Impossible 2* was filmed in Sydney. Australian Steve Courtley shared the Academy Award for best achievement in visual effects for his work on *The Matrix*, while Australian David Lee shared the Academy Award for best achievement in sound.

2000   Russell Crowe won the Oscar for best actor for *Gladiator*. George Lucas's *Star Wars: Episode II—Attack of the Clones* was filmed at Fox Studios in Sydney.

2001 Australian Andrew Lesnie won the Oscar for cinematography for *The Lord of the Rings: Fellowship of the Ring*. Baz Luhrman's *Moulin Rouge*, filmed at Fox Studios in Sydney, opened to popular and critical success. Australian Catherine Martin and Brigitte Broch shared the Oscar for best achievement in art direction for *Moulin Rouge*. Martin also shared the Oscar for best achievement in costume design with fellow Australian Angus Strathie.

2002   Nicole Kidman won the Academy Award for best actress for the film *The Hours*. Phil Noyce's *Rabbit-Proof Fence* opened to critical acclaim over its treatment of the "stolen" indigenous children issue. Rolf de Heer's *The Tracker* interrogated other aspects of Aboriginal history. **1 January:** The Australian Centre for the Moving Image (ACMI), dedicated to all media forms of the moving image, was established by the Victorian government. **17 November:** ACMI cinemas opened at Federation Square.

2003 Consolidated Press Holdings sold a 60-percent interest in the American operation of Hoyts (554 screens) to Regal Entertainment Group. Glendyn Ivin's *The Cracker Bag* won the Palme d'Or for the best short film at Cannes. P.J. Hogan's much-anticipated *Peter Pan*—filmed at the Warner Bros. studios in Queensland with a US$100 million budget—opened to mixed reviews and disappointing box office returns. **1 July:** Following a review of cultural agencies the Federal government integrated ScreenSound Australia—the National Screen and Sound Archive into the Australian Film Commission.

2004 **April:** Pioneer filmmaker Tim Burstall died.

An Introduction to Australian Film

DEFINING AUSTRALIAN FILM

Why is it important to define Australian film? After all, if one lives in the United States or elsewhere for that matter, defining an American film is never an issue because any film made in the United States falls within that category. Actually, the term "Hollywood" is a broader, if not more precise, umbrella because it encompasses any film that comes out of that vast, nongeographical production conglomeration. But there is no associated definition of the film itself; the term "Hollywood" does not define anything about the film, although it might suggest certain characteristics.

In Australia though, the question of definition is important, if difficult. Unlike the situation in the United States, Australian federal and state government financing has—since the 1970s—supported the Australian film production industry. Such assistance is available only to projects that meet the criteria of an Australian film. For that reason, defining an Australian film is essential. Such a defining process is also necessary in any discussion of the Australian film industry, for without that, there would be no rationale for writing this book.

There is no simple answer to this question. Like ideas of the nation or national character, or a particular genre in film studies, the definition can never be precise. Rather, it is a set of possibilities that are dynamic in a temporal sense. That is, instead of a single sentence definition, Australian film is inferred through a set of criteria, such as content, actors, filmmakers, the element of "creative control," and so on. At the same time, these criteria change over the course of years. Thus, in the early days of filmmaking in Australia, the subjects were always recognizably Australian, the films were made by Australian filmmakers, with Australian characters. Hence any classification was a simple process. There is an element of temporality in this argument. As the world has become a smaller place—a global village, perhaps—through new and improving communication technologies, with different business opportunities—arising from an increased agglomeration of assets—added to filmmaking technologies that required larger audiences, then the nature of filmmaking has changed. So, too, have descriptions and definitions of Australian film.

In addition, writers and critics have defined and described Australian film in different ways at different times. Thus, a description is itself a metadefinition, a discussion of how others have talked about films, noting continuities, transformations, and changes, in the significance of the various criteria. These writers and critics have delineated Australian film in particular ways (*see* Moran & O'Regan 1989: xi–xv). An exploration of these definitions not only clarifies the situation, but also explores the nature and history of the industry.

First, all films made in Australia might qualify for the label of Australian film. At one time, this was enough to classify a film. The early silent films, for example, such as *Breakers at Bondi* (1897), *For the Term of His Natural Life* (1908), and Charles Chauvel's *Forty Thousand Horsemen* (1940), clearly were made in Australia. Indeed, all but a few films in this book fit the bill. This is one criterion that a film must meet, it seems, as a precondition for the appellation of "Australian." Some films were shot partly in Australia, with other scenes being shot elsewhere. Jane Campion's *Holy Smoke* (1998), for example, is a story that crosses a number of continents. Yet other films made in Australia do not rate as Australian films. *Mission Impossible 2* (2000) is not an Australian film, even though it was shot in Australia.

Second is the criterion that Australian films are made by Australians. At first glance, it would seem safe to assert this, yet, historically, the notion of "Australian" was ambiguous, as being a Briton was the same as being an Australian. Although director Raymond Longford was born in Australia, many of his contemporaries were born in the United Kingdom and subsequently migrated to Australia. Like many Britons who came to Australia, even up until the last 20 years, becoming an Australian citizen was never an issue because Britain was the "home country," and a British passport was a key to the world, and gave holders the right to vote in Australia. British citizenship meant that the Briton could enjoy all the rights and privileges of Australian citizens, exofficio. But

AN INTRODUCTION TO AUSTRALIAN FILM • 27

now the idea of "an Australian" is even more ambiguous. Jane Campion, for example, was born and educated in New Zealand, yet was one of the first intake into the Australian Film and Television School (later, Australian Film Television and Radio School). She made many films in Australia and lives in Australia, and is claimed by the Australian industry as an Australian. At the same time, many Australian filmmakers now reside overseas, having all but abandoned the Australian industry. Some return for a time to make films, such as Phillip Noyce and Gillian Armstrong, and such films have a strong claim to be Australian. But even this criterion is difficult. Consider the films of Fred Schepisi. *The Devil's Playground* (1976) and *The Chant of Jimmy Blacksmith* (1978) are quite clearly Australian, and *Plenty* (1985) and *Roxanne* (1987) are clearly not. What of *A Cry in the Dark* (also *Evil Angels*) (1988)? Shot in Australia from an Australian story, it stars Meryl Streep and Sam Neill, and was produced by the US companies Warner Bros. and Cannon Entertainment. Increasingly, this is the kind of question that is raised more often as cast and crew move across national borders, as do the companies that make the films and the stories that are the subject of the films. The participation of other significant Australian crew members, such as the writer, cinematographer, or editor, might be enough to suggest a film be designated Australian. Certainly, the globalization of the industry is an interesting and dynamic subject.

Third, it seems reasonable to argue that Australian films need to be about Australia, and, to a very great extent, this was the case. Indeed, they could hardly be about anything else. Yet, to follow this argument to its logical conclusion would be to assert that national films (of any country or nation) would be about that nation or country, leaving films with some kind of international subject to be made elsewhere, which could be taken to be Hollywood. Obviously, this cannot stand up to any kind of examination. The most striking recent example of a "universal" film being made outside Hollywood is the *Lord of the Rings* trilogy (2001–2003). Certainly, the films were not about New Zealand (although New Zealand cleverly reconstructed itself as Middle Earth as a result of the success of the films). An earlier and successful example filmed in Australia was the *Mad Max* trilogy (1979––1985), which, although made in Australia, could have been made in a similar location elsewhere on the globe; certainly, the films were not about Australia.

A fourth category is films made for Australian audiences. Most films made in Australian before the 1970s revival fitted this category, as the marketing networks for such films overseas were not reliable, if they existed at all. However, notable exceptions included those films made for the US market, by American or Australian directors, such as Ken G. Hall, beginning with *Thoroughbred* (1936). Since the revival, films made for Australia have sometimes been popular overseas, if only with the arthouse circuit.

The final category is films that are made by, or involve, Australian actors and other crew working overseas on films that have no immediate relevance to Australia. It would be difficult to argue that films starring Nicole Kidman should be regarded as Australian. Yet films made by Peter Weir might be Australian. *Green Card* (1990) is often mentioned in this regard. Weir wrote the screenplay and directed the film, which was shot in New York City, and which had nothing to do with Australia. Apart from the involvement of a few Australian companies that provided dubbing and postproduction facilities, no other element of the film had Australian input. Yet the Film Finance Corporation of Australia was one of the major funding sources, meaning that the film met the Corporation's requirements for an Australian film. Another example is *Moulin Rouge!* (2001). Made by Australian Baz Luhrmann and starring Australian Nicole Kidman, the story was not Australian, nor did the film receive funding support from the Film Finance Corporation or other Australian support organizations. It was shot primarily in Australia. Yet, for the purposes of Australian Film Institute (AFI) awards, the film was Australian and won AFI awards. For other award-presenting organizations, whether the film was Australian or not seemed irrelevant, as it won Oscars and British Academy of Film and Television Arts (BAFTA) awards, among others.

According to funding bodies like the Australian Film Commission (AFC), the definition of an Australian film is now quite simple, although riders are attached. Basically, an Australian film is one where the project is under Australian creative control; that is, where the key elements are predominantly Australian and the project was originated and developed by Australians. This includes projects under Australian creative control that are partly foreign-financed. Even that definition is problematic. Take a film like *The Piano* (1993). Director Jane Campion was a New Zealander, living in Australia. The film was shot in New

Zealand, with a New Zealand subject. Yet, for the AFC, it was an Australian film, and that organization provided script development funding. The film won an unprecedented 11 AFI awards. Yet it is also claimed by New Zealand as one of theirs, with good reason. So, the grey areas are quite large. All these definitions are limited in some way. Given the increasing globalization of the industry, barriers of nation and national films can be limiting. On the other hand, such differentiation is necessary to maintain the film industry in countries like Australia.

In this book, Australian film has been defined quite broadly, but generally within the bounds of the definitions funding bodies use. The film has to have some element that is recognizably Australian and that plays some part in Australian film culture. Thus, the narrative should have some essentially Australian motifs, or concern itself with an Australian identity, or be peopled by Australian cast and/or significant Australian crew. The film might be supported by Australian funding, either in the form of government assistance or through its production in an Australian or New Zealand studio. Thus, *The Matrix* (1998) and *Holy Smoke* fall into the Australian category; *The Lord of the Rings* is a New Zealand film, as is *The Piano*.

HOLLYWOOD AND AUSTRALIA

Cinema is of great significance in Australian culture. Australians have always enjoyed an outing to the "pictures," as cinema was called from the earliest days up to the 1960s. As in the United States and New Zealand, the heyday of the cinema—in terms of frequency of attendances—was in the 1940s, when, on average, Australians went to the cinema twice each week. Before the 1980s, the lowest wage that could be paid to a worker was the basic wage, and unlike the minimum wage concept, the basic wage was determined on the basis of its capacity to feed, house, clothe, and generally maintain a family. The significance of the cinema in Australian life is attested to by the fact that one of the elements in determining the basic wage was the price of cinema attendance.

Although cinema is significant, it is dominated by the United States. In 2002, Australia had a population of just under 20,000,000. There were 1,872 cinema screens across the country, with a gross box office in 2002 of $844,000,000 derived from 93 million admissions. In comparison with the figures from either the United States or the United Kingdom, the Australian industry is in a different, much smaller, league, yet the market is still important to profit margins and shareholder returns. The statistics from 2002 are representative of the degree of domination. A total of 258 films were released, of which 22 were Australian (19 features and three documentaries), which is just 8.5 percent of all films released. On the other hand, two-thirds of this total—172 films—were from the United States. The total budgets of Australian films represented just 1 percent of the total budgets of American films released in Australia in that year. The share of box office revenue for Australian productions was 4.9 percent, or $41.8 million, but that for the United States was 80 percent of the gross annual box office.

Revenue from Australian films in the Australian market is minimal compared with Hollywood films. Films that make over $1 million are considered successful, and in 2002 there were 10 such films, ranging from $7.7 million to $1.3 million. In contrast, the average budget for a major American studio film (for example, Disney, Warner Bros., Universal) in 2001 was US$47.7 million and the average for a minor studio (for example, Miramax, New Line) was US$32.5 million. Thus, in terms of the overall market, the Australian film industry plays only a small part, but, in terms of its place in the cultural life, the industry is of great importance.

The domination of the industry by the United States began early, but it was not necessarily a case of American interests simply taking over. In 1906, Australian filmmaking declined because an exhibition monopoly, which was Australian based, favored imported film because it was cheaper. In 1913, a similar rationale on the part of the exhibition and distribution monopoly effectively destroyed production in Australia. In order to redress the balance, the federal government imposed a tax on imported film in 1914, but this was reduced in 1918. By 1923, the domination was almost complete: 94 percent of all films screened in Australia were made in the United States. Although various attempts were made to address this problem, the most successful were those taken since the 1970s, when state and federal governments supported the production of films.

However, there is another side to this matter. First, many Hollywood studios are owned by non-American companies, such as Sony and News Corp., which tends to qualify ideas of American imperialism through films, although clearly, many of the values, ideas, and subjects exported in American films are American-centered. (In the reverse of this argument, News

Corp is, at the time of writing, applying to move its headquarters from Australia to Delaware.) Today, non-American actors play Hollywood characters, and non-American filmmakers direct Hollywood films. For example, at the 2004 Academy Awards, three of the best director nominations were not American, and New Zealander Peter Jackson won the award. The best film Oscar was won by his film, *The Lord of the Rings: Return of the King*, which was clearly a New Zealand film, but appropriated by Hollywood. The Oscar for best actress was won by South African Charlize Theron. And there is some dissatisfaction in Hollywood over the perception that production had moved overseas: Tim Robbins, winner of the Oscar for best supporting actor, urged filmmakers to bring productions back to the United States, as local actors were suffering from a lack of work.

Other characteristics of the industry differentiate it from that in other countries. One of the most significant elements of the industry in comparison with the United States is the lack of studios. Australia has no tradition of large corporations making films in their own studios. But in the last 30 years, it has developed a number of state and federal studios. For example, state film organizations support film development and production in a number of ways: through the provision of script development support, location advice, production financing and facilities, and postproduction facilities. That is, these state industries offer the same kind of infrastructure that a Hollywood studio might offer. Of course, the details vary. In Queensland, for example, the studios are owned by private interests, but the films shot in them are supported in the ways mentioned previously. The distribution and exhibition elements of the film industry have yet to be documented in a comprehensive way. Some work has been done on various sectors, but a complete history is lacking (*see*, for example, Brand 1983; Collins 1987). Ownership of Australian theater chains is in an ongoing state of flux, and, as the chronology indicates, discovering who owns what at any one moment in time is a problem of unraveling cross-ownership details.

THE STORY OF AUSTRALIAN CINEMA

To understand Australian cinema, it is essential to understand something of its history. In the early part of the 20th century, Australians embraced not only going to the cinema, but also making films, beginning in about 1896. Following the model of the earliest Mèliés' films—and the limitations of technology—these short, unedited documentaries focused on the lives and events of Australia, and important among these were the horse races, capturing a national pastime for posterity. One of the most interesting linkages of this Australian film history was that between the industry and the Salvation Army, which seized on the new media as an appropriate tool for its work. From 1897 to 1910, the Army's Limelight Department made religious films but, because it had such extensive knowledge and experience, it was commissioned by government and others to produce secular films, including the inauguration ceremonies of the Commonwealth of Australia in 1901.

In the first decade of the 20th century, Australia was the largest film-producing country in the world. Between 1910 and 1912, almost 90 narrative films were made; looking wider, between 1906 and 1928, 150 narrative films were made. From 1906 to 1911, the Australian industry made more of these films than anywhere else. Included in this is arguably the world's first feature film, *The Story of the Kelly Gang* (1906). As would be expected, these films reflected Australian life, interests, and history, such as horse racing, convict life, gold mining, and the perennial favorite, bushranging, and films on this subject often viewed the bushrangers sympathetically, to the chagrin of the constabulary. Few of these films have survived, but *The Sentimental Bloke* (1910) has. The foundations of a filmmaking tradition were laid, because of the efforts of filmmakers like Raymond Longford, and actors like Lottie Lyell, Louise Lovely, and Bert Bailey. This golden age was not to last. Rationalization of the industry followed in 1913, in a classic case of the accountants taking over the business, and of the expansion of American interests. The various small production houses and theaters amalgamated to form a vertically integrated company called Australasian Films and Union Theatres, which controlled production, distribution, and exhibition. This combine decided to cease local production and focus on the distribution and exhibition of overseas films. This effectively curtailed investment in the local industry, although films were still made.

After World War I, the industry revived somewhat, although it never returned to the levels reached in the first decade of the century. The US domination of the industry was complete, as in 1922 and 1923, 94 percent of all films screened in Australia were made in the United States.

Nevertheless, while the features of Raymond Longford, Charles Chauvel, the McDonagh sisters, and Beaumont Smith were significant achievements in this period, so too were the documentaries of Frank Hurley. On the other side of the camera, Australian Louise Lovely worked in the Hollywood industry in films like *Jewelled Nights* (1925), and in the 1930s, Errol Flynn acted in films in Australia before moving to Hollywood. The exhibition sector continued to expand and restructure, so that two cinema chains, Union and Hoyts—with substantial shareholding from the United Kingdom and the United States respectively—became dominant. "Talkies," such as *The Jazz Singer* (1927), required sophisticated and expensive sound recording equipment, making the production of local films even more costly, and financially risky. Fewer films were made at this time, although some companies, notably Frank Thring Sr.'s Eftee Film Productions but also A.R. Harwood's Talkie Productions, continued to pursue profits in filmmaking. However, while the market for homegrown features was limited, another market for newsreels opened, as theaters began to screen newsreels before the feature film, and the Cinesound company filled this niche market. Cinesound also made features, and Ken G. Hall, one of the most successful filmmakers of the time, made 16 features for the company, up to World War II when it ceased making features for the war's duration, and never restarted these operations.

The period between the wars was marked by renewed government interest in the industry. A Royal Commission was established in 1927 to enquire into the industry and reported in 1928, but did not propose a firm agenda for supporting local production, apart from the recommendation that cash prizes be given to Australian films. In 1934, the New South Wales government established an inquiry into the industry, with the aim of protecting it. The recommendation was a quota system, materializing in the 1935 law that required that 5 percent of all films distributed within the state had to be of Australian origin. If anything, this law shows the extent to which overseas films dominated the market. However, the legislation was doomed to failure for various reasons—it applied in only one state, for example—and the quotas were gradually removed from 1937. Yet, the New South Wales government did continue to support the industry through cash grants.

Other concerns besides filmmaking held the attention of Australians during World War II, but soon after the Australian government moved into documentary production with the establishment of the Australian Film Board and the subsequent making of important documentaries like *Mike and Stefani* (1950) and *The Back of Beyond* (1954). On the other hand, the feature film industry languished from World War II to the end of the 1960s. Greater Union and Cinesound did not resume filmmaking after they had postponed such production during World War II. Only one or two features were made each year; nevertheless, some of them are noteworthy. The English company, Ealing, set up a production facility after the war, making *The Overlanders* (1949), *Eureka Stockade* (1949), and *Bitter Springs* (1950). Ken Hall's final feature, *Smithy* (1946) was released, along with Charles Chauvel's significant *Sons of Matthew* (1949) and *Jedda* (1955), and Cecil Holmes' *Captain Thunderbolt* (1953). The participation of Ealing in the Australian industry ceased when Prime Minister Robert Menzies legislated financial restrictions through the Capital Issues Board, which also stopped the projects of Ken Hall.

By the 1960s, feature film production had almost ceased, in part because of the challenge of television, and because distributors and exhibitors were not interested in supporting local production. Yet other developments suggested a slowly awakening industry. In 1958, the Australian Film Institute was established to promote an awareness and appreciation of film. Commercials were regulated to protect the local industry, to the extent that they had to be shot in Australia using Australian personnel. In addition, the Vincent Committee recommended in 1966 some form of government aid for the industry. Some film workers could also find work in coproductions, such as those of Southern International, a joining of the talents of Lee Robinson and Chips Rafferty. Their first film, *The Phantom Stockman* (1953), made a healthy profit at home and overseas. Later, in 1966, the Anglo-Australian coproduction *They're a Weird Mob*—which focused on some idiosyncrasies of the Australian character—was released to popular acclaim, and contained the seeds of the ocker cycle that was to follow.

The 1970s were the first decade of the Australian film revival. Financial assistance for the production of films was to be expedited through the newly established Australian Film Development Corporation (AFDC). The first film of the ocker cycle, Tim Burstall's *Stork*, was released in 1971, and his second film, *Alvin Purple* (1973), became the most profitable film at the box office since *On Our Selection* (1932). The ocker films showed that Australians would watch films about Australians, especially those that exaggerated the comic elements of character. State governments, beginning with South Australia, recognized the cultural and employment potential of a film industry and established their own funding offices over an eight-year period. In 1975, the Australian Film Commission (AFC) replaced the AFDC, paralleling the demise of the ocker films and the rise of the art and period genre, beginning with Peter Weir's *Picnic at Hanging Rock* (1975). Other films of the same genre—known as the "AFC genre" because such films were favored by the AFC for funding—followed, such as Donald Crombie's *Caddie* (1976) and Fred Schepisi's *The Devil's Playground* (1976). Yet these directors and other crew were assisted by the Australian Film and Television School, which was established in 1973. Gillian Armstrong, Jane Campion, and Phillip Noyce were among the first intake.

Although the ocker style and art/period genre were significant during this period, other films of various styles and genres were also released. On the one hand, Peter Weir's *The Cars That Ate Paris* (1974) and Sandy Harbutt's *Stone* (1974) were examples of popular if not critically acclaimed films that contrasted with the two genres of film that dominated contemporary film output. On the other, a series of low-budget, social-realist films were released between 1974 (*27A*) and 1978 (*Mouth to Mouth*). However, both of these were overwhelmed by the new Australian blockbusters, which not only found large audiences at home, but achieved significant overseas box office success as well. Dr. George Miller's *Mad Max* (1979) ushered in this new success, which was followed by the even more successful *Mad Max 2* (1981), and another action/adventure film, *The Man from Snowy River* (1982), directed by a different George Miller. *Crocodile Dundee* (1986) and *Crocodile Dundee II* (1988) continued the blockbuster tradition.

Other aspects of the industry changed as well with this revival. In 1975, the Greater Union theater chain resumed investment in film production, and the second chain, Hoyts, followed in 1978. In the same year, the government liberalized tax laws to allow a 100 percent write off for investment in film, and reduced the time over which the deduction could be spread from 15 to two years. In 1981, the 10BA tax regulations changed this to a 150-percent deduction, with an additional clause that 50 percent of returns were to be tax free. After some years, this deduction was reduced to 133 percent—with 30 percent tax free—and further reduced to 100 percent in 1988. The result of this tax liberalization was, of course, greatly increased film production. In the 1970s, the average number of films made each year was 15; this rose to 27 in the 1980s, as did production budgets. A great number of these films were simply tax-minimization projects, but even those films were the training ground for performers and crew who went on to greater things. Although the AFC was charged with funding film development, the Film Finance Corporation was established in 1988 to provide finance, generally in the form of equity, for film projects, replacing the 10BA schemes with direct funding. In the exhibition sector, the first multiplexes built in suburban shopping complexes began exhibiting in the late 1980s.

In the 1990s and the early 21st century, Australians have taken their talents to Hollywood and elsewhere and succeeded, both in films that are Australian and in more general, international films. At the same time, some Australian films have been widely acclaimed within this globalized industry.

PROBABILITIES AND POSSIBILITIES

The Australian industry might appear to have a secure future. It has, after all, been in a continuous state of production on a reasonable scale since the revival, that is, for at least 30 years. It boasts two studio complexes, one on the Gold Coast and one in Sydney, with two major American corporations owning significant stakes. The Australian government supports the industry through the Australian Film Commission and the Film Finance Corporation, and filmmakers can often gain additional funding for development and production from one or more of the state funding organizations. Investors in films have tax concessions accorded them, which, although not as generous as the 150-percent deduction that once existed, is still significant at 100 percent. Filmmakers have honed their skills and many have achieved critical and popular success at home and abroad, as have actors and other crew. American filmmakers and companies have found it cheaper to make films in Australia because wages and salaries are lower, and the expertise in most areas of filmmaking is comparable to that of anywhere in the world. At the same time, Australian audiences still enjoy watching Australian films, making the films profitable, even if this is a small profit. Overseas audiences sometimes respond favorably to these films. The new technology of

DVDs has created a new market, as more people watch films at home. Thus, it might appear that the industry is secure.

Yet a number of elements in the equation are not secure. One is the variable of government support. This is never certain. For example, a free-trade agreement between Australia and the United States might stipulate that the Australian government stop supporting, or subsidizing, the industry, in order to allow the free market to determine what Australians watch on television and in the cinema. If this situation recurred, the industry would be in a similar situation to some time in the past. A second variable is the value of the Australian dollar in relation to the US dollar; that is, the exchange rate. While the US dollar is high in value, then it makes sense for American companies to make films in Australia. However, when the dollar drops in value, the economic advantage reduces, and when added to the logistics of transferring cast and crew to Australia, the advantage disappears. In addition, American film becomes cheaper to exhibit, and Australian film becomes more expensive in the United States, while American returns are less. A third variable is the decisions by organizations, such as the American Screen Actors Guild (SAG). In May 2002, the SAG ordered its 98,000 members to refuse to work anywhere in the world unless they are offered SAG contracts, which stipulates minimum rates in US dollars that many Australian projects running on tight budgets could not afford.

Despite these reasons for a future downturn in the local industry, downturns in recent years have occurred even though it seemed that the industry was on a stable footing. One such downturn occurred in the 2002/2003 financial year when feature film and TV drama production activity dropped for the first time in eight years. Total expenditure fell 23 percent from $663 million to $514 million. Twenty-six feature films were made, compared with 39 in the previous year. However, the downturn in economic terms was even more pronounced. The value of feature film production fell by 63 percent from $131 million to $49 million, due largely to a lack of foreign-financed local features. In addition, there were no Australian features with budgets over $10 million, compared with three the previous year; only one film budget was in the $6–$10 million range, compared with three in the previous year.

One of the economic models used to characterize the Australian film industry is "boom and bust." In the past, this has been a reasonably accurate description of the production aspect of Australian cinema; that is, filmmaking has been subject to the various and changing government policies, business plans, vertical integration, and other economic factors that pervade the industry, with the result that filmmaking has sometimes boomed, but, just as often, the bubble burst. The bubble has been expanding now since the 1970s, and although there is some hope that the industry is now on a secure footing, providing a consistent film output, recent downturns suggest that the bubble might be slowly contracting. Certainly, without government support—public financing—of the industry, it would collapse, as it has in the past. The possibility of a free-trade agreement between the United States and Australia is a threat to this public funding, and to the filmmaking industry. At the same time, the success of films in holding up a mirror to Australians—however distorted—would seem to guarantee a future. These narratives of Australia, the stories that are essential for any culture to establish a history, must continue.

The Dictionary

– A –

ABORIGINES AND FILM. Aboriginal history is a history of the conquered, and contains all the elements that appear in such histories, including stories of brutality, rape, and murder, generally on the part of the conqueror, and sometimes enacted by the conquered. Historians and cultural critics argue the extent of such maltreatment, and no clear consensus is apparent. The films where Aborigines appeared or starred reflect, through a glass darkly, different elements of their stories. Aborigines appeared only rarely in the first 70 years of Australian film. Early documentaries explore Aboriginal culture ethnographically, creating a sense of otherness and strangeness, from which the viewer may have drawn conclusions about the ability of that culture to survive in a Social Darwinist universe. In silent films such as *Robbery under Arms* (1907) and *Dan Morgan* (1911), Aborigines were the sidekicks of white protagonists, exhibiting contemporary "qualities" of loyalty and subservience. They were white actors in blackface, a tradition that continued in various films up to 1967, in *Journey out of Darkness*. The films included Australian and United Kingdom coproductions by **Ealing** studios such as *The Overlanders* (1946) and *Bitter Springs* (1950). The narrative of the latter film prefigures, in a general sense, the land rights debates of the 1990s, as it is a story about the conflict between white settlers and Aborigines over a limited water supply.

   Charles Chauvel's *Uncivilised* (1936) was a clumsy film about race and desire, while ***Jedda*** (1955) was a much more effective film in its representation of Aboriginal culture and the juxtaposition with white culture. As well as being the first Australian color film, this was the first to feature Aborigines in leading roles, and was significant for its exploration of issues surrounding assimilation and integration of Aboriginal people into the particular white culture depicted in the film. The film deals with these questions in a balanced way, while the tragic finale has its seeds in that balance. *Jedda* was the first Australian film exhibited at the Cannes Film Festival.

Since the **revival**, Aborigines have had more and diverse treatments. Directors who have gained an international reputation—for example, Charles Chauvel, **Peter Weir**, **Phillip Noyce**—have often returned to, or sometimes began their careers with, films featuring Aboriginal actors and focused on Aboriginal issues as a kind of interrogation of their understanding of the treatment of the indigenous people of Australia.

Weir's *The Last Wave* (1977) exhibits elements of the supernatural, the surreal, that infuse his early work. Here, Aboriginal spirituality generates the supernatural strangeness that provides the film's coherence, rather than the usual classical style of linear narrative. **Fred Schepisi**'s *The Chant of Jimmy Blacksmith* (1978) retells events in 1901—significantly, the year that the separate states federated to become the Commonwealth of Australia. Both the traditional Aboriginal community and the white community reject a part-Aborigine, and the white community's rejection of him because of his race results in an explosion of hatred and violence. The reality of the rejection and dehumanizing of a person based on color, and its consequences, are Schepisi's concern in this film. With a similar realism, **Bruce Beresford**'s *The Fringe Dwellers* (1986) is a serious narrative that does not romanticize Aboriginal culture. Rather, the film portrays Aboriginal culture as complex, contradictory, and essentially human, through a story of the life of an adolescent daughter within a family, which is part of an Aboriginal community in a camp or settlement on the outskirts of a **country** town in northern Australia. Few whites appear in this film; rather it is a story about the effect of the juxtaposition of cultures, from an Aboriginal perspective as seen by Beresford.

Noyce made two films, *Backroads* (1977) and ***Rabbit-Proof Fence*** (2002). *Backroads* explores the matrices of race, class, and gender through the story of two fringe-dwelling Aborigines and a white itinerant, who is racist and sexist, but like the Aborigines Gary and Joe, is a social misfit, abandoned by his tribe. The film explores the commonalities, differences, and outgrowths resulting from this juxaposition of character and culture. *Rabbit-Proof Fence* is an award-winning film derived from a true story in the period of Australian history when bureaucrats removed part-Aboriginal children from their parents and resettled them in institutions where they could learn the ways of white society, and learn a menial role that would enable them to survive in that society. The film is a narrative about the indomitableness of the human spirit, in this case, in three Aboriginal girls who escape from such an institution to return to their mothers deep in outback Australia. The film romanticizes Aboriginal culture while portraying white culture as essentially evil, and while ascribing positive motivations to Aboriginal characters and culture, the film ascribes negative motivations to white characters. As in *Rabbit-Proof Fence*, **Rolf de Heer**'s *The Tracker* (2002) has **David Gulpilil** once again playing the part of the tracker, this time in a lead role, and now on the trail of a murderer rather than escaped girls. The characters have no names, only roles, and the film's plot derives from the confluence and shuddering interaction of the Tracker with the Fanatic, the Veteran, the Follower, and the Fugitive, leaving the non-Aboriginal Australian viewer with a sense of shame about the history of the relationship between Aboriginal people and white people. The last scenes, however, remove any sense of guilt and points to a different future.

Other recent films are less successful in their reconstruction of history and culture. *Black and White* (2002) is based on a true story of the trial and appeal of a part-Aborigine accused of the rape and murder of a young girl in the 1950s (*see* NGOOMBUJARRA, DAVID). *Australian Rules* (2002) is a simplistic story with good characters comprising all Aborigines, bad characters comprising all white adult fathers, victims (of white men) comprising white **women**, and children. As a result of such stereotyping, the film loses any credibility as an interrogation of the issues of relations between Aborigines and others in Australia.

Two films have popularized Aboriginal characters for international audiences: ***Crocodile Dundee*** (1986) and ***Crocodile Dundee II*** (1988). *Dundee* is a popular, mainstream **comedy** that constructs an Aboriginal character, Nev, in the same mould as other, non-Aboriginal people; that is, he participates in a traditional ceremony—a corroboree—because his parents expect it. He subverts the stereotype of the "noble savage," revealing instead a cosmopolitan, nonromantic character. **Paul Hogan** played Crocodile Dundee and David Gulpilil played Nev. The Aboriginal character Charlie in *Crocodile Dundee II* is less significant to the narrative, because Mick Dundee attempts to speak on behalf of Aborigines, voicing a particular position about the contemporary and controversial issue of land claims.

Recently, Aboriginal filmmakers have made films like the **documentary *Black Chicks Talking*** (2001). Brendan Fletcher and Leah Purcell record the lives of five Aboriginal women who are not accepting the victim stereotype, but who are carving their lives into the totem of contemporary Australia.

While filmmakers wrestle with issues concerning the juxtaposition of Aboriginal culture with Australian-European culture, on the level of the film industry, Aboriginal actors appear to suffer from lower remuneration than others. For example, Gulpilil reportedly earned only US$6,500 playing the role of Nev in *Crocodile Dundee.*

Other films are *Walkabout* (1971), *Eliza Fraser* (1976), ***Storm Boy*** (1976), *Journey among Women* (1977), *Maganinnie* (1980), *Wrong Side of the Road* (1981), *We of the Never Never* (1982), *Backlash* (1986), *Deadly* (1992), and *Blackfellas* (1993).

See also ADAPTATIONS.

ACTION/ADVENTURE. Action/adventure is one of the broadest generic classifications, and contains films where the Australian twist or characteristic is quite evident as the grounding of the narrative. The term "action-adventure" suggests a number of qualities about **masculinity** common to this group of films. These include a propensity for physical action; in recent times—and budget permitting—of spectacular special effects; narratives including fights, chases, and explosions; and acting performances that include physical feats and stunts. The ***Mad Max*** trilogy, especially *The Road Warrior* (1981) and *Beyond Thunderdome* (1985), is the quintessential example of the **genre** since the **revival**. In turn, patterns of action and character relationships link these representative elements. Like the romance of medieval literature, a protagonist either has or develops great and special skills and overcomes insurmountable obstacles in extraordinary situations to successfully achieve some desired goal, usually the restitution of order to the world invoked by the narrative. Whether it is driving a mob of cattle across Australia in *The Overlanders* (1946) or the duels in *The Matrix* (1999), the protagonists confront human, natural, or supernatural forces that have improperly assumed control over the world and, in many cases, eventually defeat them. In some instances they do not, as in *Ned Kelly* (2003) and *Gallipoli* (1981).

The earliest action/adventure films involved bushrangers. *The Story of the Kelly Gang* (1906) makes some claim to being the world's first feature length movie. Its subject, Ned Kelly, is a national icon, reflected in the fact that seven films have been made about the gang. The penultimate *Ned Kelly* (1970) starred Mick Jagger, but this did not help the film to achieve any success. Many other films portrayed bushrangers sympathetically, as resourceful, brave and chivalric; few were unsympathetic. Because of this sympathetic portrayal, the New South Wales Police requested the state censors ban such films, to which that body agreed in 1912. The excision of a likely 30 percent of the potential audience was a powerful disincentive to the production of more films of the genre, and production stopped until the 1950s.

Films about convicts were a symbolic catharsis of the new nation coming to grips with a past that was somewhat disreputable. *For the Term of His Natural Life* (1908) ushered in a genre of melodrama that centered on the trials and tribulations of convicts transported to Australia. The convicts were generally innocent, or shown to be acting with the highest motives, such as saving the lives of their families, even if their act contravened the law.

Another action/adventure subgenre of early Australian filmmaking was the "new chum" films. Few films still exist, yet they were significant before World War II. The new chum genre is recycled in the films of other countries; in the Australian manifestation new arrivals to Australia, generally from the aristocracy in the United Kingdom, arrive in outback Australia filled with the cultural baggage of superiority that was no longer appropriate in egalitarian Australia. Manners of speech and other reflections of an English class system are lampooned, and the unfortunate "new chum" undergoes a series of humiliating incidents that serve to show the need for a different set of behaviors in the new *country*. In the end, the Englishman is changed by the frontier and becomes a "real" person, like those already inhabiting the film. Filmmaker Franklyn Barret made the first of these films, *The Life of a Jackaroo* (1913), with others following with at least 10 films. The send-up of the monocled English twit in *The*

Adventures of Algy (1925) is recycled as "Pommy bashing" in later films, such as *The Adventures of Barry McKenzie* (1972), **My Brilliant Career** (1979), *Gallipoli* (1981), and **Breaker Morant** (1980). None of these later films could be classified as "new chum" films; however, the dislike of the Englishman is a theme, an element of narrative, rather than a generic marker as some of the films are **comedies**, such as *The Adventures of Barry McKenzie*.

An early subgenre closely associated with the bush—related to those genres described above—involved mates and larrikins. Anti-authoritarianism is arguably a strong thread in Australian culture, and the working-class larrikin is a distinctly Australian character, enshrined in film in *The Sentimental Bloke* (1919). For the larrikin, vulgarity was the defense against pretension, exhibited in the **ocker** films of the 1970s such as *Stork* (1971) and *The Adventures of Barry McKenzie* (1972). Although *Wake in Fright* (1971) showed the excesses and dark undercurrents in this larrikinism, **Sunday Too Far Away** (1975) explored the **mateship** and unique unionism of the shearing sheds of the 1950s. The democratic, egalitarian, larrikin bushman became the digger in war films like **Charles Chauvel**'s *Forty Thousand Horsemen* (1940), *Breaker Morant*, *Gallipoli*, and, to a lesser extent, *The Lighthorsemen* (1987), which focused on the experiences of four participants in the mythic Charge of the Light Brigade.

Not all films of the early period were concerned with the new settlers alone. A corpus of films explored the earlier settlers, the **Aborigines**, and interrogated the stresses and consequences of two cultures grinding in juxtaposition. As one would expect, the narrative arguments adopted by the films over time have changed considerably. Charles Chauvel made *Uncivilised* (1936) and **Jedda** (1955), **Ealing** studios co-produced *The Overlanders* and *Bitter Springs* (1950), which was the first film to deal seriously with the question of land rights. Since the revival of the 1970s, films dealing with this cultural dislocation and its consequences been made regularly and will continue to be made until the issues are resolved. These films include *The Chant of Jimmy Blacksmith* (1978), **Rabbit-Proof Fence** (2002), and *The Tracker* (2002).

The plots in recent Australian action/adventure films are usually episodic, allowing for wide variations in tone, the inclusion of different locations and incidentally introduced characters, and moments of spectacle, generally involving fights, explosions, or other types of violence. Even where locations are restricted, the control of space and the ability to move freely through space or from one space to another is always important. Indeed, given the budgetary limitations that are generally placed on the genre in its Australian adaptation, the hero is defined as much by his physical expressiveness as by his heroic deeds. Although most Australian films that fall into the category of action/adventure appear to accept its characteristic emphasis on white male mastery, several of the more interesting qualify and modify such assertions. *Crocodile Dundee* (1986), for example, deliberately slips into **comedy** and parody such as to interrogate this kind of myth. Similarly, *Shame* (1987) also inverts the gendering by making the protagonist a very capable woman who, in terms of ingenuity, skill, and intelligence, is able to meet the more brutal forms of masculinity that come her way. Finally, too, *Razorback* (1984) also engages in parody pitting the protagonists against a monster that is so gigantic that it constitutes a parody and caricature of more serious action/adventure films.

As suggested in passing above, the action and adventure genre is well represented in Australian filmmaking. However, two factors militated against Australian work in action/adventure as currently defined. The first of these is budgetary. For the most part, unless there is substantial international production finance available, Australian producers are unable to afford the high cost special effects spectacle and mise-en-scene available elsewhere. Secondly, Australian government sources of film finance, often aided by film critics, have not looked on this genre with approval until recently (*see* FILM FINANCE CORPORATION). Thus, work in other genres including the period/soft art film and **social realism** gained greater cultural legitimacy even if audiences often stayed away. Nevertheless, despite these handicaps, Australian film producers have shown a distinct capacity to work in this most international of film genres, and the new commercial imperatives of the Film Finance Corporation give such films a greater chance of receiving funding. These factors probably account for the fact that there have been no intensive cycles of production. Rather, most of the later films that conform to the type have been produced as one-offs; the singular exceptions are those of the *Mad Max* trilogy and the **Man from Snowy River** quartet.

Historically and in the period of the revival, then, Australian film **history** is dotted with examples of the action/adventure films. The period since 1970 also includes others that conform to the type including at least one swashbuckler, *The Pirate Movie* (1981). More to the point is the fact that the genre in Australia also includes a good deal of overlap and hybridism with other genres. Thus, for example, part of the genius of *Crocodile Dundee* is its ability to balance and reconcile the generic demands of action/adventure, comedy, and romance.

ADAPTATIONS. While film has become the dominant mode of storytelling in the 20th and early 21st centuries, much of the material for the stories is adapted from written sources, particularly the novel. Australian films draw on both literary and popular novels, and occasionally plays and poems, to provide the raw material for the narratives of film. This tradition is long embedded in the industry: Rolf Boldrewood's novel *Robbery under Arms* had wide and enduring appeal, and five films with this title have been made, from 1907 to 1985. While the films depicted the bushranging life in some detail, Marcus Clarke's *For the Term of His Natural Life* wove a story around the life of a convict transported to New South Wales, and was the basis for three feature films from 1908 to 1927. These history-based novels captured significant elements of early Australian life, and the narratives of bushranging and convict life have been noteworthy themes in Australian filmmaking (*see also* GENRE). Other elements of **country** life, such as the events that comprised the life of simple farming families on small farms, or "blocks" (selections), and the **comedy** that arises from interactions of such characters are significant chapters in the Australian legend. The characters, plots, and locations from Steele Rudd's stories were the basis for the "Dad and Dave" series of films: *Dad and Dave Come to Town* (1938), *Dad Rudd, M.P.* (1940), and *Dad and Dave: On Our Selection* (1995).

Novels were not the only source for early Australian film. Comic strip characters such as Fatty Finn found motion picture life in *The Kid Stakes* (1927), as did Ginger Meggs. In addition, popular poetry, especially long narrative poems, has been a rich lode for Australian film. The feature film *The Sentimental Bloke* (1919) drew on the series of popular poems, *The Songs of a Sentimental Bloke* by C.J. Dennis, for characters and narratives. Other versions were made in 1932,

1968, and 1982, suggesting the enduring attraction of the narrative over time. Bush poet A.B. "Banjo" Paterson wrote one of the most popular poems in the Australian legend, *The Man from Snowy River.* **George Miller** turned this into an internationally successful commercial film in 1982, where he combined the narrative of the poem with traditional dramas of love and action in a high-country, western environment (*see MAN FROM SNOWY RIVER*). Occasionally, plays have been used as the source of films. John Powers wrote the play from which *The Last of the Knucklemen* (1979) was derived.

Before the **revival**, the relatively few films that emerged from the industry continued to draw on print sources. D'Arcy Niland's novel was the basis for **Ealing** studio's production of *The Shiralee* (1957), a quite topical story of adultery, divorce, child custody arguments, and the adventures of an itinerant country worker and his daughter. New possibilities for an Australian film industry arose in the 1970s, and an obvious source of Australian material lay in the novels and plays—popular and literary, historical, and contemporary—about Australian life and characters. One of the first films of the revival, *Wake in Fright* (1971), was based on a Kenneth Cook novel. *Stork* (1971), another film about aspects of the Australian male character, was based on the **David Williamson** play, *The Coming of Stork.* **Peter Weir**'s *Picnic at Hanging Rock* (1975), based on Joan Lindsay's novel, was a counterpoint to the masculine focus of other films of the time, and was grounded in a literary tradition, firmly ensconced in an artfully reworked past, and defined by tales of gentility. *Picnic* catapulted the Australian film industry into national and international markets.

It was followed by other period films where any critique was muted and placed in a gentler past. That subject of that past is often the coming-of-age, or maturing, of the character, a theme that is relatively common in this phase of the Australian industry. Colin Thiele's children's novels were the basis for *Storm Boy* (1976) and *Blue Fin* (1978); Henry Handel Richardson's novel was adapted for **Bruce Beresford**'s *The Getting of Wisdom* (1977), and Colin McKie's novel was the source of *The Mango Tree* (1977). Elizabeth O'Connor wrote the novel that gave rise to *The Irishman* (1978), while **Gillian Armstrong**'s feminist film *My Brilliant Career* (1979) came from a Miles Franklin novel. Sumner Locke Elliott's novel about the life of a young boy caught in a custody battle between two diametrically opposed aunts was the source for *Careful, He Might Hear You* (1983). Peter Carey's novel *Bliss* was the source for the 1985 film of the same name, and more recently, Gillian Armstrong directed the US-Australian coproduction of Carey's *Oscar and Lucinda* (1998). Although Carey wrote about Ned Kelly, the latest version of the legend, Gregor Jordan's *Ned Kelly* (2003) was based on Robert Drewe's *Our Sunshine*.

Less literary, but nonetheless popular, novels transmogrified into films from the same time. **Bruce Beresford** directed the adaptation of the novel by Kathy Lette and Gabrielle Carey, *Puberty Blues* (1981). Ken Cameron's *Monkey Grip* (1982) arose from Helen Garner's novel. In the same year, Peter Weir's adaptation of C.J. Koch's novel, *The Year of Living Dangerously*, launched his international career as a director. The comedy *Death in Brunswick* (1991) arose out of a novel by Boyd Oxlade.

Novels by non-Australian authors have provided the screenplays for films made in Australia. **Tim Burstall** adapted D.H. Lawrence's novel about Australia, *Kangaroo,* into a film of the same name in 1986. *Dead Calm* (1989), directed by **Phillip Noyce**, starring **Nicole Kidman** and **Sam Neill**, and filmed by **Dean Semler**, was an adaptation of a novel by American author Charles Williams.

Novels about the juxtaposition of Aboriginal and white cultures have reached a wider audience on the silver screen. The confronting and violent **Fred Schepisi** film about an Aboriginal man's attempt to come to terms with white society, *The Chant of Jimmy Blacksmith* (1978), was based on Thomas Keneally's novel of the same name. Phillip Noyce's *Rabbit-Proof Fence* (2002) was based on the book by Doris Pilkington Garimara. Phillip Gwynne wrote the novel *Deadly Unna*, made into *Australian Rules* (2002).

The narratives and themes of Australian cultural **history**, initially limited to a reading audience, have been recycled as visual narrative, ensuring their enduring presence within that history.

ADVENTURES OF PRISCILLA: QUEEN OF THE DESERT, THE **(1994).** *Priscilla* is the eighth most popular film at the Australian box office, grossing $16.5 million to January 2003. Directed by Stephan Elliott, the film relates the adventures of an aging transsexual (Terence Stamp) and two drag queens (**Hugo Weaving** and **Guy**

Pearce) on their way to a gig in central Australia. Priscilla is the name they give to the bus, which is their home and mode of transport from Sydney through the desert—both geographically and culturally—to Alice Springs. As in all road movies, trouble ghosts their passage as they battle the outback environment and human cultural differences. Cinematographer **Brian Breheny** revels in the color and big sky isolation of the outback dunes and hills. The spectacular scenery is matched by the spectacular, gaudy, and overwhelming costumes; yet while the scenery is spectacular in its emptiness and desolation, the costumes are spectacular for their riotous, contrasting color. Shots of the bus speeding along dirt tracks to the sounds of classical music as Guy Pearce sits atop a stiletto-throne with yards of silver fabric trailing behind him contrast dramatically with the subdued outback tones, mirroring the cultural rift that exists between this flamboyant minority group and the strong but straight people of the Australian outback. *Priscilla* is not just a diatribe about the characters of straight Australia: the film explores the nature of love on the one hand; on the other, it is a high-camp display of bitchiness and excess.

Costume design won the film an Oscar and a BAFTA award in 1995 and an **Australian Film Institute** (AFI) award in 1994. In 1994, the film was nominated for seven AFI awards, including best film, best director, and best actor for both Stamp and Weaving. BAFTA nominated *Priscilla* for four awards, including best actor (Stamp) and best screenplay.

ALISON, DOROTHY (1925–1992). Alison was born in New South Wales, and appeared in *Eureka Stockade* (1949) and *Sons of Matthew* (1949). To further her career, she traveled to the United Kingdom, appearing in *Mandy* (1952) and *Reach for the Sky* (1956), as Douglas Bader's nurse. On returning to Australia, she played in the minor films *Two Brothers Running* (1988), *Rikky and Pete* (1988), and *Malpractice* (1989). Her tenderness and sincerity underpinned her characters, especially Lindy Chamberlain's mother in ***Evil Angels*** (1988).

ALVIN PURPLE **(1973).** *Alvin Purple*—touted accurately as the "**Ocker** smut classic!"—was a significant production in the Australian film industry for two reasons. First, it was the most successful film at the Australian box office between 1971 and 1977. Second, it was, arguably, the most significant film in the ocker cycle of films that emerged and then fell from favor in the first half of the 1970s. The film was popular in part because it reflected and defined the Australian male's attitude and wish-fantasies about sex, which made the film a soft-core porn film without it degenerating into the category of the straight porn that was to come later. Although he just wants to live the quiet normal life of suburbia, Alvin (**Graeme Blundell**) is constantly pursued by girls who cannot refrain from offering themselves to him, or ravishing him. As a normal man, wanting both to respond to a request from a woman—no matter what the request—and to respond as a sexual being, there is little choice for Alvin. His psychiatrist, Dr. Liz Sort, has a voracious sexual appetite, and as the only authority figure in the film, she plays a large part in his final downfall.

The film was the third directed by **Tim Burstall** and paved the way for Australian films being accepted by mainstream distributors and exhibitors. Distributors *Village Roadshow* formed a partnership with Burstall after his success with his previous ocker film, *Stork* (1971), in order to profit from *Alvin*'s marketing in mainstream cinemas, but also to show the other funding bodies, the state funded bureaucracies, that they were not averse to supporting the local industry. Unfortunately though for Village Roadshow, *Alvin* was one of the last of the cycle. A tidal wave of influence arising from both a backlash to this kind of humor and stereotyping of men, **women**, and the relationships between them, and some embarrassment at the representation of Australians, forced funding bodies to change the criteria for funding, resulting in the rise of the **art and period** film. Doubtless though, the ocker cycle made possible the success of later cycles in establishing that Australian films would draw audience and critical attention, both domestically and overseas.

ANGEL BABY (**1995**). Like *Shine* (1996), *Angel Baby* deals with the effect of mental illness on those who suffer from it, and their families. Unlike *Shine* though, this film did not find a US distributor, possibly because there is no uplifting denouement; rather, the raw and jagged lives are not relieved. The schizophrenic Harry (John Lynch), becomes attracted to a new client, Kate (Jacqueline McKenzie), at the psychiatric outpatient facility he attends and, after some tentative meetings, they fall in love. Their feelings are powerful and intense, and while they believe that love can overcome anything—even their need for medication—it is clear that the reality is far less auspicious and doom is impending. Colin Friels plays Harry's brother and Deborra-Lee Furness his sister-in-law. Although unsuccessful at the box office in Australia and overseas, the film won six **Australian Film Institute** (AFI) awards in 1995, including best film, best director (Michael Rymer), best lead actress (McKenzie), and best original screenplay (Rymer).

ANNIE'S COMING OUT **(1984).** Based on a true story written by the central figure, this feature is one of the very few commercial ventures produced by the government **documentary** production company, **Film Australia**. Also known as *A Test of Love*, it stars Angela Punch McGregor as Jessica and Tina Arhondis as Annie. The story concerns the protracted attempt to allow a disabled, deaf and dumb young woman to live in the community. This "coming out" is achieved mainly through the efforts of Jessica, a sympathetic teacher. However, over and above human effort, the film is also symptomatic of its time in terms of its emphasis on the central role of communication in this process. Thus, *Annie's Coming Out* divides into three sections. First Jessica teaches Annie to use her tongue to say "yes" and "no." At an art gallery, Jessica senses the girl's intelligence when Annie responds to a caricature. In turn, she then learns how to spell, using the latter's body as instrument. As Jessica realizes Annie's intelligence, the film moves into its second phase wherein the teacher attempts to have Annie released from the hospital into her care. Gradually convincing some others of Annie's intelligence, Jessica still faces bureaucratic obstruction and refusal. However, in a third stage of the film, the matter goes to court in an appeal against Annie's incarceration. She is tested twice by the judge and passes. Jessica is able to take her out of the hospital, which was closed subsequently, and the children were placed in special homes in the community. Overall, then, *Annie's Coming Out* can be seen as part of a pluralist discourse about Australian society. Just as **women**, gays, and others have come out in the past 30 or so years, so too have the disabled, as human beings entitled to the same respect and dignity as others.

ARMSTRONG, GILLIAN (1950–). Gillian Armstrong was one of the wave of filmmakers that included **Peter Weir**, **Bruce Beresford**, and **Fred Schepisi** to begin their career in the early days of the **re-vival**. She was also the only woman to come to the fore at this time. Born in 1950 in Melbourne, she graduated from the film school at Swinburne Institute of Technology, completing the short *The Roof Needs Mowing* in 1971. In turn, she was a student in the first interim intake at the newly constituted **Australian Film Television and Radio School** in Sydney in 1973. There she cut her directorial teeth on *One Hundred a Day* (1973) and *The Singer and the Dancer* (1974). The fact that both of these short films were **adaptations** of literary sources—short stories by Alan Marshall—was a clue to what was to be a recurring feature of her career, the literary basis of a significant number of her feature films. However, before moving to features, she directed the **documentary** study of young teenage girls in Adelaide, *Smokes and Lollies* (1976). Finally, after several years in preparation, she and producer Margaret Fink brought Miles Franklin's classic Australian novel *My Brilliant Career* to the screen in 1979 to much critical and popular acclaim.

The film launched Armstrong's career on the international stage and highlighted her capacity to work with women here including writer Elinor Whitcomb and later producers Sandra Levy and Jan Chapman and writers Laura Jones and Helen Garner. Now began a flow of important works from Armstrong. These included a follow-up to the earlier documentary that picked up the real life story of the Adelaide teenage women some four years later—*14's Good, 18's Better* (1981)—and Australia's only feature **musical** of the 1980s, the underrated *Star Struck* (1982). By then, Armstrong was in Hollywood undertaking her first feature there, *Mrs. Soffel* (1984). However, despite this successful career move, Armstrong did not abandon her roots. Indeed, she remained interested in documentary as was evidenced by *Bob Dylan in Concert* (1986) and, most especially, two further follow-ups to the true-life "diary" type portraits of the young Adelaide women, *Bingo, Bridesmaids and Braces* (1988), and *Not 14 Again* (1996). Moving backward and forward across the Pacific, she survived the "10BA" period, where her oeuvre included *Hightide* (1987). Films produced under the reign of the **Film Finance Corporation** included *The Last Days of Chez Nous* (1992) and the less than glorious *Oscar and Lucinda* (1996), the latter under producer Chapman based on the novel by Peter Carey. Meanwhile in Hollywood there have been a string of films, most notably *Fires Within* (1991) and *Little Women* (1994). Altogether, Gillian Armstrong is a giant in the landscape that is Australian cinema. Equally at home with period settings and modern subjects, she shows herself to have a special affinity and insight into the plight of her women characters and figures, not only as single subjects but also in their intergenerational relationships. Not surprisingly she has been highly important in the screen career of several actors including **Judy Davis**, **Claudia Karvan**, and **Cate Blanchett**, as well as *Sam Neill.

ART AND PERIOD FILMS.   The first films of the **revival**—that is, those released between 1970 and 1973—were the **ocker** comedies like *Stork* (1971), *The Adventures of Barry Mackenzie* (1972), and *Alvin Purple* (1973), which celebrated the more vulgar side to an alleged typical "Australianness." These films had financial success at home and were popular overseas, and thus pointed the way to the possibility of a revived Australian film industry. However, critics and the relatively new federal and state government funding bodies were less than enamored; their desire was that Australian films would represent Australia as a sophisticated place with manners and a style that approximated the best European traditions. A review of government financial assistance in 1975 changed the criteria for that assistance, so that commercial success was no longer as important as the ability of the films to act as cultural lighthouses; to generate some form of cultural capital (Turner 1989: 99–101). Thus, over the next five years, approval for financing was given to films that had a distinctive visual and narrative style, and such films became known as the "AFC genre" (**Australian Film Commission** genre) because of this favoritism.

   The model for emulation was the European art film, but the stories were often sourced from literary novels. The films were set in the past, they highlighted Australianness through re-creations of history and the representation of landscapes, they were lyrically and beautifully shot, with many long, atmospheric takes, and they avoided direct action or sustained conflict. Key films include **Peter Weir**'s *Picnic at Hanging Rock* (1975), Donald Crombie's *Caddie* (1976), **Bruce Beresford**'s *The Getting of Wisdom* (1977), **Gillian Armstrong**'s *My Brilliant Career* (1979), and **Phillip Noyce**'s *Newsfront* (1978). Other films include *Between Wars* (1974), Ken Hannam's

Sunday Too Far Away (1975) and *Break of Day* (1976), *Mad Dog Morgan* (1975), **Fred Schepisi**'s *The Devil's Playground* (1976) and *The Chant of Jimmy Blacksmith* (1978), **Tim Burstall**'s *Eliza Fraser* (1976), *The Mango Tree* (1977), *Journey among Women* (1977), *Raw Deal* (1976), *The Picture Show Man* (1976), and Crombie's *The Irishman* (1978). Thus, although not always given the status of a **genre**, the art film in Australian cinema **history** assumes an importance that makes a separate generic title appropriate.

At the edges of the spectrum, art films have elements in common with both the classical **Hollywood** cinema and the modernist films of **Europe**. Generally though, they do not have the same fixation with cause-effect linkages of events that the classical narrative has. Nevertheless, the art film is realistic, in that its characters are psychologically complex, and the problems that it addresses are real problems of alienation, of lack of communication, for example. In the art film, the author becomes a formal component, the consciousness that constructs and composes the film, which is then presented to the audience for consideration. Thus, the films often have authorial codes, and the audience asks questions like: who is telling this story? How is the story being told? Why is the story being told this way? (Bordwell 1979: 57). A further property of the art film is ambiguity, leading to an open-ended narrative, so that the story often lacks a clear-cut resolution. Mysticism, or some kind of supernatural presence, is often a key element of art cinema and, in the Australian version, the characterization of **Aborigines** suggests a mystical strain, rather than the more common social realist perspective. The camera too becomes significant in the narrative, using techniques to suggest themes and moods. For example, in *The Chant of Jimmy Blacksmith*, the camera work suggests containment, entrapment, and enclosure, by using shots through eyeholes in prison doors and claustrophobic shots inside houses, for example.

Yet, *Picnic at Hanging Rock* remains the most well known of the art/period films, with long shots, visually stunning and evocative scenes of fog in the Australian landscape juxtaposed with the European values epitomized in the Victorian architecture of the buildings. The content of the story is ambiguous; events can be seen in a number of different organizing structures. Disappearances are not explained, nor are they shown on screen; all is implied, rather than asserted. The film contained other elements that assisted its marketing in the United States and the United Kingdom, and that were demanded by those markets (Walsh 2000–2001: 36). For various reasons, in the late 1970s there was a recession in the American art film circuit, and Australia was seen to be a possible supplier. Thus, in that market, the "British" quality is important, often manifesting as a timeless Victorian past, and these qualities are apparent in many Australian films. It is significant that many of these films were screened in the American art theater circuits, and the films were submitted and acclaimed at Cannes and other European festivals.

These films began a tradition in Australian filmmaking that has continued in the work of some filmmakers. Jonathan Teplitzky's *Better Than Sex* (2000) was filmed almost entirely within a single location, a studio apartment in Sydney, and comprised a three-day blossoming of love between two people, one of whom (**David Wenham**) might be judged to be physically attractive, while the other (**Susie Porter**) does not have the qualities of traditional Hollywood femininity. Writer, producer, and director **Rolf de Heer** could be classified as an auteur filmmaker, with films like *The Old Man Who Read Love Stories* (2001), *The Tracker* (2002), and *Alexandra's Project* (2003) as contenders for the art film appellation. *The Tracker*, for example, had no characters, just types: The Tracker, The Fanatic, The Follower, The Veteran, and The Fugitive. The characters had no history, apart from that suggested by their type. Scenes of violence were replaced by paintings of those events. Cause-effect relationships were never clear, while the interpolation of Aboriginal Australians was often mystic, rather than socially realist. The acceptance of de Heer's films, especially in European film festivals, attests to his expertise in this genre.

ASIA. Despite its geographic proximity to Southeast Asia, Australia and New Zealand are regions of recent white settlement that retain strong cultural, linguistic, and historical ties with **Europe**, most especially the United Kingdom, but also the eastern Mediterranean region as well as northern and eastern Europe. Thus, it should come as no surprise to find a relative paucity of films, whether features or documentaries, that deal with the region. Indeed, five of the six feature films that have appeared only in the past two decades tend to follow a familiar narrative trajectory. Frequently taking the form of a thriller or mystery melodrama, the archetypal film follows the adventures of a white Australian soldier of fortune, whether he is an investigator or photographic journalist, seeking to get to the root of injustice and corruption and save some helpless Asians from this threat. Romantic melodrama is also favored as this crusade involves romance with a white woman often against an Asian setting which if indistinguishable is definitely exotic and threat-laden. It is also confined to that part of the region closest to Australia, there being no film engagement with either East Asia or South Asia.

Meanwhile, the Asians of the proximate are relegated to the background where they function in minor roles or in crowd scenes. The feature films that constitute this cycle can be summarily noticed here. *Far East* (1982) is a remake of Warner's *Casablanca* exchanging that location for Manila and Humphrey Bogart for actor **Bryan Brown**. The latter, initially cynical and passive in the face of political and social oppression, is stirred into action by the presence of an old girlfriend and her investigative journalist husband. A character added to the original format is an Asian woman activist who is potentially a heroine but is reduced to victim status by being raped and brutalized. The same year also saw a second Asian feature, *The Year of Living Dangerously*, which turned Indonesia's political crisis around the downfall of Sukarno into the background for a suspense thriller. Again, there is a splitting of hero. Foreign correspondent **Mel Gibson** pursues romance with British diplomat Sigourney Weaver. Meanwhile, Billie, a Chinese-Australian photojournalist supporter of Sukarno ultimately falls victim to forces of reaction and is killed. Indonesia is both beautiful and sinister, densely populated with large crowd scenes adding to the deliberate feeling of "foreignness." In turn, this is compounded further by the casting of a female in the male role of Billie, a decision that also invokes the myth of the androgyny of Asians.

In 1990, Asia was featured again in *Blood Oath*, a courtroom drama set on the island of Ambon in Indonesia. The film was set in the immediate aftermath of World War II and concerned an Australian court prosecutor, Bryan Brown, who has to put various Japanese on trial for war crimes against Australian prisoners of war. The film deliberately avoids controversy in its dramatization of these issues of power and abuse differentiating between both American and Japanese forces. It also finds dramatic space to differentiate between the Japanese officers themselves and finds a "good" Japanese in the shape of a Christian. Meanwhile, *Turtle Beach* (1992) used the same formula of crusading white journalist exposing Asian corruption. By way of variation, this film concerned the plight of Vietnamese boat people, was set in Malaysia, and starred a woman actress, Greta Scacchi.

However, if this group of films defines a structure of narrative and feeling, two other features vary the pattern. The first of these, *Echoes of Paradise* (1987), is a **woman**'s melodrama. The central figure is a middle-aged housewife (Wendy Hughes) who departs Sydney and a philandering husband for Thailand. Here she responds to Thailand in all its variety and otherness. An androgynous Asian gigolo sensuously arouses her, enabling her to return to her former life with new-found confidence and sexuality. Finally, *Traps* (1994) is set in former Indochina in 1954 with the Vietminh struggling against French colonial rulers. Australian husband, journalist Michael, and British wife, photojournalist Louise, again find themselves caught up in this struggle. However, this film is in fact much more sensitive to issues of orientalism and subtly critiques the thinking and actions of the couple rather than endorsing them as the other films in this cycle are want to do. In addition, there is a stream of **documentary** films having to do with Asia that offer a much wider range of subjects and a more interesting diversity of perspective. Undoubtedly, an important precursor of the latter is the feature length documentary, *Indonesia Calling* (1946), directed by noted Dutch documentarist Joris Ivens with extensive support from Australian trade unions, political activists, and filmmakers. Appointed Film Commissioner by the Dutch government, Ivens found that the Indonesian peoples wanted not the reimposition of Dutch colonial rule after the Japanese defeat but independence. His film graphically highlights their plight. By the 1970s, other notable filmmakers had begun to make films in the region. These included James Darling on Bali, Solrun Hoaas on Japan, Curtis Levy on Indonesia, Dennis O'Rourke on the Pacific, and Mike Rubbo on Vietnam and Indonesia. Thus to round out this account, three recent documentaries that indicate this greater outlook can be identified. In 1989 appeared John Mercen's *Road to Xanadu*, which looks at a three-way interchange between China, the West, and Japan over a millennium. Similarly, in 1992, appeared Christine Olsen and Curtis Levy's *Riding the Tiger*, a meditation on what is Indonesia. The film traces the influence of both the Dutch and the Japanese in shaping modern-day Indonesia and subtly raises the epistemological problem of nationalist knowledge. Finally, the controversial *The Good Woman of Bangkok* (1992), Dennis O'Rourke's complex inter-rogation not only of the subject of Thai prostitution but also of his own motives as failed savior of Aoi, the central figure of the film's ti-tle. Altogether, then, Australia has had only a fleeting engagement with Asia in cinema in the past 50 years. Still, if more of the open, exploratory impulse to be found in documentaries were to find its way into feature films, then there would be more chance of breaking free of the stereotypes to be found there.

AUSTRALIAN CENTRE FOR THE MOVING IMAGE (ACMI). The Australian Centre for the Moving Image (ACMI) was established on 1 January 2002 by the *Film Act 2001 (Victoria)*, which provided for a new cultural institution in Victoria dedicated to the moving im-age in all its forms. ACMI (formerly CineMedia) promotes the mov-ing image and has a charter to develop collections, exhibitions, events, and educational resources in Victoria within a national and global environment. The focus of its activities is within its new facil-ity at Federation Square, in the center of Melbourne, but the Centre is also a lending collection, an online presence, and an international contributor to research and development of screen works. This new cultural body brings together leading-edge digital technology and the screen, providing its visitors, both in person and online, with access to the creation and viewing of the moving image. ACMI features the world's largest screen gallery—over 1,500 square meters; two multi-format cinemas; hands-on interactive, education, and production zones; and the largest public lending collection of moving image for ACMI members. A four-story purpose built venue at Federation Square houses the Screen Gallery, Cinemas, and public activity spaces. The ACMI Lending Collection is located elsewhere. ACMI presents a program of regular free screenings in the cinemas.

A visit to Australia in 1940 by Dr. John Grierson led to the estab-lishment of the Australian National Film Board in 1945. Dr. Grier-son's recommendations also led to the formation of state-based government film bodies and the State Film Centre of Victoria was established (*see* COMMONWEALTH FILM UNIT; FILM AUSTRALIA). The aims of the Centre were to maintain "a list of all suitable **documentary** and educational films" with a responsibility to promote the material for public consumption. It was in this capacity that the State Film Centre established and maintained its own film library in addition to supporting regional lending services, especially for schools, and mobile projection units that screened films to isolated audiences.

The introduction of **television** to Melbourne in 1956 saw the State Film Centre become involved in television production. The organization also played a valuable role as an archive of important Australian films such as *The Sentimental Bloke* (1919)—acquired in 1957—and *On Our Selection* (1920) in 1958. During the 1960s, the State Film Centre increasingly provided advice on film treatments, production, scripts, and distribution outlets to local filmmakers, demonstrating the growing importance of the facility to the local industry. In 1969, the Centre assumed management of the newly constructed State Film Theatre, providing the community with an important facility exhibiting material not screened in commercial cinemas. In the 1970s, the scope for the State Film Centre's acquisitions changed to include examples of student films generated by the introduction of film studies to universities. During this period, the Australian production industry experienced significant change, driven by new levels of government funding and emerging filmmakers producing confident, original films drawing acclaim from Australian and international audiences (*see* REVIVAL).

In 1983, *The State Film Centre of Victoria Council Act 1983* facilitated a new governing structure for the State Film Centre and foreshadowed a change in direction in terms of its policy. The initial push for development recognized the changing nature of screen industries in an environment of emergent digital media forms, and a need for an exhibition space free of the restrictions imposed in traditional display facilities. The State Film Centre further developed plans for the Australian Centre for the Moving Image in the early 1990s, evaluating several sites around Melbourne for suitability, finally settling on Federation Square. On 1 January 2002, the ACMI was established by the *Film Act 2001* (Victoria). On 26 October, the first stage of the ACMI was opened. On 17 November, the ACMI cinemas officially opened.

AUSTRALIAN CHILDREN'S TELEVISION FOUNDATION (ACTF). The ACTF is a national nonprofit organization, created to encourage development, production, and dissemination of high-quality **television** programs, films, and other audiovisual media for children. It promotes these productions in the community. Since 1982, the ACTF has assisted in the development of a production environment and of children's programming. The foundation has supported 165 hours of programs, which have been sold in more than 100 countries. These productions have received 70 nominations and have won 90 national and international awards, including an International Emmy Award and Prix Jeunesse.

The role of the ACTF includes the initiation, development, and production of innovative programs; the provision of development finance to writers and filmmakers; the undertaking of research into and evaluation of productions; advice to filmmakers; marketing of programs in Australia and overseas; and promotion of programs in the community. Although the major thrust of the Foundation's work has been in television, it is supporting feature length films and telemovies. The Foundation's first **action** feature film was *Jolngu Boy* (2001).

AUSTRALIAN FILM COMMISSION (AFC). The Australian Film Commission is the federal government agency that supports the development of projects in film, **television**, and the interactive digital media, particularly in the independent sector. The AFC provides financial and information resources to assist people in developing projects.

The federal government established the AFC in 1975 because of the Tariff Board's inquiry into the industry, to address issues of **national identity** and culture. The Commission was preceded by the Australian Film Development Corporation, which provided direct financial assistance to commercial film production. The AFC has a much wider brief and is the most powerful of the plethora of federal and state government agencies concerned with film. It has many responsibilities: project development through script and other preproduction assistance; postproduction grants, and low-budget production funding; grants in support of a vigorous and diverse screen culture; international promotion of Australian productions and marketing advice; creative, interactive media development, production and exhibition; development of indigenous film and television program makers; monitoring of film, television, and multimedia industry performance; and information services.

The AFC provides direct financial assistance to project development, including script development and production financing, using cultural and commercial criteria. Offices in Los Angeles and in the United Kingdom, as well as the Australian office, handle the promotion of films at the Cannes and other film festivals. Less commercial films, such as experimental and **documentary** film, may be funded through the commission. Recently, like other Australian government agencies, the commission has entered into multimedia as well.

Critics of the AFC argue that it has forced the development of films in a particular mould, that it has indulged in cronyism, and that it is providing subsidies in what should be a purely commercial industry. On the other hand, argue others, it has provided a strong impetus for the development of the industry, and without the AFC, the Australian industry might have withered on the vine.

Some of the criticisms are pertinent. The AFC was established at a time when the commercial criteria used by the Australian Film Development Corporation resulted in funding for films like those of the **ocker** cycle. The AFC changed the criteria so that the commercial imperative gave way to cultural and aesthetic criteria in the determination of funding (*see* ART AND PERIOD FILMS). At the same time, the AFC ignored certain films, and some directors were marginalized, for whatever reason (*see STONE*).

AUSTRALIAN FILM DEVELOPMENT CORPORATION. *See* AUSTRALIAN FILM COMMISSION.

AUSTRALIAN FILM FINANCE CORPORATION (FFC). *See* FILM FINANCE CORPORATION AUSTRALIA.

AUSTRALIAN FILM INSTITUTE (AFI). The Australian Film Institute is proof of Melbourne's importance in the national film industry and culture and also proof of its marginality. Incorporated in 1958 as an offshoot of the Melbourne Film Festival, a clone of the prestigious British Film Institute, the AFI quickly managed to find a reason for its existence in the shape of an industry award event. This took the form of the organization of annual awards for achievements in film production. In its early years and often, indeed, since, the AFI has managed to continue to do this often when there is little or no competition because of low levels of industry output. Until around 1972, the AFI operated much as a private club for members, which was not open to the general public. By then, however, the federal government had decided to kick start a film industry and a film culture. To do so, it needed a pre-existing instrument to administer such programs as its newly created Experimental Film Fund. The AFI took over this function and prospered over the next decade adding film distribution, film exhibition venues in Melbourne, Hobart, and Sydney, a Melbourne Research and Information Centre, and the operation of the National Film Theatre of Australia.

Meanwhile, the jewel in the crown continued to be the annual AFI awards, an event that then and now falls somewhere between the cultural prestige of a Venice or Cannes film festival and the commercial ballyhoo of the **Hollywood** Oscars. However, starting in 1975 and accelerating in the second half of the decade, the federal government began trimming the budgets that it made available to its various film instrumentalities. One by one, the AFI lost its various programs, sometimes because of broader bureaucratic restructuring and sometimes because of budget constraints. However, with most federal agencies in the overlapping areas of film, media, and culture generally located in Sydney, the continued existence of the AFI was, in effect, not negotiable. In any case, in order ensure its own survival, the AFI had adopted a new constitution that made membership available to all who would pay an annual membership fee. Hence, the body continues down to the present, still running the annual awards, research library, distribution of shorts and documentaries, a modest exhibition program, and cinemas in Hobart and Sydney.

AUSTRALIAN FILM TELEVISION AND RADIO SCHOOL (AFTRS).

The Commonwealth Government established the AFTRS as a statutory authority in 1973. The school is the national center for professional education and advanced training in film, broadcasting, and interactive media. The main campus is in Sydney, where full-time postgraduate students study aspects of the film industry, such as scriptwriting, producing, directing, cinematography, editing and sound, in graduate diploma and masters-level programs. In other cities, the school offers short courses for industry professionals who wish to broaden their area of expertise, upgrade current skills, or learn new skills.

The alumni are a *who's who* of Australian film. Directors include ***Jane Campion, Phillip Noyce, P.J. Hogan, Rolf de Heer**, and **Alex Proyas**; scriptwriters include Chris Noonan and Denny Lawrence; cinematographers include **Andrew Lesnie** and **Dion Beebe**.

AUZINS, IGOR (1949–). Auzins was a cinematographer, director, and producer for the Crawfords *television* production house in the 1970s. He directed *High Rolling* (1977), and later, telemovies, miniseries, and **documentaries** for the **South Australian Film Corporation**. He directed a number of films for television: *All at Sea* (1977), *The Night Nurse* (1978), *The Death Train* (1978), and *Water Under the Bridge* (1980). He has since directed two feature films, *We of the Never Never* (1982) and *The Coolangatta Gold* (1984).

– B –

***BABE* (1995).** *Babe* is the second most popular film at the Australian box office, taking $36.8 million in revenues up to 2003. It has won many awards: in 1996, it won an Oscar for best visual effects, a Saturn award for best fantasy film from the United States Academy of Science Fiction, Fantasy, and Horror Films, a cinematographer of the year award for *Andrew Lesnie* from the Australian Cinematographers Society, a Film Critics Circle of Australia award for best director (Chris Noonan) and for best original music (Nigel Westlake) in 1997, a German Golden Screen award, as well as many others. The film was nominated for Oscars (best actor in a supporting role, best art direction, best director, best editing, best writing, and best film) as well as BAFTA awards.

The animated fairytale follows the adventures of a pig that has an identity crisis while trying to escape the fate of being presented on the table as Christmas pork. Orphaned at birth, Babe is won by a farmer at a **country** fair, and taken to the Hoggetts' farm where he meets the other animals and decides he wants to become something other than a pig. The Hoggetts are quiet, unassuming, and kind to the animals, but are oblivious to the intelligence and secret lives led by the farm animals, which is the backdrop for many comical scenes.

As well as producing the film, **Dr. George Miller** wrote the screenplay from the story *The Sheep-Pig* by Dick King-Smith, the successful author of some 70 children's stories. Chris Noonan—*Bulls* (1973), *Stepping Out* (1980)—assisted Miller with the screenplay and directed the film. The film featured the voices of Christine Cavanaugh as Babe, Miriam Margolyes (better known as Professor Sprout in the Harry Potter films) as Fly, the female sheepdog, **Hugo Weaving** as Rex, the male sheepdog, and many others, including Magda Szubanski.

***BABE: PIG IN THE CITY* (1998).** The sequel to *Babe* (1995), was also written by Miller—in collaboration with Judy Morris and Mark Lamprell—and directed by him. It was not as successful as *Babe* on the awards circuit, but it was nominated for many including an Academy award for best original song. Nor was it as commercially successful. While *Babe* took US$66 million at the American box office, the sequel made only US$18 million. The reasons are not difficult to find. Although the original was clearly and simply made for children, the sequel moves into mature satire evolving from a sophisticated narrative about a pig with a huge ego, as befits a star of another blockbuster. Babe rescues a pit-bull terrier, who then performs service to the pig by enforcing a utopian society, echoing images from George Orwell's *Animal Farm*. Although the film is excellent viewing for adults, it did not attract the audience who were enamored by the saccharine sweetness of the original.

***BAD BOY BUBBY* (1993).** Written and directed by **Rolf de Heer**, *Bad Boy Bubby* marked new ground in the Australian industry. Produced by the **Film Finance Corporation**, *Bubby* was filmed in Adelaide, South Australia. The abused child of a drunken mother and estranged father—who disguises himself as a priest—Bubby remains locked up for 30 years, to avoid the poisonous air that his mother has convinced him exists in the outside world. A visit from his father breaks the spell, and Bubby murders both his parents, and then continues to rape and pillage, employing every act of perversion, violence, and degradation that de Heer could shoehorn into the available film time. Finally though, Bubby's cathartic activity leads him to change his life, and he ends up a happily married, suburban man. The film is another of de Heer's essays on the nature of alienation on the individual, and its consequences, although that brief exposition tends to downplay the significance of the film. Interestingly, the happily married suburban man is the subject of de Heer's later study in alienation, the one-sided *Alexandra's Project* (2003). *See also ROMPER STOMPER.*

BAILEY, BERT (1868–1953). Bert Bailey was born in New Zealand, but moved to Sydney at an early age. He wrote and appeared in the popular plays and films that portrayed the life of the Australian pioneer farmers, through **comedy** rather than drama. He cowrote, with Edmund Duggan, the play *The Squatter's Daughter*, and directed and starred in the film of the same name in 1910. In 1911, he starred in *The Christian* as Archdeacon Wealthy. Inspired by the stories of Steele Rudd, Duggan and Bailey wrote the play *On Our Selection*, which **Ken G. Hall** made into a film in 1932 starring Bailey as Dad Rudd. With Ken Hall in 1938, Bailey wrote the screenplay for *Dad and Dave Come to Town*, in which Bailey starred again as Dad Rudd. Sequels were a way of capitalizing on the popularity of a **genre** even in the 1930s, and Hall and Bailey wrote *Dad Rudd, M.P.* (1940) in which Bailey starred once again as Dad Rudd. In all these films, Dad is the icon for so-called traditional values of home and hearth and family, representing the innocent **country** folk juxtaposed against the experienced, and thereby somehow corrupted, people from the **city**.

BANA, ERIC (1968–). Eric Bana built a strong career in Australian **comedy television** from 1993 to 1996 in *Full Frontal*. He debuted on the big screen as Con Petropoulous in **Rob Sitch**'s *The Castle* (1997). He then played the lead role of Mark Brandon "Chopper" Read in the film about the life of this particular criminal, *Chopper* (2000). The film is based on Read's autobiography, which he wrote while in prison serving a sentence for murder. Both the film and the book sold well, and the film showed that Bana was capable of sustaining a strong lead in a noncomic role. The **Australian Film Institute** awarded him the prize for best leading actor in 2000. He made a successful and sudden transition to **Hollywood**, transmogrifying effectively into the strong supporting role of American marine SFC

"Hoot" Gibson, complete with authentic southern accent, in Ridley Scott's *Black Hawk Down* (2001). Returning to Australia, Bana showed that he had not lost his sense of comedy, playing the road worker Lotto who, with his friends, found a large gold nugget, in Bill Bennett's *The Nugget* (2002). He had a small part in *Finding Nemo* (2003) as the voice of Anchor, before winning the lead role of Bruce Banner in Ang Lee's superhero tale *Hulk* (2003).

BARRETT, RAY (1926–). Ray Barrett is one of the elder statesmen of the Australian film industry. Born in Brisbane, Queensland, he worked in radio in the dark days of Australian filmmaking. Nevertheless, he first appeared in a strong supporting role in the American-made *The Desperate Women* (1955) before immigrating to the United Kingdom. There, Barrett was cast in **television** and film roles, in which he thrived, appearing in many television series and some 12 films, including the lead role of Sgt. Henry Fraser in the Herbert Wise **crime** film, *To Have and to Hold* (1963). Other lead and supporting roles followed.

By 1975, the Australian industry was in the throes of **revival**, so, even though his career in the United Kingdom seemed secure, Barrett returned to Australia and has worked consistently since then on stage, in television, and in films. His craggy features and relaxed appearance suggest the laconic Australian character, and while he plays these roles well, he is an accomplished character actor, moving seamlessly across parts that have different demands. He played the abusive failed psychiatrist, Mal, in **Bruce Beresford**'s *Don's Party* (1976), and a corrupt, mean policeman in **Fred Schepisi**'s *The Chant of Jimmy Blacksmith* (1978) for which he won the **Australian Film Institute** (AFI) award for best actor in a supporting role in 1978. As the hard-boiled private detective in the film noir-inspired *Goodbye Paradise* (1983), Barrett stalked the streets of Brisbane with such conviction that he easily could have been mistaken for one of the real-life crime characters of the pre-Fitzgerald era. The AFI awarded him the best lead actor award for this role in 1982. He played in Werner Herzog's story of the clash of **Aboriginal** culture and values with non-Aboriginal extractive mining culture in *Where the Green Ants Dream* (also *Wo die grünen Ameisen träumen*) (1984).

As president of the bench in *Prisoners of the Sun* (1990), he presided over the trials of Japanese prisoners-of-war. In *Hotel Sor-*

rento (1995), even though his character dies half way through the film, Barrett won the AFI best lead actor award in 1995. He gave an outstanding performance as **Russell Crowe**'s father in the uneven Craig Lahiff's *Heaven's Burning* (1997), a road movie that traversed Australia. In the **comedy** *Dalkeith* (2002), Barrett offered another strong performance as a retired barrister living anonymously in a retirement home, who again takes up the barrister's robes and wigs to fight for the residents of the home.

Other films in the United Kingdom and the United States include *Touch of Death* (1961), *Time to Remember* (1962), *Mix Me a Person* (1962), *Jigsaw* (1962), *80,000 Suspects* (1963), *The Reptile* (1966), *Just Like a Woman* (1968), *Revenge* (1971), *Little Laura and Big John* (1973), *The Amorous Milkman* (1974), *The Hostages* (1975). Other films in Australia include *Let the Balloon Go* (1976), the American produced (but shot in Australia) *The Earthling* (1980), *Dangerous Summer* (1981), *The Empty Beach* (1985), *Relatives* (1985), *Rebel* (1985), *Frenchman's Farm* (1987), *As Time Goes By* (1988), *Waiting* (1991), *No Worries* (1993), *Dad and Dave: On Our Selection* (1995), *Brilliant Lies* (1996), *Hotel de Love* (1996), *In the Winter Dark* (1998), *Deluge* (1999), *Visitors* (2003).

BERESFORD, BRUCE (1940–). Another of the first wave of feature film directors associated with the **revival** of the early 1970s, Beresford was born in Sydney in 1940, attended Sydney University and directed his first film *The Rifle* before journeying to England, part of a wave of departures that included Germaine Greer and Clive James. Indeed the latter reveals in *Unreliable Memoirs* a thinly disguised Beresford already single-handedly pursuing his craft of filmmaking director in Sydney before this departure. While overseas in the second half of the 1960s, Beresford had stints with both the British Film Institute and the Rhodesian Film Unit that saw him working in the area of film production. However, the establishment of the **Australian Film Development Corporation** lured Beresford back to Australia. Here he embarked on his first commercial feature film, *The Adventures of Barry McKenzie* (1972), which he cowrote with Barry Humphries, and directed. Its commercial success launched Beresford on a career that continues to the present. Showing remarkable commercial tenacity and determination to continue to make films, he worked briefly for

Reg Grundy Enterprises, where he directed both a feature **documentary** *The Wreck of the Batavia* (1974) and the "Bazza" sequel *Barry McKenzie Holds His Own* (1974). Although there was a congruence of sorts just then between his career and that of **Tim Burstall**, Beresford soon showed more ability and good fortune in his choice of projects. One part of this probably lies in his capacity to work in several **genres** and types of film in different film industries, notably in Australia and in **Hollywood**. His last film in the **ocker comedy** cycle *Don's Party* (1976) was among the very best of that genre. However, the shift toward the **art and period** film that occurred in Australia following the success of *Picnic at Hanging Rock* (1975) saw Beresford direct two of the most notable films of this cycle, *The Getting of Wisdom* (1977) and *Breaker Morant* (1980). Meanwhile, there was still time to make one of the very best **action** thrillers of the decade in *Money Movers* (1979) and to reunite with a **David Williamson** stage project in *The Club* (1980).

By the early 1980s, Beresford spread his wings further and showed himself sympathetic in dealing with a female teenage story in *Puberty Blues* (1981). He was then in a position to venture further afield to pursue other feature projects. These included the Canadian coproduction *Black Robe* (1991), the ridiculous extravaganza of *King David* (1985), and the more modest but more impressive *Tender Mercies* (1983). The latter fetched him an Oscar nomination and he achieved the award itself for a later Hollywood feature *Driving Miss Daisy* (1989), although a later thriller, *Double Jeopardy* (1999), was not well received; neither was his biopic of Alma Mahler, wife of Gustav and others, *Bride of the Wind* (2001). He bounced back with *Evelyn* (2002), a story about a father in 1950s Ireland attempting to win back custody of his children from the state.

Beresford was by no means lost to the Australian industry returning from time to time for such notable films as *The Fringe Dwellers* (1986), *Paradise Road* (1997), and the documentary *Sydney: A Story of a City* (1999). Altogether, he has been an enormously significant figure both in the Australian film industry and in the international industry. He has shown a remarkable ability to demonstrate a fine sensibility and is at ease working with both male and female ensembles of actors sensitively exploring human vulnerabilities and feelings. While several of his films are excellent observations of characters caught in physically and psychologically confining spaces, he is equally adroit in the outdoors of a *Black Robe* or a *Tender Mercies*. Finally, too, it is also worth noting the extent to which Beresford has worked on projects based on existing literary works indicating not just a *metteur en scene* as *Cahiers du Cinema* once put it but a strong and robust sensibility that is able to constantly marshal its power and insight in bringing these works to the screen.

BIRCH, CARROLL AND COYLE (BCC). Although **Greater Union** and **Hoyts** dominate Australian film exhibition, nevertheless, this very large, Queensland-based exhibitor is crying out for a solid history and organizational study. Despite this scholarly neglect, it is possible to follow the contours of its structure and growth against a general backdrop of exhibition in Australia. Historically, American companies achieved extensive penetration of the Australian film distribution market in the early decade of the 20th century and this was solidified by 1914. Although none of the American motion picture companies owned and operated theaters in Australia during the most lucrative period of cinema exhibition history, nevertheless a familiar enough pattern has existed, in this case in the state of Queensland. A dominant chain that owned cinemas in the lucrative exhibition markets there characterized this. The roots of Birch, Carroll and Coyle lie in the very early years of the 20th century when itinerant cinema-photographers also acted as traveling projectionists and exhibitors. The threesome who gave their names to the merged company were located in southern, central, and north Queensland respectively. As early as 1907, two brothers—E.J. and Dan Carroll in Brisbane—bought the Queensland exhibition rights to the film *The Story of the Kelly Gang*, one of the first full-length features made in Australia. In turn, this led to them launching the first open-air screening in Brisbane in 1909, operating at the Exhibition Ground and the Woolloongabba Cricket Ground. They also included the Ipswich Sports Reserve in this developing exhibition circuit. Being open-air, their exhibition screenings were confined to summer. In winter, they ran skating rinks in different North Queensland centers. By 1910, the two had established the first dedicated continuous picture theater in Brisbane. Shortly after, the company added two more picture theaters to their circuit: the Majestic (1915) and the Wintergarden (1923).

Meanwhile, paralleling the development of exhibition circuits in the United States, the Carrolls looked elsewhere to expand. In 1918, George Birch joined the company with his Earl Court Theater in Rockhampton. Similarly, in late 1922, Virgil T. Coyle in North Townsville further expanded the network by adding his two theaters to the circuit. More theaters were acquired and it was decided to form a new parent company out of these mergers. Thus, in 1923, Birch, Carroll and Coyle Limited came into existence. By then, the group operated 13 cinemas in seven provincial cities in the state. The new company immediately developed plans to further extend, building cinemas in the coastal cities of Rockhampton and Townsville and several smaller towns. In keeping with theater design and scheduling at the time, these accommodated both live stage shows and films. Although the company wired its theaters for sound, the onset of the Great Depression followed by World War II meant that plans for further expansion had to be put on hold. Nonetheless, in 1946, the group acquired the Roxy Theater in Townsville. Some further growth occurred although shortly curtailed by the onset of **television** between 1959 and 1962 in regional Queensland. To help create a new market, BCC began opening drive-ins, beginning in 1961 with the Tropicaire in Mount Isa. Progressively divesting of single hard-tops, BCC also moved into multiplexes. Thus, in 1975 it closed its Wintergarden in Townsville and replaced it with an air-conditioned twin-cinema complex. About the same time, the company also built its first twin drive-in, the Rockhampton Twin Drive-In. In addition, the city received the Rockhampton Twin Cinemas, making it the first provincial city in Queensland to gain this kind of double exhibition arrangement. Meanwhile, expansion was also moving across state borders. In 1972, it opened cinemas and drive-ins in northern New South Wales and an air-conditioned hard-top in the adjacent Northern Territory capital of Darwin. By early 1980s, BCC had acquired the Maroochy Cinema and opened the Mermaid Twin Cinema, together with the first multiplex on the Gold Coast.

However, video home rental was booming and the company began to close drive-ins as well as some hard-tops. By 1989, it was again looking for opportunities around the development of multiplexes. That year, in conjunction with Warner Brothers and **Village Roadshow**, the group began building in Brisbane shopping centers. Parallel expansion occurred in provincial Queensland cities and adjoining areas. BCC also acquired leases to complexes in the rapidly expanding, sun-belt southeast corner of Queensland. By late 1990s, multiplexes were succeeded by megaplexes of 12 to 16 cinemas in the Brisbane shopping centers. In the meantime, BCC had come to exist in name only following a Greater Union takeover in 1991.

BLACK CHICKS TALKING (2001). This **documentary**, inspired by the book of the same name, takes the viewer into an eye-opening journey into contemporary **Aboriginal** society, to investigate what it means to be a **woman** and Aboriginal in contemporary Australia. Director Leah Purcell maps the lives of five indigenous women who are influencing current Australian culture. For example, Deborah Mailman is a star of Australian **television** and film, including *Rabbit-Proof Fence* (2002), while Kathryn Hay won the 1999 Miss Australia competition. The documentary won the most popular film at the 2002 Brisbane International Film Festival.

BLANCHETT, CATE (1969–). Born in Melbourne, Cate Blanchett graduated from the National Institute of Dramatic Art into a role with the Sydney Theatre Company's production of *Top Girls*, and then into *Kafka Dances*, which won her critical acclaim. That same critical acclaim has followed the various performances of this talented actress, whether on the Shakespearean stage, in present-day **television** dramas, or in contemporary or period roles on the big screen. She has made an easy transition to the international industry and is in great demand as an accomplished artist. Blanchett first appeared on the big screen in a film of a television series, *Police Rescue* (1994), which was followed by the lead role of Rosie in Kathryn Millard's *Parklands* (1996), a drama about corruption in law enforcement agencies. In **Bruce Beresford**'s *Paradise Road* (1997), she played one of the women interned in a Japanese prison camp in Singapore during World War II. Another superb performance followed in the romantic **comedy** *Thank God He Met Lizzie* (1997), which won Blanchett an **Australian Film Institute** award for best actress in a supporting role in that year. It was in **Gillian Armstrong**'s *Oscar and Lucinda* (1997) that she came to the attention of international critics and audiences, playing Lucinda opposite Ralph Fiennes as Oscar. Lucinda is a protofeminist heiress whose gambling activities link her with Oscar. The film was shot in the United Kingdom, with American and Australian production funds, and from here Blanchett landed her next role, that of Elizabeth I in *Elizabeth* (1998), playing opposite **Geoffrey Rush**, Richard Attenborough, and Joseph Fiennes. That film and her role were of such power that they were nominated for and won many international awards, including best actress in a leading role from the British Academy of Film and Television Arts (BAFTA), and Academy Awards nominations for best picture and best actress in a lead role.

That performance secured her status as an actress of the highest order, and her career blossomed. Jumping a time zone and a cultural time warp, she played the New Jersey-accented wife of Nick Falzone (John Cusack), in the comedy about air traffic control, *Pushing Tin* (1999). In another period film set in the 1950s, *The Talented Mr. Ripley* (1999), she played Meredith, involved in a plot to kill a playboy so that another can assume his identity. Blanchett starred as the gold-digging Russian chorus girl, Lola, in *The Man Who Cried* (2000), and in the same year appeared in the gothic thriller *The Gift*, as a clairvoyant living in the southern bayou region of the United States who leads police to a murdered woman's body. Teaming up with Bruce Willis and Billy Bob Thornton, she took the role of the kidnapped girl who is in the fortunate position of having both her captors fall in love with her, in the crime/comedy *Bandits* (2001), and played the lead role of Charlotte in **Gillian Armstrong**'s film of an extraordinary woman who joined the French Resistance during World War II, *Charlotte Gray* (2001). Between 1999 and 2001, she was involved in the filming of ***Peter Jackson**'s **Lord of the Rings* trilogy, in the role of the distant and beautiful elven queen Galadriel. The films were released in 2001, 2002, and 2003. She played Kevin Spacey's ex-wife Petal in the critically acclaimed story of love and death in Newfoundland, *The Shipping News* (2001). As Philippa, she takes the law into her own hands when her husband is murdered, and is herself arrested in the European co-production, *Heaven* (2002). Blanchett continued with leading roles in Joel Schumacher's *Veronica Guerin* (2003) and Ron Howard's *The Missing* (2003).

Other films include the romantic comedy *An Ideal Husband* (1999), *Bangers* (1999), and *Coffee and Cigarettes* (2003).

BLISS* (1985).** Raymond Lawrence has directed only two films, *Bliss* and ***Lantana (2001). Both have been critically acclaimed and both tell of the developments in and unraveling of the lives of characters. Peter Carey and Lawrence collaborated in writing the screenplay, which was based on Carey's novel of the same name. The film tells the story of the ethically compromised advertising executive Harry Joy (Barry Otto), who lives a normal, but nightmarish existence with a partner who has cuckolded him, a shrewish wife and obnoxious children. After a heart attack and near death experience, Harry abandons his lifestyle to run off to a hippielike existence, where he woos ex-prostitute Honey Barbara for the eight years it takes to grow a grove of honey-producing native trees. The film is a masterpiece of black humor spliced into a series of surreal stories and images, while never moving into the realm of fantasy. *Bliss* was nominated for a Golden Palm award at Cannes in 1985, and for 10 **Australian Film Institute** (AFI) awards in the same year. It won three AFI awards for best director, best film, and best adapted screenplay.

BLUNDELL, GRAEME (1945–). Graeme Blundell is almost the face of the **ocker** films that drove the renewal of the Australian film industry in the early 1970s (*see* REVIVAL). He teamed with director **Tim Burstall** to play a part in *Two Thousand Weeks* (1969), a little-known film now. However, at the time it was the most important film of the late 1960s, although it did not live up to the expectations of critics, even though it was modeled on the European art films that were later to figure so prominently in Australian filmmaking (*see* ART AND PERIOD FILMS and GENRE). Blundell then took on a persona that was to become almost larger than him. In John B. Murray's *The Naked Bunyip* (1970), he starred as an inept market researcher, exploring the sexual mores prevalent in Australia at the time. He played opposite such later personalities as Barry Humphries, Harry M. Miller, Russell Morris, and Malcolm Muggeridge, who all played a significant part in the Australian cultural scene in subsequent years. In 1971, he again worked with **Tim Burstall** as Westy in *Stork* (1971), the first ocker **comedy**, and the first major commercial success of the new Australian cinema. *Stork* took a satirical swipe at the Australian establishment in intellectual, political, and cultural fields.

However, his next film, also directed by Burstall, was one of the seminal films of the history of the industry, and the most commercially successful film of the 1970s. Blundell played the lead in *Alvin Purple* (1973), a comic story of Alvin's attempts to come to terms with his magnetic irresistibility to women, through psychiatry. Blundell starred in the first sequel, *Alvin Purple Rides Again* (1974), but not in the second, *Melvin, Son of Alvin* (1984). He had a small part in this film where the context had changed after a decade, and where audiences no longer appreciated this particular style of humor. He appeared in a small role in *Mad Dog Morgan* (1976), an Australian Western starring Dennis Hopper and many Australian actors whose names were later to become synonymous with the industry: **Jack Thompson**, **David Gulpilil**, Frank Thring, and **Bill Hunter**.

Blundell has played in many films since then, but none of those roles has had the impact of his ocker roles. As the pipe-smoking Liberal Party supporter in the **David Williamson**-written *Don's Party* (1976), he argued with a room full of aggressive, Labor party supporters. He played in the antiwar black comedy about the Australian soldiers in Vietnam, *The Odd Angry Shot* (1979). He has continued with an array of films through the 1980s, 1990s, and into 2000.

Other films include *Weekend of Shadows* (1978), *Kostas* (1979), *Pacific Banana* (1981), *Doctors & Nurses* (1981), *The Best of Friends* (1981), *Midnite Spares* (1983), *Those Dear Departed* (1987), *The Year My Voice Broke* (1987), *Australian Dream* (1987), *Gino* (1994), *Idiot Box* (1996), and *Looking for Alibrandi* (2000).

"BREAKER" MORANT (1980). Directed by **Bruce Beresford,** *"Breaker" Morant* tells the story of three Australian carabineers fighting with the English in the Boer War. The screenplay was adapted from a true story of three Australian officers who were court-martialed for allegedly executing Boer prisoners-of-war, but who may have been scapegoats, betrayed by their British superiors including Lord Kitchener. The three soldiers were executed. Edward Woodward starred as "The Breaker" while **Jack Thompson** and **Bryan Brown** added to their screen portfolios. Along with *Gallipoli* (1981), *"Breaker" Morant* is one of Australia's most popular war films, exploring the nature of hierarchies and the notion of loyalty within those hierarchies. The film was critically and popularly ac-

claimed and Thompson won a best supporting actor award at the 1980 Cannes Film Festival. Nominated for three **Australian Film Institute** (AFI) awards including best lead actor (Woodward), *"Breaker"* won another 10, including best film, best director, best actor (Thompson), best supporting actor (Brown), and best cinematography (Donald McAlpine). The film was nominated for an Oscar for best screenplay in 1981.

BREALEY, GIL (1932–). Born in Melbourne in 1932, Brealey took a degree in Commerce at Melbourne University. He was active in the University Film Society, and from there joined the Victorian Department of Education as an art teacher stationed in the Visual Arts section of Coburg Teachers College. By now his film credits included work on the documentaries *Sundays in Melbourne*, *Grampian Highlands*, and *Waiting for Thursday*. In 1962, he joined the ABC as a film director and in the mid-1960s became a producer on *Chequerboard*. From there, he moved to the **Commonwealth Film Unit** as a producer. Among his more notable work there was *Three To Go* (1971) and *Flashpoint* (1972). In 1972, he moved again, this time to the newly inaugurated **South Australian Film Corporation** as its first chairman. Although his tenure there was short—only remaining until 1975—nevertheless he is credited with the decision to back the feature *Sunday Too Far Away* (1975) which, in turn, persuaded other state governments to follow the South Australian lead and establish separate state film bodies. By then, Brealey had again moved on. After briefly lecturing in Drama and Film at Flinders University in Adelaide, he became the first chairman of the newly established Tasmanian Film Corporation. However, film production eventually drew him back from administration. He was executive producer on *Manganinnie* (1980) and producer on *Dusty* (1983) while in 1984 he directed the first feature film of **Film Australia** intended for commercial film release, *Annie's Coming Out*. Although the film was interesting, it failed to attract a great deal of attention either critically or commercially and Brealey's career went quiet thereafter.

BREHENY, BRIAN J. Brian Breheny has worked on many feature films as director of photography, working with producer **Al Clark** on four occasions. He won a Film Critics' Circle Award and nominations from BAFTA and the **Australian Film Institute** for *The Adventures of Priscilla, Queen of the Desert* (1994), his first feature film. Since then, he has been widely sought after, and his arresting work with color and the outback—a powerful element in *Priscilla*—continued in other films, such as *Siam Sunset* (1999) and *Heaven's Burning* (1997), which were both produced by Clark. His other feature film credits include the antibank, UK-Australian coproduction *The Hard Word* (2002), the Australian made *My Mother Frank* (2000), *Dear Claudia* (1999), and *The Roly Poly Man* (1993). Outside Australia, he worked on the Singaporean *Forever Fever* (1998), and in the United States, *The Other Side of Heaven* (2001).

BROWN, BRYAN (1947–). In his late twenties, Bryan Brown went to London to train with the National Theatre. That may have been the key to his success, as, on his return to Australia, he quickly became one of the most accomplished and popular actors on Australian screens. His star has risen in parallel with the film industry and he has been prominent since the **revival**, gaining popularity in a proliferation of films in the late 1970s. They include *Third Person Plural* (1978), *Weekend of Shadows* (1978), *The Irishman* (1978), the arresting *The Chant of Jimmy Blacksmith* (1978), **Newsfront** (1978), *Money Movers* (1979), *The Odd Angry Shot* (1979), and *Cathy's Child* (1979). The number of roles has continued since then, while his prominence within films has increased. In the 1980s he played in *Palm Beach* (1980), *Blood Money* (1980), *Stir* (1980), **Breaker Morant** (1980), *Winter of our Dreams* (1981), *Far East* (1982), *Rebel* (1985), *The Empty Beach* (1985), and *The Good Wife* (1987).

In many of these films, he was the laconic Australian, sometimes in the outdoors, sometimes outside Australia. His character stood outside the morality of the orthodoxy, whether that orthodoxy was represented by government, business, or the military, and much of his success lay in his characters' lack of respect for those institutions. That lack of respect was epitomized in *Breaker Morant*, where he played Lt. Peter Kadcock, one of the three Bushveldt Carabineers sentenced to death by a military court determined to punish a scapegoat, and where he first came to international attention. In these roles, he represents the archetypal Australian male. He has perfected these characterizations in later films in which he has starred. In *Risk*, he played the insurance assessor Kriesky working scams with a lawyer (**Claudia Karvan**), and thumbing his nose at the insurance industry in the process. In *Two Hands*, he played the Kings Cross mobster, an Australianized **crime** boss who talks to his child about origami immediately before discussing the latest hit with his cronies, and who wears thongs (flip-flops) and shorts, while in *Dirty Deeds* he plays a crime boss who thinks about forming an allegiance with American crime.

Brown is perhaps better known in the United States for his role as the special effects wunderkind in *F/X* (1986) and *F/X2* (1991), as Tom Cruise's suicidal mentor in *Cocktail* (1988), as the romantic interest for Sigourney Weaver in *Gorillas in the Mist* (1988), and opposite Peter Weller in *Styx* (2001).

In 1999, Brown won the **Australian Film Institute** (AFI) award for best supporting actor for his role in *Two Hands*, following a similar award in 1980 for *Breaker Morant*. The Film Critics Circle of Australia (FCCA) granted him the best supporting actor award for *Two Hands* in 2000, and in 1997 he won the special achievement award for his contribution to Australian films.

His other films include *Grizzly Falls* (1999), *Dear Claudia* (1999), *On the Border* (1998), *Dead Heart* (1996), *Age of Treason* (1993), *Blame it on the Bellboy* (1992), *Sweet Talker* (1991), *Prisoners of the Sun* (1990), and *Tai Pan* (1986).

BURSTALL, TIM (1927–2004). Tim Burstall was very much a forerunner director whose career was already in train when the **revival** began around 1970. Born in the United Kingdom in 1927, Burstall finished school and university in Melbourne. He produced, wrote, and directed his first film, a short, in 1960. Entitled *The Prize*, the film won him a Bronze Medal at the Venice Film Festival. In turn, this enabled him to secure a job at the **Commonwealth Film Unit**. One of his more notable films there was the children's film *Nullarbor Hideout,* which he both wrote and directed. Then a Harkness Scholarship enabled him to study at the Actor's Studio in New York. From there, it was back to Australia to cowrite a script with producer Patrick Ryan for his first feature film *Two Thousand Weeks* (1969). The film was made in difficult circumstances and its fictional situation of a frustrated teacher undecided whether to follow his artistic vocation that would take him to England was partly autobiographical.

However, the film's failure both at the box office and with critics and reviewers created a watershed for Burstall who now resolved to become a more determinedly commercial director rather than attempting to engage in a personal filmmaking career. His next film, *Stork* (1971), was more rewarding both at the box office and also in terms of Burstall being able to take advantage of a burgeoning wave of artistic activity coming out of Melbourne.

With the establishment of **Hexagon Productions**, an offshoot of **Village Roadshow**, Burstall began a period of consistent output. His features in this period included *Alvin Purple* (1973), *Petersen* (1974), *End Play* (1975), and *Eliza Fraser* (1976). Additionally, he was engaged in several other films made by other directors at Hexagon with Burstall serving as producer. In addition to the Hexagon period, he directed other films including "The Child" episode of *Libido* (1973), *The Last of the Knucklemen* (1979), *Attack Force Z* (1979), *Duet for Four* (1981), *The Naked Country* (1985), *Kangaroo* (1987), and *Nightmare at Bitter Creek* (1988). However, since around 1990, Burstall's directorial career appeared to have been on hold. He busied himself in several other ways. With his university degree in literature and history, Burstall was a prolific writer of poetry, children's stories, art criticism, and film screenplays. More significantly, he was also fiercely partisan on behalf of the Australian film industry, contributing to public debate and controversy about the local film culture. Burstall died in 2004.

BUSH. *See* COUNTRY.

– C –

CAESAR, DAVID. David Caesar is one of the new wave of Australian directors, raised in **television** drama and just beginning to make his mark in feature films. Caesar cut his directorial teeth with a **documentary**, *Body Works* (1988) written by Dr. Karl Kruszelnicki, which looked at the industries that deal with the deceased, followed by the little-known *Greenkeeping* (1992), which he wrote and directed. He then moved to television, directing episodes of the gritty, realistic ABC series, *Wildside* (1997), followed by episodes of *Hali-*

fax ("Isn't It Romantic" episode) in 1997, *All Saints* (1997), and *Stingers* (1998), among others. He returned to the silver screen, turning out *Mullet* (2001) and the **crime/comedy** *Dirty Deeds* (2002), both of which he wrote and directed. However, neither film made much of an impact at the box office, although the former did receive critical attention. Caesar has more recently returned to television.

CAMPION, JANE. *See entry in New Zealand section.*

CANTRILL, ARTHUR AND CORINNE. Making films for over 40 years, the artistic career of Arthur and Corinne Cantrill has had a consistency and purity that is remarkable both in Australia and internationally. The two began making **documentary** films on children's craft activities in Brisbane for the Children's Library and Crafts Movement in 1960. Simple narrative fictions including *Kip and David* (1961–1963) followed these. However, the two decided to break with this kind of representational mode. Lone voices at the time, they decided to publish a film journal. Thus, the first issue of *Cantrills Filmnotes* that appeared in 1971 carries a manifesto calling for films more concerned with matter and form that would "defy analysis" than with content. Remarkably, the journal remained in production, introducing ideas, nurturing talent, and stirring hornets' nests, until 2000. It was Australia's foremost journal of independent and avant-garde film and video production. Meanwhile, the two continued to pursue their vision of cinema. A series of biographical films (on Robert Klippel [1963-65], Charles Lloyd [1966], Will Spoor [1969], and Harry Hooton [1969]) followed. These challenged traditional documentary and culminated in the autobiographical grand opus *In This Life's Body* (1984). This latter tells Corinne's personal story at the same time as it addresses issues of the writing of autobiography. Meanwhile, the two had left Brisbane for London (1965–1969), Canberra (1969–1970), before settling in Melbourne.

Other sojourns in New York (1973–1975) and Berlin (1985) connected with the international avant-garde cinema movement. The materiality of film is evident through all their work, but becomes explicit in films such as *Three Color Separation Studies—Landscapes* (1976) and those concerning ethnographer Walter Baldwin Spencer including *Reflections on Three Images by Baldwin Spenser* (1974).

Corinne's early training as a botanist is apparent in their many films that focus on the Australian landscape such as *At Uluru* (1976–1977) and *Tidal River* (1996). They rework their earlier films, often presenting them as performance pieces. Much of their work has been on 16mm although since 1990, they have worked on 8mm film. Publishing a film journal and making films has brought them very little in the way of income and they have singularly lacked much institutional support. Nevertheless, they have worked on with energy, imagination, and enormous tenacity.

Over their long careers, the Cantrills have been well known and more appreciated abroad than within Australia, where the lot of the independent, experimental filmmaker can often be bleak indeed. Their filmwork is well known internationally: they are represented in several film collections including those of The Royal Film Archive of Belgium, Freunde der Deutschen Kinemathek (Berlin), Deutsches Filmmuseum (Frankfurt), Musée national d'art moderne (Centre Georges Pompidou, Paris), New York Museum of Modern Art, PRÉA (Avignon), The British Council, and the National Library of Australia. Their films have been shown at the Centre Pompidou and The Louvre in Paris, the New York Museum of Modern Art, as well as other art museums and film festivals. Arthur Cantrill has given lectures on 19th Century Proto-Cinema, Len Lye, Color in Cinema, and other topics at Deutsches Filmmuseum in Frankfurt, Kino Arsenal in Berlin, The National Library of Australia, **ScreenSound** Australia, and other places.

For a time, Arthur Cantrill held the position of associate professor of Media Arts in the School of Creative Arts, University of Melbourne, and now holds the emeritus position of senior associate there.

CAREFUL, HE MIGHT HEAR YOU (1983). Adapted from the novel of the same name by Sumner Locke Elliott, *Careful, He Might Hear You* tells the story of a battle for custody of the child PS (Nicholas Gledhill), fought by his two aunts Lila (Robyn Nevin) and Vanessa (Wendy Hughes). Lila is working class; Vanessa is from the upper end of town. PS's father, Logan (John Hargreaves) is a shiftless and lazy man. Told through the eyes of PS, the story does not explore the advantages and disadvantages of the environments of wealth and simplicity. Rather, the film explores the meanings of those environments from the child's perspective, ranging across the coldness of the objects of wealth because of the coldness of Vanessa, to the warmth of Lila's home.

Careful, He Might Hear You was nominated in five categories in the 1983 **Australian Film Institute** (AFI) awards, and won awards in eight categories including best film, best director (Carl Schulz), best cinematography (John Seale), best adapted screenplay (Michael Jenkins), best leading actress (Hughes), and best supporting actor (Hargreaves).

CASTLE, THE (1997). *The Castle* was the first film to come from the collaboration of **Rob Sitch**—who also directed the film—Santo Cilauro, Tom Gleisner, and Jane Kennedy, known collectively as Working Dog. The team drew on their successful **television comedy** writing skills to tell the story of the Kerrigans and their home, neighbors, and their resolution in the face of overwhelming odds. Their castle comprised not only their home at the end of the runway of an international airport, but also the associated elements of a home: family relationships, meals together, good neighbors, and contentment. Thus, when the authorities decide to acquire the land, the Kerrigans do not lie down and take it. Australian filmmaking has many examples where the little man, poor but proud, takes on the faceless and unfeeling bureaucracy and wins—for example, *The Man Who Sued God* (2001). Yet few films manage to do it so well, without falling into acts of stupidity. The Kerrigans and their friends resonate within the psyche of many Australians.

Released in the United States and the United Kingdom, *The Castle* performed well. It was nominated for three **Australian Film Institute** (AFI) awards in 1997 and won the award for best original screenplay.

CENSORSHIP. For the most part, film censorship in Australia has followed the path of censorship elsewhere although it has also been the site of moral panics unique to a state with authoritarian leanings. Indeed, in the period between 1930 and 1970, Australian censorship, including that of imported film, rivaled that of the Republic of Ireland in terms of its prurient narrowness of outlook. As occurred elsewhere, film censorship in its earliest years in Australia was a health-inspired regulation of place rather than a concern with film content.

Subsequently, there has been much oscillation around censorship. For example, before 1910, boxing films were objects of criticism not only because of violence but also because they showed black victories. During World War I, a film of labor struggle was banned from screening. However, from the 1920s on and at different times, the censors have taken most exception to matters of violence and sex.

Meanwhile, the Australian Federation of its colonies in 1901 had brought into existence a dual system of censorship under which the Commonwealth controlled imports of printed material and cinematographic films. Initially, the Commonwealth was sparing in its import controls. But exhibitors also had state authorities to contend with as they too took a hand in the censorship and regulation of film. To make matters worse, national distributors had six different state authorities to deal with, each with its own standards and procedures. The late 1920s onward saw a considerable tightening of censorship generally and that of film in particular.

Mostly, up to this point, the states' censorship officials had made the running as far as literature and film were concerned. However by the 1930s, the Commonwealth took over, denying Australians the right to read works by contemporary writers. This was part of a drive that was not only antimodern but also anti-American. Thus, concerns about their corrupting influence on Australian youth also led to the banning in 1938 of American comics. Nor, despite the best efforts of American film producers through the instrument of the Production Code, could many Hollywood films escape the same fate of either heavy cuts or outright banning. Thus, for example, the Charles Laughton film *The Night of the Hunter* was banned in 1955, not so much because of its suppressed sexuality but rather because of its subject matter that focused on a homicidal preacher, played by Robert Mitchum, who preyed on young widows, including Shelley Winters, marrying them and then strangling them for their savings. The film was banned because, in the eyes of the censor, it brought **religion** into disrepute. Although the film has since been screened several times on **television**, its theatrical ban has never been lifted.

Meanwhile, some states had kept their own censorship covering local productions, and giving them the opportunity to intervene in any federal decision with which they disagreed. In Victoria, for example, a 1926 act made state classification mandatory, preventing children six to 16 attending films deemed unsuitable. However, over the next 40 years, in concert with the general drift of powers from the states to the Commonwealth, several states ceded film censorship powers to federal bodies. In recent years, though, some states have reappointed advisory classifications systems.

By the 1960s, with the increasing pluralization of Australian society, opposition to film censorship grew considerably. With the spread of film culture, particularly as it was registered in the **film festivals**, there occurred major controversies around the cutting or banning of foreign art films. A compromise that allowed such films to escape the censor's scissors provided they were screened only at the Sydney or Melbourne festivals actually opened the floodgates, forcing a more general liberalization of censorship. In fact, from the 1960s, literary and artistic censorship declined generally. By 1968, significant relaxation of Commonwealth controls had occurred, especially under the Liberal-Country Party customs minister, Don Chipp. Film censorship was eased, leading, in 1971, to the introduction of the "R" certificate. The cutting of films dropped noticeably and only extreme films were banned. Despite their initial fears, mainstream commercial cinema exhibition did not suffer but rather gained from this liberalization. Meanwhile, small newsreel theaterettes became specialist "R"-houses while drive-ins began two screenings, an early session for families with "G"-rated movies and an "M"-rated movie for younger adults.

Censorship's internal impact on the local film production industry is unclear. Some earlier films inspired controversy for reasons that are now hard to gauge. The local producer/director **Charles Chauvel** frequently orchestrated censorship disputes in order to help market his films. In the early 1970s, films such as *Alvin Purple* (1973) deliberately set out to flout regulations concerning nudity and so on as a means of promotion and publicity.

However, by the late 1980s, the censorship pendulum was swinging the other way. Some feminists argued that pornography fostered violence against **women**. Others claimed a need to protect the rights of vulnerable minorities. Additionally, over the past 20 years, technological change, including the introduction of the video recorder, subscription television, and the Internet, have brought back arguments for stricter controls over graphic depictions of violence and pornography. In turn, film censors have become party to these disputes. With video, existing regulations were expanded but this was not enough, as the classifications proved insufficient to protect children from pornographic and violent material. The lack of uniformity of state and territory laws led to a boom in nonviolent pornography distributed and sometimes produced by the Canberra-based Eros Foundation. Meanwhile, sexual violence in both film and video began to excite the censor's concern, which was now institutionalized in the Office of Film and Literature Classification. The fate of Pasolini's *Salo* (Italy, 1975) is indicative of the different ways in which the winds of censorship have blown in Australia recently. The film was banned in the late 1970s. In 1993, judging that community standards were seen to have altered, censors allowed it to be released. However, *Salo* was banned again in 1998 as part of a more recent political and moral backlash.

CHAUVEL, CHARLES (1897–1959). Charles Chauvel is undoubtedly the great romantic, even heroic figure of Australian cinema from the 1920s to the 1950s, a compelling primitive as Stuart Cunningham (1991) has persuasively argued. In ambition and scope, his films deserve comparison with such **Hollywood** giants as Cecil B. de Mille and King Vidor. Yet if these comparisons are illuminating, they also underline just how difficult were the circumstances of filmmaking in Australia in this period as against the opportunities available to the others in Hollywood. Chauvel, "the boy from Warwick," was born in southeast Queensland in 1897. With a family whose roots went back to the French Normans, Chauvel was well connected: his uncle was a key figure in the Australian Light Horse in World War I. This was an important first entry point to cinema and underlined the fact that Chauvel would need every connection at his disposal in the difficult project of pursuing a film career in Australia in these years.

Equally sympathetic and supportive were the various Hollywood film distributors in Sydney who were instrumental at key moments in Chauvel's career in helping him raise the finances for his films. Nevertheless, pursuing a directing and producing role in Australia exacted a decisive toll in terms of his output and the often epic difficulties that sometimes surrounded the making of a number of his films. Altogether Chauvel made nine feature films, four wartime shorts, a wartime **documentary** re-edited from Soviet film, and *Walkabout*, a 13-episode documentary series that he produced for **television** for the BBC.

Working as writer, director, and producer on these, Chauvel was intimately dependent on his wife Elsa who worked as cowriter and erstwhile secretary on all these productions. Elsa herself had first worked for Chauvel as star in several of his silent films although after marriage she moved into production. Chauvel was active both before and after World War II so that his is one half of continuous output that complements the career of **Ken G. Hall** and **Lee Robinson**. The latter was to be a partner with actor **Chips Rafferty**, and Chauvel was central not only to that acting career but to those of **Errol Flynn** and Michael Pate. Chauvel's career now appears to fall into two halves, not least because of the loss of many of the earlier films. These include *Robbery under Arms* (1920), *The Shadow of Lightning Ridge* (1920), *A Jackeroo of Coolabong* (1920), *The Moth of Moombi* (1926), *Greenhide* (1926), *In the Wake of the Bounty* (1933), *Heritage* (1935), *Uncivilised* (1936), *Rangle River* (1936), and *Rats of Tobruk* (1944).

However, it was another, mostly later, group of films whose subject matter and narrative concerned epic adventure that was frequently matched by equally epic adventures in the areas of financing and production. This work included such films as *Forty Thousand Horsemen* (1940), *Sons of Matthew* (1949), and *Jedda* (1955), all of which occupy the position of classics in the Australian film canon. Possibly exhausted from the sheer vicissitudes of his projects, Chauvel died in 1959. Since then, his reputation has steadily climbed. Admired in his lifetime for his sheer capacity to keep going and to make films with a highly personal stamp, he was a genuine cinematic primitive who, although naive in his political and moral outlook, nevertheless could make films that had a dynamism of theme and style that more than matched their subject matter.

CHUBB, PAUL (1949–2002). Until his death from complications of heart-related surgery, the rotund figure of Paul Chubb added intensely effective characters to films ranging from **comedy** to hard-boiled **crime**, sometimes mixing those extremes. He appeared in some 40 films—some of which were made for **television**—and miniseries, beginning as a policeman in *The Night Prowler* (1978), developing as a character actor through *Hoodwink* (1981)—in which **Geoffrey Rush** also appeared—*Kitty and the Bagman* (1982), a detective in *Heatwave* (1982), and a debt collector for organized crime in *Goodbye Paradise*

(1983). He continued the criminal characters as Syd, a petty but, in inverse proportion, vicious character in *With Love to the Person Next to Me* (1987), and later changed to a flinty private detective in the comedy *The Roly Poly Man* (1994). He appeared in two short films directed by ***Jane Campion**, *Passionless Moments* (1983) and *A Girl's Own Story* (1984). His last film was *Dirty Deeds* (2002), a crime film related in this way to his early and most significant films.

Other films include ***Bliss*** (1985), *Takeover* (1987), *Danger Down Under* (1988), *Shotgun Wedding* (1993), *Cosi* (1996), *The Well* (1997), and *Road to Nhill* (1997).

CINESOUND. Like **Efftee** Film Productions, Cinesound was a product of the early 1930s. However, unlike its rival, the company proved to have much greater stability than its erstwhile Melbourne opposition. Indeed with its "bread and butter" output of newsreels and its more prestigious output of one or two features a year, Cinesound was the closest to a **Hollywood** film production studio that the Australian cinema managed to produce in the period before the **revival**. The company's parent was the exhibitor, **Greater Union Pictures**. During the silent phase of the Australian cinema, the latter built up an enviable list of interesting and entertaining films ranging from before World War I with *Shepherd of the Southern Cross* (1914), through substantial postwar productions including *Painted Leaders* (1925), *The Pioneers* (1926), *For the Term of His Natural Life* (1927) to *The Adorable Outcast* (1928).

Stuart Doyle who was in charge of both the exhibition and the production companies decided to reorganize the latter. **Ken G. Hall**, his personal assistant, assumed control of the production company and renamed it as Cinesound, a name that heralded the entry into "talking pictures." This appointment was a shrewd move as Hall had a showman's flair for popular entertainment and under his stewardship Cinesound failed only once—with *Strike Me Lucky* (1934)—to make a profit on the 16 feature films that he was to direct over the next 10 years. His first film was *On Our Selection* in 1932 and its success saw Hall continue making one or two features each year for screening in Greater Union cinemas across the country. Thereupon followed *The Squatter's Daughter* (1933), *The Silence of Dean Maitland* (1934), *Strike Me Lucky*, *Grandad Rudd* (1935), *Orphan of the Wilderness*

(1936), *Thoroughbred* (1936), *Lovers and Loggers* (1937), *Tall Timbers* (1937), *It Isn't Done* (1937), *Let George Do It* (1938), *The Broken Melody* (1938), *Dad and Dave Come to Town* (1938), *Gone to the Dogs* (1939), *Mr. Chedwortti Steps Out* (1939), *Come up Smiling* (1939), and *Dad Rudd, M.P.* (1940). Hall produced all of these and, with the exception of *Come up Smiling,* also directed them. His style was unremarkable and unobtrusive, very much in the Hollywood classical tradition. However, Hall was no one man show and it is important to take account of the production team that he brought together. Arthur Smith and Clive Cross originated Cinesound's sound equipment. George Heath was in charge of photography although both Walter Sully and **Frank Hurley** also contributed. Bill Shepherd edited, while Fred Finlay was in charge of direction for the early films. Later this fell to Eric Thompson and Alan Kenyon. Finally, Hamilton Webber wrote much of the music.

Meanwhile throughout the decade, Cinesound continued to make its weekly newsreel. The outbreak of World War II caused the interruption of feature film production and, despite high hopes, this was not to resume after the cessation of hostilities. However, the output of the weekly newsreel and the occasional Cinesound **documentary** was to continue, the former up until 1970. By then, Hall had long left the company. Already a veteran, he took up an offer from Frank Packer to act as general manager of the new commercial **television** station TCN9 Sydney, which he oversaw from 1956 until his retirement in 1965. However, even then, Hall continued as a kind of elder statesman to the new production industry that emerged around 1970, frequently drawing on business wisdom and aesthetic ideas gained in his time at Cinesound.

CITY IN FILM. Two basic aspects suggest themselves as a key to understanding the relationship between cities and cinema in Australia. The first lies in the realization that this cinema always has been produced for, has circulated across, and has been engaged at particular sites, most especially in the Australian city. Inspired by the Lumière actualities, cinematographers were at work in the streets of cities such as Melbourne and Brisbane around 1900 constructing rich, anthropological records of people, places, and movement. And whether the ostensible **genre** is nonfiction or fiction, such a tradition of filmmaking in urban streets, buildings, and open city spaces has come down to the present, reminding contemporary and future viewers of the living texture of particular slices of city life. Additionally, one can chart a succession of further developments in urban film production, most heavily concentrated in Sydney and Melbourne but occurring in other cities and using a repertoire of different technologies 35, 16, and 8mm film, video, and computer animation. This tradition of independent city production has given rise to a veritable archive of city films. Here, by way of example, just one can be mentioned: John Prescott's feature *Bootleg* (1986) made in Brisbane, which casts that place as a *noir* city full of its own corruptions.

A fuller consideration of production's insertion in Australian cities must also consider the advent of particular film studio complexes. Historically, these include **Efftee** in Melbourne, Pagewood in Sydney, Warner Bros. at the Gold Coast, **Fox Studios** in Sydney, and an intended Columbia in Melbourne (*see also* WARNER BROTHERS MOVIE WORLD STUDIOS). These add to city infrastructures for film production, an infrastructure that includes film schools and tertiary institutions. Another dimension of urban cinema infrastructure concerns the changing complex of spaces wherein films are accessed. The most obvious of these has, of course, to do with patterns of cinema locations both in cities and in suburbs, a history that would trace the emergence, development, and successive transformations of public cinema attendance. The venues in question include open-air cinemas in the more tropical cities, the building of chains of hardtop cinemas in urban locations, rivaling, and eventually displacing earlier forms of public entertainment and leisure. The trajectory of Australian cinema forms from hardtop stand-alone cinemas, drive-ins, cineplexes, and multiplexes have also done much to enrich the patterns of everyday life in Australian cities, both in the central districts and in the suburbs.

Over and above cinema's physical shaping of Australian cities, there is also its virtual mediation of a population's understanding of the Australian city. As a visual and narrative form, it has conditioned perceptions and understandings of places, showing particular pictures as "locations" for drama, for example, or narrating documentaries from a particular point of view. Thus, the Australian cinematic city is more than buildings and streets but is, instead, the arena of small as well as big time dramas of living in the city. There is, accordingly, a spectrum of filmic response ranging from the optimistic, utopian pastoralism to be found, for example, in *The Kid Stakes* (1927) through to the darker, less sanguine vision of *The Sentimental Bloke* (1919). In turn, these polar responses enable us to predict some of the generic forms of the urban film to be found in Australian cinema in the recent present. Since the **revival**, the favored form of this latter kind of film has been the genre of **social realism**. A list of representative titles would run from *Three to Go* (1971) through *Hard Knocks* (1980) and *Return Home* (1990) to *Metal Skin* (1994) in the recent present. Such films are by no means necessarily concerned with the more famous icons and tourist locations of cities such as Sydney and Melbourne but are, rather, concentrated on different geographies of the city and the living of city life whether on the streets or amid the quiet satisfactions and hidden anxieties of middle-class suburbs. What these films collectively offer is a repertoire and "structure of feeling" of the iconography of locations and encounters that give texture and significance to the audience's own experience of Australian city life. Again, this social realism cycle varies and overlaps other genres, especially as it reveals an optimism on the one hand and a darker cynicism on the other. With the first, there is the overlapping of the **musical** (*Star Struck* [1982], **Strictly Ballroom** [1992]), romance (*The Heartbreak Kid* [1993], **Muriel's Wedding** [1994]) and, especially, **comedy (*Death in Brunswick*** [1991], *Spotswood* [1992], and **The Castle** [1997]). Such films tend to mitigate the raw, harder effects of city life in terms of suggesting the presence of social enclaves, local communities, that shield against the harsher, brutal effects of urban living.

However, the Australian city film is by no means only wedded to this pole. At the other end is a vision of city life as nasty, brutish, and short. Some recent representations of this dystopian vision are **Romper Stomper** (1992), *Idiot Box* (1996), *The Boys* (1998), and *Black Rock* (1997). Indeed, a number of short distinctive cycles of this kind of film have enabled audience, producers, and critics to claim distinctive traditions of cinematic urbanism, such as a Melbourne wave of social realism whose output includes *Queensland* (1976), *Mouth to Mouth* (1978), *Love Brokers* (1988), *Romper Stomper*, and *Metal Skin*. Collectively, this kind of film provides a distinctive iconography of the modern Australian city. This cycle, for example, is set in the working-class Melbourne western suburbs and follows tough, hard-edged stories that concern males with no way out from nihilistic futures; those caught in the dislocations of unemployment, alienation, violence, racism, and psychological breakdown. Meanwhile, elements of this vision also attach themselves to more familiar generic forms that find city settings for their narratives. These include **crime** and the thriller. Coming full circle, this latter kind of urban film seeks not the everyday lives and settings of ordinary people but more spectacular urban arenas for their actions and adventures. Not surprisingly, then, in films such as *Mission Impossible 2* (2000) and *The Matrix* (1999), the notable tourist features of Sydney including harbor, bridge, beach, and water become the markers of Sydney as a world city, a suitable arena for global finance or global crime. Thus, despite the alleged prevalence of rural myth in Australian culture, including film, the fact is that Australian cinema has been, is, and seems likely to continue to be intimately engaged with the city. *See also* COUNTRY.

CLARK, AL. Born in Spain, Al Clark worked in various capacities with the London magazine *Time Out* and the Virgin group before coproducing *Nineteen Eighty-Four* (1984) and *Aria* (1987). He was executive producer for *Secret Places* (1984), *Absolute Beginners* (1986), *Captive* (1986), and *Gothic* (1986). He moved to Sydney and was appointed to the board of the **Australian Film Commission** from 1989 to 1992. Since then he has produced two films featuring **Russell Crowe**—*The Crossing* (1990) and *Heaven's Burning* (1997)—and two directed by Stephan Elliott—the multiple award winning *The Adventures of Priscilla, Queen of the Desert* (1994), and *Eye of the Beholder* (1999). In addition, he produced John Polson's *Siam Sunset* (1999), *The Hard Word* (2002), and was executive producer for *Chopper* (2000), featuring **Eric Bana**.

CLARKE, JOHN. *See entry in New Zealand section.*

COLLETTE, TONI (1972–). Toni Collette has won international acclaim for a breadth of roles across **genres** and national boundaries. She has been involved in acting from her teenage years. She won a scholarship to the Australian Theatre for Young People in 1989, and then studied at the National Institute for Dramatic Art in 1991–1992. While not in the mold of a "glamorous" actress, her characters are generally potent and consistent, and she is one of the most productive of recent Australian actresses. Her talent was obvious in her earliest roles: she had a small role in *Spotswood* (1992), for which she was nominated for an **Australian Film Institute** (AFI) best supporting actress award. Her role in ***Muriel's Wedding*** (1994) as a marriage-focused, ABBA-loving heroine won the AFI Best Actress award. Since then she has been in demand both in Australia and overseas. She played in the Australian-produced *The Boys* (1998) and the unfortunately timed *Diana and Me* (1997). Her voice was used as Meg Bluegum in the children's animated film *The Magic Pudding* (2000)—which also featured the voices of actors **Geoffrey Rush**, John Cleese, *****Sam Neill**, **Hugo Weaving**, and **Jack Thompson**— and followed with her role as the voices of the nurse and good witch in the United States and United Kingdom production of the animated *Arabian Nights* (1995). Collette played the young Lillian in the harrowing *Lillian's Story* (1995), for which she won an AFI best supporting actress award. Other Australian films include *This Marching Girl Thing* (1994), *Cosi* (1996), and *The Boys* (1997).

Collette has been in demand outside Australia. In the British *Velvet Goldmine* (1998), she played the discarded wife of a glitzy rock-star. In *The Sixth Sense* (1999), she played the worried mother Lynn Sear.

In 2002, she played in four films that display the versatility in roles and nationalities, and the trend to a global, rather than a national cinema: *Changing Lanes*, *About a Boy*, *Dirty Deeds*, and *The Hours*. *Changing Lanes* is a thriller set in New York; Collette plays Michelle. In the British comedy *About a Boy*, she plays Fiona. *Dirty Deeds* is a **crime/comedy** film set in Sydney, Australia; Collette plays the wife of mobster Barry Ryan. The drama *The Hours* was made in the United States, about Virginia Woolf, and stars **Nicole Kidman** with Collette as Kitty. *Japanese Story* (2003) won Collette an AFI best actress award as a geologist who falls in love with the son of a Japanese shareholder in an extensive mining interest in Western Australia.

Other films include: *The Pallbearer* (1996), *Emma* (1996), *James Gang* (1997), *The Clockwatchers* (1997), *Velvet Goldmine* (1998), *81/2 Women* (1999), *Hotel* Splendide (2000), and *Shaft* (2000).

COLOSIMO, VINCE (1966–). Vince Colosimo plays in roles that are seemingly worlds apart, and his ability in playing these roles is evident in the award of Australian Star of the Year (2002) by the Australian Movie Convention. In *Lantana* (2001), he was the househusband Nik Daniels, resident father to the children, while his wife worked. He won the best supporting actor in the 2001 **Australian Film Institute** (AFI) awards for this role. He successfully changed sexual orientation in *Walking on Water* (2002), where he played the gay Charlie, participating in passionate scenes with his lover, for which he was nominated for best actor in the 2002 AFI awards. Before that he had been at the other end of the spectrum, playing the thug Neville in *Chopper* (2000), and then larger-than-life Frank in the **comedy** *The Wog Boy* (2000), following with Dimitri in *The Nuggett* (2002) and Detective Mick Kelly in *The Hard Word* (2002), a film about ex-prisoners who are qualified butchers.

Colosimo's first film appearance was in the coming-of-age film *Moving Out* (1983), where he starred as Gino, the son of immigrant parents struggling to find a balance between the wishes of his parents, and the pull of contemporary Australian culture. He received an AFI nomination in the 1982 awards as best lead actor for that role. He played Vince in *Street Hero* (1984), and then dropped out of commercial films to focus on a **television** career until *The Wog Boy*, and he has now returned, at least for the moment, to the big screen.

COMEDY. The first comedy from the early part of the century, **Raymond Longford**'s *The Sentimental Bloke* (1919), has some elements in common with the more recent **ocker** films of the 1970s in that it reflects the Australian context, which differentiates the film from imported material. The use of the vernacular is a comic element, as is the drinking and gambling that were part of **mateship** rituals up to the late 1970s, and the urban, working-class milieu. At the same time—and in contrast to the ocker films—the bush and its inhabitants, and its particular characters, situations, and innocence, became suitable subjects for a kind of affectionate comedy. The "Dad and Dave" stories, where the bush legend coalesced, appeared in the national magazine, *The Bulletin*. The bush character was defined by way of contrast to the "gilded youths" from the **city** in A. B. Patterson's poem "The Man from Ironbark." The **country** innocent was much beloved of Australian audiences, and was seized on by filmmakers like **Ken Hall**, resulting in a stream of films from 1920 (*On Our Selection*) to 1940 (*Dad Rudd, M.P.*). For Australian audiences, the country bumpkin encapsulated the innocence and naiveté of a hard-working country life, compared with the apparent sophistication and experience of the city. The happy conclusion, affirming the value of a simple family life outside the corrupting influence of the metropolis, is a feature that appears in later films of the century. As well, other traces of this **genre** are apparent in later films like ***Crocodile Dundee*** (1985), albeit reflecting the globalized nature of the film audience in the comparison of the Australian bush with metropolitan New York.

A tangent in the development of Australian comedy was the ocker films of the 1970s, which contrasted strongly in many ways with the country naiveté framed in the earlier films. These films emerged in immediate response to the tax concessions for filmmakers that drove the **revival** of the industry in 1969. The significant films were *The Naked Bunyip* (1970), *Stork* (1971), *Adventures of Barry McKenzie* (1972), **Alvin Purple** (1973), and *Number 96* (1974). These films showcased a version of the language called "strine," which included copious mention of the nonformal terms for bodily functions, sex, women, and drinking.

Recent comedies have clear links to the earlier bucolic films, where the "little man" stands up to powerful institutions, and with the help of the community, overcomes. *Spotswood* (1992) shows the ordinary person, supported by family and communal solidarity, standing up to innovations in industrial rationalization. A similar narrative underpins **The Castle** (1997), and *The Man Who Sued God* (2001), which starred Billy Connelly as the David taking on the Goliath of insurance companies. The background for the "little man" theme in *Crackerjack* (2002) is a metropolitan bowls club, threatened by irrelevance and a poker machine licensee.

Another comic style is derived by taking character and situations to extremes, and then allowing them to interact. Thus comedy occurs through an exaggeration of the traits that exist in reality. *Crackers* (1998) tells the story of the Christmas gathering of a dysfunctional extended suburban family, with characters who do little more than hold a distorting mirror up to certain traits in Australian culture. *Doing Time for Patsy Cline* (1997) is a gentler comedy, drawing on the inequities of social life in an Australian setting of country music, rural life, and the less idyllic drug scene. The characters in *Cosi* (1996) come from a psychiatric institution and are to put on a play, drawing on a convention from *Marat/Sade* (1967), but there the resemblance almost ends, except that the offbeat comedy parallels events happening in the lives of the characters.

Comedy thrives on taking people from one environment and placing them in another—the "fish-out-of-water" narrative—and then watching the situations unfold. Australia's most successful film, both in Australia and in the United States, was *Crocodile Dundee* (1986), with **Crocodile Dundee II** (1988) following closely. These films revolve around the relocation of a country innocent, though still wise, from the Australian outback to cosmopolitan USA. Within Australia, the reality of a multicultural society provides similar "fish-out-of-water" narratives. *They're a Weird Mob* (1966) tells the story of a recently arrived Italian journalist who works as a builder's laborer and learns, through many comic situations, something of Australian society and culture. In a different vein, but arising from the narratives of difference, is the black comedy **Death in Brunswick** (1991), where cemeteries become sites for comedy. In a suburb of Melbourne populated by Greek and Turkish families, the Australian character played by *Sam Neill is drawn into the feuds between warring ethnic families, a war that involves the elements of death and dying (*see also* ETHNIC REPRESENTATION). *The Wog Boy* (2000) takes the stereotypes of multicultural Australia to the extremes when they become comic, once again playing on the juxtaposition of cultures and idiom for the comic effect. ("Some people think I know farck nothing. But I know farck all!"). *Fat Pizza* (2003) continues the trend, less successfully.

A less visible subgenre of comedy is romantic comedy. To some extent, the subgenre has been the domain of new **women** directors, such as Emma-Kate Groghan (*Love and Other Catastrophes* [1996]), Megan Simpson Huberman (*Dating the Enemy* [1996]) and Cherie Nowlan (*Thank God He Met Lizzie* [1997]). *Love* is a hectic pastiche of events in the life of a university student, collapsing the drama of student life into 24 hours, bringing together mismatched couples into new formations for a happy denouement. *Dating the Enemy* involves characters switching from one body to another, as well as switching gender. The comedy arises once again from "fish-out-of-water" narrative; in this case the strangeness is not in the geographic location but in the physical body. *Lizzie* tells the story of a man torn between two women. The problem is that he is about to marry one of them, and the comic situations arise out of a series of flashbacks, which compare the women.

COMING OF AGE FILMS. *See* MATURATION/COMING OF AGE FILMS.

COMMONWEALTH FILM UNIT (CFU). The Commonwealth Film Unit was the de facto name given to the Australian government film production body between about 1956 and 1973 when its name changed to **Film Australia**. The organization had a long ancestry going back to at least 1911 when the federal government appointed a photographer and filmmaker to make information films. These tended to focus on such subjects as the produce of Australia's primary industries and were intended both to promote agriculture and migration from the United Kingdom. After the end of World War II, the government decided to act on the advice of John Grierson and reestablish the film body on a larger scale with a twin brief, both to produce films for particular government departments and agencies and also to produce films in the more general, national interest.

Known informally as the Film Division, an arm of the News and Information Bureau of the Department of the Interior, the body found itself referred to as the Commonwealth Film Unit from 1956 onward. The chief presence at the Unit in these years was **Stanley Hawes**, who had learned his craft and its supporting ideology at the British Post Office film division in the 1930s. He followed Grierson to the Canadian National Film Board toward the end of that decade and later came to Australia to help set up and run the newly expanded film production instrument. Under Hawes' leadership over the next two decades, the CFU was responsible for the making of over 400 information films, most of them consisting of a single reel but with one or two running to feature length. The most notable of the latter was *The Queen in Australia* (1954), which was, undoubtedly, its most prestigious (and among its dullest) films. Overall, this period of Australian history was marked by postwar affluence and consensus and this found articulation and expression in many films of the period.

The pillars of this affluence were, variously, those of material development, social and physical improvement, a consensual populace, a suburban society, and renewed and expanding consumption. The preferred mode of film at the unit, at least until the mid-1960s, was that of the classical **documentary** style. Such an approach bespoke not just the legacy of Grierson's role in establishing the expanded film production effort but was also suited to a consensualist view of Australian society. The most important feature of these films was undoubtedly the use of an expository voice, "the voice of God." Always confident and authoritative, the speaker is invariably male, neither obviously young, old, nor ethnic, and apparently classless in accent. In other words, as a means of affirming and maintaining its authority, this voice is impersonal, objective, acting on behalf of the general interest, and able where necessary to conjure up voices as well as images in support of its exposition. Thus, for example, *The Earth Reveals* (1960) calls up both images of the new mining technologies now in operation as well as a controlled cacophony of voices of miners and others at work in these fields.

However, the consensus implied by these films was beginning to erode by the early 1960s and this was paralleled by shifts in the style of film emerging from the CFU. The obvious driving force for this change in the preferred mode of filmmaking lay not in any ideological determination to reflect the new, emerging mood and tone of the society. Rather, it came about in part because of the advent of new filmmaking technologies and the desire on the part of the unit to remain contemporary in this arena. Thus, color became increasingly common in its films and, toward the end of the 1950s, films such as *Paper Run* were made in a Cinemascope format. However, the advent of new sound equipment and film techniques fractured the style of the classical documentary's reign at the CFU. Meanwhile, the CFU itself was changing. In 1962, it moved to more spacious premises specially designed to meet its needs. Its budgets rose sharply over the next dozen years and the political/bureaucratic attacks that had dogged it now fell away. New younger staff was recruited and the unit briefly won a reputation as Australia's de facto national film school.

The paradigmatic film of this phase was *From the Tropics to the Snow* (1964), a reflexive film about the CFU itself and the impossible and irreconcilable claims of people and place involved in making a film about Australia. Paralleling the social shifts in Australian society toward a more pluralist outlook, the film used its more flexible sound resources to create and hold together the competing claims of both tropics and snow and everything in between. However, this was not the only impressive work to emerge at this time and mention should be made of two anthropological series to do with indigenous peoples—*People of the Western Desert* and *Towards Baruya Manhood*—which were completed in the late 1960s. Completing these were the fictional trilogy of the early 1970s—*Michael*, *Judy,* and *Toula*—and another trilogy dealing with social outsiders who were also remarkable visionaries—*The Man Who Can't Stop* (1973), *Mr. Symbol Man* (1974), and *God Knows Why but It Works* (1975). The change of name to Film Australia in 1973 was prophetic of other changes in Australia itself and in the film organization. The oil crisis of 1973–1994 heralded the disruption of the postwar consensus and the commencement of a neoliberalism that would shortly begin to affect staff levels and budgets at the unit.

CONNOLLY, ROBERT (1967–). Robert Connolly entered the filmmaking world as associate producer on the poorly received **comedy** *All Men Are Liars* (1995). This film was the first in a series that interrogated the representation of gender and relationships between different genders. He produced the dramatic *The Boys* (1997), depicting the activities of a violent and misogynist group of brothers, including **David Wenham**, and *The Monkey's Mask* (2000), a **crime** thriller where the protagonists are lesbian. He was consultant on *Better Than Sex* (2000), a light-hearted examination of the growth of something other than sex—the title suggests that it cannot be named—between two people, also starring Wenham. He then broke with this mold, writing and directing *The Bank* (2001), a thriller revolving around one man's desire for revenge on the bank that caused his father to commit suicide. The film was nominated for nine **Australian Film Institute** (AFI) awards, including best film, best director, best actor, and best original screenplay, which it won.

CORNELL, JOHN (1941–). John Cornell is the silent partner in the **Paul Hogan** success story. As a producer for the **television** news magazine program "A Current Affair" in the 1970s, John Cornell spotted Hogan in the new talent show "New Faces," where Hogan reached the finals with a blistering take-off of the show itself and its judges. Cornell contracted Hogan to appear on "A Current Affair," where he became the resident comic. He then produced the television series, "The Paul Hogan Show" in 1977, acting as well as Hogan's foil, "Strop." He was the cowriter and producer of the immensely successful *Crocodile Dundee* (1986), and was the director of *Crocodile Dundee II* (1988) and the light-hearted *Almost an Angel* (1990), also starring Paul Hogan, which he also produced. There is no doubt that the success of the Paul Hogan character, as well as the astute business decisions surrounding the character, are due not only to Hogan, but also to John Cornell.

COUNTRY. Australian filmmakers and others will not use the term "country" for that which is outside the larger cities, for rural and even remote areas. Instead, the preferred terms are "the bush" and "the outback." Nevertheless, the intention is the same—to designate that part of the territory where the presence of land, nature, isolation, and, sometimes, danger, are the realities of cinematic life. As a "white settler society," Australia has shared in a common Western cultural legacy, itself part of the ideology of colonialism, having to do with the myth of the "frontier." Thus, the frontier is that border between civilization and barbarity, between the land as garden and the land as wilderness. However if the country as a site of cinema shares elements with "frontier" films in South Africa, Canada, and, especially, the United States, then it also partakes of a far older tradition to do with dualities, binary opposites between the idea of the country and the **city**. In such a linkage, the one is the opposite, shadow or complement of the other. Armed with these ideas, one can begin with the assertion that in cinema, the country has been seminal in shaping the Australian imagination. Two films of the midcentury made by the same director, **Charles Chauvel**, can ground these observations. *Sons of Matthew* (1949) is set in the country and is an epic narrative of heroic men wresting a living in the bush against such natural catastrophes as bushfires and cyclones. In this kind of film, generally, the realities of colonial appropriation are displaced by constituting the land as an empty space populated only by natural challenges and catastrophes. In overcoming these and wresting a living in such a place, the settlers are metaphysically legitimated.

Such a story of "frontier" achievement is a narrative of the manly independence and fortitude that transforms a wilderness into a garden. What is almost entirely missing from the cinematic account, except for the recent present, is the registration of those who were displaced in this process of colonial settlement. However, Chauvel's next film, *Jedda* (1955), rebalances the account. Giving narrative prominence to such landscapes as rain forests, desert, and pastoral countryside, the film is concerned to dramatically juxtapose liberal white settlers and both uprooted and nomadic **Aborigines**. However, these two films with their assorted rural types hardly exhaust the repertoire of figures found in the Australian films of country. Instead, the checklist should also include rich squatters, poor selectors, and others, manual laborers of all kinds, miners, drovers, small farmers, shopkeepers, and shearers.

What should be apparent in this list, as is also the case in the two Chauvel films, is the masculinist emphasis of many Australian films set in the country. Even in early Australian feature films, the narrative structures could range from the countryman as hero, in the shape of settler, drover, and shearer to the figure as villain embodied in the form of villainous overseer, bushman, and so on. These polarities were embodied perfectly in a cycle of films about bushrangers running from around the turn of the century until 1918 when they were banned. Recurring right down to the 2003 remake of *Ned Kelly*, such films focus on an ambiguity of the central figure as both hero and outlaw. However, the bushranger/Western is not the only generic variation that Australian films of country have been capable of.

Indeed, here it is relevant to mention a cycle of films made by overseas companies in Australia between the 1940s and 1960s that mostly subscribed to the myth of the Australian rural landscape as the site of epic adventure. Films in this group included *The Overlanders* (1946), *Kangaroo* (1952), *Bitter Springs* (1950), *Smiley* (1956), *The Back of Beyond* (1954), *Robbery under Arms* (1957), **The Shiralee** (1957), and *The Sundowners* (1960). Nor is this tradition completely dormant as **The Man from Snowy River** (1982) demonstrated. Hailed as a break from the tradition of the period film and its overtones of nationalism and nostalgia, the film had a narrative rhythm and sense of movement more familiarly encountered in **Hollywood**. Like the Hollywood Western, the film's ideological project was the reintegration of **masculinity** and landscape.

An opposite strain to this tradition has been that of **comedy**. Here, two particular cycles of bucolic comedy surrounding the figures of both the Hayseeds and the Rudd family have been important. Nor were the two exactly alike. For after the farce and broad comedy of the former, the latter combined comedy with a degree of what passed for realism with an enduring stress on the hardship and heroism involved in wresting a life from the bush. Thus, films such as *Dad and Dave Come to Town* (1938) and *Dad Rudd, M.P.* (1940) are comedies of country, pitting rural figures and values against those of the city and civilization. Arguably, this "fish out of water" theme inaugurated in these rural comedies continues. It can, for example, be seen as one powerful mechanism behind the **ocker** comedies of the 1970s where the comic crassness of, say, Barry McKenzie is implicitly seen as testimony to Australia's condition of hinterland as against the metropolitan centeredness of London and Britain. In 1986, *Crocodile Dundee* made this link patently apparent in comically juxtaposing the bush outlook of the central figure with New York as the embodiment of civilization.

However, beyond these occasional connections, the primary and most consistent use of landscape occurred in the features of the period film cycle that began in 1976 with *Picnic at Hanging Rock*. What this group of films looked at primarily was country so that their characteristic register was landscape, their vision was one of light, and their primary emphasis was that of the physical. Additionally, many of these such as *Gallipoli* (1981) deliberately interlaced this with nationalistic overtones. In other words, land and landscape were central to this ideological undertaking. Overall, though, the Australian countryside has tended to be viewed in three distinct but related ways in films of the 1970s and early 1980s. First, in the **art and period** film, country and landscape become the site for an obvious nostalgia. The passing of a kind of traditional society is embedded in a country background in films such as *Sunday Too Far Away* (1975), *The Picture Show Man* (1977), and *The Irishman* (1978). Secondly, beginning with *Hanging Rock*, there is also a cycle that extends both backward and forward constructing a more existential connection and encounter between individual, group, and land. Such a cycle sometimes suggested the notion of a powerful, mysterious, and archaic nature, menace, and sublimity that is embodied in landscape. Some representative titles include *Picnic at Hanging Rock*, *The Long*

Weekend (1978), *The Chant of Jimmy Blacksmith* (1978), *Gallipoli* (1981), and *We of the Never Never* (1982). In turn, linked directly to this sense of rural foreboding was that of a fear and dread of dissolution, a descent into nature from which there was little or no return. Films embodying this nightmare include *The Back of Beyond* (1954), *Jedda*, *Wake in Fright* (1971), *Little Boy Lost* (1978), and *Walkabout* (1971). This same sense of something alien and, often, menacing even extends to several films in which the country town is represented including *Country Town* (1971), *The Cars That Ate Paris* (1974), *Shame* (1987), and *Road to Nhill* (1997). In summary, then, country has acted and continues to act as a powerful polarity in Australian cinema.

CRACKNELL, RUTH (1925–2002). Ruth Cracknell first appeared in film as Mrs. Gaspen in the Australian *Smiley Gets a Gun* (1959), starring **Chips Rafferty**. From 1962 to 1975, she appeared in many **television** series where she had her greatest impact, especially as Margaret Whitlam in *The Dismissal* (1983) and the impossible mother Maggie Beare in *Mother and Son* (1983). Her film career was less successful, with some notable exceptions. She starred as Rose Dougherty in *Spider & Rose* (1994), a **comedy** directed and written by Bill Bennett, about a road trip that an ambulance driver and an old lady undertake. Earlier, in **Gillian Armstrong**'s *The Singer and the Dancer* (1977), Cracknell starred as the older woman who never speaks to her daughter and detests everything about her. She played a strong supporting role as Mrs. Heather Newby in **Fred Schepisi**'s award-winning *The Chant of Jimmy Blacksmith* (1978). As Doris Bannister in Jim Sharman's *The Night, the Prowler* (1978), she played the mother in the dark, seething, and comic undercurrents of suburban life. She was nominated for best leading actress by the **Australian Film Institute** for this role. While **Toni Collette** played the role of the young Lilian Singer in *Lilian's Story* (1995), Cracknell portrayed the adult, released from a mental institution after 40 years. The film addresses issues of physical and mental abuse, and tells of the triumph of the human spirit over the worst adversity.

Other films are *That Lady from Peking* (1970), *The Best of Friends* (1981), *Molly* (1983), *Emerald City* (1988), *Kokoda Crescent* (1989), *Joey* (1997).

CRAWFORD, HECTOR (1913–1992). Hector Crawford was a dynamic force in radio program production, which he repeated in **television** with his company Crawford Productions. In the 1960s and 1970s, this "Hollywood on the Yarra" was Australia's *de facto* film school and was responsible for teaching many hundreds of actors, directors, writers, and others their craft.

CRIME. The hard-boiled crime fiction is, in the historical spectrum, a more recent **genre**. *Goodbye Paradise* (1983) re-creates Raymond Chandler's Los Angeles of the 1940s in Brisbane, the capital city of Queensland, in the 1970s and 1980s, with a culture that paralleled the corruption and crime that was a feature of Los Angeles. A corruption inquiry in Queensland a few years later showed that the film had certain parallels in reality. The film registers a kind of earthy distaste of the corrupt values of the metropolis, and sees the alternative beach cultures as little better, but unlike other films in the **action/adventure** genre, for example, nothing was suggested by way of contrast. However, the film deviates from its American model in the denouement, when the lead character wanders, in a state of alcoholic meltdown, into a fight between rebels and the army. Here the plot resembles an early James Lee Burke novel—although not sourced from that—rather than the usual Raymond Chandler novel.

    Bryan Brown has been an effective actor in crime films, beginning with *The Empty Beach* (1985), based on a novel by the Australian crime writer Peter Corris. The detective, Cliff Hardy (Brown), is a tough, no-nonsense guy in the manner of earlier models, but unlike in other films of the genre, he has no private narrator who is able—through direct explanation to the audience—to offer some relief from and explanation of the "tough-guy" character. Thus, we see only a hard-bitten, cryptic character who appears to overreact. Brown continued with lead roles in the caper films *Two Hands* (1999) and *Dirty Deeds* (2002), both of which juxtapose serious criminal acts with comic or endearing family scenes, following *Pulp Fiction* (1994). In *Two Hands*, Brown becomes the "T-shirts, shorts-and-flip-flops" criminal boss Pando, the epitome of the casual, working class, beer-drinking, joke-cracking Australian thug. He is also a devoted family man, moving easily from making origami with his young son to discussing the shooting of a recalcitrant crook. There is no hard-boiled detective here, just a gang of medium-level criminals who end up dying at the hands of a young streetkid, whose friend they inadvertently killed. The criminals operate seemingly without intervention from an effective police force represented generally through the tough, cynical detective. In *Getting Square* (2003), the detective is corrupt. Satisfaction lies in the personal extinction of people who are unutterably evil, who have no respect for the lives of anyone. The karma of living unethically strikes the corrupt John Kreisky (Bryan Brown) yet again in *Risk* (2002). Here, the insurance adjustor Kreisky and his lover, the lawyer Louise Roncoli (**Claudia Karvan**), fleece the company Kreisky works for in an increasingly complex swindle, that goes wrong when Ben Madigan (**Tom Long**) has second thoughts.

An earlier film, *Grievous Bodily Harm* (1988), like *The Empty Beach* and *Goodbye Paradise*, constructs a social logic where redemption is not possible at the social level through a newfound commitment to community values; rather redemption is a personal catharsis, within the contemporary world and not some other. Crime and the criminal world is outside the realm of normal experience for most people, but a simple sequence of events can lead a normal, relatively well-adjusted person into the upside-down and frightening world of crime and the grey zone between those who populate it and those who fight it. That grey zone is filled with ambivalent motives and actions.

Two other films fall into this genre, and both are based on the same true-life event. **Phillip Noyce**'s *Heatwave* (1982) and Donald Crombie's *The Killing of Angel Street* (1981) were inspired by the death of investigative reporter Juanita Nielsen while exposing the corruption surrounding the development of a block of older-style houses in favor of expensive high-rise apartments. The developers have no mitigating traits, and are involved with criminal enforcers, corrupt police, compromised lawyers, and greedy politicians. On the other hand, the residents of Angel Street are sweetly innocent. The **city** is once again the site of corruption, and those who indulge in it are protected from prosecution because of the privileges of power.

Other films in the genre include *The Surfer* (1988), *The Custodian* (1994), and *The Hard Word* (200x).

CROCODILE DUNDEE (1986). *Crocodile Dundee* is the most popular Australian film to be exported to the United States, grossing

US$175 million in the first four months at the American box office and a further US$70 million in American rentals alone. In Australia, it was the best box-office performer in 1986, as was *Crocodile Dundee II* in 1988. *Dundee* remains the best box-office performer of all time in Australia, grossing $47.7 million, three times the box-office of the critically acclaimed *Muriel's Wedding* (1994) and *The Adventures of Priscilla, Queen of the Desert* (1994). Its total gross was US$350 million, the 10th largest in history. Despite being nominated for, and winning, awards overseas, *Dundee* was not nominated for any awards by the Australian industry, perhaps reflecting the "high-culture" pretensions of that industry. In 1987, the American Academy nominated the film and writers **Paul Hogan**, Ken Shadie, and **John Cornell** for the best screenplay written directly for the screen. The British Academy of Film and Television Arts (BAFTA) nominated Paul Hogan as the best actor, and the three writers for the best original screenplay. The film won the B.M.I. film music award in 1987, and the Golden Screen (Germany) best film award. In the same year, Paul Hogan won a Golden Globe award for best actor, and Linda Kozlowski was nominated for best performance by an actress in a supporting role.

Although the humor wears thin for audiences today, in 1986 the film crystallized and codified a new Australian legend in the person of the laconic, weather-beaten, self-deprecating crocodile hunter Crocodile Dundee, spinner of the tall tales to entertain and enthrall unsuspecting visitors and tourists, such as American journalist Sue Charlton (Linda Kozlowski). After experiencing his expertise in the tropical wetlands of Australia, she persuades him to accompany her back to New York. He is the naïve and not-quite-innocent outback icon transferred to the urban jungle of Manhattan, where his skills and understanding of human nature put him in interesting and comic situations. Research had suggested that the character of Dundee would be accepted immediately, and the excellent script and release timing ensured the film would be immensely popular.

The sequels, *Crocodile Dundee II* (1988) and *Crocodile Dundee in Los Angeles* (2001) did not enjoy quite the same success. While *Dundee II* enjoyed good box office support, the third film just covered costs at the American box office.

CROCODILE DUNDEE II (**1988**). *Crocodile Dundee II* is the fourth most successful Australian film at the Australian box office, taking

$24.9 million, and the second most successful at the American box office, taking US$109.3 million. Its success, though, was measured by audience response rather than in critical acclaim. The narrative is similar to that of the original, in that the **comedy** arises out of the clash of certain, exaggerated cultures existing in modern USA and outback Australia. We see, for example, Mick Dundee fishing in New York Harbor, using dynamite. The plot revolves around the drug trade, photos of killings, the kidnapping of Mick's girlfriend, Sue Charlton (Linda Kozlowski), her rescue, a cunning plan designed to catch the mobsters through outwitting them back in outback Australia, and a denouement where Linda, Mick, and their friends return to a state of stability and happiness. While not living up to the novelty of the original, the film remains a warm-hearted adventure, popular in both Australia and the United States, and in northern Europe. The film won a German Golden Screen award in 1988.

CROWE, RUSSELL (1964–). Russell Crowe was born on 7 April 1964 in New Zealand, still maintains his New Zealand nationality, and holds a New Zealand passport. He moved to Australia when he was three, until moving back to New Zealand at 14. He moved again to Australia in his late teens. His acting career began with successful stage appearances as Eddy in *The Rocky Horror Stage Show* in New Zealand, and he starred in *Blood Brothers* in 1988. The play attracted enthusiastic reviews, and New Zealand *Women's Weekly* interviewed him in 1989. His first film was *Prisoners of the Sun* (1990)—also known as *Blood Oath*—concerning the Japanese mass executions of (mainly Australian) prisoners of war in World War II on the island of Ambon. In one of the worst atrocities of the war, Australian POWs were tied together at the hands, and then, as a group, were made to coil up like a neatly coiled rope, when they were doused in fuel, and incinerated. *Crossing* (1990) and *Proof* (1991) followed. In his first starring role in *Crossing*, he was nominated for best actor in a lead role at the 1990 **Australian Film Institute** (AFI) awards for his performance as Johnny, the **country** boy dealing with feelings of love he has for a girl left behind when he moved to the **city**. A 1991 AFI award for best supporting actor resulted from *Proof*, where Crowe worked with **Hugo Weaving** to explore reality and the nature of truth through photographs taken by a blind person. The film was exhibited at Cannes, giving Crowe international exposure. Crowe had a supporting role in

Spotswood (1991)—which preceded *Proof*—a **comedy** where the practical and human effects of downsizing return to confront the efficiency expert.

In *Hammers over the Anvil* (1991), Crowe played East Driscoll, a laconic Australian horse-trainer who falls in love with the aristocratic, already married, Grace. Driscoll tries to drag her away from the marriage, with tragic results. Crowe won the Best Actor award at the 1993 Seattle International Film Festival for this film, and for ***Romper Stomper*** (1992). Before filming *Romper Stomper*, Crowe worked with director David Elfick on *Love in Limbo* (1993), playing Arthur, a Welsh factory supervisor looking over young Ken, who is desperately trying to lose his virginity, while Arthur learns some Australian virtues. *Romper Stomper*, a socially critical film, signaled a different direction for Crowe. As Hando, the leader of a skinhead gang in Melbourne, he exhibits the mindless violence of Kubrick's Alex, couched in racist ideology and practice. Crowe's role won him the best lead actor award at the 1992 AFI awards and the best male actor award by the Film Critics Circle of Australia. *The Sum of Us* (1994) placed Crowe in the exact opposite role, that of a homosexual son's changing relationship with his father, Harry (**Jack Thompson**), both of whom are coming to terms with, and enjoying, the potential of their individual and common lives.

Turning his attention to the United States, Crowe starred with Sharon Stone in *The Quick and the Dead* (1995), followed by the science-fiction film *Virtuosity* (1995), playing a computer-generated killer opposite Denzel Washington. Crowe's next film, *L.A. Confidential* (1997), allowed him to reach his potential as a character with a questionable integrity, the thuglike detective Bud White. In the same year, he played opposite Youki Kudoh in *Heaven's Burning*, an underrated Australian road movie. This film redraws the Australian mise-en-scene and populates it with a cast of misfits, deviants, no-hopers, and outlaws. Three out of four of its father-son polarities are dysfunctional and the other characters are unable to be integrated into a myth of multicultural celebration. While Crowe takes the Australian antihero to uncharted levels of passivity, the arresting Kudoh transmogrifies Midori from bride, to hostage, to bank robber and romantic outlaw, leaving **Hollywood** heroines gasping in her wake. Crowe then played in three films—*Breaking*

Up (1997), the Disney production *Mystery, Alaska* (1999), and *The Insider* (1999)—before the award-winning role of Maximus in Ridley Scott's *Gladiator* (2000), for which he won an Oscar and a British Academy of Film and Television Arts (BAFTA) award. Yet this achievement was overshadowed by his gripping and powerful portrayal of the Nobel prize-winning mathematician and schizophrenic John Nash in Ron Howard's *A Beautiful Mind* (2001), for which he was nominated for an Oscar and an American Film Institute award. He followed this up with the lead role of Captain Jack Aubrey in the award-winning, **Peter Weir**-directed *Master and Commander: The Far Side of the World* (2003)

Although Crowe is famous for his acting ability, he has no time for the games of Hollywood, and prefers to live in Australia when he is not working. He married his long-time girlfriend Danielle Spencer in 2003.

– D –

***DARK CITY* (1998). Alex Proyas** was one of the screenplay writers, and also producer and director for this science fiction film, which was filmed in **Fox Studios**, Sydney, as well as Los Angeles. Its claim to listing is that it was, in many respects, an Australian film in a **genre** where few Australians are represented. Critics claim that it goes further than *Blade Runner*. While Blade Runner extrapolates current trends, *Dark City* presents a unique vision of dystopia. Starring Rufus Sewell, Jennifer Conwell, Kiefer Sutherland, and William Hurt, the film tells the story of a person's discovery of the world around him, and the presence of the Strangers, aliens who had come to Earth when their own planet was dying. Memory and its significance in culture play a large part in this film, and Murdoch (Sewell) tries to unravel the bits of reality that lie in tatters in his memories. But these memories might be real, or part of the fabrication of illusion. Proyas creates a realistic world through careful cinematography and mise-en-scene, even though the sense of comic-book, noir-ish characters and sets remains. The film won the Saturn award for best science fiction film, from the Academy of Science Fiction, Fantasy and Horror Films in 1999.

DAVIS, JUDY (1955–). Like **Nicole Kidman** and **Mel Gibson**, for example, Judy Davis has established her reputation as one of the best performers on both the small and wide screens. In the first part of her career in Australia, her rise to stardom parallels the development and maturing of the Australian film industry since the **revival**. She has been likened to other great character actresses like Bette Davis, and her work is often marked by a sense of tension with directors, but this tension results in performances that are something special. She has a reputation for speaking frankly, as do many of her characters, and performs with passion and genuine artistry. Her ability has been recognized in the numerous accolades that the industry has given her.

Born in Perth, Western Australia, she attended drama school with Gibson in that state, and played in *Romeo and Juliet* with him, and they both then attended the National Institute of Dramatic Art. She first appeared on the screen in a short film directed and cowritten by **Gillian Armstrong**, *Clean Straw for Nothing* (1976). A small part in *High Rolling* (1977) followed, before she teamed up with Armstrong again in the leading role of the freethinking, strong-willed writer Sybylla Melvyn in the **adaptation** of Miles Franklin's novel, *My Brilliant Career* (1979). In 1981, she won the British Academy of Film and Television Arts (BAFTA) film awards for best newcomer and best actress for this role, and was nominated for best leading actress by the **Australian Film Institute** (AFI) in 1979.

Continuing to play self-assured and eccentric **women**, Davis starred in two films directed by Australians. In John Duigan's *The Winter of Our Dreams* (1981), she played a prostitute desperate to escape the pincers of a destructive environment, in *Hoodwink* (1981), the sexually repressed, lay-preachers wife, and in **Phillip Noyce**'s *Heatwave* (1983), she played an anarchist urban militant searching out corruption and murder. In 1981, the AFI bestowed two awards on her: best actress in a supporting role for *Hoodwink*, and best actress in a lead role for *The Winter of Our Dreams*. Davis's career was not enhanced greatly by her first international appearance in *Who Dares Wins* (also *The Final Option*) (1982), a thriller that does not challenge either cast or audience, but her next role as the repressed Adele Quested in David Lean's *A Passage to India* (1984) was the opposite, where she worked with grace, skill, and subtlety in giving life to Adele. As a result, in 1985, she was nominated for an Oscar for best actress in a lead role.

Returning to Australia, Davis played in another brilliant literary role as Harriet Somers, D.H. Lawrence's wife in *Kangaroo* (1986) and reunited with Armstrong in *High Tide* (1987), as a worn-out singer who encounters the daughter she had abandoned as a child. She won another AFI award for best actress in a lead role for this performance. Much of her work since then has been outside Australia, but she has returned on various occasions. First, for *Georgia* (1988), and then the farcical **comedy** about an Australian's romance with Stalin, resulting in a love-child, in *Children of the Revolution* (1996). More recently, she played alongside Billy Connolly, as Anna Redmond in the comedy—about a battle between the unfeeling insurance corporation and the average person—*The Man Who Sued God* (2001). In a drama about a swimming family in Queensland, Australia, *Swimming Upstream* (2003), she played Dora Fingleton, winning another best actress award from the AFI in the process, and adding to that she won for *Children of the Revolution*. Her work overseas has led her to work with Woody Allen in *Alice* (1990), *Husbands and Wives* (1992), *Deconstructing Harry* (1997), and *Celebrity* (1998). She worked with the Coen brothers in *Barton Fink* (1991), and with David Cronenberg in *Naked Lunch* (1991).

Yet this brief summary of her work in film is only one half of Davis's oeuvre. She is an accomplished and in-demand performer on **television**, featuring in television docudramas and series in Australia and overseas that are too numerous to mention here. Suffice to say that her work is applauded in that medium, with five Emmy nominations and two awards, the most recent being for her portrayal of Judy Garland in *Life with Judy Garland: Me and My Shadows* (2001).

Other films include *On My Own* (1992), *Impromptu* (1991), *Dark Blood* (1993), *The Ref* (1994), *The New Age* (1994), *Blood and Wine* (1996), *Absolute Power* (1997), *Deconstructing Harry* (1997), and *Gaudi Afternoon* (2001).

DEATH IN BRUNSWICK* (1991).** Based on a novel by Boyd Oxlade and directed by John Ruane, *Death in Brunswick* is a black **comedy** of a type not often seen in Australian filmmaking, driven by a narrative of surprising convolutions, and quirky characters who are recognizable as real, or at least one step removed. Carl (Sam Neill**) is a shiftless cook who works by night in a squalid nightclub in the inner-city

Melbourne suburb of Brunswick. By day he stays at home with his dominating mother and visits his best friend Dave (*John Clarke), who is, by contrast only, a model of domesticity. However, by a strange twist of fate, Carl is involved in the killing of the Turkish kitchen-hand Mustafa (Nico Lathouris), whom he then has to secretly bury with the help of his grave-digger friend, Dave. Complicating matters is his falling in love with Sophie (Zoë Carides).

DE HEER, ROLF (1951–). Working in the industry as writer, director, and producer, de Heer has not won many critical fans—except for *The Tracker* (2002)—although his career, especially in its most recent phase, continues to be worth following. Born in the Netherlands, he moved to Australia in 1959. He cut his directorial teeth in 1984 on two features, the ABC telefeature *Thank You, Jack* and a children's film *Tail of a Tiger*. There followed, in 1988, the underrated *Incident at Raven's Gate* (a.k.a. *Encounter at Raven's Gate*), a story set in the South Australian outback that traced the effect of aliens (never seen) on a small community. De Heer both wrote and directed this work. In 1991, he made *Dingo* and followed this in 1993 with ***Bad Boy Bubby***. Depicting the picaresque adventures of an infantile adult, this was a low-budget, almost surreal, presentation of incest and murder. Nevertheless, overlaid with irony and black humor, *Bubby* produces a strong critique of contemporary Australian society. There followed *The Quiet Room* (1996), *Episolom* (a.k.a. *Alien Visitor* [1997]), *Dance Me to My Song* (1998), *The Old Man Who Read Love Stories* (2001), *The Tracker*, and *Alexandra's Project* (2003). In general, de Heer has had strong backing from the **South Australian Film Corporation** and, in recent years, it has been coproductions between the latter and interests from the Netherlands, Germany, Spain, and elsewhere that have financed his films. De Heer himself has usually written and produced these, suggesting that this is a strong creative personality in a classical European *auteur* tradition.

DEVIL'S PLAYGROUND, THE **(1976). Fred Schepisi** wrote the script, produced, and directed this autobiographical coming-of-age film that centered on growing up in a Roman Catholic seminary. Like ***Picnic at Hanging Rock*** *(1975)*, the institution of civilization was set amongst the rural peace of Australia. Yet, within this institution seethed the seemingly unnatural undercurrents of repression and an overlay of evil. The young Tom Allen, who feels for a time a strong sense of vocation, also feels a longing for the freedoms of a changing world outside the seminary, freedoms that are constantly challenged inside the walls by even harsher training. At the same time, the lives of the priests are not depicted as other than men who have fought, or are fighting, their own battles of chastity and obedience. That is, Schepisi does not demonize them.

In 1976, *The Devil's Playground* became the first Australian film to be invited to the director's fortnight at the Cannes Film Festival. It won six of the newly established **Australia Film Institute** (AFI) awards, including best film, best director, best screenplay, and best actor in a lead role (Simon Burke and Nick Tate). The film established Schepisi's reputation as a director of world standard. *See also* REVIVAL.

DIMITRIADES, ALEX (1973–). Dimitriades's first appearance in film was a starring role as the Greek teenager in *The Heartbreak Kid* (1993), a coming-of-age story about a high school student falling in love with his teacher. It seemed to herald great success for Dimitriades, and indeed, that success did manifest in lead roles in **television** series. He was nominated for best actor in the **Australian Film Institute** awards for the role of Ari in *Head On* (1998), but further success was not guaranteed. He played in the lamentable **comedy** *Let's Get Skase* (2001), which had little for Dimitriades to work on. The film's plot centered around an attempt to bring the Australian Gordon Gecko, Christopher Skase, back to stand trial in Australia, where he had fleeced many of their savings through failed investments. A starring role as Conrad followed in the R-rated science fiction thriller *Subterano* (2002), a German-Australian coproduction about 11 people trapped by remote-controlled toys in an underground car park. He followed this with a supporting role in the uneven *Ghost Ship* (2002), a horror story about the salvaging of a ship that disappeared in 1962.

DISH, THE (2000). *The Dish* is the sixth most successful Australian film, earning $18.0 million at the Australian box office. The film won the Film Critics Circle of Australia awards for best music score and best original screenplay in 2001, and the **Australian Film Institute** nominated it for best film and best original music score in the same year.

Directed by **Rob Sitch**—who also directed *The Castle* (1997)—*The Dish* tells the story of the Apollo 11 moon landing in July 1969 from a different perspective; that is, the dramas surrounding the transmission of the pictures of the landing using the 110 foot receiving dish installation at Parkes, New South Wales. This dish was the backup for the NASA dish at Goldstone, California. Six hundred million viewers watched this event, but the film relates how the transmission of the moon landing was almost botched through human flaws and the vagaries of Mother Nature. The team at Parkes is led by the quiet and introspective Cliff Buxton (*Sam Neill), with support from the technician Mitch (Kevin Harrington) and plotter Glenn (**Tom Long**). The NASA liaison person, Al Burnett (Patrick Warburton), helps the team deal with the problems, both actual and contrived for the film, that threaten to prevent the transmission of **television** pictures to the expectant audience.

DOCUMENTARY. Australian documentary cinema is the sprawling, frequently unrecognized twin of Australian feature film. Like its sibling, it has been present from the birth of filmmaking. Yet, it has tended to flourish while the other languished and vice versa. Of course, this bifurcation of cinema into these two types has been widely recognized. Thus, for example, documentary has been seen to lean toward information and education while the other strives toward entertainment; the one prefers realism while the other verges toward fantasy; the former adopts factualism while the latter employs fiction. Clearly, the actual **history** of documentary—including its employment in Australia—contradicts these binaries. The 1952 classic, *Mike and Stefani*, for example, employs a narrative mode of presentation and engages in a fiction of re-creation. Equally, the "father" of British documentary, John Grierson's formulation of this kind of filmmaking as "the creative treatment of actuality" cautions against too strict an application of a rigid binarism.

Grierson's name is apposite here not only because of his articulation of an ideology of documentary very influential in Australia but also because of his dramatic intervention in 1940 in the institutional course of Australian documentary cinema. However, to grasp the significance of advice he gave to the Australian government about the present and future of documentary, it is necessary to understand the earlier development of this mode of filmmaking in Australia.

Unlike commercial feature film production, which lacked any state support before the period of the **revival**, documentary film was early recognized as a mode that easily made itself available to a newly created state committed to developing a centralist ideology and a **national identity**. To that end, the Australian government employed information/documentary filmmakers from as early as 1901 to record and present various events and activities that further legitimated the state. For example, The Salvation Army Limelight Department was one of the most prolific documentary filmmakers in this period up to 1904, making some 50 films, including *The Inauguration of the [Australian] Commonwealth* (1901) and *Under Southern Skies* (1902), the most elaborate film presentation of its time. In 1911, the federal government appointed an official film cameraman and photographer whose purpose it was to produce moving and still images of various aspects of Australia, frequently for purposes of promoting immigration from and sales of agricultural produce to the United Kingdom. In 1919, a permanent unit attached to the Department of Agriculture was established and this in turn became the Cinema and Photographic Branch in 1932. The output of these years up to 1940 has mostly been neglected, although some documentarists, especially **Frank Hurley**, have provoked critical interest.

Grierson's 1940 visit to Australia, then, constituted a decisive intervention for reasons of institution and ideology. Sponsored by the Imperial Relations Trust, a body concerned to reaffirm the old bonds of the British Empire, Grierson wrote a report on his visit, offering the Australian government much the same advice that he had recently furnished to those in Canada and New Zealand. Sealing a lid on feature film making, he suggested that Australia should not attempt to compete with or emulate **Hollywood**. Instead, it should concentrate on the distribution and production of shorter information or documentary films for purposes of presenting the nation to itself and to the rest of the world. At war's end, the government acted on this advice, following Grierson's Canadian institutional framework, and reconstituting the existing film bodies as the Australian National Film Board. Some of the successors to Grierson's initiative are the **Commonwealth Film Unit** and **Film Australia**.

Four related points are worth mentioning. First, since the 1950s and, especially the 1960s, documentary film institutions, particularly

Film Australia, have come to seem like de facto film schools where young practitioners can learn their craft before moving on to feature film. However, the traffic has not always been one way. Some resolutely remain in documentary while others have moved back to this mode and institutional framework.

Secondly, there is the fact that from the late 1960s onward, **television** became an important institutional player in this field. Television has become a major source for the exhibition, financing and production of documentary films both for the government production body and for independent companies and individual filmmakers.

Thirdly, over and above these agencies, there have also been other institutional sites of documentary including the Shell Film Unit—responsible for the 1954 classic *The Back of Beyond*—the Institute of Aboriginal Studies, and the Methodist Overseas Studies. These last two worked in the area of ethnographic film. At the same time, other agencies such as the Waterside Worker's Film Unit in the 1950s produced a series of films dealing with various aspects of the postwar Australian labor struggle. It is also worth recording some of the distinguished filmmakers who have produced documentaries under the aegis of these and other agencies over the past 50 years. A partial roll call includes Martha Ansara, Bob Connolly and Robin Anderson, **Ian Dunlop**, John Heyer, **Cecil Holmes**, John Hughes, Joris Ivens, David McDougall, Mike Rubbo, Dennis O'Rourke, and Tom Zubricki.

Finally, it is worth mentioning the stylistic variety found in Australian documentary cinema in these years. The dominant or classic expository mode engages in direct audience addresses, frequently through a narrator whose commentary guides the viewer's attention and understanding. Limited sound-recording technology until the early 1960s and institutional imperatives ensured that this mode became the preferred style of many hundreds of Australian documentary films. More recently, this type has been complemented by a kind of neoexpository mode that varies the style through softer commentary voices and the interspersion of commentary and on-screen interview. From the late 1960s on, Film Australia also engaged in an observational or direct cinema found, for example, in *Changing* (1976). A further kind of fracturing of the preferred mode was in

God Knows Why but It Works (1975), a more interactive kind of documentary with the interview of subject occurring before the camera. In summary, then, Australian documentary cinema has been responsive to traditions and pressures not only within the field of documentary but also within the twin trajectories of institution and changing technology.

DUNLOP, IAN (1927–). Born in London in 1927, Ian Dunlop took a BA at Cambridge University. In 1948, he moved to Sydney where he enrolled at the University. However, the degree was cut short and he joined the ABC, working in Sydney, Adelaide, and Canberra. In 1957, he took up a position as production assistant with the **Commonwealth Film Unit** (CFU), and two years later was assistant director. Meanwhile, his first visit to Central Australia occurred in 1957 to complete the film *Balloons and Spinifex* on a remote weather station. By this time, with the CFU expanding rapidly, Dunlop was being allowed to specialize in ethnographic film. His first such project concerned the **Aboriginal** settlement known as Aurukun. Among the films produced between 1962 and 1964 were *Five Aboriginal Dances* and *Dances at Aurukun*. In turn, sponsored by the Institute of Aboriginal Studies, Dunlop completed 19 archival films on *People of the Australian Western Desert* (1966–1969), and a shorter, more popular version titled *Desert People* (1966). Dunlop organized the CFU-sponsored UNESCO Round Table on ethnographic filmmaking in the Pacific Area in 1967. Australian ethnographic film, including Dunlop's own work, was received with great acclaim. In turn, for the next meeting in Florence, Dunlop compiled a comprehensive Retrospective Review of Australian Ethnographic Film and toured this around Europe. He made 23 films in the Yirrkala Film Project (1970–1982), and two large cycles of 26 films in the Baruya project in New Guinea, in association with French anthropologist Maurice Godelier. Some of these links suggest the fact that Dunlop has a highly prestigious international reputation in his field while only receiving moderate acclaim in Australia. Hence, for example, he was elected an Honorary Fellow of the Royal Anthropological Institute in 1991. Meanwhile, at home, he gained the **Australian Film Institute**'s **Raymond Longford** Award (1968) and the Medal of the Order of Australia in 1986.

– E –

EALING STUDIOS. Like other British studios, Ealing suffered a loss of skilled technicians during World War II. At the height of this problem, two thirds of the British film industry's technicians were on active service; for Ealing, this meant a loss of 50 workers out of a small workforce of approximately 200 (Perry 1981:52). To help remedy the situation, Ealing's head of production Michael Balcon looked for skilled labor in the British **documentary** movement, specifically the Crown Film Unit of the Ministry of Information. The most important of these new staff was the producer and director Alberto Cavalcanti, who had worked with Grierson in the 1930s, and later with Harry Watt (director of *Night Mail*, 1936) at the CFU. Attracted to Ealing by Cavalcani's growing influence there, Watt joined a pool of new directors who, with other directors fostered from within Ealing's own ranks, were to form the core of the studio's subsequent expansion. This group included Watt, Charles Crichton, Basil Dearden, Charles Frend, Alexander Mackendrick, and Robert Hamer (Barr 1977:46–7).

In 1946, Balcon was approached by Jack Baddington, head of the CFU, to look for suitable stories on Australia's contribution to the war effort. Watt was dispatched to Australia, in the expectation of making a semidocumentary feature along the lines of his first Ealing film, *Nine Men* (1943). On arrival, he found the Australians already making a film of this type—*The Rats of Tobruk*—but was pleased to find a suitable story of a less conventional kind; that is, the story of how, in 1942, 100,000 head of cattle were driven from the Northern Territory before the threatened landing and advance south of Japanese forces. The Royal Australian Air Force loaned Ralph Smart to the production, as associate producer. Smart, who had worked in the British film industry in the 1920s, and who later divided his working life between the Australian and British film and **television** industries, went on to direct *Bush Christmas* (1947) and—this time for Ealing—*Bitter Springs* (1950). *The Overlanders* (1946), starring **Chips Rafferty** and shot on location in the Australian outback, was a success and convinced Balcon of the feasibility of making features in Australia. The cycle lasted until 1959 and comprised five films: *The Overlanders* (Watt, 1946), *Eureka Stockade* (Watt, 1949), *Bitter*

Springs (Ralph Smart, 1950), **The Shiralee** (Leslie Norman, 1957), and *The Siege of Pinchgut* (Watt, 1959).

The Overlanders incidental adventures were played out in a spectacularly photographed Australian outback landscape. Audiences in metropolitan Britain were suitably impressed and this image of an Australian frontier was to feed into the postwar marketing of Australia as a land of opportunity. Ealing films like *Where No Vultures Fly* (Watt, 1951) and *West of Zanzibar* (Watt, 1954) were filmed in another site of colonial fantasy, South Africa. Other Ealing features—*Whiskey Galore* (Alexander Mackendrick, 1949) and *The Maggie* (Mackendrick, 1949)—were set in the comic hinterlands of the Celtic north and west of the British Isles; they had more in common with the charming small community comedies like *Passport to Pimlico* (Henry Cornelius, 1949) or *The Titfield Thunderbolt* (Charles Crichton, 1953).

Ealing's corporate decline stemmed from the increasing irreconcilability of its two main strategies: to make films of an ambitious, patriotic nature that, in Balcon's words, embodied Britain's "postwar aspirations" and showed it as a "questing explorer," and to make "films of a modest nature" (Barr 1977:62–3). By the late 1940s, the American market had begun a love affair with the Ealing comedies that was to exacerbate this strategic instability. Ealing's Australian venture was never really secure; after its initial success with *The Overlanders*, its stocks had declined with *Eureka Stockade* and *Bitter Springs*. The situation began to become serious when the Federal Government refused to renew the lease on the Pagewood studio that Ealing had equipped at considerable expense, on the grounds that filmmaking was not an essential industry and the leaseholders were, in any case, not Australian residents. The fate of the Australian venture was sealed in 1952 when Balcon dispatched the accountant John Davis to assess its financial viability. Davis had helped Rank—which underwrote Ealing's finances and distribution deals—restructure in the late 1940s. His report was negative and his personal opinion was that, in any case, "I could never understand why it was considered necessary to make pictures in Australia . . . After all, we in England have four or five modern, well-equipped studios, and nearly 4,000 people employed. We can make all the pictures you [Australians] need" (Perry 1981:148). Ealing went on to film two more features in Australia: *The Shiralee* (1957) and *The Siege of Pinchgut* (1959).

EDGERTON, JOEL (1974–). Joel Edgerton is a graduate of Sydney's Theatre Nepean. He is an accomplished Shakespearean actor and has worked in the Sydney Theatre Company as well as appearing in a number of popular Australian **television** series. His film credits include the unstable armed robber Shane Twentyman in *A Hard Word* (2002), Owen Lars in *Star Wars: Episode II—Attack of the Clones* (2002), Leo in *Praise* (1998), and Wayne in *Erskineville Kings* (1999). Other films include *Ned Kelly* (2003), *The Pitch* (2002) and as writer, *Gate* (2000), *Sample People* (2000), *Dogwatch* (1999), *Bloodlock* (1998) (also writer and producer), and *Race the Sun* (1996).

EFFTEE PRODUCTIONS. Efftee Productions was an optimistic attempt to take advantage of the introduction of sound to Australian cinema, which was to founder under the combined effect both of the Depression and the stranglehold that American distributors had over film exhibition by the 1930s. The finance to launch the company came from **Frank Thring Sr.** after he had sold his shares in **Hoyts** cinema chain in the early 1930s. In 1931, the company opened its production facilities in what had formerly been Her Majesty's Theatre after the latter had been affected by fire. The company's manager Tom Holt brought the latest in sound production equipment which was installed, complete with staff training, by American Dan Blombard. Thring himself directed all films with the exception of an early two and employed silent veteran **Raymond Longford** as uncredited assistant. Meanwhile, Efftee also employed the same production team including Alan Mill (sound) and Arthur Higgins (cameraman).

The company was also involved in documentaries produced by Noel Monkman as well as making newsreel inserts. What Efftee aimed at was supplying an exhibition package that included a feature film as well as other items and entertaining novelties. In late 1933, the company moved to a refurbished studio in St. Kilda but the next year saw production halted when release difficulties set in. By 1936, Thring was contemplating a move to Sydney when he died. Without the principal, creditors had no option but to wind up the company.

ETHNIC REPRESENTATION. Since 1788, successive waves of immigration, beginning with the settlement in Australia by convicts and soldiers from England in that year, formed and molded Australian history and culture. These waves of immigrants, over time, displaced those whose ancestors had themselves immigrated into Australia over 50,000 years before.

Free settlers followed slowly the first wave of convicts and their jailers, but the first population explosion occurred in the mid-19th century, when gold was discovered in Australia, attracting people from all over the world, especially those who were employed in shipping. Included in this group were many Chinese people, and the first interethnic tension occurred when the industry was contracting, and the Chinese were content to rework mines thus making a living. This conflict, stemming in part from a belief that Chinese workers would lower the standards for workers in Australia, produced a national xenophobia that found expression in the first law passed by the newly federated Australian nation in 1901, restricting the immigration of people to those of Anglo-Saxon descent through a ubiquitous language test. This policy was relaxed somewhat to allow European refugees from World War II to settle in Australia, and this began an immigration program that, with changes to overall numbers, continues. From 1960, the immigration laws were gradually relaxed so that by 1965 all mention of restrictions on "non-Europeans" was removed.

Given these patterns of immigration, Australia is now a multicultural society, and has policies that reflect that. For many immigrants with non-English speaking backgrounds, learning English may have been difficult; for their children it was much easier, but the downside was that the children tended to move away from the culture of their parents. Many films examine this search for a cultural identity among the sometimes competing cultures found in the broader Australian culture. At the same time, the juxtaposition of these two cultures does not always exhibit an easy acceptance and understanding. Yet such a juxtaposition cannot do other than change both cultures in some way; for example, on one level people from both cultures take parts of the other culture to use and adapt as they see fit.

These issues are represented in films, not always to the benefit of any or both cultures. For example, one of the earliest representations of Chinese people is in *A Girl of the Bush* (1921), with crude caricatures representing common views of Chinese culture in Australia. These crude caricatures were also found in political cartoons of the period. One ethnic group that did a great deal to open up the outback were people from Afghanistan, who brought camels into Australia. They are represented in *The Squatter's Daughter* (1933) in the characters of Jebal Zim, a licensed hawker, and his daughter, Xena, who travel through the outback in a gypsylike caravan selling wares. Costumes and speech assist in establishing identity. Xena is in love with Jimmy, who is the crippled brother of station-owner Jean, and the difficulties of this liaison are a significant element in the narrative of this film.

Later films explore similar issues. Significantly, actors who are from ethnic backgrounds often play in films about different cultures. **Alex Dimitriades** is one of these, as the son of first generation immigrants from Greece, who grew up in the working class suburb of Earlwood in Sydney. His first film role was in *The Heartbreak Kid* (1993), which critiques the conservatism and narrowness of middle-class Greek culture, at the same time decrying the bigotry that was a significant element of Australian culture, and that found expression in such terms as "dago" and "wog." Christina (**Claudia Karvan**) is a recently graduated school teacher coming to grips with an urge to find the liberation promised to her by the times and culture she lives in, but to do so she has to free herself from the constraints of her Greek parents and the culture they are a part of. Interestingly, she sleeps with her student (Dimitriades), a situation which, if the roles were reversed, would have caused some moral outrage. In *Head On* (1998), Dimitriades plays a young gay Greek man alienated from the immigrant culture of his parents and their home, but also his own friends. His ethnic and cultural dilemma is vaguely mediated through a rollercoaster of passion, anger, and lust. A film that is similarly violent, *Romper Stomper* (1992), focused on the anti-Asian racism and profascist skinhead culture of its main protagonist. The chief skinhead, Hando (**Russell Crowe**), portrays a deep-seated resentment common to those who have little, and he and his thugs violently confront and destroy what they perceive to be the cause of their resentment; namely, Asians and Asian culture.

However, not all films are so violent. Different ethnicities are a source of **comedy** arising out of the fish-out-of-water situation. *They're a Weird Mob* (1966) is a good-humored narrative around the experiences of a recently arrived Italian immigrant, Nino Culotta (Walter Chiari), his working life in the building industry and his romance with his boss's daughter. Elements of Australian culture are thrown into sharp relief in this examination. Three notable comedies examine cultures in juxtaposition, and the change that each culture causes to the other at this site of contact. **Death in Brunswick** (1991) is a story about the seedier side of life in working-class Brunswick, an inner-city suburb of Melbourne where many immigrant families settled in the postwar years. In 1970, for example, Brunswick High School counted 26 nationalities in its student population. No hierarchies of culture exist in this film; all are essentially strange. *Wog Boy* (2000) and *Fat Pizza* (2003) celebrate, in sometimes bizarre ways in the case of *Pizza*, the ethnic elements of Australian culture from the perspective of those ethnic elements. Those cultures are undergoing change, but an important element of change is the richness of its product. While *Wog Boy* pokes fun at the dishonesty in elements of Australian politics, *Pizza* sends up elements of all cultures. **Looking for Alibrandi** (1998) is a comedy that follows the lives of three generations of women of Italian-Australian descent, their loves, their dramas, and their family support mechanisms.

Two other films deserve mention. **Silver City** (1984) dramatizes the experiences of postwar Polish immigrants who were herded into ex-army Nissan huts before being resettled in mainstream Australian cities. The xenophobia, corruption, and bloody-mindedness the film ascribes to most (male) characters is inaccurate, but the film deals with issues that are once again extant in Australia, in the case of refugees who are incarcerated in similar huts behind barbed wire in the Australian desert. **Strictly Ballroom** (1992) is not generally regarded as being a film about ethnic culture. However, the film looks at the way mainstream Australian culture views immigrant cultures, and the reverse. The film draws on Spanish culture, and while this is generally disregarded as irrelevant, the film does address the common issues of belonging: one's personal, social and cultural identity, and relationships between generations that may be affected by ethnic backgrounds. The film is an example of the degree to which ethnic difference (and similarity) underpins narratives about Australian culture.

EUROPE. Unlike Asia, which although geographically proximate has only a fleeting screen presence here, Europe (including the United Kingdom) is a permanent, often pervasive element in the Australian film landscape. For the period since the end of World War II, one Australian film, the feature-length **documentary** *Mike and Stefani* (1952), forms an obvious reference point, telling about not only the war but also the plight of refugees and the massive immigration drive undertaken by the Australian government immediately after 1945. However, even over and above its narrative concerns, the film—with its reworkings of British documentary and Italian neorealist practices—also signals a rich European cultural and cinematic tradition from which Australia continues to be nourished. One of the important themes of Australian film has been immigration, especially that from Europe, with a large number of government information films produced up to around 1960. Even beyond that, as later series such as *The Migrant Experience* (1976) disclose, this flood of people from Europe has been a constitutive experience for the contemporary Australian imagination.

One of the first of these documentaries was the **comedy** *Double Trouble* (1949), which forced two Australians, ignorant of the linguistic difficulties facing European immigrants, to sample what life might be like in an unidentified European country if they could not speak the language. In turn, by the 1960s, this comedy of the "fish out of water" could give rise to two comedy features looking at the Italian migrant newcomer in *They're a Weird Mob* (1966) and the lesser-known *Squeeze a Flower* (1970). Meanwhile, *The Golden Cage* (1976) was a more somber take on the same subject, this time tracing the lives of three Turkish migrants in Australia. Yet, another part of this film cycle concerned with first generation European immigrants focused on some of the cultural gaps complicating romantic and marital relationships between immigrant men and women. Thus, for example, two social realist features in this period—*Sposerebbo Compaesana Illibata (Girl in Australia)* (1971) and *Promised Woman* (1975)—examined arranged marriages between a migrant and a woman from the old country. However, with growing pluralism in Australian society, the immigrant was no longer a "dago" or "wog" as is evidenced in *Kostas* (1979). Unlike the figure in *Weird Mob* who becomes a manual laborer, the Greek hero of the title, although first discovered as a taxi-driver, turns out to be a professional, a trained journalist who ultimately wins the heart of the most ultimate Anglo-Saxon, a rich Toorak divorcee. By the 1980s, the migrant flow from Europe was a thing of the past so that *Silver City* (1984), set in a migrant camp in 1949, was a bitter-sweet re-creation, a period film, an elegy to this period of massive intake of European peoples and culture.

However, there still remains a cinematic space for other related legacies of World War II in Europe. One of these concerns the second generation European migrant experience in Australia as is exemplified in more recent Australian features such as the romantic drama of *The Heartbreak Kid* (1993) and the comedy of *The Wog Boy* (2000) and *Fat Pizza* (2003). Finally, too, to round out this narrative legacy, mention should be made of two recent features whose generic influences are elsewhere. *Father* (1989) begins with the Polish holocaust of the Jews and the escape of one young victim. She traces the camp commander to Australia. In the present, Joe Mueller (the great Swedish actor Max von Sydow) is a frail, loving, family figure. Put on trial, the evidence against him is discredited and charges are dropped. However, he then reveals to daughter Anne that he was in fact guilty although he has no remorse for his crime. Meanwhile, by contrast, in *Hostage: The Christine Maresch Story* (1983), the connection with Europe proves to be contemporary. A German neo-Nazi, Walter Maresch, on the run in Australia, tricks new wife Christine into returning with him to Germany. There he exposes his involvement with the neo-Nazis and forces his wife into bank robbery to support the political ambitions of the group. There is further trouble for the two in Turkey and they return briefly to Australia only to have Walter again attempt to return to Germany, this time by sailboat.

Even beyond this subject and narrative legacy from Europe, there also exists another tradition to do with the lasting cultural repertoire that Europe makes available to Australian artists, including its filmmakers. *Breakfast in Paris* (1982) is a romantic comedy although while set in Europe owes more to the **genre** of romantic comedy found in both British and Hollywood films rather than in Europe. On the other hand, there are others such as *Devil in the Flesh* (1989), set in Paris, based on a French novel that had been made already into both a French and an Italian film. At this level also might be included Esben Storm's *In Search of Anna* (1979). The latter is deliberate in its references to the traditions of the European art film, most especially Antonioni's *L'Avventura* (1960), which concerned another missing woman called Anna.

To complete this account of contact between Australian and European cinemas, mention should be made of the particular instance of filmmakers with a distinctly European outlook and their Australian films. Thus, on the one hand, there are several Australian directors with what might be called a European sensibility. The best known and most prolific is Paul Cox. Hailed in the Netherlands as a Dutch filmmaker although often working in Australia, his is the most distinct and consistent cinematic workings in the European art film tradition, resulting in a steady stream of films, including *Illuminations* (1976), *Inside Looking Out* (1977), *Man of Flowers* (1983), *My First Wife* (1984), *Cactus* (1986), *Island* (1989), *Golden Braid* (1990), *Exile* (1994), *Molokai: The Story of Father Damien* (1999), and *The Diaries of Vaslav Nijinsky* (2001). Another in the same mold, although more interested in abstract questions and issues in the tradition of Werner Hertzog is Ian Pringle. He has written and directed three notable features. *The Plains of Heaven* (1982) is an ambiguous essay in metaphysics inscribed inside a narrative depicting two men coping both as they man a tracking station and when they return to **city** life. *The Prisoner of St. Petersburg* (1988) concerns an Australian who has ended up in Berlin after failing to discover his dream city of prerevolution St. Petersburg. More recently, *Isabelle Eberhardt* (1992) a French Australian coproduction, concerns a young Frenchwoman's adventures in North Africa around 1900, examining a host of social and political issues in its complex narrative including political manipulation, colonization, intercultural conflict, and an inner search for peace.

Finally, mention should also be made of three films made in Australia concerning local subjects by visiting European auteurs. Werner Hertzog's *Where the Green Ants Dream* (1984) explores a clash of culture between **Aborigines** and whites. Dusan Makajeve's *The Cocoa Cola Kid* (1985) based on short stories by Frank Moorehouse details a comic clash of culture, this time between the American figure of the title and Australian bureaucrats and bohemians. Meanwhile, Wim Wenders *Until the End of the World* (1992) trips across four continents with a central figure who wants to make his blind mother see. In summary, then, Europe has been a fertile source and inspiration as far as Australian cinema in the past half century is concerned. *See also* ETHNIC REPRESENTATION.

EVIL ANGELS (ALSO *A CRY IN THE DARK*) **(1988).** Director **Fred Schepisi** returned to Australia to make this film, which was based on a true story about the disappearance and assumed death of Azaria Chamberlain. The 10-week old baby was taken and killed by dingoes at Uluru, the world's largest rock, **Aboriginal** sacred site, and tourist destination in central Australia. Flawed forensic evidence was used to convict the mother, Lindy Chamberlain (Meryl Streep) and husband Michael (*****Sam Neill**) of murder. After inquiries and further evidence, the two were found not guilty and released. The trial was a saga in Australian cultural history. Rumors of child sacrifice and obscure religious practices, the seeming coldness of Lindy, the disbelief that dingoes could carry off children, and the site of the event produced a cacophony of interest in the media, which both obscured the truth and finally pressed for its uncovering.

Evil Angels was critically applauded both in Australia and overseas. In 1989, it was nominated for four Golden Globes including best director and best picture–drama. Schepisi was nominated for a Golden Palm, and Streep won the best actress award at the 1989 Cannes Film Festival. In the same year, the film was nominated for three **Australian Film Institute** awards and won five: best actor (Neill), best actress (Streep), best director, best film, and best adapted screenplay. In addition, Streep was nominated for an Oscar for best leading actress.

EVISON, PAT. *See entry in New Zealand section.*

– F –

FILM AUSTRALIA. The Australian **Commonwealth Film Unit** changed its name in 1973 to Film Australia. The same year also saw the division relocated within the Australian federal bureaucracy, shifting from the Department of the Interior to the Department of the Media and yet again in 1975 to the **Australian Film Commission.** In 1988, the organization was established as a government company: Film Australia Pty. Ltd. Denys Brown was head at the time of the name change and, in turn, he was succeeded by John Mabey (1980–1984), Robyn Hughes (1985–1989), Bruce Moir (1989–1997), Sharon Connolly (1997–2004), and Daryl Karp (since 2004). During this period, the organization made almost 2,000 mainly **documentary** films, the majority of which government departments commissioned while the others were produced from within its own budget in the national interest.

In line with changing industrial trends in the commercial production industry, a reorganization in the 1980s led to the downsizing of the permanent staff, and a policy of contracting out production, including in the 1990s increasing use of new technology. As might be expected given the orientation of the information/documentary film in general, the period from 1973 up until the present has, for the most part, seen a continuing emphasis on social issues. One of the dominant strains within this concern has been an involvement with fringe groups in the society—those that have been marginalized, invisible, and without a voice in the recent past. Film subjects that fall into this category include migrants (*The Migrant Experience* [1984]), **Aborigines** (*On Sacred Ground* [1981]), under-development in **country** areas (*Cunnamulla* [2000]), and the disabled (***Annie's Coming Out***). The latter film, released in 1984, was a fiction feature film that achieved mainstream theatrical release and was a highly prestigious film winning many awards. It was far from being the only such prize-winning film, which group also included *Leisure* (1976) and *Mabo: Life of an Island Man* (1997). Indeed, the former film, made by popular cartoonist and filmmaker Bruce Petty, won an Oscar, the second film of the unit to win such an award. The division's films have always aimed at an education market but, in the Film Australia period, **television** has replaced commercial release in theaters as the major distribution point. This, in turn, has often forced the organization to produce its material not in the form of one-off films but rather in terms of series such as the aforementioned *The Migrant Experience* and the multipart *The Human Face* (1979–1983) series. Meanwhile, Film Australia has also continued to be significant to the Australian film production industry in general in training directors, producers, and cinematographers who have gone on to illustrious careers in other parts of that industry. Turning to the films themselves, it is noteworthy that, despite continuities with the output of the late Commonwealth Film Unit period, the films produced since 1973 project a different view of Australia to those of earlier films.

Although the society is still pluralist, nevertheless, there is frequently competition and conflict that is sometimes resolved and brought into equilibrium and sometimes not. Essentially, Australia has become a darker, more diverse and anxious society. Thus, the environment has become a central image and a large cycle of the division's recent films have stressed the complexity and fragility of that phenomenon and diverse capacities both to adapt and to fail to survive. The mock documentary *Cane Toads* (1987), a film that examines the disastrous environmental consequences of introducing this species into Australia, is representative of this outlook. Meanwhile, as part of this readjustment of viewpoint toward that entity that is Australia, Film Australia's style and mode of filmmaking has also subtly readjusted in recent years. If one thinks of documentary as involving a dialectic between experience and argument, the need to affirm the validity of individual experience and the necessity to generalize, then recent division films—including the *Striving* series, *The Hurdle* (1984), *The Migrant Experience*, *The Human Face*, *Cane Toads*, and many others—have been marked by the return of an interview-based commentary.

Characteristically, these films work by accumulating a series of particular cases and experiences, thus offering, first, a dramatization of experience, and then, an interpretation of these. Epistemologically, the case studies and experiences legitimate and validate the commentary as do other strategies including the on-screen presence of the commentator. Finally, too, it can be noted that at least part of the reason for this (qualified) return to authoritative commentary has to do with the fact that, since the mid-1970s, the unit has come to rely more and more on the sponsorship of its films by different government departments. Undoubtedly, this kind of film style fits well with the pedagogic needs of these agencies.

FILM FESTIVALS. Film festivals are an important part of the cultural landscape in Australia. Not only are they important to the health and well-being of what might be called film culture but they are also important events so far as tourism, city promotion and "branding," community identity, and heritage activities are concerned. One important element in this has been the locating of several of these festivals in "showcase" cinemas that are now of considerable heritage value. Following the lead given by older, highly prestigious European film festivals established in the interwar period such as those of Venice and

Cannes, Australian film festivals began to appear in Melbourne and Sydney in the early 1950s. In turn, a second wave of city festivals located in Adelaide, Brisbane, and Perth got underway in the 1970s, often with quite varied results. More recently still, smaller cities and other centers have embraced film festivals as a means of adding to the range of cultural attractions both for tourists and for locals. Meanwhile, more recently, the larger cities with their older mainstream festivals have also become the site of a series of smaller, fringe festivals that are further enriching both culture and community.

Both the Sydney and Melbourne film festivals began in 1953, each of them growing out of film societies and their desire for a single major film event once in the calendar year. The Sydney festival was an offshoot of the Sydney University Film Society, which organized film screenings on a weekly basis during the university year. In 1952, it decided to organize a winter festival and initially screened in a series of nearby local cinemas. In turn, this event became the basis of the Sydney Film Festival. By the mid-1960s, the Festival was able to appoint a full-time director, David Stratton, and by the 1970s had settled into permanent occupation of the historic State Cinema in the center of the city. Meanwhile, in Melbourne, the Australian Council of Film Societies held an inaugural film festival in 1952 on the outskirts of the city, and its success led to the establishment of the first Melbourne Film Festival the following year. Like its Sydney counterpart, the Melbourne festival slowly moved toward professionalism and acquired permanent screening headquarters at the historic Palais Cinema in St. Kilda. These two festivals, both of them carrying accredited international status, have become the benchmark for film festivals in Australia. Since the mid to late 1960s, these have been seen by commercial distributors as important venues for building box office appeal for particular feature films so that one central component of their screenings has to do with the presentation of commercially viable features in which Hollywood has significant investments. In turn, these are mixed with other features from other centers, a kind of "world cinema," where the audience is given the opportunity to learn about unknown directors, **genres** and subject matter, and stylistic traditions.

A third component of this screening policy has to do with retrospective programs. Thus, for example, the Brisbane International Film Festival offered a season of the Westerns of Budd Boetticher as part of its 2000 offering. Meanwhile, as part of a general multiplication of particular film seasons held under the auspices of such festivals, there are now underground, **documentary**, cult, animation, and experimental programs. Additionally, short film competitions also provide opportunities for new filmmakers to display their filmic ideas. Of course, other surrounding screening sites and times become increasingly necessary to cater to this increased array.

Film festivals in the four other state capital cities had slower gestations. Organized by David Rowe, the Perth International Film Festival ran from 1972 until 1976. Its bold devotion to the exhibition of independent and avant-garde film and European art film, and to the promotion of new Australian cinema, was not enough to ensure continued funding and, eventually, it was abandoned; a victim of local cultural politics that denied it the necessary subsidies that it needed. More recently, however, Perth has reacquired a film festival. This is the "Film Screen" season, part of the summer Festival of Perth, at the Somerville Auditorium at the University of Western Australia.

Adelaide had two independent, and very successful, film festivals up to 1991. Both ran for a number of weeks, and showcased European films as well as commercial productions. Given that South Australia was the first state to establish a state-funded film production facility in the **South Australian Film Corporation**, and that the performance-oriented Adelaide festival is an internationally recognized event, then the absence of a state-supported film festival was incongruous. However, in November 2002, the state government announced the establishment of the Adelaide International Film Festival, a biennial event that began in 2003. Although a film festival occurred in Brisbane as early as 1976, nevertheless, the current festival, the Brisbane International Film Festival, is a much younger creature, which dates back to 1991. Although it draws its films from across the globe, it particularly highlights the work of Australian filmmakers. Two of its newer seasons consist of a Fast Film competition, designed to showcase local films, and a Brisbane Underground Film Festival that screens cult, trash, and other marginal genres and types of films. Finally, Hobart's "Edge of the World Film Festival" is the most recent of these and includes a program of contemporary international feature and short films, a national short-film and video program, and a Super-8 competition.

Meanwhile, with the major city film festivals hosting fringe festivals, it was little wonder that a new crop of such festivals should become established as stand-alone entities. Recently, for example, the short film has become an object of a festival in its own right. In 1993, the Sydney Tropicana Short Film Festival was launched with a single screening at the Tropicana Cafe in Darlinghurst. By 1998, "Tropfest" sold over 8,000 places, spilling onto nearby Victoria Street, which was closed to traffic. The annual St. Kilda Short Film Festival, dedicated to the short film as a legitimate form in its own right, avoids prescription and encourages diversity among entrants. In turn, Melbourne's Super-8 Festival extends this thinking further by offering a program that celebrates the variety and richness of this form. On the margins of film and art, the biennial Experimental Arts Festival offers film, new media, video installations, performances, and sound art. It encourages creativity in the making of digital images and sound generated by new technology as a means of stretching the boundaries of media arts exhibition in Australia.

Finally, it is certainly worth pointing out that film festivals are also important in the life of diverse communities. The Sydney Mardi Gras Film Festival and the Melbourne Queer Film and Video Festival celebrate the achievements of queer cinema. The latter, which began in 1991, has been particularly successful with audiences of up to 10,000 patrons, and has recently initiated a national tour of program highlights.

FILM FINANCE CORPORATION AUSTRALIA (FFC). The Film Finance Corporation Australia (FFC) is a wholly owned Commonwealth company providing support for feature films, telemovies, miniseries, and **documentaries**. It supports a diverse range of culturally relevant material through equity investment, undertaken in partnership with the film and **television** marketplace, including distributors, sales agents, broadcasters, and private investors.

In the 1980s, investors in film were entitled from 100 percent to 120 percent tax deductions and other benefits in an attempt by the government to fund films of higher quality that might not appear to be commercially viable. However, this resulted in investors searching for film investments that gave the best tax deduction. A changing tax framework meant that the actual return to investors was decreasing, and investments in film subsequently fell. As a result, the **Australian**

Film Commission, in 1986, proposed a single funding agency, and in 1988, the Film Finance Corporation Australia was launched. Since then, the FFC has been the main agency for financial support of productions judged on commercial criteria alone. Initially, private investors had to provide 30 percent of capital, but this rose to 35 percent, and then 40 percent in 1991. However, changing government policies were reflected in the first review of the FFC in 1991, and funding decreased from $68 million in 1998 to $40 million a decade later. While the commercial imperative is strong, the FFC is sometimes more flexible in providing funding for films that do not have known actors or directors, which may result in a lower level of marketplace support. The distinction between the FFC and other funding bodies is clear: the FFC provides equity investment; it does not fund development. The Australian Film Commission and state funded film agencies provide development funding in the form of script and marketing assistance.

In recent times, the FFC has financed many major films, like *Muriel's Wedding* (1994), *The Adventures of Priscilla, Queen of the Desert* (1994), *Shine* (1996), *Chopper* (2000), *The Man Who Sued God* (2001), *Rabbit-Proof Fence* (2002), *Dirty Deeds* (2002), *The Tracker* (2002), *Australian Rules* (2002) and **documentaries** like *Black Chicks Talking* (2002).

FINCH, PETER (1916–1977). Following a similar pattern to many Australian performers in being born and raised elsewhere, Peter Finch was born in London and raised in France and India, before arriving in Australia as a teenager. For the decade before his return to England in 1949, he was one of Australia's leading stage, screen, and radio performers, and was the archetype for the laconic, rugged, yet intelligent "Aussie." His first film was *Dad and Dave Come to Town* (1938), where he played a young farmer, then a German spy pretending to be an Australian in *The Power and the Glory* (1941), before an English soldier in *The Rats of Tobruk* (1944). Although he left Australia, he returned to make three films. He won his first of five British Academy of Film and Television Arts (BAFTA) awards for his portrayal of the bushman, cowboy, and prisoner of war Joe Harmon, in *A Town Like Alice* (1956), a part resuscitated by **Bryan Brown** in the **television** miniseries of the same name in 1981. In the

Ealing film, *The Shiralee* (1957), he played the footloose itinerant rural worker Macauley, who takes his child Buster out of a dysfunctional urban setting to spend time with her on the road, where they develop a strong bond that surpasses the "burden" suggested by the name "shiralee." He starred in *Robbery under Arms* (1957) as the bushranger Captain Starlight.

Finch also had a strong **documentary** thread in his output. During World War II, he supplied the narration for a film about Australian troops entitled *Jungle Patrol* (1944). In 1947, he worked on a documentary about the Arnhem Land **Aborigines**, *Primitive Peoples* (1947).

Finch's output numbered some 50 films, all of which cannot be listed here. His other Australian films are *Mr. Chedworth Steps Out* (1939), *Red Sky at Morning* (1945), *A Son is Born* (1946), *Eureka Stockade* (1949).

FLAUS, JOHN (1934–). The Renaissance man of Australian film, John Flaus has had a series of identities that spill across the different components of the industry. Born in Sydney in 1934, he was initially a public servant. However, an overwhelming love of cinema led him to the notice of the newly established La Trobe University film program. Taking up an academic career as a film lecturer, he also found time to play a lead role as himself in David Jones' *Yaketty Yak* (1973). Having already appeared in other early films by Michael Thornhill and Richard Brennan, he willingly helped his students by appearing in their low-budget films. Hence, over the past quarter century, he has appeared without cost in well over 100 of these films, that still await full documentation and review. After lecturing appointments at the Australian Film and Television School (now the **Australian Film, Television and Radio School**) and elsewhere in Melbourne where he continued to appear before student cameras, he found himself in demand for more serious higher budget projects that included *Queensland* (1976), *Newsfront* (1978), *Palm Beach* (1979), *Plains of Heaven* (1982), and *Blood Money* (1980). The first and last of these featured Flaus in lead roles where he played the classic loser, a familiar type in some of the 1940s Hollywood B features that he most admired and celebrated in his academic writings.

By this time, he was moving toward a full-time acting career. In feature films and in **television** fiction, he has been an ever-reliable character actor registering memorable cameos for the cognoscenti as a grizzled, experienced, and sometimes weary presence, whether as a policeman or manual worker. However, working in low-budget features—including straight-to-video or television films such as *Archer* (1985), *Bootleg* (1985), *My Country* (1986), *Traps* (1986), *Hungry Heart* (1987), *Stroker* (1987), *Raw Silk* (1988), *Devil's Hill* (1988), *In Too Deep* (1989), *Jigsaw* (1989), *A Kink in the Picasso* (1990), and *Breakaway* (1990)—gave the actor much more scope and flexibility in building characters. During this period Flaus also perfected his grizzled screen persona for a string of other more critically acclaimed features including *Warm Nights on a Slow Moving Train* (1988), *Grievous Bodily Harm* (1988), *Ghosts...of the Civil Dead* (1989), **Death in Brunswick** (1991), and *Spotswood* (1992). Meanwhile, the theater also beckoned and again he acted in many fringe productions including a one-man show, *Caught* (1989–1990). Through the 1990s the same dedication to his craft was evident in a further cycle of films including *Nirvana Street Murder* (1991), *The Nun and the Bandit* (1992), *Point of No Return* (1995), *Lillian's Story* (1995), and **The Castle** (1997). Finally, as though this prodigious output was not enough, the actor was also increasingly in demand for radio commercials, **documentary** narration, and other voice work, his being a kind of working class accent that was rapidly becoming outdated.

FLYNN, ERROL (1909–1959). Errol Flynn was born in Hobart, Tasmania, the son of Marrelle Young who was a descendant of a mutineer on HMS *Bounty*. Ironically, Flynn played the leader of the mutineers, Fletcher Christian in his only contribution to Australian cinema, **Charles Chauvel's** *In the Wake of the Bounty* (1933). His contribution to the English language is the phrase "in like Flynn," which originated as a reference to his prowess as a seducer. He traveled to the United Kingdom and then to the United States, where he replaced Robert Donat in the lead role of *Captain Blood* (1935), and he proceeded to play similar roles in *The Charge of the Light Brigade* (1936), *The Prince and the Pauper* (1937), *The Adventures of Robin Hood* (1938) and *The Private Lives of Elizabeth and Essex* (1939). His character was based on the freedom-loving rebel, a man of action who fought against injustice and he became the original swashbuckler, winning the hearts of damsels through his principles and actions.

During World War II he played in war films like *Desperate Journey* (1942) and *Objective Burma* (1945), but his physical appearance began to lose attractiveness, perhaps because of his wanton and decadent lifestyle, and his roles became less significant, in inferior films. However, in the few years before his death, his characters took on a new and powerful life, and often they were alcoholics, as in *The Sun Also Rises* (1957) and *Too Much Too Soon* (1958). Although many charges were laid against him during his life, and many false accusations about him after his death, his contributions to the industry are being reevaluated and doubtless, his place as an actor of some stature and strength is assured.

FOX STUDIOS AUSTRALIA. Fox Studios Australia is built on the former site of the Royal Agricultural Society's Sydney Showground. After some initial controversies over the terms of the deals made to secure the valuable inner-city heritage site, the studio facilities opened in May 1998. They comprise eight stages, production offices and workshops, and ancillary businesses covering a wide range of filmmaking and retailing activities, and offer entertainment, shopping, and dining to the public. Indeed, the studios are less production facilities than a unique entertainment precinct. Fox Production Services, the professional arm of the complex, hires out the studio facilities and acts as an Australian base for offshore producers, who are required by law to work through an Australian company when filming in the country; it provides budgeting services, government and union liaison, casting advice and crew hire, and travel and equipment hire. This vertical and horizontal combination is a feature of Fox's Australian venture, which also includes an Australian TV development and production company, Fox World Australia. Fox Studios Australia's credits include: *Dark City* (**Alex Proyas**, 1996-97); *Babe: Pig in the City* (**Dr. George Miller**, 1998); *The Matrix* (The Wachowski Brothers, 1999); *Mission Impossible 2* (John Woo, 1999); *Holy Smoke* (***Jane Campion**, 1999); *Moulin Rouge!* (**Baz Lurhmann**, 2000); *La Spagnola* (Steve Jacobs, 2000); *Star Wars: Episode II—Attack of the Clones* (George Lucas, 2000); *Kangaroo Jack* (David McNally, 2001); *The Quiet American* (**Phillip Noyce**, 2001); *Matrix Reloaded and Matrix Revolutions* (The Wachowski Brothers, 2001–2002), *The Night We Called It a Day* (Paul Goldman,

2002); *Looking for Natalie Wood* (Peter Bogdanovich, 2003); *Star Wars: Episode III* (George Lucas, 2003). *See also* WARNER BROTHERS MOVIE WORLD STUDIOS.

– G –

GALLIPOLI (1981). Written by **David Williamson** from a story by **Peter Weir**, who also directed the film, *Gallipoli* is set in a significant historical moment for Australians. The Gallipoli campaign was the first time Australia had fought on the battlefield as a commonwealth, a federation of states. It is also significant in that the campaign was a precursor of what was to follow in France in subsequent years; namely, the futile loss of life by soldiers of all nations at the hands of some commanders who often felt that the death of their own troops alone signified an appropriate battlefield strategy. Gallipoli is now regarded as the crucible in which the Australian nation was tragically and heroically born.

The film sits in a significant historical moment in the **history** of the Australian industry as well. It represented a development of the industry a decade after the beginnings of the **revival**, and was a strong performer at the box office in Australia, as well as in the United States, where it took over US$5.5 million as the first film in a decade to achieve mainstream distribution. It was widely acclaimed in Australia, being nominated for four **Australian Film Institute** (AFI) awards, and winning eight awards including best film, best director, best leading actor (**Mel Gibson**), best supporting actor (**Bill Hunter**), and best screenplay. Cinematographer Russell Boyd won the 1982 Cinematographer of the Year from the Australian Cinematographers Society. In the United States, the film was nominated for a Golden Globe for best foreign film.

The film tells the story of two men. The young Frank Dunne (Gibson) and Archy Hamilton (Mark Lee) are two young athletes who come from diametrically opposed backgrounds. Archy is a farmer who lies about his age (as did many Australian soldiers in this conflict) in order to enlist in a war that was threatening the mother country, England. Frank is an urban youth, streetwise, and a survivor. They meet in a **country** athletic meet, and their friendship continues and develops in the rest of the film, in Australia, Egypt, and finally Gallipoli. In one sense, it is a film about **mateship**. On the other, it is a film about the tragedy of war, and the stupidity of some British commanders. Although criticized in some circles, the film is historically accurate in this depiction.

GARCIA, ADAM GABRIEL (1973–). Adam Garcia was born in Wahroonga, New South Wales. He arrived on the international film scene via his tap-dancing expertise. He played in two **musicals** on the London stage, before appearing in the tap-dancing sequence in the opening ceremony of the 2000 Sydney Olympic Games. Subsequently, he cofounded the dance troupe "Tap Dogs," which quickly won international attention. His film career began with a small part in *Wilde* (1997), a European and Japanese production of the biography of Oscar Wilde. He played Kevin O'Donnell, the boyfriend of the lead character, in the Bruckheimer production of *Coyote Ugly* (2000), and the lead role in the Australian made *Bootmen* (2000), set in the sixth-largest Australian city of Newcastle, a city once famous for industrial capacity, and the home of the Australian steel industry. The film turns on its head the notion that tap-dancing is for sissies. As Drew Barrymore's son in the Hollywood production *Riding in Cars with Boys* (2001), he played the son that no one would want to have, and followed with the lead role of Andy Caspar in Mick Jackson's **comedy** *The First $20 Million Is Always the Hardest* (2002). He has joined that select group of Australian actors who perform in the international film milieu as either Australians, or in roles that are not defined by national boundaries.

GENRES OF AUSTRALIAN FILM. "Australian film" may itself be viewed as a genre, as Australian films may exhibit one of more of these characteristics: an emphasized "Australian-ness"; and/or references to known Australians, Australian works, Australian events, Australian geography, and Australian idiom. However, given the blurring of distinctions between "Australian" and "other" films, that generic classification is difficult to support. Genres of Australian films are similar to those of films in the classical Hollywood tradition; it is the specifics of theme and content of Australian films that may differ from others in a genre. The genres are **action and adventure**; **comedy**, romance, and **musical**; **crime** and thriller; **art and period films**; **social realism** or "urban surreal"; science fiction; **documentary**; short and experimental; and pornography. These last two are significant in any discussion of the Australian film industry, but examples of the genre may be difficult for people to access, so no further mention will be made of them outside this entry, apart from stating that the work of **Arthur and Corinne Cantrill** is of international significance and has been screened to acclamation throughout the world.

While genres have specific markers and narratives, individual films may slide easily into different genres depending on the interests of the audience, the research of the marketing department, and the reaction of critics. Thus, ***Crocodile Dundee*** (1986) can be construed as comedy, romance, and action/adventure. Whether an individual film is of one genre or another is not significant; rather, the organizing principle of genre theory makes it possible to generalize and classify film, and thereby analyze and interpret cultural interests and preoccupations. At the same time, filmmakers like to market films as multigeneric, as including the conventions of as many genres as possible, in an effort to reach as wide an audience as possible.

The action and adventure genre represents a large proportion of films, although the nature of such films has changed. Early examples of this genre reflected the narratives of Australia: stories of convicts and bushrangers; of new settlers in a strange environment and the contrast between "real Australians" and these "new chums"; of the importance of egalitarianism, mateship, and the rise of the larrikin; and of the situation of **Aborigines**. These early films are imbued with Australian characters, settings, and narrative. The films were produced relatively inexpensively, as the market was small, limited to Australian cinemas, and occasionally the films were exported to the United States or the United Kingdom. After the **revival**, the action and adventure genre was the domain of explosive and expensive special effects, funded because the international market was of greater size than the local market. Thus the narratives became more global (read "suitable for the United States"), and Australian characters and settings were used only within an international context. Films of war—most filmed after the revival—recycled stories of masculine adventure and Australian courage for a different audience of arguably more sophisticated, urban filmgoers. In the last decade or so of the

20th century, the costs of film production in Australia, the availability of technology and the expertise to use it, and the ease of travel has ensured that the new globalized, international action/adventure genre is well-represented in Australian filmmaking.

The bushman as a **country** bumpkin is a significant element of the national character that underpinned Australian comedy. Films like *On Our Selection* (1920) through to *Dad Rudd, M.P.* (1940) capitalized on this trait. Traces of this construction of national character are apparent in later films like *Crocodile Dundee* (1985), albeit reflecting the globalized nature of the film audience in the comparison of the Australian bush with metropolitan New York. Recent comedies have clear links to these earlier bucolic films, where the "little man" stands up to powerful institutions, and with the help of the community, overcomes. Examples are *Spotswood* (1992), *The Castle* (1997), *The Man who Sued God* (2001), and *Crackerjack* (2002). Another narrative style is the comic characters in Australian life, where the comedy is simply an exaggeration of the traits that exist in reality. *Crackers* (1998) and *Doing Time for Patsy Cline* (1997) have this narrative focus, as does *Cosi* (1996) to a lesser extent. The musical is included here in the same genre as comedy, being tied to it as a kind of light entertainment. There are few examples of musicals in Australian film, although music has always been a significant nondiegetic element in Australian film.

The hard-boiled crime fiction is, in the historical spectrum, a more recent genre. *Goodbye Paradise* (1983) re-creates Raymond Chandler's Los Angeles of the 1940s in Brisbane, the capital **city** of Queensland in the 1970s and 1980s, with a culture that paralleled the corruption and crime that was a feature of Los Angeles. More recent films follow the generic reconfiguration exemplified in, for example, *Pulp Fiction* (1994), such as *Two Hands* (1999) and *Dirty Deeds* (2002), both of which juxtapose serious criminal acts with comic or endearing family scenes. Other films in the genre include *The Surfer* (1988), *Grievous Bodily Harm* (1988), and *The Custodian* (1994).

Art and period films figure strongly in the corpus of films made in the period immediately after the change in tax laws that caused the revival. These films had art-cinema models and were made with those conventions, in response to a government need for films that were worthy of notice by a critical, sometimes overseas, audience.

Social realism is a genre that needs little explanation in an international sense, although the added "urban surreal" may require some. But social realism means something different here: it is a kind of "faithfulness to reality" that is different from **Hollywood** genres.

Science fiction is represented by *The Chain Reaction* (1980), *The Salute of the Jugger* (1989)—known as *The Blood of the Heroes* in the United States, and starring Rutger Hauer—*The Time Garden* (1987), **Dark City** (1998), and the **Mad Max** trilogy, which is often categorized as action, but the films are, in their narrative subject, science fiction. Recent examples include the **Matrix** trilogy. Science fiction is a genre that is, in recent manifestations, difficult to locate in a particular nation; it is a genre that fits easily into a globalized world. The dystopic films since the 1980s feature cities and people without nations, and thus the films can be made anywhere the appropriate technology and expertise (for filmmaking and special effects) is available at competitive prices, and Australia is an example of such a location.

Documentary is almost another form of cinema, divorced in many ways from feature fiction films. However, there are many crossovers in themes, styles, and crew. Documentary was also a tool of a state that wanted to establish national unity and support for its own policies through filming *actualité*. Thus the making of documentary was supported in a way that feature film was not.

Relaxed **censorship** laws, and changing community values, opened the way for softcore pornographic films in the 1970s. *The Set* (1970) is attributed as the first Australian sexploitation film, but this may be because it was the first such film that was openly screened, in keeping with the "liberated" seventies. It is difficult to believe that no pornographic films were made before this, as Australia took to filmmaking as easily as other nations, and Australia was no more puritanical than the United States. Even in the 1970s, the nudity in *The Set* caused a furor. *Fantasm* (1976) was banned in Queensland, resulting in greater interest and the film became one of the most profitable of the decade. In *Felicity* (1979), John Lamond tells of the sexual rites of passage of a young girl. The film's portrayal of a schoolgirl enjoying the sexual gaze of the gardener is both incorrect as adjudged by current ideologies about such matters, and an example of the value of film as cultural artifact. Since then, pornographic films have not been recognized in any discussion of Australian film. Only recently has serious work been done on the industry.

GIBNEY, REBECCA. *See entry in New Zealand section.*

GIBSON, MEL (1956–). Like **Nicole Kidman**, Mel Gibson left Australia after being recognized as an international star and now returns only occasionally to Australia. While many people believe Gibson to be the true all-Australian boy, this is not the complete story. He was born in Peekskill, New York, and when he was 12 his father brought the family to Australia. He trained as a stage performer at the National Institute of Dramatic Art, graduated in 1977, and went straight into the South Australian State Theatre Company. While still a student, he made his **television** debut in the series *The Sullivans* (1976). Later that year he made his big screen debut, in a teenage surfing film—*Summer City* (1977)—in which he played Scollop, who lives for the surf.

However, the film that won him national and international recognition was **Dr. George Miller**'s *Mad Max* (1979) (*see MAD MAX TRILOGY*). Picked to play Max Rockatansky, he validated the choice by making the character of Mad Max known around the western world. In this film, Max fights a gang of outlaw motorcyclists in the postapocalyptic world of the outback roads and territory of Australia, where no law exists except that of might. His motivation is explained by the death of his wife and child at the hands of these outlaws. He gives up the law, in order to effectively deal with those outside the law. In the American edition of this film, Max's voice had been dubbed by another actor with an American accent, which sounds, to Australian ears, appalling. *Mad Max 2: The Road Warrior* (1981) continued the tradition, but this time the location was less obviously Australia. In *Mad Max Beyond Thunderdome* (1985), Max had become a little more introspective and more of the everyman searching for a simpler and more balanced way of life.

Other films allowed for Gibson's acting abilities to be further refined and broadened. He played the mentally impaired son of parents who are concerned about his future in the realist film *Tim* (1979), a story about the love or lust that an older woman has for Gibson's character after seeing his shirtless torso in the garden. The **Australian Film Institute** (AFI) awarded him best actor in a lead role for this performance, and again for his performance in **Peter Weir**'s *Gallipoli* (1981). In the latter film, Gibson played the part of the street-hardened Frank, the best friend of Archie, and the narrative revolved around the mateship of these two both as athletes and then as soldiers. It is fitting that, in this period that reclaimed and celebrated an Australian culture, a film would be made about two significant cultural moments: mateship and the killing fields of Gallipoli. Weir contracted him for his next film, *The Year of Living Dangerously* (1982), playing opposite Sigourney Weaver in a story about the near revolution in Indonesia that was suppressed viciously by a government that was assisted by both the Australian and the US governments. The plot surrounding Gibson's Indonesian liaison has been repeated in films like *Good Morning Vietnam* (1987).

After this successful career in Australia, in films that were seen outside Australia as well, Gibson moved to **Hollywood** and has not made another film in Australia, nor does he return often. In transition to the United States, he played Fletcher Christian's Mate in *Roger Donaldson*'s *The Bounty* (1984), filmed in New Zealand and French Polynesia. His transmogrification into a Hollywood and international star was seamless, and he has received critical and popular acclaim. As a slightly deranged, yet good-natured policeman he teamed up with Danny Glover to destroy powerful, drug-dealing criminals and other lowlifes in the *Lethal Weapon* (1987, 1989, 1992, 1998) series of comedy/crime/action films. At the other end of the spectrum, he played Hamlet in Franco Zeffirelli's *Hamlet* (1990), which was both a recognition of his early training and an affirmation of his extensive capabilities. Gibson turned his understanding of film to directing and producing for the films *Man without a Face* (1993) and *Braveheart* (1995). In the latter, he also starred as the Scottish hero William Wallace, and his expertise at the other end of the camera was critically acclaimed for he won an Academy Award and a Golden Globe for best director for this film, and the film won an Academy Award for best film. His interest in the story of Jesus, if not his strong fundamental Catholic faith, is evinced in his production and direction of *The Passion of the Christ* (2004). In his oeuvre, Gibson has played in a diverse range of roles that have enamored him with audiences as an actor of vast capacity, as well as a director of great skill and courage in tackling difficult projects.

The AFI recognized Gibson's contribution to the international film industry as an actor and director in awarding him a Global Achievement Award in 2002.

Lead roles in other films include *Attack Force Z* (1982), *The River* (1984), **Gillian Armstrong**'s *Mrs. Soffel* (1984), *Tequila Sunrise* (1988), *Bird on a Wire* (1990), *Air America* (1990), *Forever Young* (1992), *Man without a Face* (1993), *Maverick* (1994), *Pocahontas* (1995), *Ransom* (1996), *Conspiracy Theory* (1997), *Payback* (1999), *The Million Dollar Hotel* (2000), *Chicken Run* (2000), *The Patriot* (2000), *What Women Want* (2000), *We Were Soldiers* (2002), *Signs* (2002), and *The Singing Detective* (2003). Other films include *Chain Reaction* (1980), *Earth and the American Dream* (1992), *Fathers' Day* (1997), *Fairy Tale: A True Story* (1997).

GILLIES, MAX (1941–). Max Gillies first appearance was at the beginning of the **revival** in the film industry. He appeared as Uncle Jack in *Stork* (1971), Gerry in *Libido* (1973), Rojack in the experimental *Dalmas* (1973), and Metcalfe in *The Cars That Ate Paris* (1974). He starred as Deadeye Dick in the bawdy but unsuccessful *The True Story of Eskimo Nell* (1975), and appeared in *The Great McCarthy* (1975) and *Pure S* (1975), before coproducing and playing a major role in the ambitious *Dimboola* (1979). He is most successfully a satirical writer and actor, and his **television** shows and anarchic characters are legends in Australian television history.

Other films include *The Firm Man* (1979), *The Trespassers* (1976), *The Coca-Cola Kid* (1985), *As Time Goes By* (1988), *A Woman's Tale* (1991), and *Lust and Revenge* (1996).

GILLING, REBECCA (1953–). Gilling first appeared as the biker's moll Vanessa in *Stone* (1974) and the beautiful, evil cabin attendant in *Number 96* (1974). She followed these with the role of Angelica in *The Man from Hong Kong* (1975), an imitation of a Bruce Lee **action** film. While her subsequent successful career has been in **television**, she did star as the insecure wife of a cattle station (ranch) owner in *The Naked Country* (1985), based on a novel by Australian author Morris West. She played Annie in *Heaven Tonight* (1990) and the city-bred Fran in *Feathers* (1987), a film comparing **city** and **country** polarities.

Other films include *Stone Forever* (1999).

GINNANE, ANTONY (1949–). Anthony Ginnane was born in Melbourne, Australia, and has worked in the film industry since the 1970s. In 30 years, he has produced some 54 films in various countries, such as the United States, the United Kingdom, the Philippines, Canada, and New Zealand. He has worked as producer, writer, crew member, and director. Although his productions have not often achieved critical acclaim, there is no doubt that the impact on the industry in Australia and overseas has been very significant. He wrote, produced and directed the little-known Australian drama *Sympathy in Summer* (1971), and then provided the idea for and produced the R-rated comic sex romp *Fantasm* (1976), and the sequel *Fantasm Comes Again* (1977). His next production, *Patrick* (1978), was more up-market, and the Richard Franklin-directed horror/thriller was well received and nominated for best film by the **Australian Film Institute**. The multigeneric, **Simon Wincer** film *Harlequin* (1980) received a good response from critics, and *The Survivor* (1981) told the story of a lone survivor of a 747 crash.

Ginnane's next film marked his transition to an international context. *Strange Behavior* (1981) was set in the United States and produced by American, United Kingdom, and New Zealand companies, while *Race for the Yankee Zephyr* (1981) was set in New Zealand and made by New Zealand and Australian companies. His next production exemplifies the global nature of filmmaking, even in 1984. *Second Time Lucky* (1984) was filmed by a British director in New Zealand—but these settings were presented as international locations—financed by New Zealand investors, cast in Los Angeles, New Zealand, Australia, and the United Kingdom, with a story that had nothing to do with New Zealand. The Simon Wincer-directed *The Lighthorsemen* (1987), a war story about the part played by the Australian Light Horse in the British advance in Palestine in 1917, received good reviews and has remained something of a classic, as has **Gillian Armstrong**'s *High Tide* (1987). The horror film *Dark Age* (1987) tells a different crocodile story in an Australian outback location, while Roger Scholes' *The Tale of the Ruby Rose* (1988) continues the slightly weird and supernatural threads in the narrative. *The Everlasting Secret Family* (1988) continues the offbeat tradition of Ginnane's films, with a narrative that reveals how a secret homosexual society has infiltrated the upper echelons of Australian politics and spheres of influence. *The Siege of Firebase Gloria* (1989), on the other hand, is an Australian-made film about the war in Vietnam, without any distractions from the old-style battle tale about a sergeant who whips his new command into shape.

Ginnane produced the **action** film *Minnamurra* (1989), a film shot in Australia about a feud between a greedy station owner (rancher) who lusts after a woman and her station. He was the executive producer for the Australian film *Mull* (1989), and then was the supervising producer for the science fiction *Screamers* (1995), scripted by Dan O'Bannon from a story by Philip K. Dick. He was the executive producer for *Bonjour Timothy* (1995), a light comedy based on a coming-of-age theme and set in New Zealand. He produced *Ian Mune's award-winning *The Whole of the Moon* (1997), a Canada/New Zealand production about the effect of cancer on the lives and relationships of boys and their understanding of life.

Ginnane has produced a number of films in Canada, and has produced Australian–Canadian coproductions. The Canadian made *Men with Guns* (1997) was violent and did not impress at the box office, *Black Light* (1998) was a reasonable thriller, *Captive* (1998) and the comedy *Reluctant Angel* (1998) were not well received. The coproduction *Sally Marshall Is Not an Alien* (1999) is a good **adaptation** of a children's novel by Amanda McKay and is set in Adelaide's western suburbs. Recently he has been producer and executive producer for some American-made films that have had uneven reviews. While *Reaper* (2000) was considered to be a reasonable murder mystery, later films have been panned, including the rarely seen *Torrent* (2001), *Sweet Revenge* (2001), *The Hit* (2001), and *Blind Heat* (2002).

Other films he produced or was the executive producer for include *Blue Fire Lady* (1977), *Snapshot* (1979), *Thirst* (1979), *Prisoners* (1981), *Escape 2000* (1981), *Mesmerized* (1986), *The Time Guardian* (1987), *Slate, Wyn and Me* (1987), *Killer Instinct* (*Behind Enemy Lines* in the United States) (1987), *Initiation* (1987), *Grievous Bodily Harm* (1988), *Savage Justice* (1988), the second **Rolf de Heer**-directed *Encounter at Raven's Gate* (1988), *The Dreaming* (1988), *Boundaries of the Heart* (1988), the Philippines-made *A Case of Honor* (1988) and *Demonstone* (1989), *Driving Force* (1989), the science fiction film *Fatal Sky* (1990), the Canadian-made action film *No Contest* (1994), and *The Truth about Juliet* (1998).

GLOBALIZATION. Globalization challenges ideas of a national cinema. While a national cinema is part of a wider project of developing and describing—and perhaps in some cases defining—a national culture, recent moves in the industry suggest a widening and changing structure, one that is not purely Australian, but rather the product of an international collaboration. To some extent, funding imperatives both drive and reflect this change, as Australian funding agencies view co-productions favorably. That is, a film project that has the backing of companies outside Australia, as well as an Australian company, have a different set of criteria to meet to gain funding.

Yet, if the film industry is a child of the 20th century, it follows that such a child would have the characteristics of the century, a century marked by an urge to globalization, to a global village. Actors, production crew, funding, studios, and locations have become fluid, and this has been the characteristic of the industry since its inception. For example, **Louise Lovely** was one of a number of expatriate Australian actors in early **Hollywood**; she was followed by stars like **Errol Flynn**, and more recently, **Mel Gibson**, **Nicole Kidman**, and **Russell Crowe**.

The ability to cross national boundaries was not only a characteristic of individuals, but corporations as well. Overseas film corporations established facilities in Australia, such as the British studio **Ealing**. The studio established a production facility in Australia in the 1940s, producing films like *The Shiralee* (1957), which explored, rather than exploited, Australian culture for an audience outside Australia. The film starred Australian **Peter Finch**, who is an example of an international actor beginning his career in Australia, working successfully in England and Hollywood, before returning to Australia to play an Australian character. Ealing also established a production network in post-World War II Australia and recent history has seen the establishment of Hollywood studio facilities in Australia. For example, these films were shot at **Fox Studios** in Sydney: *The Matrix* (1999), *Babe: Pig in the City* (1998), *Farscape* (1999), *Mission Impossible 2* (2000), *Moulin Rouge!* (2001), *Star Wars: Episode II* (2002), *Kangaroo Jack* (2003), and *The Quiet American* (2002). The **Warner Brothers Movie World studios** on the Gold Coast of Queensland have hosted productions by Twentieth Century Fox, Disney Television, Paramount Pictures, Universal Pictures, Warner Brothers, and many other Hollywood-based, United Kingdom, and Australian companies.

This breakdown of national barriers in the film industry has created some confusion in the classification of films as belonging to, or emanating from, a discrete country. For example, the US-produced *The Matrix* was written and directed by Chicago-born Andy and Larry Wachowski; an Australian company was one producer; Australian companies worked on the special effects; Australian **Hugo Weaving** played a lead role; New Zealander Julian Arahanga played another role; the filmmakers utilized other Australian actors; and the film was made partly in Australian studios.

To some extent, globalization means that the industry has recognized the permeability of national barriers, reflected in the internationalization of audiences, the international appeal of certain stories, the internationalization of corporations, the international attraction of stars, the international mobility of crews, the inimitability of locations, and the availability of facilities. While the attraction of particular stars such as Nicole Kidman is not new, the number of Australians at all levels of the industry and their movement from international films to national films is notable. For example, director **Phillip Noyce** directed the Australian *Newsfront* (1978) before working in Hollywood, where he made films like *Patriot Games* (1992) and *The Bone Collector* (1999), before returning to local Australian issues in ***Rabbit-Proof Fence*** (2002).

Globalization suggests a monolithic structure, a form of cultural imperialism by, in this instance, the United States, which according to the model, gobbles up the film industry of small nations, with all the negative effects on the local industry that often accompanies such rationalization. Yet there are many qualifications to this simplistic view. The companies themselves are global in their ownership. News Limited, the Australian company effectively owned by the expatriate Australian (but US citizen) Rupert Murdoch, owns Twentieth Century Fox. (However, News Limited is changing its home location to Delaware, USA.) Sony bought out Columbia and Tristar to form Sony Pictures Entertainment. The shareholders in these companies may not be nationals of the country where the company is owned or has its head office, thus the companies themselves may be classified as international.

Another unexpected event that challenges the argument of monolithic cultural imperialism is the broadcast of films that originate in non-American nations to ethnic communities (*see also* ETHNIC

REPRESENTATION). Typically in Australia, the process involves the recognition of a demand in a particular ethnic community, the interest of a group of businessmen from that community, who then lease a satellite channel and transmit **television** and film programming that originate in the "home" country. Members of that community buy satellite dishes and decoding cards for that channel. Thus the technology associated with globalization (satellite) becomes important for the maintenance of cultural identity, a process that is the antithesis of monolithic globalization.

An effect of globalized audiences is an increase in interest in countries where popular films are made, and a subsequent increase in tourism to that country. For example, films like ***Crocodile Dundee*** (1986) and the ***Lord of the Rings*** trilogy exposed Australia and New Zealand respectively to the international world, placing those countries on the world stage—if only for a brief time—and resulting in an increase in international tourism to those countries.

The globalization of the Australian film industry has been a continuing process since the early years of the 20th century. It has had both positive and negative effects, as judged by those who stand in different ideological and economic positions, and depending on the particular plane of the globalization sample that is under the microscope. *See also* GENRES.

GREATER UNION ORGANISATION (GUO). The Greater Union Organisation is Australia's oldest and largest film exhibitor. G.U. came about through the amalgamation of Spencer Pictures with West's Pictures and Amalgamated Pictures to create the General Film Company of Australasia. In 1913, this organization joined Greater J.D. Williams Amusement Company to form Union Theatres/Australasian Films. Australasian Films was a distribution company, with buyers in cities like London and New York, while Union Theatres was an exhibition chain, which formed a partnership with **Birch, Carroll and Coyle** in Queensland in 1928, and which still exists today, owning many multiplexes in regional Queensland as well as in Brisbane. During the Depression in the 1930s, cinema attendances fell, and the English, Scottish, and Australian Bank as the major shareholder forced the liquidation of Union theaters. One of the managers of Union Theatres, Stuart Doyle, purchased the old company, sold off the distribution arm, Australasian films, and resurrected the exhibition arm, Greater Union Theatres. Doyle directed the company into film news magazine production through the **Cinesound** company, while competing with the **Hoyts** organization for the audience dollar. However, the Depression continued and their bank financiers forced an unpopular merger.

During World War II, audiences flocked to the silver screen again, and in 1945, the United Kingdom-based J. Arthur Rank Organization bought 50 percent of Greater Union. The company was loathe to support local production, preferring product from overseas with proven generic pedigree, and it rejected **Ealing**'s overtures to coproduce films in Australia in 1948. However, it did support the 1949 production of *Sons of Matthew*, but lost money and made no further attempt to invest in local production until the **revival**. The 1973 Tariff Board Review criticized the exhibition and distribution chains for their lack of investment in local production, resulting in a radical change of direction for the three major exhibition chains, and significant funding of local productions, including *The Man from Hong Kong* (1975), *Oz* (1976), *Break of Day* (1976), and *My Brilliant Career* (1979), among others.

During this time, the industrial shakeout and reorganizations continued, along with improvements in exhibition venues. In 1955, in partnership with Hoyts, Greater Union built the first drive-ins, and introduced stereo and 70mm film in an attempt to compete with **television**. This refurbishment and upgrading continued in the 1960s, along with changes to the corporate entity. The renamed Greater Union Organisation bought a 33 percent interest in Village Theatres. In a complex corporate restructure, GUO became a part of Amalgamated Holdings Limited, which owns other leisure facilities, and in 1984 the company bought out the Rank holdings so that the company was once again Australian owned, as is Hoyts. On the distribution side, the distribution arm Greater Union Film Distributors merged with **Village Roadshow** Distributors, to become one of the three major distribution companies. Greater Union has moved into partnerships with other companies; for example, the Movie World Theme Park on the Gold Coast of Queensland is a joint venture of Greater Union, Village Roadshow, and Warner Brothers, as are multiplexes in major cities (*see also* WARNER BROTHERS MOVIE WORLD STUDIOS). As might be expected from these mergers and vertical integration, Greater Union has been the subject of monopoly investigations by the Australian Competition and Consumer Commission (ACCC), in particular over the acquisition of the cinema advertiser Val Morgan by Hoyts, Greater Union, and Village Roadshow; however, the ACCC did not find that the merger was inconsistent with its policies.

GRIFFITHS, RACHEL (1968–). Rachel Griffiths lived on the Gold Coast of Queensland until she was five years old. She is an acclaimed performer on the stage as well as in film, has an education degree in dance and drama, and has written and directed two short films. Her role as the sharp-tongued Rhonda in **P. J. Hogan**'s *Muriel's Wedding* (1994) won her international recognition, and she was nominated for an Oscar with her performance as Jacqueline du Pre's sister Hilary in *Hilary and Jackie* (1998). In Australia, she took the lead in *Me, Myself, I* (1999) and *Amy* (1998). With **Geoffrey Rush**, **Judy Davis**, and *****Sam Neill**, she appeared in *Children of the Revolution* (1996). As the bottle-blonde Carol Twentyman in *A Hard Word* (2002), she played a morally ambiguous, hard-edged wife to **Guy Pearce**'s Sam.

Griffiths' international credits include the lead in Sara Sugarman's *Very Annie-Mary* (2001), opposite Pete Postlethwaite in *Among Giants* (1998), *Blow Dry* (2001), *Divorcing Jack* (1998), *My Son the Fanatic* (1997), *Jude* (1996), and a cameo in *My Best Friend's Wedding* (1997). Her recent work has been in the United States, where she appeared as Johnny Depp's mother in *Blow* and opposite Dennis Quaid in *The Rookie* (2002). Other films include *Ned Kelly* (2003), *Blow* (2001), *Welcome to Woop Woop* (1997), *To Have and to Hold* (1997), *Cosi* (1996), and *Small Treasures* (1995).

GROSS, YORAM (1926–). Born in Poland in 1926, Gross attended both the University of Krakow and the Polish Film Institute. By 1958, he was in Israel and made his first animated films, *Chansons Sans Paroles* and *We Shall Never Die*. Four years later appeared his and Israel's first feature film, the puppet animation *Ba'al Hahalomot* (*Joseph the Dreamer*). Meanwhile, a year later, he made the commercially successful live-action comedy *Rak Ba'Lira* (*A Pound Apiece*). By 1968, he had settled in Australia, later establishing Gross Film Studios in Sydney. First though, he had to postpone features in favor of whatever was on offer. Over the next nine years, this was to include short films, **documentaries**, commercials, protomusic videos for **television**, and feature titles and graphics. To teach others the craft of animation, he published *The First Animated Step* in 1975, which was accompanied by a demonstration film of the same name.

Finally, in 1977, he made a triumphant return to features with *Dot and the Kangaroo*. This was carefully pitched to work both in Australia and internationally. Most especially, it was planned to fit the dominant Disney-feature animation format. Later, in 1986, Gross began selling to the Disney cable television channel. *Dot and the Kangaroo* also initiated what would become a trademark for Gross—the constant mixing of animated characters and settings with live-action footage of actors, landscapes, and animals. In turn, the enormous commercial success of *Dot* enabled Gross to spinoff the character into a series of features. In succession there appeared *Around the World with Dot* (1982), *Dot and the Bunny* (1984), *Dot and the Koala* (1985), *Dot and the Whale* (1986), *Dot and Keeto* (1986), *Dot Goes to Hollywood* (*Dot in Concert*, 1987), and *Dot and the Smugglers* (*Dot and the Bunyip*, 1987). Paralleling Dot was a second recurring character. Beginning in 1992, the feature *Blinky Bill: The Mischievous Koala* spun off a television series. This sold to 80 countries and, later, became an interactive CD-ROM.

Outside of these two cycles, Gross has produced a string of other features. The *Little Convict* (1979) concerns two young convicts transported to labor on a forbidding government work farm. At the same time, this story is frequently interrupted by Rolf Harris as narrator who comments and leads sing-alongs. Next came *Sarah* (1980), which included Mia Farrow in a live-action part. This film was set in **Europe** and drew on Gross' childhood experiences in World War II. In 1981, he adapted his novel *Save the Lady* into the script for a live-action film of the same name. Meanwhile his next two films were set in the Australian outback. *Camel Boy* (1984) concerned the role of camels in outback exploration while *Epic* (1985) involved baby twins orphaned and raised by dingoes. By 1991, Gross made his first fully animated feature, *The Magic Riddle*, a children's story concerning fairy tales. Altogether then, Gross is an artist of the first order. Where others have resorted to computer animation, he has steadfastly continued to make films that are traditional full animation. The mainstay of Australian theatrical feature animation for over a quarter of a century, he is deeply committed to Australian subjects.

GULPILIL, DAVID. Arguably, David Gulpilil is one of the two most well-known Aboriginal actors. Before appearing as the guide for lost children in *Walkabout* (1971), he lived in a traditional way in eastern Arnhem Land, where he spoke little English. When he is not filming, he still lives in that way with his extended family, a lifestyle that he loves.

He costarred with Denis Hopper in *Mad Dog Morgan* (1976), as the only ally of the bushranger. His major role in that year was in *Storm Boy* (1976), a film set in the arid Coorong saltwater wetlands area of South Australia, in which he becomes the surrogate father to a boy whose own father has grown distant. Gulpilil's Fingerbone Bill teaches the boy to be in harmony with the environment and with the pelican, which the boy befriends. The film achieved both critical and box-office success, and Gulpilil was nominated for the best actor in the **Australian Film Institute** (AFI) awards for 1977. He showed his immense versatility in following this naturalistic, poetic film with his characterization of a tribal **Aborigine** transposed to the slumlike urban setting of inner-Sydney in **Peter Weir**'s *The Last Wave* (1977). He appeared briefly in *The Right Stuff* (1983), and then in *Crocodile Dundee* (1986), as the tribal Aborigine who jokes with Dundee about taking part in a ritual corroboree as a way of keeping the old folks happy.

A few minor roles followed in the unreleased *Dark Age* (1987), Wim Wenders's German-French-Australian coproduction *Bis ans Ende der Welt (Until the End of the World)* (1992), *Dead Heart* (1996), and *Serenades* (2001). He followed this with the role of the tracker Moodoo in **Phillip Noyce**'s *Rabbit-Proof Fence* (2002), where his character and powerful screen presence reflected the depths of 50,000 years of Aboriginal lore. In that year, he starred in **Rolf de Heer**'s *The Tracker* (2002) in the character that carries the film title, and won best male actor in the AFI awards and the Film Critics Circle of Australia awards. He was nominated for best supporting actor for *Rabbit-Proof Fence*.

This success has to be seen in context though. While applauding his ability and powerfully wrought roles, filmmakers pay him token sums, in a kind of parody of the colonial payment of trinkets and mirrors for land in the early days of European settlement. Now, however, the payment is for acting ability. For example, he allegedly earned US$6,500 (AU$10,000) for his part in *Crocodile Dundee*, which grossed over $200 million at the box office. For his role in *Rabbit-Proof Fence*, he earned $20,000, and a similar amount for the starring role in *The Tracker.*

– H –

HALL, KEN G. (1901–1994). Hall was Australian cinema's most commercially successful filmmaker before the **revival**. Born in Sydney in 1901, he worked briefly in journalism and as a theater manager before becoming national publicity director for Union Theatres and Australasian Films (*see* GREATER UNION ORGANISATION). From 1924 to 1929, Hall was publicity director for the Australian branch of First National Pictures. In this role, he traveled to Hollywood in 1925 to acquire a fuller understanding of production and marketing. The former was to prove especially useful to his subsequent career. In 1928, for example, he directed new sequences of Australians for First National's *The Exploits of the Emden* (1928). Its commercial success impressed Union Theatres' managing director Stuart Doyle. Hall rejoined the company as Doyle's personal assistant. When, in 1931, Doyle reorganized the company's production arm as **Cinesound**, he put Hall in charge. Hall's bent as showman now came to the fore as he both managed the company and also produced a string of features over the next decade. Under his stewardship, Cinesound failed only once — with *Strike Me Lucky* (1934) — to make a profit on the 16 feature films that he was to direct. His first film was *On Our Selection* (1932) and its success saw Hall continue making one or two features each year to be screened in **Greater Union** cinemas across the country. Thereupon followed *The Squatter's Daughter* (1933), *The Silence of Dean Maitland* (1934), *Strike Me Lucky*, *Grandad Rudd* (1935), *Orphan of the Wilderness* (1936), *Thoroughbred* (1936), *Lovers and Luggage* (1937), *Tall Timbers* (1937), *It Isn't Done* (1937), *Let George Do It* (1938), *The Broken Melody* (1938), *Dad and Dave Come to Town* (1938), *Gone to the Dogs* (1939), *Mr. Chedworth Steps Out* (1939), *Come up Smiling* (1939), and *Dad Rudd, M.P.* (1940). Hall produced all of these and with the exception of *Come Up Smiling* also directed them. His style was unremarkable and unobtrusive, very much in the Hollywood classical tradition. Many of his most popular films were **comedies** but he also succeeded in other genres including melodrama, **action/adventure**, and even one **musical**. In 1942, the Cinesound Review newsreel special *Kokoda Front Line*, edited under his supervision, won an Academy Award.

Hall's biography of pioneering aviator Charles Kingsford Smith— *Smithy* (1946)—was a box-office success, and was modeled on the Hollywood biopic. The fact that it was his final feature would be an increasingly sore point, since he had expected Greater Union to resume regular feature production after the war. But he spent another decade making documentaries and steering the fortunes of Cinesound Review, the company he had started in 1931. In 1956, he quit Cinesound to join the first commercial **television** station in the country, TCN9 Sydney. Here, as general manager, he ran a smooth operation that combined business and entertainment to the satisfaction of the station's owner, Frank Packer. Although there was little commissioning and even less screening of independent films, nevertheless in this period, he was able to encourage some independent directors (commissioning the Project series of documentaries, buying and screening films of **Cecil Holmes** and **Bruce Beresford**). Indeed after his retirement in 1966, Hall became very much the "Grand Old Man" of Australian film. At first a fierce critic of government film-funding, he later modified this stance and saw such funding as encouraging writers and producers. Championing the work of directors such as **Dr. George Miller** and **Peter Weir**, he advised **Phillip Noyce** on the making of *Newsfront* (1978). Later, Noyce had him direct a sequence in the television miniseries *Cowra Breakout* (1984). This proved to be his last venture behind the camera, as the veteran died in 1994.

HARBUTT, SANDY (1941–). In the annals of the Australian film industry, Sandy Harbutt is unique. He is the only person to have made a very popular, commercially successful film with the backing of the state-funded bureaucracy at the time—the **Australian Film Development Corporation**, then the **Australian Film Commission** (AFC)—and then not to have been offered work again in the industry. He was certainly and inexplicably ignored by the industry, even though he had appeared in **television** and film before *Stone* (1974).

Harbutt cowrote, directed, produced, and played a lead role in the first Australian biker film *Stone*. Before this he worked in the Ensemble Theatre in Sydney as a gifted stage actor, and had roles in the television series *You Can't See Round Corners* (1967), *The Long Arm* (1970), and in two little-known films *Color Me Dead* (1969) and *Squeeze a Flower* (1970). *Stone* was his first film, and although it has weaknesses, it has stood the test of time, and remains popular. His cooperative style of working was both a feature of the film's making, and its culture. In the face of disdain from the AFC, Harbutt was dedicated to making a success of the film, re-editing it significantly and marketing it independently in Cannes in competition with the AFC screenings.

He appeared in the **documentary** *Stone Forever* (1999), about the Stone Memorial Run and the saga of the original film.

HAWES, STANLEY (1905–1991). Born in England, Stanley Hawes joined John Grierson in **documentary** filmmaking in the 1930s and 1940s. After a stint with the National Film Board of Canada, he had come to Australia in 1947 as producer-in-chief at what was to become **Film Australia**, guiding this body until his retirement in 1970.

HEXAGON PRODUCTIONS. This company represented a concerted attempt by Melbourne-based distributor Roadshow to be a significant player in the production arena in the newly revived Australian cinema of the 1970s (*see* REVIVAL). Bringing together the considerable business and artistic abilities of former Melbourne cineastes, Alan Finney and **Tim Burstall**, Hexagon made a considerable profit on its early films only to see these dry up in the second half of the 1970s. Linked to such artistic developments as the Melbourne University's interest in *auteur* cinema and to the theatrical scene at the Pram Factory, Finney and Burstall were in agreement in seeking to marry commercial success with popular **genres**. Burstall achieved such success with *Stork*, a broad **comedy** based on a play, which was released through **Village Roadshow** in 1972. Thereupon, Roadshow proceeded to invest heavily in the newly created Hexagon.

The company embarked on a full slate of films with a broad appeal for audiences. First cab off the rank was ***Alvin Purple*** (1973), a sex comedy, which proved immensely successful at the box office even if most critics felt it unworthy of subsidy from the public purse. Many of the production personnel—several of them recruited from Crawford **television** productions including **Homicide**—who worked on this and *Stork* were to appear on many of Hexagon's other films over the next six years. This roll call includes editors Edward McQueen-Mason and David Bilcock, photographer Robin Copping, art director Les Binns, and sound recordist Peter Fenton. The sequel, *Alvin Rides Again* (1974), was directed by Copping and Bilcock although it proved not nearly as popular as its predecessor. Meanwhile, Burstall was particularly involved with Hexagon's output directing five more films. He also acted as producer on several others including *Alvin Rides Again*, *The Love Epidemic* (1975), and *High Rolling* (1977), the last two directed by Brian Trenchard Smith and **Igor Auzins**, respectively. Finney, too, was immensely busy with his name appearing on all films either as associate or executive producer. By this time, Hexagon was well into its stride. The Burstall-directed *Petersen* (1974) was an interesting attempt to engage with more serious adult subject along the lines of his earlier *2000 Weeks* (1969). However, in 1975–1976, it embarked on its most ambitiously budgeted film, *Eliza Fraser*. A kind of female version of *Tom Jones*, this comic historical piece, directed by Burstall, used expensive imports Trevor Howard and Susannah York. It also featured well-known Melbourne television and theater personality Noel Ferrier as the heroine's cuckolded and unfortunate husband. However, the film was less comic than expected and failed to deliver the strong box office result expected.

Although the company fulfilled its slate over the next several years, the writing was on the wall. Hexagon's last release was *The Last of the Knucklemen* (1979), a tough male-centered film set in a remote mining camp in the desert. Although it received good critical notices, the film was only mildly successful with the public. As a result, Hexagon wound down and Finney and Burstall went their separate ways. As a result, Hexagon soon became inactive.

HICKS, SCOTT (1953–). Hicks is living proof of the nursery role that an Australian state film corporation could provide in the past. Born in Uganda in 1953, Hicks undertook a degree in drama and cinema at Flinders University in Adelaide. While a student, he first appeared on screen in David Stocker's *Ten Minutes* (1973) before working as director with writer Kim McKenzie on *The Wanderer* (1974) and *Down*

The Wind (1975). From there, he began to gain regular work at the **South Australian Film Corporation** (SAFC). Apprentice films made there in the very late 1970s and early 1980s include *You Can't Always Tell* (1979), *Bert Flugelman: Public Sculpture* (1979), *The First Ninety Days* (1980), *Women Artists of Australia* (1980), *Attitudinal Behaviour* (1980), *The Hall of Mirrors* (1982), and *One Last Chance* (1983). Meanwhile, Hicks was also finding work on feature films in an assistant capacity including **Storm Boy** (1977), *The Last Wave* (1977), *The Irishman* (1978), *Harvest of Hate* (1978), *The Money Movers* (1979), *Dawn!* (1979), *Final Cut* (1980), and *The Club* (1980).

Finally, in 1982, he got his first chance to direct a feature, the SAFC's *Freedom*. The latter was a road movie, which, although it began well, soon fell away. It excited neither critics nor public and Hicks' talents still went unrecognized. For over a dozen years, his career limped along with his name attaching to such works as different as *Call Me Mr. Brown* (1986), *Sebastian and the Sparrow* (1989), and a **television** film *The Space Shuttle* (1994). Finally, his luck broke with the astonishing national and international success, both commercially and critically, of the feature **Shine** in 1996. Hicks was nominated for various awards—including two Oscars, two British Academy for the Film and Television Arts (BAFTA) awards, and a Golden Globe—and won the best director award from the **Australian Film Institute** in 1996. The film paved his way to **Hollywood** where he has worked ever since, as writer and director of *Snow Falling on Cedars* (1999) and as director of *Hearts in Atlantis* (2001).

HISTORY. Various elements contend for the central spotlight under this heading. However, the most significant is that to do with the history of Australian film production considered both in terms of the key structures and developments, and in terms of just how that history itself has been written. In other words, what has been looked at and who has done the looking. Broadly speaking, Australian film history consists of two entirely different trajectories. These two cinemas are in effect completely different having only two things in common. The first of these is the name "Australian film." The second is a recurring cyclical pattern in the events of its narrative, familiarly known as "boom and bust." Otherwise, this cinema falls into two major epochs:

an earlier commercial feature film production sector and a later, state-supported commercial industry.

The early period runs from before the turn of the century down to the 1950s and early 1960s and follows the general trajectory of "boom and bust." The story is a familiar one in world cinema and is that of a local production sector that at first dominates its local market but is increasingly displaced by the advent of imported films from the United States. Comparative research on the advance of the latter has shown that even before World War I, US interests had come to dominate local film distribution and exhibition. Australia was one of the first overseas countries to capitulate to US film interests, but that is a story that would be repeated globally. The increasing effect of this dominance was that Australian film directors and producers found it increasingly more difficult to obtain distribution that, in turn, directly affected their ability to produce films. This situation grew worse by the 1920s when the federal government set up a Royal Commission (in 1927) to examine the industry and to look at what measures it might enact to assist the industry. However, by then the situation was largely irretrievable especially given the fact that the film sector was a commercial industry where distribution/exhibition and production interests did not see eye to eye about either problems or solutions. Although two state governments did enact some measures of protection, these were ineffective so that the decline in feature production continued. Although some new parties entered the field of filmmaking in the 1950s, the production sector had expired almost completely by around 1960.

This and the interregnum that followed set the scene for the **revival**. Claiming itself to be a continuation of an already existing film industry, a new infrastructure came into being as an effect of the federal government subsidization of feature production beginning around 1970. The new industry was to be a hybrid. Unlike its predecessor it was to be oriented to both commerce and culture, encouraging the making of films that would make money and develop and record a **national identity**. Effectively, this is the film industry that is still in place at the beginning of the new millennium. Unlike its predecessor it has not followed an overall pattern of "bust." This is not to say, however, that this trend is not found at a more micro level. For, indeed, it is. Despite the hopes that the cinema of the revival would become financially independent, it has not reached this goal and shows no signs of doing so. Thus, although many films funded through state support have been very successful at the box office, overall Australian feature films of the revival period, the period stretching from 1970 to the present, have lost millions of taxpayers' dollars. That is, obviously, not the end of the story however, and any financial audit must be balanced by a far more positive account of particular films and film careers. Obviously, these triumphs must be followed up elsewhere.

However, if one steps back from these details of loss and profit to a brief consideration about how these historical facts have been treated by Australian film historians, then, it is clear that some obvious strategies and explanatory schema have been employed to make further sense of the pattern. Overall, the basic model employed by Australian film historians is chronological. The premodern epoch before the revival, usually labeled as the early period, is frequently periodized both around decades and major historical events. Hence, for example, World War I, the 1920s, the coming of sound, the Great Depression, and so on. In turn, stitched into this are individual stories of particular companies and isolated producers and directors working within an ever constricting industry: **Eftee Productions**, **Raymond Longford**, **Cinesound**, **Ken Hall**, **Charles Chauvel**, and so on. Meanwhile, in case the ledger seems perilously thin, Australian film is defined expansively so that it includes any feature film made inside the country. In other words, the productions of overseas British and American companies can, and are, included in the archive.

Dealing with the revival period, historians have adopted a different explanatory method. Here, feature films have been periodized in terms of a linked bipart schema: the particular government agency or subsidy arrangement in place at the time of a particular group of films' production and some of the dominant formal and stylistic features apparent in the films themselves. Accordingly, for example, some critics have delineated one cycle in the revival as the "AFC (**Australian Film Commission**) film," in place between 1976 and 1983. Meanwhile, a second strategy that was briefly begun but seems to have fallen into abeyance is one oriented around the identification of Australian directorial auteurs. **Peter Weir** and **Bruce Beresford** have been singled out for this kind of attention. However, with the increasing critical bypassing of this approach in film studies generally, other would-be filmmaking Australian geniuses have gone unrecognized. Both these approaches seem increasingly unsustainable in terms of an ever-expanding feature film production output that is increasingly both *sui generis* and a part of international cinema. In other words, the near future will see new patterns become apparent in Australian film history and this, in turn, will hasten a revised understanding of the history of this trajectory. *See also* GLOBALIZATION.

HOGAN, PAUL (1939–). Paul Hogan was born in a small, opal-mining town in the northwest of New South Wales, called Lightning Ridge, on 8 October 1939. His life was decidedly uneventful in terms of his later career. He was a scaffolder on the Sydney Harbour Bridge when he appeared on **television** at the age of 31, appearing on a talent quest show, "New Faces," with an act that brutally satirized that show. Yet it created the character most associated with Hogan: popular, working-class, laconic, unassuming, and unpretentious. He appeared on various other shows, most notably as a regular comic commentator on the nightly news magazine show, "A Current Affair." **John Cornell**, Hogan's partner in business, production, and scriptwriting (and comic foil as "Strop" in "The Paul Hogan Show") was the producer for "A Current Affair." In 1977, the *Paul Hogan Show* cemented his Australian character, which in turn became one of the most successful marketing icons for the cigarette brand Winfield, Fosters beer, and US tourism to Australia. This marketing success proved to Hogan and Cornell that a film like *Crocodile Dundee* (1986) would be a success, which it was, of course. It remains the most successful Australian film ever made. Ignored by the local intelligentsia and industry film groups (*Dundee* was not even nominated for any awards by the **Australian Film Institute**, although international awards were more forthcoming), the character of Crocodile Dundee became a legend, used by the Australian prime minister and others. *Crocodile Dundee* changed other elements of Hogan's life as well. He married Linda Kozlowski, his costar, after divorcing his wife of 30 years, Noelene.

For Hogan though, that level of success did not continue. *Crocodile Dundee II* (1988) was an interesting and quite successful sequel to the original, but *Crocodile Dundee in Los Angeles* (2001) was a failed attempt to resurrect a lifeless manikin. The character of Dundee had palled. Hogan's other films, *Almost an Angel* (1990) and *Lightning Jack* (1994) portrayed Hogan as a different character, but it was not one that audiences were attracted to. However, it is worth noting, as Hogan himself once said, that the unsuccessful *Jack* has made more money at the US box office than ***Muriel's Wedding*** (1994), which Australian critics rate much more highly. Financial success, then, is a relative criterion in the world of the box office. Without a doubt, Paul Hogan changed the perception of Australia and Australians in the United States, and foregrounded the positive elements of the Australian character(s).

Other films include *Fatty Finn* (1980), *Flipper* (1996), and *Floating Away* (1998).

HOGAN, P.J. (1962–). Very much a product of the latest wave of Australian feature films, P.J. Hogan first developed his talent as a writer and started directing in the late 1980s. Among his first films were *The Humpty Dumpty Man* (1986) as writer/director and *Vicious* (1987), which he wrote. However, these were less than successful and his career marked time. Married to Jocelyn Moorhouse, he worked as second unit director on her debut feature, *Proof* (1991). Finally, Hogan struck gold with ***Muriel's Wedding*** (1994). Not only did he direct but he also wrote the screenplay, basing it on a short story that he had written earlier. The film's success at the box office and also with critics propelled him to **Hollywood** where his first film was *My Best Friend's Wedding* (1997). Both these latter films demonstrate that Hogan has a particular flair for black comedy and knows how to pace a narrative to keep his action humorous and thus please his audience. Further work in Hollywood included *Unconditional Love* (2002) and *Peter Pan* (2003), both of which he wrote and directed.

HOLLYWOOD. Hollywood forms one of the permanent corners of Australian cinema, just as Australia constitutes one of the peripheral hubs of the movie colony and the movie industry. In other words, the intersection of these two entities is a complex, shifting site with various different fault lines. This overlap can be considered both in the past before the Australian **revival** and in the more recent present of New Hollywood.

First is the physical fact of film, the material presence of Hollywood in Australia, which is an element of distribution rather than of production. Australia has the dubious honor of being one of the first countries to fall under the control of US film distributors, a situation that developed as early as 1911. So, one of the first elements of the Hollywood influence has to do with the reconfiguration of film exhibition in early Australian theaters, a new system whose thoroughness ran from matters of management down to the provision and marketing of such foodstuffs as ice cream and popcorn in the theater foyer. Early film exhibitor and distributor Millard Johnson began his career in the fledgling Australian exhibition and production industry, then in 1913 went to work for Adolph Zukor of Famous Players, becoming one of the very many show business figures that constitute the burgeoning film trade in the United States. In turn, Johnson was succeeded by many others who made the journey to the new production and business mecca in Los Angeles; some settled there but others learned their craft and returned to Australia to apply Hollywood lessons. One such representative figure was **Ken Hall** who began his Australian film career in exhibition and marketing but learned the craft of filmmaking and advertising in Hollywood, then returned to Australia. Again, Hall is not alone in this regard and Australian film scholarship requires well-researched career biographies of the Australian heads of the various distribution arms of the Hollywood majors—such as Herb McIntyre—who acted as important gatekeepers in the economic and cultural traffic between the two places.

One other element of this pattern also deserves mention. This has to do with a surprisingly large number of Australians who made their way to the world's film capital in other capacities. Some such as the woman who married Stan Laurel of Laurel and Hardy fame never appeared before the camera. But others including **Errol Flynn**, Cecil Holloway, **Louise Lovely**, Michael Pate, Ann Richards, Rod Taylor, and **Frank Thring Sr.** are only the tip of an iceberg. These are matters of history and their individual impact and contribution has been documented.

Other aspects of the connection still await more thorough analysis. One of these is the social place of going to the "pictures" in a country like Australia in the sound era from the early 1930s to the coming of **television**. Almost invariably what was on screen came from Hollywood. What was the social place of cinema-going? Who went, when, and why? How were these films watched and absorbed by the population? What was the more general impact of Hollywood on the Australian population and upon the Australian imagination? These are significant and inviting questions whose answers will shed as much light on Australian society and character as they will on Hollywood.

Of course, not all films made in Hollywood had to do with the United States. Indeed, on some rare occasions, Hollywood could offer to the world, including Australia, representations of the Australian experience. How otherwise to understand a film such as *The Kangaroo Kid* (1950), a B Hollywood film that recast its Western hero, Jock Mahoney, in an Australian setting? The Twentieth Century Fox feature of the D.H. Lawrence novel *Kangaroo* (1952) should be regarded as a similar kind of enterprise, a recasting of the **action/ adventure genre** in an Australian setting. At least this film was actually filmed on location in South Australia, which was not the case with such costume melodramas as *Botany Bay* (1953) and Alfred Hitchcock's *Under Capricorn* (1949). However, by the 1960s, Hollywood, for its own internal reasons, was much more inclined toward "runaway" productions such that features like *On the Beach* (1959), *Summer of the Seventeenth Doll* (1959), and *The Sundowners* (1960) were all filmed and produced in Australia.

The more recent period of New Hollywood and the Australian revival has seen a reconfiguration of the pieces on the board. Hollywood continues to be a dominant, overweening presence at the Australian film and video box office. However, Hollywood is itself transformed in such a way as to call into question any easy cultural and economic assumptions about a "them" and "us." Two Australian film trilogies are especially important in this transition, the ***Mad Max*** and ***Crocodile Dundee*** trilogies. With the exception of the last in the second series, all these films (distributed by Warner Brothers) were immensely popular at the international box office. Both cycles also recovered two of Hollywood's most cherished and venerable genres, the action melodrama and the **comedy**, although an equally strong argument can be mounted that these are international genres rather than ones unique to Hollywood. In any case, these and other films from Australia helped give Australians useful "calling cards" when it came to relocating their work to Los Angeles. Some of the more famous actors who have permanently crossed the Pacific include **Mel Gibson**,

Guy Pearce, **Russell Crowe**, **Nicole Kidman**, **Cate Blanchett**, and **Naomi Watts**. These are complemented by such directors as **Peter Weir**, **Fred Schepsi**, **Gillian Armstrong**, and **Phillip Noyce** and cameramen such as **Dean Semler** and Russell Boyd. This confluence creates real problems not only for film researchers but also for funding bodies and agencies when it comes to deciding whether such films as *Green Card* (1990) and *Evil Angels* (also *A Cry in the Dark*) (1988) are American, Australian, or both. However, this blurring is symptomatic of a more general convergence across cultural industries, including that of cinema, in the era of **globalization**. By way of example is the case of the Australian-born Rupert Murdoch who became an American citizen to pursue his international media interests, acquiring the Twentieth Century Fox Studios, branching into a new Fox television network, and opening **Fox Studios** including one in Sydney, Australia.

All of which goes to show that Hollywood is not somewhere else but has rather been at the heart of the Australian experience and imagination for the best part of the last century.

HOLMES, CECIL (1921–1994). Born in New Zealand in 1921, Holmes managed to get a job at the newly established New Zealand Film Unit in 1945. Initially, he worked as an editor on newsreels and soon began directing. One of his more worthy projects at this stage was *The Coaster* (1947). However, as a left-wing activist, he soon fell under the baleful eye of authority and was sacked. Holmes fought back and a strike at the Unit led to his being awarded a year's back pay. But the writing was on the wall and he moved to Australia in 1948. However, his reputation preceded him and he found it difficult to get work apart from that on the **documentary** *The Food Machine* released by the Shell Film Unit in 1952. Astonishingly, Holmes next project was the feature film *Captain Thunderbolt* released in 1953. Starring Grant Taylor and *Charles Tingwell*, this uneven film featured political drama, **action/adventure**, and **social realism**. His next feature film project came about through an association with socialist writer Frank Hardy. The two collaborated on a short film based on the latter's "The Load of Wood." Faced with the difficulties of gaining a theatrical release, they decided to make this the basis of a trilogy that was released in 1957 under the title *Three in One*.

The 1950s were especially difficult for a man of the left and most of Holmes' energy went into simply surviving (*see* HISTORY). The next decade was to see a marked improvement in his fortunes so far as work continuity was concerned. From 1960, he was involved in over 20 different film projects. By then, ABC Television had instigated a film pool and Holmes' work there included *I the Aboriginal* (1960) and *An Airman Remembers* (1963). At the **Commonwealth Film Unit**, he made *The Islanders* (1968) and *Gentle Strangers* (1973). For the Institute of Aboriginal Studies he directed *Return to the Dreaming* (1971). He even directed and produced films for the Methodist Overseas Missions including *Lotu* (1962) and *Faces in the Sun* (1965). However, the **revival** had little space for the stormy petrel of Australian cinema and his last years were spent working on various projects that did not come to fruition. Holmes died in Brisbane in 1994.

HORLER, SACHA (1971–). The daughter of the founders of Sydney's legendary—but now extinct—Nimrod Theatre, Sacha Horler studied at a Sydney clown school as a teenager and then the National Institute of Dramatic Art. Her first film appearance was in *Billy's Holiday* (1995), followed by a role as the teacher in *Blackrock* (1997), a story about the code of silence in the surfing culture following the rape and murder of a young schoolgirl. She played the lead role of the sex-, weight-, and drug-obsessed Cynthia in the slice-of-life, left-leaning drama *Praise* (1998), before a small part as the voice of the night nurse in **Babe: Pig in the City** (1998), and then as Nadia, one of the three sisters returned home to nurse their dying mother, in *Soft Fruit* (1999). The role of Margaret, an upper-middle class mother of two, who enjoys commanding others, in Mark Lamprell's *My Mother Frank* (2000), followed. As the girlfriend Bonita of the lead character Coco in *Walk the Talk* (2000), she once again showed her ability in the face of a tired script. In the romantic comedy *Russian Doll* (2001), she played Liza, then moved to the small screen for roles in the miniseries "Changi" (2001) and other **television** films. In 2003, she starred as Bronwyn White in Kathryn Millard's *Travelling Light* (2003), a one-eyed tale of the alleged conservatism of the **city** of Adelaide in the 1970s. Horler is the wife of a man who does not allow her to go to work, preferring that she stay at home, even though she is a qualified teacher.

HOYTS CINEMAS. Hoyts Cinemas is one arm of the Hoyts Corporation, and is one of three film exhibition and distribution companies in Australia. The company is one of the oldest film-related companies in the world, beginning in 1909 when Melbourne dentist Dr. Arthur Russell leased a hall in Bourke Street, Melbourne, and started showing short films on Saturday nights. Emboldened by the success of this exhibition, Russell formed Hoyts Pictures, which had expanded into Melbourne and its suburbs and Sydney by the time of Russell's death in 1915. In 1926, Hoyts Pictures, Electric Theaters, and Associated Theaters (owned by George Tallis and **Frank Thring Sr.**) merged to become Hoyts Theatres, and by 1932, in an early example of the global nature of the industry, the US-owned Fox Film Corporation had bought a major shareholding in the company. This expanded capital base funded further expansion, including the building of Regent theaters in the cities, and smaller copies of these comfortable theaters in regional towns and cities.

The 1930s Depression saw a forced merger between Hoyts and their only national competitor, **Greater Union Theatres**, but this merger was never complete and the two firms parted company again in 1937, and remained the two major players in film exhibition until joined by the third player, the **Village Theatre** chain, in the 1950s. Hoyts were responsible for the first drive-in theater chain in that decade, and while "ozoners" or drive-ins were one element in the face-off with **television**, technical innovations were another. Cinerama and Todd-AO delineated the difference between cinema and television. However, as the baby boomers of the postwar generation had children, their interest in ozoners declined, and these closed throughout the 1960s, as much a victim of technology as of maturing generations. The ozoners could not compete with the new sound and other technologies being installed in cinemas, nor with the multiplexes pioneered by Hoyts in 1976 in Sydney, that were themselves the product of new film-projecting technologies. These technologies allowed one or two operators to control the operation of a bank of projectors, from one projection room.

Hoyts entered production in 1978, partly as a result of the 1973 Tariff Board report that resulted in the film **revival** in Australia. In 1978, the corporation backed the making of *The Chant of Jimmy Blacksmith*, and continued supporting filmmaking as Hoyts Productions in 1987.

This venture was not as successful as executives and owners may have wished. In a kind of reverse process to the vertical integration prohibited by the 1947 Paramount Decree in the United States, Hoyts entered the distribution sector in 1979, releasing, as Hoyts Distribution, the two box-office hits, *The Man from Snowy River* (1982) and *Crocodile Dundee* (1986).

After five decades of ownership by Twentieth Century Fox, control returned to Australia when four Melbourne businessmen bought out Fox in 1982. One of the four, Leon Fink, bought out the other partners in 1985, merging his own substantial entertainment interests with Hoyts to form Hoyts Corporation, of which Hoyts Cinemas was but one component. As well as distribution, exhibition, and production interests, the corporation had interests in television and cinema advertising though the Val Morgan company. The new ownership encouraged new creative talent to manifest within the organization: one manifestation was the public listing of two of the companies in the corporation, Hoyts Media and Hoyts Entertainment, on the Australian Stock Exchange in 1987.

Another manifestation was the internationalization of the organization, not through ownership of the company by overseas interests, but by the building and purchasing of cinemas in New Zealand, the United States, and South America. Many of these were multiplexes, built in cooperation with the exhibition subsidiary of Paramount and Universal, Cinema International Corporation. Within Australia, new multiplexes were built in major shopping centers, and new screens were added to older multiplexes in an expansion that accurately predicted the rise in attendances, and turned these shopping complexes into small "inner-cities," with bustling, after-hours activity of wining and dining. During this time, shares in the company were sold to interests outside the Fink family with the purpose of raising capital for this expansion. As a result of this expansion and building program, by 1994, Hoyts had become the 10th biggest cinema company in the world, and was once again a globalized company: an American investment company, Hellman and Friedman, held 47 percent of the shares; the directors and senior management held 21 percent; and the Australian company Lend Lease Corporation held 10 percent.

Following other companies in the corporation, Hoyts Cinemas was floated in 1996, but this public ownership did not last long. The Packer family, through their company Consolidated Press Holdings, purchased the last parcel of shares from Hellman and Friedman in 1999, and is now the private owner of Hoyts Cinemas. Consolidated Press Holdings is second only to the Murdoch group in ownership of media interests in Australia. At that time, Hoyts Cinemas was still in the top ten in the world exhibition market, with 1,500 screens in Australia, the United States, Mexico, Europe, and New Zealand. Hoyts withdrew from the European market, selling cinemas in Poland in 1999 and the United Kingdom in 2000. In 2003, Consolidated Press Holdings sold a 60 percent interest in the US operation of Hoyts (554 screens) to Regal Entertainment Group, the largest US cinema chain, although the deal included C.P.H. obtaining an interest in Regal. *See also* REVIVAL.

HUNTER, BILL (1940–). Bill Hunter's film career started at the beginning of the **revival**, and has continued to develop and grow through the various changes in **genres** and — consequentially — roles that have occurred in that time. He has appeared in many more films than many stars of the Australian cinema, often just one step away from the leading role, but always offering suitable and compelling foils for the leading characters to play off, and through which their own characters become more clearly defined. He has had roles in some 70 features and **television** films and series. He first appeared as a police officer in *Ned Kelly* (1970), and as the barman in *Stone* (1974). Since then, there have been only a few years where he has not acted in at least one film. He was nominated for a 1977 **Australian Film Institute** (AFI) award for best supporting actor for the role of Sergeant Smith in *Mad Dog Morgan* (1976).

A significant role occurred with **Phillip Noyce**'s statement about the culpability of non-Aboriginal Australians in the poverty and destitution of Aboriginal "fringe dwellers," *Backroads* (1977). Hunter played the lead of Jack, the drifter who teams up with a militant **Aborigine**, Gary, and tears around western New South Wales in a stolen car. Hunter's fine performance established him as an actor with finesse in the portrayal of difficult characters. He teamed up with Noyce again in *Newsfront* (1978), where he played Cinetone cameraman Len Maguire, fighting to keep both his company afloat against competition from the television industry, and his life in some kind of order in the wake of failed relationships. The role met with critical acclaim, and Hunter won another AFI award for best actor in a lead role. Further critical plaudits greeted his portrayal of Major Barton in **Peter Weir**'s *Gallipoli* (1981), with the AFI awarding him the prize for best actor in a supporting role. In the final scene, knowing that his men would be decimated, he followed orders and led them into the Turkish machine guns, in what would prove to be the model for trench warfare for the next four years of World War I. Hunter worked with Noyce and **Judy Davis** again in *Heatwave* (1982), and played Walker in John Duigan's Casablanca-inspired *Far East* in the same year, with **Bryan Brown** and Helen Morse.

For the 10 years that followed, Hunter's career seemed to be on hold, in film at least. He made many films, but with few memorable performances. His television roles continued apace, both in films and series. This changed in 1992, when he played the farcical Australian Dance Federation President Barry Fife, intent on maintaining his petty autocracy, in **Baz Lurhmann**'s romantic comedy *Strictly Ballroom*. This was followed immediately by another strong performance as Beth's father in **Gillian Armstrong**'s *The Last Days of Chez Nous* (1982), winning Hunter another nomination for an AFI best supporting actor award. He then played the sensitive outback man Bob, who accompanies the drag queens and transexual after repairing their bus, in *The Adventures of Priscilla, Queen of the Desert* (1994). As Bill Heslop, the father of Muriel in **P.J. Hogan**'s *Muriel's Wedding* (1994), he was at once the small-town greedy businessman and failed politician, as well as Muriel's father. He led the band of old lawn bowls players in the battle against the "pokies" in the comedy *Crackerjack* (2002), which was Paul Moloney's second directing stint in feature films—the first was in 1985—after a 25-year career directing for television.

Other films include *27A* (1974), *The Man from Hong Kong* (1975), *Eliza Fraser* (1976), *Weekend of Shadows* (1978), *In Search of Anna* (1978), . . . *Maybe This Time* (1980), *Hard Knocks* (1980), *Dead Man's Float* (1980), *The Return of Captain Invincible* (1983), *Street Hero* (1984), *The Hit* (1984), *An Indecent Obsession* (1985), *Rebel* (1985), *Sky Pirates* (1986), *Death of a Soldier* (1986), *Call Me Mr. Brown* (1986), *Rikky and Pete* (1988), *Fever* (1988), *Mull* (1989), *Deadly* (1991), *Broken Highway* (1993), *Shotgun Wedding* (1993), *The Custodian* (1993), *Everynight . . . Everynight* (1994), *Race the Sun* (1996),

River Street (1996), *Road to Nhill* (1997), *Crackerjack* (2002), *Kangaroo Jack* (2003), *Horseplay* (2003), the voice of the dentist in *Finding Nemo* (2003), and *Bad Eggs* (2003).

HURLEY, FRANK (1888–1962). Almost the Robert Flaherty of early Australian cinema, Frank Hurley was not only a photographer, a cinematographer, producer, and director of feature films and, especially, **documentary** films but also a showman, explorer, traveler, soldier, and adventurer. His early career in particular emphasizes the links between adventure and colonialism on the one hand and photography and cinema on the other. Born in 1888, Hurley soon became a nature photographer whose works eventually would be shown in galleries, books, newspapers and magazines, and even in films. From this passion, he moved into recording moving images. He accompanied the Mawson expedition to the Antarctic in 1911 and his edited record was given theatrical release as *Home of the Blizzard* in 1913.

He toured with this as he would with his later films, exhibiting it throughout Australia, the United Kingdom, Canada, and the United States, acting as both showman and narrator. Like Flaherty and Murnau, he was also attracted to warmer climes. His record of a journey through the tropical north of Australia with Francis Birtles was released as *Into Australia's Unknown* (1915). Almost immediately, he was traveling back to the Antarctic, this time as part of the expedition led by Ernest Shackleton, the cinematic diary released as *In the Grip of the Polar Ice* (1917). War briefly interrupted this cycle. From June 1917, armed with the title of Captain, Hurley was Australia's first official cameraman.

Then it was back to further cinematography associated with exploration and expeditions beginning with *The Ross Smith Flight* (1920) and continuing to Papua New Guinea. The documentary outcomes of the latter stay were *Pearls and Savages* (1921) and *With the Headhunters in Unknown Papua* (1923).

The popular success of his films on his various tours together with comments about the potential of Papua New Guinea as an exotic location, led him to undertake the production of two fiction feature films, *The Jungle Woman* (1926) and *The Hound of the Deep (Pearl of the South Seas)* (1926). Although these proved to be money-spinners, Hurley went back to documentary when the opportunity arose to make two further trips to the Antarctic with Mawson. From these came *Siege of the South* (1931). Meanwhile, the film of the Shackleton expedition was re-released with sound in 1933 as *Endurance*.

Hurley was very busy in the 1930s shooting several of the **Cinesound** features, including *The Squatter's Daughter* (1933), *The Silence of Dean Maitland* (1934), *Strike Me Lucky* (1934), *Grandad Rudd* (1935), and *Lovers and Luggers* (1937), the last two with George Heath. Cinesound also employed Hurley on commission to produce documentaries sponsored by government and private companies. A large output included *Symphony In Steel* (1933), *Treasures of Katoomba* (1936), and *A Nation Is Built* (1938). He also undertook some second-unit work for Chauvel's *Forty Thousand Horsemen* (1940), and was again an official cameraman during World War II. After 1945, he confined himself to photography and published several books. Hurley died in 1962 whereupon in 1973 came Anthony Buckley's filmic memorial *Snow, Sand and Savages*.

– J –

JEDDA (1955). The last feature film to be made by producer/director **Charles Chauvel**, *Jedda* is his most compelling and interesting, a great classic of the pre**revival** period. In terms of its melodramatic intensity and its unflinching ability to marshal irresolvable differences around gender and ethnicity, the film can bear the closest of comparison with King Vidor's great Hollywood classic, *Duel in the Sun* (1946). The narrative of the Australian film is deceptively simple. On a remote cattle station in the Northern Territory, a newly born Aboriginal baby is adopted by a white woman, Sarah McMann, in place of her own child who has died. Sarah names the baby Jedda, after a wild bird, and raises her as a white child, forbidding contact with the **Aborigines** on the station. Years pass, and Jedda, a beautiful teenage girl, is drawn by the mysteries of the Aboriginal people, but is restrained by her upbringing. Like the half-caste Pearl Chavez in *Duel*, this ethnic "doubleness" lays the base of the tragedy that is to follow.

One day a powerfully built-full blood Aborigine, Marbuck, arrives at the station seeking work. As though to emphasize his sexuality, Marbuck is marked as physically darker than the other Aborigines.

Jedda is fascinated by him and one moonlit night is drawn by his song to his campfire. He takes her away as his captive. Dragging the half-willing but frightened girl across the desert, Marbuck returns to his tribal lands, only to find himself rejected by his tribe for breaking its marriage taboos. Pursued by the men from Jedda's station and haunted by the death wish of his own tribe, Marbuck is driven insane. He and Jedda fall to their death over a cliff. On the face of it, the film was interesting in its time in placing Aborigines in the central roles and is, depending on one's point of view, either reactionary or progressive in its first half in tracing the white-black encounter. However, these considerations fall away in the second half that is concerned with the drive of the chase and the relationship between Marbuck and Jedda. Like Pearl and Lewt in *Duel*, their love is impossible and the film reaches a magnificent pitch of romanticism in tracing out the logical and emotional outcome of this union.

JONES, GILLIAN (1947–). Since 1982, Gillian Jones has appeared in strong and diverse supporting roles over almost 20 years, yet rarely has she played lead roles. Her characters are often in a state of change and growth, and are narratively significant. In the **Phillip Noyce** directed *Heatwave* (1982), she was a prostitute in a web of corruption and crime in the seedier Sydney inner-city areas. Subsequently, in the critically lauded but unpopular *Shame* (1987), she played the working-class, **country**-town girl who gains strength through her involvement with an out-of-town avenging angel. In 1987, she played three characters in *Twelfth Night*, and in *Echoes of Paradise* (1987). She played a lead in *Lover Boy* (1988) and *What I Have Written* (1995), and appeared in *Oscar and Lucinda* (1997) and *Terra Nova* (1999).

Other films include *Fighting Back* (1982), *I Own the Racecourse* (1986), *Echoes of Paradise* (1987), *Alterations* (1988), and *Cody: A Family Affair* (1994).

– K –

KANTS, IVOR (KANTZ, IVAR; KANTS, IVAR) (1949–). Ivor Kants has acted in the theater and on screen, in both **television** and film, although he is probably more well known for his television characters. He is of Latvian descent, and is a graduate of the National Institute of Dramatic Art. Two television films began his career, *The Puzzle* (1978) and **Peter Weir**'s early thriller *The Plumber* (1979), in which he played the plumber, disrupting and terrorizing a housewife. Lead roles followed in quick succession: in *Brothers* (1982), *Moving Out* (1983), the Thomas Kenneally-written *Silver City* (1984), **Tim Burstall**'s *The Naked Country* (1984), *Jenny Kissed Me* (1986), with **Geoffrey Rush** in *Twelfth Night* (1987), *Gallagher's Travels* (1987), *Edge of Power* (1987), and *You and Me and Uncle Bob* (1993). None of these films reached the heights of commercial or artistic success, and Kants continued working in television up to 1994. He appeared in the unexciting *Counterstrike* (2003), a television film.

KARVAN, CLAUDIA (1972–). Unlike other Australians who have left Australia to pursue careers overseas, Claudia Karvan has been happy to remain in Australia, honing her considerable talents and ability across a range of characters and **genres**. As well as a relatively long and fruitful career on the big screen, she has a long list of **television** credits. Acting has been a part of her life since childhood; she made her first appearance in *Going Down* (1983) as a disgruntled child. She first appeared in a lead role in *Hightide* (1987) as Ally, a teenager living in a caravan on the coast of New South Wales, torn between her alcoholic mother—played by **Judy Davis**—who had abandoned her, and her grandmother, who had been looking after her since that time.

Karvan excels in **comedy**, and in the romantic comedy *The Big Steal* (1990), she played the young girl to whom Danny (Ben Medelsohn) is attracted. As an Australian of Greek descent in *The Heartbreak Kid* (1993), she played a high school teacher who falls in love with one of her students, and depicts the trials and tribulations of this love, which is rather tragic. However, if the roles were reversed—if the film were about a young male teacher who fell in love with a female student—the representation of the situation and the audience reception of the film would have been arguably quite different. In the comedy *Dating the Enemy* (1996), Karvan exchanged bodies with her sexist ex-boyfriend, who experiences the travails of the female world. Paul Cox has directed her in a number of films, including the comedy *Lust and Revenge* (1996), written by Cox and ***John Clarke**. In the romantic comedy *Paperback Hero* (1998), Karvan (Ruby Vale) played opposite Hugh Jackman (Jack Willis) as the alleged author of romance novels, which, in fact, the truck-driving Jackman wrote. As a **country** woman, Karvan is independent, strong, and although lacking the graces of an urbanite, makes up for it with her exuberance and *joie de vivre*. With **Naomi Watts**, **Hugo Weaving**, and **Tom Long**, she played one of the three women living together in Sydney and three male friends in the otherwise inconsequential romantic comedy *Strange Planet* (1999).

Karvan works effectively in other genres. *Redheads* (1992) provided her first lead in a thriller, where she is an inmate who has an affair with a lawyer, who is later murdered. The short, erotic, Paul Cox film, *Touch Me* (1993), shows Karvan in the role of a lover. Perhaps her best role to date was the corrupt lawyer Louise Roncoli, playing opposite Tom Long and corrupt insurance assessor John Kriesky (**Bryan Brown**) in the cynical *Risk* (2000).

Other films include *Molly* (1983), **Phillip Noyce**'s *Echoes of Paradise* (1987), *Holidays on the River Yarra* (1990), *Broken Highway* (1993), *The Nostradamus Kid* (1993), *Exile* (Paul Cox 1994), *Natural Justice: Heat* (1996), *Flynn* (1996), *Two Girls and a Baby* (1998), and *Passion* (1999).

KENNEDY, BYRON (1952–1983). Until his accidental death in a helicopter accident in 1983, in Warragamba Dam, New South Wales, Byron Kennedy was the other half in the Kennedy Miller production-direction team responsible for *Mad Max* (1979) and *Mad Max 2: Road Warrior* (1981) (*see* MILLER, DR. GEORGE). These films had their genesis in *Violence in the Cinema Part One*, produced by Kennedy and written and directed by Miller, an unsettling film that exploited the potential of cinematography, location, editing, and mise-en-scene; potential that reached fruition in the Mad Max films. Kennedy acted in *The Office Picnic* (1972), was cinematographer for *Come Out Fighting* (1973), and produced *Last of the Knucklemen* (1979). He also produced the **television** miniseries *Cowra Breakout* (1984) and *The Dismissal* (1983).

The **Australian Film Institute** established the Byron Kennedy Award in 1983 to recognize an individual working in any area of Australian film or television—usually early in their career—whose work is marked by excellence.

KENNEDY MILLER PRODUCTIONS. Byron Kennedy and **Dr. George Miller** established the Kennedy Miller production company in 1972. The pair had met in the summer of 1969 at a film course run by the Australian Union of Students at Melbourne University. After Kennedy had gone on to work as an actor and cinematographer in the film industry and Miller had completed his medical training in Sydney, they met again and founded the company. Miller's medical career was to help finance the company's productions for some time to come. Kennedy quickly settled into the role of producer, while Miller concentrated on writing and directing. In 1975 Miller and James McCausland wrote the script for *Mad Max* (1979). Because it was a **genre** picture, rather than the kind of art cinema then being financed by government, Kennedy and Miller organized financing for the film themselves, from the distributor Roadshow and a syndicate of 20 investors. Following the international success of this film, the much bigger and more expensive sequel, *Mad Max 2* (1982), was easier to finance (*see also MAD MAX TRILOGY*). For this film, Terry Hayes joined the production team as a scriptwriter. Hayes went on to write much of the company's first **television** miniseries, *The Dismissal* (1982).

In 1983, Byron Kennedy was killed in a helicopter crash, yet despite this blow, Kennedy Miller continued to grow as a company, gaining a reputation in the 1980s as a leading Australian producer of quality TV miniseries. Its credits include: *Bodyline* (1983), *The Cowra Breakout* (1984), and *Vietnam* (1986). Films produced by Kennedy Miller and directed by Dr. George Miller include: *Mad Max*, *Mad Max 2*, *Mad Max: Beyond Thunderdome* (codirector, 1985), and ***Babe: Pig in the City*** (1998). Films the company has produced (but that were not directed by Miller) include: *Heaven Before I Die* (1997), ***Babe*** (1995), *Flirting* (1991), *Dead Calm* (1989), and *The Year My Voice Broke* (1987).

KIDMAN, NICOLE (1967–). Born in Hawaii to a nursing instructor mother and a biochemist and psychologist father—both Australians—Nicole Kidman spent the first three years of her life in the United States, near Washington, D.C. The family returned to Australia where Kidman learned ballet and participated in school theatrical presentations. By the age of 15, she had appeared in small roles in the successful *Bush Christmas* (1983) and *BMX Bandits* (1983) and was a regular in the **television** series *Five Mile Creek*, which gave her the time and developed her confidence in front of the camera. Her talent and compelling screen presence even then was noticed and roles in other films followed in quick succession. *Wills & Burke* (1985) was a lampoon of historical epics, *Windrider* (1986) was a teenage film about a surfer who built a high-tech surfboard. However, a part in the **Kennedy Miller** television miniseries *Vietnam* (1986) — directed by John Duigan — was a watershed in this early part of her career as her ability was affirmed in the **Australian Film Institute** award for best leading actress. Terry Hayes wrote the miniseries, and he was so impressed that he wrote the part of Rae Ingram in **Phillip Noyce**'s thriller *Dead Calm* (1989) with her in mind. Although only 19, Kidman played the part of a 30 plus year old woman grieving for her lost child. She then reverted to a snotty teenager in John Duigan's *Flirting* (1991), working with **Noah Taylor** and Thandie Newton. It was the last Australian film she made, although she went on to work with Australian directors like *****Jane Campion** and **Baz Luhrmann**.

Dead Calm* brought her to the notice of the international art-house circuit and to Tom Cruise, who invited her to work with him in Hollywood on *Days of Thunder* (1990), and with whom she was subsequently married. Film parts followed rapidly, although none matched the success of her earlier work. With Dustin Hoffman, she played a society girl in the period drama *Billy Bathgate* (1991); with Cruise she appeared as Drew Preston in Ron Howard's epic *Far and Away* (1992). Two films in 1995 revealed the range in the spectrum of her work. In *Batman Forever* she played the part of Bruce Wayne's (Val Kilmer) romantic interest, and in the satirical *To Die For*, Kidman played a television weather girl who will do anything to succeed, a role which generated a degree of gender-aligned, and mean-spirited controversy about whether she was playing a role, or just playing herself. Jane Campion made her audition for the role of Isabel Archer in the film version of Henry James novel *The Portrait of a Lady* (1996), but her ability shone through the sometimes uneven direction. The role of Dr. Julia Kelly opposite George Clooney followed in the action thriller *The Peacemaker* (1997).

With Cruise, she played the part of a wife who confesses having a sexual fantasy with another man, starting a series of responses from her husband (Cruise), and marking the disintegration of a relationship, in Stanley Kubrick's *Eyes Wide Shut* (1999). In a completely different role, she played the beautiful courtesan Satine in Baz Luhrmann's ***Moulin Rouge!*** (2001), for which she was nominated for an Oscar and won a Golden Globe. Exploiting her icy reserve, Kidman played the high-strung mother living in isolation in World War II in *The Others* (2001). The marriage with Cruise broke down in 2001, but Kidman's work continued unabated. In Australia, where she now spends much of her time, the women's pulp press had a field day with the breakup, labeling Kidman as the innocent, wounded victim "our Nic" and demonizing Cruise as the womanizing bounder who broke her heart. Generous critical acclaim followed her portrayal of Virginia Woolf in *The Hours* (2002), where she costarred with Julianne Moore and Meryl Streep, and further down the cast list, Australian **Toni Collette**. Kidman won an Academy Award, a British Academy for the Film and Television Arts (BAFTA) award, and a Golden Globe for best performance in a leading role. Audiences were divided over the film, however.

Other films include, *Archer's Adventure* (1985), *Watch the Shadows Dance* (1987), *The Bit Part* (1987), *Emerald City* (1988), *Malice* (1993), *My Life* (1993), *The Leading Man* (1996), *Practical Magic* (1998), *Birthday Girl* (2001), *Dogville* (2003), *The Human Stain* (2003), *Cold Mountain* (2003).

– L –

LANTANA **(2001).** Directed by Ray Lawrence (***Bliss*** [1985]), *Lantana* is a thriller that explores the webs of intrigue that people weave, and the explosive consequences that occur when these webs have common threads with other webs. **Anthony LaPaglia** returned from the United States to star as the conflicted family man and detective Leon Zat, who is cheating on his wife Sonja (Kerry Armstrong). Psychiatrist Valerie (Barbara Hershey) listens to her anger and frustration but her own marriage to John (**Geoffrey Rush**) has also been shattered. Househusband Nic (**Vince Colosimo**) and wife Paula (Daniela Farinacci) live next door to Jane (Rachael Blake), who has separated from her husband, Pete (Glen Robbins) and is having an affair with Leon. This festering mass is highly unstable, and Lawrence choreographs the consequences as the façade implodes. *Lantana* was successful at the Australian box office, taking over $12 million in Australia, and was the 11th most successful film by this criteria. Critics applauded the film: the Film Critics Circle of Australia nominated it in eight categories in 2002 and awarded it five prizes including best film, best male actor, and best female actor. The film was nominated for thirteen 2001 **Australian Film Institute** (AFI) awards and it won seven including best leading actor (LaPaglia), best supporting actor (Colosimo), best leading actress (Armstrong), best supporting actress (Blake), best film, and best director. In addition, the AFI conferred a screenwriting prize on Andrew Bovell.

LAPAGLIA, ANTHONY (1959–). Anthony La Paglia's career is different in that he made his name in **Hollywood** before he starred in any Australian films. Born in Adelaide, South Australia, he was a schoolteacher before moving to New York City to work in theater. He appeared in **television** series, and then became typecast as an Italian gangster in subsequent films, but also continued theater work, where he was widely acclaimed. His US film credits are too numerous to mention in this context. Suffice to say that by the time he played Michael Andretti in *Looking for Allibrandi* (2001)—a story about an Italian-Australian teenager trying to juggle the demands of the final year of high school and those of clashing cultures—he had some 40 television and feature film roles to his credit. The Film Critics Circle of Australia nominated him for an award for the *Allibrandi* role. He later returned to Australia to play the lead of Detective Leon Zat in the award-winning *Lantana* (2001), winning an **Australian Film Institute** (AFI) award for best lead actor in the process. In 2001, he returned again to play the chief executive officer, Simon O'Reilly, of the finance house in the *The Bank* (2001). His greed causes him to back Paul Jackson's (**David Wenham**) strategy for making vast amounts of money, which is actually Jackson's strategy for bankrupting the bank.

LESNIE, ANDREW (1956–). Andrew Lesnie began his career during the early years of the **revival** in 1977, as a runner for *The Getting of Wisdom*, assistant camera operator for *Patrick* (1978) and the clapper loader for *The Killing of Angel Street* (1981). He moved up to be **documentary** cameraman for *Mad Max 2: The Road Warrior* (1981) with some additional work behind the camera in other films until he filmed the little-known *Stations* (1983). He honed his skills quietly on many films until *The Delinquents* (1989), which was well received at the box office. Still, none of these films—they were not first rate films—nor those that followed, allowed him to reach his full potential, although the Australian Cinematographers Society recognized his ability in naming him cinematographer of the year for *You Seng* (1993). In 1994, he received further recognition with his filming of *Spider and Rose*, a quirky comedy about a different road trip, followed by *Babe* (1995) and *Babe: Pig in the City* (1998), both of which brought him an international reputation. Then came *Doing Time for Patsy Cline* (1997), for which Lesnie won the **Australian Film Institute** award for best cinematography.

In 1999, his credits paused as Lesnie worked as cinematographer for three years on the **Lord of the Rings* trilogy, which has been recognized as his masterpiece, at least for the time being. He coordinated the efforts of up to nine photography units at any one time, and was a significant player in bringing **Peter Jackson*'s shared vision to the screen. Lesnie has won awards from numerous international organizations for each of the three films. For *Lord of the Rings: The Fellowship of the Ring* (2002), he won an Academy Award for best cinematography in 2002. In 2002, the Australian Cinematographers Society voted him into the Hall of Fame for his achievements.

As cinematographer, his other films include *Unfinished Business* (1985), *Fair Game* (1985), *Emoh Ruo* (1985), *Dark Age* (1987), *Australian Dream* (1987), *Boys in the Island* (1989), *Girl Who Came Late* (1991), *Fatal Past* (1993), *Two If by Sea* (1996), *The Sugar Factory* (1998), and *Love's Brother* (2004).

LONELY HEARTS (1982). **John Clarke* and Paul Cox wrote the screenplay for this film, which Cox subsequently directed, and which marked a different direction for the Australian industry. Wendy Hughes plays Patricia, an unattractive bank clerk who falls in love over a considerable period of time, and after numerous self-conscious stutters and blind alleys, with Peter, played by Norman Kaye—a 55-year-old piano tuner and occasional shoplifter. Both have difficulty relating to others, especially members of the opposite sex, and the film treats their growing attraction with great sensitivity and affection.

Lonely Hearts was nominated in four categories in the 1982 **Australian Film Institute** (AFI) awards and won the best film award.

LONG, TOM. Tom Long was born in Boston, while his Australian parents were visiting in the United States. He grew up on a farm in New South Wales, where he learned to break in horses and shear sheep. These skills provided his income when he left school, but he was not satisfied and went overseas for some years. Returning to Australia, he entered the National Institute of Dramatic Art and graduated in 1996. He has played in many **television** series and television films. He had a small part as Billy Livingstone in the feature *Country Life* (1994), on the same bill as ***Sam Neill** and Greta Scacchi in this **adaptation** of Chekhov's "Uncle Vanya," transposed to Australia and Australian concerns in the 1920s. In 1997, he played Brad Goodall in *Doing Time for Patsy Cline*, a **comedy** road film about the life and times of an Australian country music singer. He played Wally in the **Gregor Jordan**-directed **crime** thriller *Two Hands* (1999), and in the same year, appeared in *Strange Planet*. He then played the starring role of Ben Madigan opposite **Claudia Karvan** (Louise Roncoli) and **Bryan Brown** (John Kriesky) in *Risk* (2000), where those two introduce him to increasingly complex insurance scams, while Roncoli assists further with his sexual education, to Kriesky's dislike. In the same year he played Glenn Latham, the scientifically focused but romantically naïve scientist who was one of three manning the radio telescope at Parkes, New South Wales, in **Rob Sitch**'s *The Dish*, a gentle dramatic comedy about the part played by the facility in transmitting vision and sound of the first moon landing. Other films include *Hildegarde* (2001) and *Boomerang* (2002).

LONGFORD, RAYMOND (1878–1959). Very much the D.W. Griffith-like figure of Australian cinema, Longford was both a hero of the silent film era and a victim of the increasing stranglehold that American feature films were exerting on exhibition schedules in Australian cinemas during and after World War I. Renowned in Australia for his partnership with a woman actor, Lottie Lyell—just as Griffith was linked with Lillian Gish—Longford soldiered on after his film career had come to an end, a walking testament to the power of studios to overcome the efforts of the independent producer/director.

Longford was born in Melbourne in 1878 and by around 1909 had become a stage actor. By this time, he had paired with Lyell, often playing the stage villain to her heroine. His first film roles were in two bushranger melodramas of 1911, *Captain Midnight* and *Captain Starlight*. It was then time to cut his directorial teeth with screen **adaptations** of two stage successes, *The Fatal Wedding* (1911) and *The Midnight Wedding* (1912). For the next dozen years, until Lyell's unfortunate death in 1925, Longford was part of a filmmaking partnership that reached its peak in the 1919 production of *The Sentimental Bloke*. Very much Longford's *magnum opus*, the film is also intimately dependent on the performance of Lyell as Doreen, girl friend and then wife of the Bloke.

Longford's credits include the **documentary** *The Naming of the Federal Capital* (1913) and two government immigration films made in 1923. Other documentaries and features include *The Life of Rufus Dawes* (1911), *Sweet Nell of Old Drury* (1912), *The Tide of Death* (1912), *Australia Calls* (1913), *'Neath Australian Skies* (1913), *The Silence of Dean Maitland* (1914), *The Mutiny on the Bounty* (1916), *Ginger Mick* (1920), *The Dinkum Bloke* (1923), *The Hills of Hate* (1926), *Diggers in Blighty* (1933), *Dad and Dave Come to Town* (1938), and *That Certain Something* (1941). However, despite this output, his career as a feature director was effectively finished by the mid-1920s as he had more and more trouble with his own projects. His work in the 1930s and into the 1940s was small second unit tasks given him as acts of charity. Worse still, only four features from his actual output survive—*The Romantic Story of Margaret Catchpole* (1911), *The Woman Suffers* (1918), *The Sentimental Bloke* (1919), and *On Our Selection* (1920). Longford gave comprehensive and insightful evidence of the plight of feature film production to the 1927 Royal Commission on the Moving Picture Industry in Australia although, by then, the stranglehold of American distribution firms on Australian screens was all but complete. In the late 1950s, when sentiments began to emerge about the possibility of reviving the Australian film production industry, Longford was rediscovered, reduced to working as a night watchman. Dying in 1959, he was not to know that seeds he had helped to plant would germinate into a **revival** that would bear fruit a little over a decade later.

The **Australian Film Institute** (AFI) has recognized his contribution and stature in the industry by establishing the Longford Lifetime Achievement Award. It is the highest accolade that the AFI can bestow on an individual, and recipients will have shown an unwavering commitment to excellence in filmmaking and thus will have contributed to the enrichment of Australian culture.

LOOKING FOR ALIBRANDI **(2000).** The Kate Wood's-directed *Looking for Alibrandi* was based on the popular novel of the same name by Melina Marchetta, who also wrote the screenplay. It tells the story of Josie Alibrandi (Pia Miranda), a year 12 student living in an extended Italian-Australian family, in love with one person who is out of reach, but loved by another who is quite accessible. Because the characters are free of stereotyping, they present as quite human, which is itself an achievement in a film where multicultural Australia is highlighted, not as a backdrop, but as one of the causes for dramatic action.

The film was nominated in four **Australian Film Institute** (AFI) categories in 2000, including best direction and best cinematography. It won AFI awards for best film, best lead actress (Pia Miranda), best supporting actress (Greta Scacchi), best adapted screenplay, and best editing.

LOVELY, LOUISE (1895–1980). Louise Lovely was born Louise Carbasse in Sydney. As, arguably, the first international star from Australia, her career was the model that others were to follow. She made nine films in Australia between 1911 and 1912, in the flourishing period of the Australian film industry. She moved to **Hollywood**, where Universal placed her on contract and changed her name to Louise Lovely. She resembled Mary Pickford in her slight stature, blond curly hair, and facial features, and played in the romantic melodramas that were a mainstay of many Hollywood studios. Her contract with Universal expired in 1918. One of the terms of the contract was that Lovely could not use that name for nine months after the contract's expiry, so she found it difficult to revive her career after that period. Nevertheless, her total Hollywood output was about 50 films. She toured Australia again in 1924 with a vaudeville show, and returned permanently in 1925 to make *Jewelled Nights* (1925) in Tasmania, which flopped. She retired from filmmaking at that time.

Some films are *One Hundred Years Ago* (1911), *A Tale of the Australian Bush* (1911), *A Daughter of Australia* (1912), *Stronger Than Death* (1915), *Tangled Hearts* (1916), *The Social Buccaneer* (1916), *The Outlaw and the Lady* (1917), *The Girl Who Wouldn't Quit* (1918), *The Butterfly Man* (1920), *While the Devil Laughs* (1921), and *Shattered Idols* (1922).

LOWENSTEIN, RICHARD (1959–). Lowenstein is a graduate of the Swinburne Film School, and made a number of short films before *Strikebound* (1984), a social realist film drawing on the experiences of strikers working at a coal mine in Victoria in 1937. His fascination with alternatives, with antiestablishment classes and cultures, is apparent in this film and subsequently. His second feature, *Dogs in Space* (1987), moved from the industrial working class to the alternative, but still politicized student culture of sex, drugs, and rock- 'n'roll in Melbourne. The interrogation of this culture continued in the Australian-Italian coproduction *He Died with a Felafel in his Hand* (1999), a slow-moving comedy about the life of a nomad, who trundles through Australian shared house cultures, taking in while registering the absurdity of the complex of lives that jigsaw with his. Other films include *Evictions* (1979), *White City* (1985), *Australian Made: The Movie* (1987), and *Say a Little Prayer* (1993).

LUHRMANN, BAZ (1962–). Bazmark Anthony Luhrmann was born in Sydney, New South Wales, living for some of his early life in the country before returning to metropolitan Sydney to attend the National Institute of Dramatic Art. His first interest was in acting, and he appeared with **Judy Davis** in the film *Winter of our Dreams* (1982). However, his interest turned to **musicals**, and, in 1992, he worked on the stage version of *Strictly Ballroom*, which he later turned into the film released in 1992. Other musical theater and opera productions followed, including La Bohème in 1990. The film of *Strictly Ballroom* set many of the parameters for Luhrmann's later work, including a mise-en-scene of garish colors, Goyaesque make-up and costumes, exuberant dancing that overflows the frame, and sincere, romantic narratives. The film was acclaimed at Cannes, and won many international awards. Returning to the past for a story, but locating it in the postmodern present of "Verona Beach," he directed

Romeo and Juliet (1996), starring Leonardo di Caprio and Claire Danes, which was also a box-office success. The next film was slow in the making, but *Moulin Rouge!* (2001) followed Luhrmann's previous success in reinterpreting old narratives in a postmodern clash of color, music, discordance, and frenzied dance.

Baz Luhrmann married his collaborator—Oscar winner in art direction and costume design—Catherine Martin, in 1997.

– M –

MAD MAX TRILOGY (1979–1985). In the 1970s, **Dr. George Miller** and **Byron Kennedy** joined forces to make *Violence in the Cinema Part One*, an experimental film produced by Kennedy, and written and directed by Miller. This was the genesis for the Mad Max films, comprising *Mad Max* (1979), *Mad Max 2: The Road Warrior* (1981), and *Mad Max Beyond Thunderdome* (1985). A fourth film was made, but has not been released. The first film reintroduced the **action and adventure genre** to the Australian industry, after some years of **art and period** films, at a time when the industry was in a renaissance (*see* REVIVAL). However, this action-and-adventure style was unlike those that had come before in the Australian industry, and was more in tune with those films of the same genre being released in the United States. Much of the films' success was due to the initial coming together of the production/direction team of Kennedy and Miller, and **Mel Gibson** as Max. Miller is a master story-teller with a camera, and his understanding of the dynamic of the story and the kinetic sense of filmmaking is a primary element of the success of the three films.

The first in the series, *Mad Max*, was a resounding success in Australia, and did achieve considerable notice in the United States. Fear of the Australian accent caused the film to be overdubbed for its US release, which did not seem to harm the film's success. However, it was re-released in 2000 in the original, Australian version. Max Rockatansky (Mel Gibson in his first internationally recognized leading role) is a cop in a postapocalyptic dystopian Australia. When a biker gang murders his wife and family, Max gives up the law to extract revenge, in the same way that Clint Eastwood and others have done in similar, Western-style films. The film documented the transition from the world of innocence and beauty to the amoral and violent outlaw world that then pervaded all three films. *Mad Max* was nominated for a number of **Australian Film Institute** (AFI) awards, including best film, best director, and best original screenplay, and for Hugh Keays-Byrne—the Shakespearean actor from the United Kingdom, who had starred as a biker in *Stone* (1974)—best actor in a supporting role, as Toecutter. The film won AFI awards for editing, sound, and original music score.

Mad Max 2: The Road Warrior (1981) continued the story of the loner, Max, now no longer with any affiliation with the law, and his ongoing battle with the bike gang, who have now become even more evil and rapacious. This time though, Max is protecting a small settlement, whose gentler members have access to the most precious commodity in the postapocalyptic desert wasteland, fuel. The AFI nominated **Dean Semler** for cinematography and Brian May for music. Miller won the award for best direction, and other awards included best costume design and best achievement in editing, production design, and sound. Recognized as a science fiction film, *Mad Max 2* won a Saturn award for best international film.

Mad Max Beyond Thunderdome (1985) starred Tina Turner as Aunt Entity, the governor of Bartertown, a trading post in the desert, filled with criminals and thieves. Here Max has to fight for Aunt Entity, but is thrown out of the town. He stumbles on a group of orphans, who survived a plane crash during the nuclear war, and who believe that he is their pilot, Captain Walker, returned to them. This is a much more reflective film, exploring elements of greed and consciousness, innocence and rebirth, with the sort of questioning that is often found in films set in postapocalyptic times. The film returns to the innocence that was lost in the first film, in a cyclical movement through unconsciousness and evil and a rebirth into what might be a better world. Although the popular success of this film was not as marked as the second, it has elements that may enhance its timelessness. The action elements are not neglected, however. One of Miller's achievements is the thunderdome, one of the first-class and unique ideas for staging a fight.

The *Mad Max* trilogy catapulted a number of people to international success: Miller, Gibson, and Semler. The trilogy also drew international attention to the Australian film industry, at a time when many films exported from Australia were for arthouse release.

MAN FROM SNOWY RIVER, THE **(1982).** *The Man from Snowy River* is the seventh most popular film in Australia, as measured by box-office revenue, grossing $17.2 million since its release. It won an **Australian Film Institute** award in 1982 for best original music score, was nominated for cinematography and sound awards, and in the same year won the most popular film award at the Montreal Film Festival. In 1983, it was nominated for best foreign film in the Golden Globes awards.

Australian critics were initially ambivalent in their appraisal of the film, as it was another film since the **revival** that spurned both the quasi art film mood exemplified by *Picnic at Hanging Rock* (1975) and the lowbrow **ocker** films that were released at the same time. The film was a commercial success, deriving much of that success from the Western and **Hollywood genres**. Director **George Miller** drew on his knowledge and experience of Westerns and adventures to make a film of **action**, romance, and the Australian bush, that tapped into a growing appreciation of the bush in Australian culture, exemplified in the blossoming of both Australian country and Western music, and outback clothing stores catering to middle class professionals in the **city**. The title is that of a famous poem by A.B. (Banjo) Patterson, which is an epic of adventure, horses, and the high **country**, but without the romance of the film. Like the poem, the film recalls a simpler lifestyle, told with simple filmic effects in a story that spurns gratuitous violence and sex.

The young man who becomes the Man from Snowy River, Jim Craig (Tom Burlinson), has to leave his father's mountain property to earn self-respect and some money on the lowlands, where he also finds love in the person of fiery Jessica Harrison (**Sigrid Thornton**). After many adventures, he returns to claim his rightful legacy in the high country of the Australian Alps and proves himself through his pursuit of valuable horses.

MASCULINITY. An analysis of the representation of both men and their relationships tells us something about masculine traditions in Australia. As films are both cultural artifacts and contain explicit messages, any interpretation of masculinity must address the context of the time in which the film is set, as well as the time the film was made. Clearly, such a project is beyond the scope of this entry, and it is adequate here to explicate some threads in the weaving of the masculinity tapestry in Australian film.

A significant element of masculinity in Australian cultural history, and therefore Australian film, is mateship. European settlement of the east coast of Australia took the form of a penal colony in 1788, supported later by free settlement. Survival depended on loyalty to one's "mates." Later, this loyalty was required in order to explore and settle the vast, inhospitable environment. In times of war, mateship was a measure of the quality of relationship, as a mate was one whom a soldier would happily accompany into the jungle; that is, one who would be dependable and able to offer support. In *The Australian Legend* (1958), Russell Ward defined mateship as the "strongly egalitarian sentiment of group solidarity and loyalty . . . [which] was perhaps the most marked of all convict traits." Mateship was not an explicit theme explored until the first films of the **revival**, like *Wake in Fright* (1970) and **Sunday Too Far Away** (1975), suggesting that its reality may have been unconscious in earlier history. In addition, the conscious use of mateship as a story line occurs only after it had been recognized as being significant in the Australian legend.

The relationships between men are often both explained by the concept of mateship, but are limited by it. For example, when a film like **Crocodile Dundee** (1986) is classified as a film about, in part, mateship, it tends to cast a pall over it, as mateship is not necessarily a positive characteristic. For many, who see mateship as having similar traits to "redneck" culture in the United States, mateship is a negative characteristic, with overtones of homosexuality, violence, abuse of alcohol, racism, and exaggerated testosterone episodes. For those same people, when mateship appears in some form on screen, then it is symbolic of negative elements in the character of Australian men. However, both national and international film audiences seem to enjoy other representations, as evinced by the success of films like *Crocodile Dundee*, where masculine traits are positively represented, including characteristics like courage, a laconic attitude, a certain innocence, and naivety. At the same time, the film does not take such characteristics too seriously, and neither do the characters themselves.

Mateship and the growth of unionism in Australia are one and the same, as the collectivization of men into groups to fight the tyranny of the "cockies," or sheep farmers, was seen to be an egalitarian movement toward fairness for all, and the ideal of a fair day's pay for a fair day's work. Unlike the situation in many countries where unionism developed in the industrial centers, the shearer's union—the Australian Workers' Union (AWU)—grew and was most powerful outside the industrial cities, in the towns and shires of rural Australia. *Sunday Too Far Away* tells of a group of men, some of whom were fiercely competitive in their determination to be the best shearer, but who worked in unison to achieve their aims. Those who attempted to break a strike, the "scabs," were seen to be quite low on the scale of humanity. Masculinity here is sometimes tough, but it is also considerate to those mates who are unable to perform. In this context, being a man meant standing up for one's integrity, not to accept humiliation, and to stand up for one's mates. As the endnotes to *Sunday* state, "The Strike lasted nine months. The shearers won. It wasn't the money so much. It was the bloody insult." A similar theme was the subject of *Strikebound* (1984), about the strike of miners on the coalfields of Gippsland in eastern Victoria in the 1930s, who struck over low wages and dangerous working conditions. In this instance, **women** were active participants in the industrial action, boycotting local businesses that supported the colliery. Masculinity did not imply a marginalization of women; rather an understanding of difference. (This was not "an accepting of difference" as this would imply some kind of rejection of the idea that they were the same. Rather, the fact of difference was clear and unequivocal.)

Other elements of the masculine are exhibited in the **ocker** films of the 1970s, including *The Naked Bunyip* (1970), *Stork* (1971), *The Adventures of Barry Mackenzie* (1972), **Alvin Purple** (1973), and *Number 96* (1974). Ocker came from the term applied to men who were unabashed Australians; these films celebrated this "Australianness." The male leads were boorish, obsessed with sex and bodily functions, and also antiauthoritarian, antitraditionalist, antipomp, antipretense, and anti-British. If the 1960s was a period of liberation for women, then the 1970s was, at least in film, a liberation for men, but such liberation was subverted by its "over-the-top" extremism, and the send-up by the characters of the stereotypes. Psychological motivation did not drive these character; social stereotypes did. The dialogue contained plays on language that were not understood by English or US audiences, so the films were popular only in Australia. And they were very popular. *Alvin Purple* was the most successful feature film released between 1971 and 1977.

The ocker films were tied to a particular moment in government policy about films. Between 1969 and 1975, the Australian government wanted to promote a film industry, and subsidized films. However, such films were to be "about" Australia and the Australian identity, and were to be commercially viable. Thus, new filmmakers from university experimental film courses, and experimental theaters, seized on the opportunity to use government funds to make films, and the ocker films were the commercially successful result. Never has the nexus between government policy and the construction of a particular cultural identity been so clear.

Other films have shredded the positive construction of masculinity. *Shame* (1988) is a scathing critique of the mateship that suppresses truth, that creates a prison of silence for women, that builds a façade of civilization over a pit of criminal and violent behavior. Mimicking *Shane* (1953), the hero rides into the small, isolated town on her motorbike, and proceeds to tear down the charade of lies on which the local, small-town masculine culture is founded.

Masculinity has many manifestations in Australian film, just as in other national film. Some elements of masculinity are unique to Australian films, and some are shared across cultures and across film **genres**, such as the **action/adventure** genre. The representations of masculinity are products of culture, sometimes assisted by government policy.

MATESHIP. *See* MASCULINITY.

MATRIX, THE (1999). Although arguable, *The Matrix* is regarded as an Australian film as it was shot on location in Sydney, New South Wales. **Fox Studios** were used for studio shoots, and some special effects were manufactured by Australian companies. Not that this makes a lot of difference, as many of the scenes are unrecognizable as Sydneyscapes. Interestingly, while produced by **Village Roadshow** (in partnership), the studios that are associated with Village on the Gold Coast were not used. **Hugo Weaving** achieved further fame, yet little critical acclaim, for his role of Agent Smith, the leader of the agents who work for the controllers of reality. **Robert Taylor** played one of his offsiders, Agent Jones. With its story based on ancient Vedic scriptures regarding the illusory nature of everyday reality, *Matrix* was regarded as the benchmark for science fiction films for a short time. A computer hacker, Neo, discovers that the world of the everyday is actually a virtual reality called the matrix, and controlled by a malevolent cyber-intelligence. The aim of this complex reality is to harness the energy of humans for the matrix's campaign of further domination. Neo, and his newly found friends, are pursued by the agents as they try to destroy the web of illusion. The film spun off two sequels, *The Matrix Reloaded* (2003) and *The Matrix Revolutions* (2003), which were not as successful.

MATURATION/COMING OF AGE FILMS. Coming-of-age is a continuing theme in Australian feature films, especially in the **revival** period. Hence, before looking at particular films that conform to this template, it is worth asking just why such a preoccupation has been so favored. The answer would appear to be three-fold. First is the myth perpetuated by white Australian society that the country is a "young" one. With the different independent British colonies federating together to form a new political entity, the Commonwealth of Australia, in 1901, such a notion would seem plausible. However, with very many other nation-states across the planet laying claim to also being new and young, this particular notion is not especially sustainable. The second level that appears to support the proposition of youth has to do with the Australian feature film production industry being given state support as a new emergent industry in 1972. It too can make claim to the notion of adolescence, ever growing into a future maturity. Not surprisingly, even in the first cycle of **ocker** comedy between 1970 and 1975—films such as *The Adventures of Barry McKenzie* (1972) and ***Alvin Purple*** (1973)—offer the prospect of the Australian male innocent, which the rest of the world (mostly in the shape of sexually predatory females) wants at any price. Finally, too, maturation and coming of age is a key ingredient of the 19th-century *bildungsroman*, the novel depicting the coming of age, a significant precursor to the Australian period (art) cinema (see ART AND PERIOD FILMS). The latter was at its height in the second half of the 1970s and has continued in a more muted way down to the present. Not surprisingly, then, the visual and narrative rite of passage of a young person, male or female, has been a recurring theme in Australian cinema in the recent present.

Various different constructions and permutations within this pattern are, of course, possible. The basic gender dichotomies will suffice as the initial point of departure. For the male, maturation may lie in the arms of an experienced, usually older woman, as in *The Mango Tree* (1977), a film echoed nearly 20 years later in *The Heartbreak Kid* (1993). In the former, the young man, played by Christopher Pate, is tutored by his grandmother even while he is sexually initiated by his French teacher. However, other films can overlay this kind of narrative of maturation with another one of physical and public maturation through **action and adventure**. Hence, in ***The Man from Snowy River*** (1982), the boy finds his manhood in the saddle among the other riders and this is coupled with the plot of romance. There is obviously a strong homoerotic element at work in these films and this is made explicit in others, especially those involving war. The pattern is especially evident in ***Gallipoli*** (1981), a war film set in Turkey during World War I. The film concerns two youths who join up for military service and finally fall under the slaughterous gunfire of the Turks. As though to mark their difference in class and maturation, one is dark-haired and experienced in the ways of the world while the other is blond and more naive. However, to deflect attention from the fact that this is a love story between two men, there is an obligatory visit to a brothel in Egypt on the way to battle. Moreover, in battle, the more experienced one survives while the more heroic and naive one is killed. In turn, too, some of these elements of "Boys Own Adventure" are repeated in *The Lighthorsemen* (1987) where heroism is again measured by the young male protagonist's ability to stay in the saddle.

On the other side of the ledger are films concerning the maturation of young **women**. Here **Peter Weir**'s ***Picnic at Hanging Rock*** (1975) is a seminal work concerning a narrative of female maturation with a deliberate interpretative invitation to the viewer. On a hot summer's day, a handful of teenage schoolgirls disappear while on a picnic. The film refuses to resolve this puzzle and ambiguously allows it to be linked to the maturation of the girls. Two other notable features in this general cycle are *The Getting of Wisdom* (1977) and ***My Brilliant Career*** (1979). However, in these, the young woman protagonist seeks emancipation from inscription in a patriarchal order rather than in the cinematic excesses of Romanticism.

With the period film cycle petering out in the early 1980s, one would have thought that this might have spelled the end of this theme as an object of continued interest for Australian filmmakers. That has not proved to be the case. Instead, perhaps reflecting the ongoing conflation both of "youth" as a continuing desirable demographic in the cinema as well as in **television** and also because new feature directors and writers are usually young themselves, maturation and rites of passage continue as main themes. Hence, for example, in the wake of the period film, several more contemporary films in a social realist **genre** such as *Freedom* (1983), *The FJ Holden* (1977), and *Fast Talking* (1984) reaffirmed a continuing interest in youth, especially young men, cars, the road, and working-class male culture. Equally, *Puberty Blues* (1981) also signaled that many of these same elements could be reconfigured around young women and their coming of age. While the young girls finally find mature company with each other rather than with males, so the heroine of *Muriel's Wedding* (1994) comes to leave behind her fantasies about heterosexual coupling in favor of the joys and securities of female friendship.

A common narrative in maturation films generates from the activities and attitudes of the adolescent of immigrant background. Waves of predominantly European immigrants after World War II influenced Australian society, adapting to and changing life in Australia. Although the generation gap cleaved Australian children from their parents, for immigrant families adapting to Australia as well as dealing with their Australianized offspring, the disjuncture was sometimes greater. *Moving Out* (1983) works through the trials and tribulations of an Italian-born migrant family, where the parents cling desperately to their old ways in the face of rapidly changing teenage expectations (*see also* ETHNIC REPRESENTATION).

Other films include *Careful, He Might Hear You* (1983), which explores the custody battle waged by two aunts, through the eyes of the orphaned boy. The film won eight **Australian Film Institute** awards. Less successful was *The Year My Voice Broke* (1987), a tale of teenage pregnancy and its consequences. *Flirting* (1991) tells the story of a boy's affair with an African girl, brought together by the proximity of their boarding schools, while others attempt to thwart their love.

In summary, coming-of-age films have been a major element in the visual and narrative repertoire of Australian feature film in the period of the revival and show every sign of continuing in this position into the future.

MCDONALD, GARY (1948–). McDonald's first, most widely known character in Australian **television** was the spectacular and bizarre Norman Gunston, but he has appeared in many films since that time. He is one of the most successful character actors in the Australian film industry, appearing in some 15 films since 1973, and at least as many television series, as well as film released to video. He graduated from the National Institute of Dramatic Art in 1967, appeared as the mechanic in the cult film *Stone* (1974), then in *Picnic at Hanging Rock* (1975), *The Picture Show Man* (1977), *Pirate Movie* (1982), *Ginger Meggs* (1982), and *Molly* (1983). He played the lead role of Robert O'Hara Burke in the unsuccessful *Wills and Burke* (1985), and the director of a workshop for intellectually impaired people in *Struck by Lightning* (1990). Supporting roles in *Those Dear Departed* (1987), *Place at the Coast* (1987), and *Mr. Accident* (2000) led to strong supporting roles, first as the Doctor in *Moulin Rouge!* (2001), and then as Mr. Neal in *Rabbit-Proof Fence* (2002).

MCKERN, LEO (1920–2002). Leo McKern was born in Sydney and moved to the United Kingdom after serving in World War II. He became involved in the theater, spending three years with the Old Vic and two years with the Royal Shakespeare Company. Later, he moved into film and **television** as well, making over 60 films in a fruitful and long career, paralleling that of **Peter Finch**. He appeared in such films as *Help!* (1965) and *The French Lieutenant's Woman* (1981). He is probably most well-known for his portrayal of the denizen of the Bailey and Pommeroy's Wine Bar and terror of many a judge in the long-running series, *Rumpole of the Bailey*. His dislike of flying prevented him returning to Australia often, but McKern played the lead in two significant films. First, he played the irritable and selfish Frank in *Travelling North* (1987), a story adapted from a **David Williamson** play about a couple who find a satisfying relationship in their later years as they head to warmer climes geographically. For this role, he won an **Australian Film Institute** award for best actor in a lead role. Second, in the remake of the Steele Rudd story, *Dad and Dave: On Our Selection* (1995), he played Dad, the somewhat slow-witted and comic, but essentially fair-minded and lovable father of the bush family. He played a smaller role as Bishop Maigret in Paul Cox's *Molokai: The Story of Father Damien* (1999), along with Australian **David Wenham**. He was appointed an Officer of the Order of Australia in 1983 in recognition of his contribution to the performing arts. McKern died in 2002 after a long illness.

MIKE AND STEFANI **(1952).** Easily the most accomplished in filmic and human terms of early **documentaries** produced by the Australian National Film Board, *Mike and Stefani* was a dramatized feature-length film. The film tells of the wartime and postwar displaced people of **Europe** and in particular of the Ukrainian couple, Mike (Mycola) and Stefani. It was directed by Ronald Maslyn Williams and photographed by Reg Pearce in Europe in 1948–1949. Williams had journeyed there to make a film about the work of the International Refugee Organization. At one camp at Leipheim in Germany, he met Mike and Stefani who were about to be interviewed by an Australian immigration officer. Williams filmed this encounter and, while they waited to hear whether they had been accepted for immigration to Australia, reconstructed on film the details of their life from the late 1930s, often with thousands of other refugees acting as extras in crowd scenes. He had little in the way of film equipment, in fact only what he and Pearce could carry between them: a 35mm camera, a half-dozen or so lights, and a wire recorder. Williams was away for over a year. On his return, the footage was edited, dialogue was post-synched, commentary overlaid; a musical soundtrack of voice and orchestra added; titles inserted.

The film has been aptly described as neorealist. Loose and episodic in structure without the tight cause-effect chain of classical narratives, the ending is open ended: the two are on their way to Australia but have been warned that, because of the shortage of housing, they may have to separate again and Stefani's brother has not come with them. The narrative chain is also loose because the characters are caught up in large public historical events beyond their control. Additionally, *Mike and Stefani* has much of the same mise-en-scene and iconography of neorealism with the characters appearing as ordinary people, much location shooting and the film depicting a set of contemporary events. Finally, voice-over narration by an omniscient unidentified commentator constantly works to link the story of Mike and Stefani into the larger arena of public, historical events.

Two other elements in the film also warrant attention. The first of these is a sparer, more poetic, observational style that generally runs across the surface of the film, thereby connecting it both with a handful of other Australian documentary films of the period, a comparable impulse to be found in some of the contemporary films of the Canadian National Film Board and even the films of Robert Flaherty. The second element in the film anticipates later developments in the documentary film generally. The sequence in question is the interview of Mike and Stefani by an Australian immigration official in the long climactic segment, filmed and sound recorded as it happened, anticipating by 20 years the impulse toward cinema vérité. The fact that the film was a documentary carried its own label of truth. Certainly Australian government officials saw the segment with the tight, relentless questioning by the formal, unsmiling official as unfavorable. The film was not given wide distribution. Nevertheless, despite this official neglect at the time, the greatness of the film has become clearer with the passing of years. Fittingly, in 2002, the National Film and Sound Archive unveiled a newly restored print.

MILLER, DR. GEORGE (1945–). Sharing the same name as another director who graduated through the Crawford TV police dramas and won universal acclaim with *The Man from Snowy River* (1982), this figure is often referred to as Dr. George Miller. Born in western Queensland in 1945, he graduated as a medical doctor and practiced in Sydney for 18 months. Films were his first love though, and he began his craft as first assistant director in *In Search of Anna* (1978). On a weekend filmmaking course, he met **Byron Kennedy** from Melbourne and the two decided to become partners to pursue a mutual love of filmmaking. With the recent controversy over brutality in films, such as *Clockwork Orange* (1971) and *Straw Dogs* (1971), still fresh, their first film, a 1972 short called *Violence in the Cinema, Part 1* was memorable for such juxtapositions as a critic reading a sanctimonious tome against violence in the cinema even as an assassin was chopping off bits of his head with an axe. This was a forecast of things to come. Securing financial backing outside state agencies, Miller and Kennedy as director, producer, and joint writer made *Mad Max* (1979), a film that rewrote the rules about Australian feature film. For here was an **action/adventure** film set in a futuristic society but was nonetheless recognizably **Hollywood**. Telling a classic story of revenge that was more usually associated with a **genre** such as the Western, *Mad Max* featured a lawman who turns his back on the law when road gangs who have swapped horses for bikes and cars destroy his wife and child. The state film agencies were aghast at the film with critic Phillip Adams (Miller and Kennedy had used an actual newspaper diatribe of his as the tome in *Violence*) recklessly and foolishly asserting that the film had the moral uplift of *Mein Kampf*.

However, the public loved the film, as did overseas distributors in Japan and the United States. After a trip to Hollywood, Miller and Kennedy were ready to follow the adventures of the former lawman again using actor **Mel Gibson** in the central role. The result was *Mad Max 2: The Road Warrior* (1981), a stunning opus in pure cinema that demonstrated the mastery of film form and style that Miller and Kennedy could attain once they had commensurate budgets. Set in the desertlike landscapes around Broken Hill in New South Wales, the film swapped the revenge tale for that of the beleaguered fort so beloved not only of Westerns but also of war, foreign legion, and other adventure films. *Mad Max 2* was an enormous hit internationally and allowed Gibson to start his career in Hollywood as a star. Meanwhile in Italy, the film spawned a host of imitations and might even be seen behind such Hollywood efforts as *Escape from New York* (1985). Kennedy died in a helicopter crash in 1983 and Miller then turned to other production partnerships. With the shift of Australian commercial **television** into a stage that can now be recognized as one of "quality," Miller seized on an opportunity to make a miniseries about the most momentous event in recent Australian political history. The result was *The Dismissal* (1983), which Miller codirected with **Phillip Noyce**, George Ogilvie, Carl Shultz, and John Power. The miniseries told the story of the dismissal of the government of Prime Minister Gough Whitlam by the governor-general, Sir John Kerr, on 11 November 1975, a radical and still controversial episode—it boasts its own website (whitlamdismissal.com)—in Australian political history. The Kennedy Miller company had remained in place and this was a conscious effort to begin to build a company style. It certainly was successful for over the next dozen years the company would give rise to a host of both television series and feature films where the actual name of the individual director was less important than the company brand itself.

The cycle of television miniseries in these years included *Cowra Breakout* (1984), *Vietnam* (1987), and *Bangkok Hilton* (1989). Meanwhile, feature films also appeared including *The Year My Voice Broke* (1987), *Dead Calm* (1989), *Flirting* (1991), and, later, **Babe: Pig in the City** (1998). He produced this film as well, and had produced the earlier **Babe** (1995). These works, whether for television or for the cinema, were very different in tone, mise-en-scene and narrative to *The Road Warrior* and one could be forgiven for thinking that there was both a filmic internationalist as well as a nationalist inextricably linked in Miller's vision. In any case, the third part of the *Mad Max* trilogy had appeared in 1985 as *Mad Max, Beyond Thunderdome*. Co-directed by Miller and Ogilvie, the two made the unfortunate mistake of shaving about 20 minutes from the film's screen time, which had the effect of making the film a less perfect masterpiece than its two predecessors. Curiously, Miller seems not to have pursued a Hollywood career with the same commitment and energy as other Australians of his generation. In 1983, he directed an episode of the film *The Twilight Zone* for Stephen Spielberg; in 1987, he made *The Witches of Eastwick*; and in 1992, *Lorenzo's Oil*. Instead, he has given a good deal of time to producing for Kennedy Miller in Australia. Indeed, still apparently calling Australia home, he wrote, produced, and directed his personal overview of Australian cinema, *40,000 Years of Dreaming*, in 1996 as part of the international recognition of the centenary of cinema.

MILLER, GEORGE (1943–). Remarkably and confusingly in a relatively small film industry, two directors with the same name and the same spelling came to public attention at roughly the same time. They can be separately identified by the fact that the other is slightly older and first trained as a medical doctor (*see* MILLER, DR. GEORGE). Born in 1943, this George Miller left Scotland as a child and grew up in Melbourne. He worked at Crawford Productions and soon began directing **television** series such as *Homicide* (1964), *Di-*

vision 4 (1969), and *Matlock Police* (1971). Miller was a solid crafts-man and continued his television work with other Crawford series such as *The Sullivans* (1976), *Bluey* (1976), and *Young Ramsey* (1977). At the same time, he was also in demand as a freelancer and worked for such independently produced series as *Cash and Company* (1975) and on prestigious miniseries such as *Against the Wind* (1978), *The Last Outlaw* (1980), and *All the Rivers Run* (1984).

Meanwhile, his career was taking him in the direction of feature films. It was the immense commercial success and the more guarded critical success of his feature directorial debut, **The Man from Snowy River**, in 1982 that made this Miller known to a much wider public. But, unlike Dr. George Miller and the **Mad Max** films, this Miller was not involved in a producer capacity. Instead, he had been en-gaged for the project as a journeyman director by producer Geoff Burrows, a fellow graduate from the Crawford police series of the late 1960s and early 1970s. This success helped consolidate Miller as a feature film director, indeed his only other miniseries work was *Anzacs* (1985) and *The Far Country* (1986). He continued his work in features putting his name on such Australian films as *Cool Change* (1986), *Bushfire Moon* (1987), *Les Patterson Saves the World* (1987), *Over the Hill* (1992), and *Gross Misconduct* (1993). But Miller has also moved offshore, directing such films as *The Aviator* (1985), with Christopher and Rosanne Arquette, *The Neverending Story 2: The Next Chapter* (1991), *Andre* (1994), *Zeus and Roxanne* (1997), and *Robinson Crusoe* (1997). He has directed many television features in recent years. Altogether though, there is little to say about Miller's di-rectorial output. Clearly, *The Man from Snowy River* did much to en-hance his name as a craftsman across both the Australian and the in-ternational film industries but, equally, 20 years on, his oeuvre provides no compelling reason for any critical revaluation.

Other features include *Frozen Assets* (1992) and *Andre* (1994).

MILLIKEN, SUE (1940–). One of the most energetic and influential **women** in the Australian film industry, Sue Milliken has worked both on set in a management capacity and also at a bureaucratic level op-erating with and in various of the Australian film agencies. Born in 1940, she trained as a journalist. She learned about television conti-nuity in the Australian Broadcasting Commission and her first drama was the Fauna children's series *Skippy*. After further continuity work with Fauna, Milliken was production manager on the Disney telefeature *Born to Run* (1976). The latter's profits helped spawn the production company, Samson Films, whose first film was *Weekend of Shadows* (1978). By now, Milliken was associate producer. Her first full credits as producer were on *The Odd Angry Shot* (1979) and *Fighting Back* (1982). Meanwhile, since 1980, she has managed the Australian branch of the completion bond company, Film Finances. Other films that have involved her as producer include *The Fringe Dwellers* (1986), *Les Patterson Saves the World* (1987), *Black Robe* (1991), *Sirens* (1994), *Dating the Enemy* (1996), and *Paradise Road* (1997). Meanwhile, wearing her other bureaucratic hat, Milliken undertook major reviews of two state film bodies, the **South Australian Film Corporation** in 1988, and chaired one concerning the Western Australian film industry in 1992. In 1993, the **Australian Film Institute** presented her with the **Raymond Longford** Award, which recognizes people who have made significant contributions to the industry. That same year also saw her become chair of the **Australian Film Commission**, a position she held until 1997.

MINOGUE, KYLIE (1968–). Kylie Minogue was born on 28 May 1968, in Melbourne, Victoria. While she is best known as a singer and for her music videos, she became internationally famous for her **television** roles. Her acting career began as Charlene in the television soap *Neighbours*, a hit in the United Kingdom as well as in Australia. Her film debut was *The Delinquents* (1989), as Lola, followed by *Street Fighter* (1994), as Cammy. She starred in the Australian independent short film, *Hayride to Hell* (1995), appeared in the comedy *Biodome* (1996) and the short film *Misfit* (1996). She played herself in the Australian film *Diana and Me* (1997), about the paparazzi and Princess Diana, unfortunately released at the time of Princess Diana's death, and promptly forgotten. She appeared in the thriller *Cut* (2000), a coproduction of Australian and German companies, starred in *Sample People* (2000), and then appeared as the Green Fairy in ***Moulin Rouge!*** (2001).

MOULIN ROUGE! (2001). *Moulin Rouge!* is the third most successful film at the Australian box office, grossing $27.7 million. It is also the fifth most successful Australian film at the US box office, returning US$57.4 million in the few years since its release. Written by Craig Pierce and **Baz Luhrmann**, and directed by Luhrmann—who directed *Strictly Ballroom* (1992) and *Romeo + Juliet* (1996)—the film has a multinational cast, including Ewan McGregor, John Leguizamo, Jim Broadbent, Jacek Koman, and Australians **Nicole Kidman**, Richard Roxburgh, **Gary McDonald**, Christine Anu, Matthew Whittet, and **David Wenham**.

The star is Satine (Kidman), the star dancer and singer in the production at the famous nightclub and bar, the Moulin Rouge, and object of the affections of the financier of the musical production, the villainous Duke (Roxborough). The writer of the production, young English poet Christian (McGregor), had escaped from his home and traveled to the Parisian district of Montmartre, where he had fallen in with the bohemian crowd and was befriended by Toulouse-Lautrec (Leguizamo). He falls in love with Satine, but the Duke of Worcester threatens their joy, as his financial support for the production depends on his unconditional access to Satine. The production is woven through a set design that is as intensely rich as the imaginations can provide. The film is a **musical**, and the traditional songs weave the narrative in this Goyaesque world of fancy.

Moulin Rouge! was nominated for and won many awards, making it one of the most critically acclaimed Australian films. It won two Academy Awards for best art direction and best costume design, and was nominated in six other categories, including best picture and best actress in a leading role. It won five **Australian Film Institute** (AFI) awards for best editing, best cinematography, best sound, best costume design, best production design, and was nominated in five other categories. The film won three Golden Globes, including best picture—musical or comedy. The British Academy of Film and Television Arts (BAFTA) conferred three awards on the film (best sound, best performance by an actor in a supporting role, and film music). In addition, *Moulin Rouge!* won awards from the American Film Industry, the American Latino Media Arts (ALMA) awards for positive portrayals of Hispanics in the media, the American Society of Composers, Authors and Publishers (ASCAP), the United States Academy of Science Fiction, Fantasy and Horror Films, the Film Critics Circle of Australia, and many others.

***MURIEL'S WEDDING* (1994).** *Muriel's Wedding* is the ninth most popular film at the Australian box office, having grossed $15.8 million. It won four **Australian Film Institute** awards for sound, best lead actress, best supporting actress, and best film, and was nominated for seven other AFI awards. In addition, it won an Australian Performing Rights Association award for best film score. Some critics rated *Muriel* highly, others thought it was a poor blend of comedy and tragedy about a woman who was an empty-headed loser, albeit among many others. Muriel (**Toni Collette**) is shunned by her own dysfunctional family, as well as by her dysfunctional friends, partly because she has no redeeming features. Instead, she likes to listen to Abba songs and to daydream. Moving from Porpoise Spit to the big city, that is in this case Sydney, she meets Rhonda (**Rachel Griffiths**) who proceeds to help her become, if not liberated, then a little more than she was. She marries, not because she loves the man, but because a big wedding is her dream.

MUSICALS. The musical is included here in the same **genre** as **comedy**, being tied to it as a kind of light entertainment, often involving romance. There are few examples of musicals, although music has always been a significant nondiegetic element in Australian film. One reason for the lack of musicals in the Hollywood tradition is the sheer size of the financial and human resources that such productions require. Large casts and high-fidelity recording and playback facilities were expensive, and filmmakers needed to attract large audiences to such films. This scenario was not possible in Australia. Nevertheless, with changing technology making the production of music a simpler affair, some musicals were produced. If a musical is a film where the narrative is carried in the lyrics of the songs, or in some other way in the music, then only a few examples of musicals would exist, most notably the films of **Baz Luhrmann**; namely *Moulin Rouge!* (2001) and perhaps *Strictly Ballroom* (1992). However, if musicals are classified by the centrality of music in and to the narrative, then other films might be classified as narrative, such as *Star Struck* (1982), *Bootmen* (2000), and *The Adventures of Priscilla, Queen of the Desert* (1994). Certainly, *Moulin Rouge!* and *Priscilla* have reached the global audiences that justify the financial outlay.

MY BRILLIANT CAREER **(1979).** Based on the book of the same name by Miles Franklin, *My Brilliant Career* is another coming-of-age story made at the height of the **art and period genre** cycle of the **revival** (*see* MATURATION). Directed by **Gillian Armstrong**, the film is a showcase of the early work of **Judy Davis**, *****Sam Neill**, and Wendy Hughes, and it was through this film that Davis and Neill achieved international recognition. The story follows the career of Sybylla Melvyn—in the days when careers for **women** were limited—from her father's dilapidated farm, to her grandmother's home, where she meets Harry Beecham, who is both a good catch and is interested. Sybylla is anything other than willing to settle down to such an existence, and her strong will points her in the direction of her chosen career, writing.

My Brilliant Career won critical acclaim around the world, and established Armstrong as a director of high stature. She was nominated for a Golden Palm at Cannes in 1979. At the **Australian Film Institute** (AFI) awards in the same year, the film was nominated in five categories and won six awards, including best film, best director, best adapted screenplay and best achievement in cinematography. Judy Davis won two 1981 British Academy for Film and Television Arts (BAFTA) awards, for best actress and best newcomer, and the film was nominated for a Golden Globe for best foreign film in the same year. In addition, the film was nominated for an Oscar for best costume design, and Don McAlpine won the cinematographer of the year award from the Australian Cinematographers Society.

– N –

NATIONAL IDENTITY. The idea of a national identity is as problematic as the idea of a nation. A nation is a changing semiosphere of influences and emerging tendencies, rather than a permanent, fixed entity waiting to be discovered, analyzed, and classified. National identity is a question, not an answer, depending on the context in which the question is asked and the contemporary cultures that, in a sense, only become real when certain elements in the semiosphere are identified, and concretized.

In Australia, a separate national identity became an issue over a period of time, when the notion of "an Australian" became important because what had gone before was no longer adequate. Through changes in global politics and economics, Australia in the late 1960s and 1970s was forced to question its position in the world, possibly because of changes forced on the nation through its involvement in Vietnam, but also because of the changes in market structures that occurred in Europe and effectively closed the European market to Australian primary products. The nation had to develop new markets in the booming Japanese economy, as well as in other Southeast Asian nations. For whatever reason though, conscious affirmations of Australian identity appeared on theater screens, as a direct consequence of the newly state-supported film industry in the 1970s (*see* REVIVAL). In retrospect, any kind of uniform national identity was problematic and always open to question and revision. Australian national identity first seemed to be masculine, coarse, vulgar, and anti-intellectual (*see* OCKER FILMS). Missing in this cycle were representations of **women** as the focus or driver of the narrative. This was rectified in some films of the subsequent cycle, where filmmakers focused on women in films like *Picnic at Hanging Rock* (1975), but those representations were hardly iconic (*see* ART AND PERIOD FILMS). Outside that **genre**, the peculiarities of growing up for some teenage girls in a certain Australian culture was the subject of **Bruce Beresford**'s *Puberty Blues* (1981). Also outside both these genres was the forerunner to *Mad Max* (1979), *Stone* (1974), where the national identity propounded by the ocker films was seriously questioned, replacing it with a considered and defiant outlaw who was alienated from mainstream society. Max Rockatansky is also alienated in a world that is Australian, but which could just as easily have been the American Midwest. Thus the notion of Australian identity becomes blurred with global, Western-culture identities.

Certainly, since *Mad Max*, many films have focused on unique Australian situations created by unique Australian characters. *Muriel's Wedding* (1994), *Mullet* (2001), *The Sum of Us* (1994), and *Strictly Ballroom* (1992) are populated by characters who are recognizably Australian, but who do not define what it is to be Australian. Thus, any description of national identity is now a plurality of possibilities, a panoply of potentialities, rather than a distinct type imbued with specific qualities. Characters are more obviously human (or not), even when they are also Australian. Only in such a world is it possible to have *The Adventures of Priscilla* (1994), with three strange Australians traveling among other strange Australians.

Defining a national identity is no longer a necessity for a film. If there is such a thing, it is only as a consequence of particular behaviors and attitudes that characters may have, and that may be different from those of other characters in other films. The spectrum of the Australian identity comprises characters as diverse as The Tracker (**David Gulpilil**), Crocodile Dundee (**Paul Hogan**), Tick/Mitzi (**Hugo Weaving**), Muriel Heslop (**Toni Collette**), and Cin (**Susie Porter**). The humanity of different Australian individuals rather than their conformity in their difference from non-Australians is now significant.

NEILL, SAM. *See entry in New Zealand section.*

NEWSFRONT (1978). *Newsfront* is one of the most original films to come out of the **revival**. The story of the life of newsreel cameraman Len Maguire, interwoven with those of his wife, lover, and colleague, is contextualized within actual news footage taken at the time; that is, the late 1940s and early 1950s. Real-life footage of events like the coming of international competition in newsreel production, the election of the Liberal-Country Party coalition after years of Labor Party rule, and the subsequent controversy over the Communist Party are seamlessly woven into the fiction of Maguire's life, not just as a backdrop to it, but as cause for various episodes. The round-Australia Redex trial is the episode leading to the marriage of his sound technician; the Maitland floods then take the life of this technician, and so on. In Len's personal life, events are similarly powerful, with his wife distancing herself from him over his questioning of elements of Catholic practice, as well as the fact that his job keeps him away from home at times. He later takes up with Amy MacKenzie, ex-partner of his brother, Frank, who has gone to the United States for bigger things in the media industry. She takes up with Frank when he returns to offer Len a job on a series that would be shot in Australia, in part, with an American lead.

Phillip Noyce wrote the script from a screenplay by Bob Ellis—who disowned Noyce's version and later reclaimed it—and then directed the film. Funding came from the **Australian Film Commission**, the New South Wales Film Corporation (*see* NEW SOUTH

WALES FILM AND TELEVISION OFFICE) and **Village Road-show**. The cast included people who were to have a lasting impact on the industry: **Bill Hunter** as Len Maguire, Wendy Hughes as Amy MacKenzie, Gerard Kennedy as Len's brother Frank, Angela Punch-McGregor as Fay, **Bruce Spence** as a Redex trial driver, and **John Flaus** as Father Coughlan. *Newsfront* reached audiences in Italy and the United Kingdom through its release at Cannes. It was nominated for all 15 categories at the 1978 **Australian Film Institute** (AFI) awards, and won eight including best film (David Elfick), best director, best original screenplay, and best lead actor (Bill Hunter). Doubtless the film will remain a classic in Australian film **history**, as well as the film that established the reputation of Noyce as a director of international stature.

NEW SOUTH WALES FILM AND TELEVISION OFFICE (NSWFTO). The New South Wales Film and Television Office is a state-funded statutory organization established under the *New South Wales Film and Television Office Act 1988*, whose aim is to foster and facilitate excellence and growth in the film and **television** industry in New South Wales. A board, comprising six representatives of the film and television industry with a nonindustry chairman, directs and oversees the activities of the office. Since 1997, Jane Smith has been chief executive and Shane Simpson was appointed chairman in 2000. The NSWFTO grew out of the New South Wales Film Corporation, originally established in 1977 in the eight years where most states established similar organizations. Its brief was to develop feature films as well as **documentaries** about the government and its departments. The Corporation was disbanded in 1988, with a significant deficit. Although the NSWFTO did not have a mandate to invest in production, in 1992, the government allocated $1,000,000 for strategic investments in production and similar allocations have continued because of the financial success of these investments. The NSWFTO now supports the production of features, documentaries, television series, and animations, and advertises the benefits of the state to overseas organizations that might be interested in film production in New South Wales. Support for the industry is similar to that provided by parallel organizations in other states; namely, for script development, production investment, skill enhancement, advice on government policy changes, and expert advice on locations and other aspects of the industry. The office promotes the films it has supported at overseas festivals, especially in China, which it sees as an important market for Australian films.

Recent films supported by the NSWFTO have won critical acclaim. **David Caesar**'s *Mullet* (2001) won the award for best director at the 2002 Shanghai International Film Festival and other awards from Australian organizations. Ray Lawrence's *Lantana* (2001) won seven **Australian Film Institute** awards, including best film and best direction. New Director Ivan Sen's *Beneath Clouds* (2002) won the premier first movie award at the Berlin International Film Festival. Other films include Mark Joffe's *The Man Who Sued God* (2001), Tony Ayres' *Walking on Water* (2002), and **Robert Connolly**'s *The Bank* (2001).

NEWTON-JOHN, OLIVIA (1948–). Whether Olivia Newton-John is actually Australian is arguable, but as she now lives in Australia, as she did when she was young, then she deserves an entry here, even though she has been more of a music star than a film star. She was born in the United Kingdom, but her family moved to Australia in 1953 when she was five and she attended High School in Melbourne. In 1971, she moved to the United States, where she became a leading singer in popular and country music. Her first screen appearance was in Australia, in the lead role in the little-known 65-minute, Joe McCormick-directed *Funny Things Happen Down Under* (1965). In the science-fiction thriller *Tomorrow* (1970), she played the lead role in this US-made film. The role that cemented her career was as Sandy Olsson, playing opposite John Travolta, in the smash-hit **musical** *Grease* (1978), and she followed with the lead in the fantasy musical *Xanadu* (1980). In the early 1990s, Newton-John began a long fight with breast cancer. In 1994, she moved back to Australia and settled on the north coast of New South Wales.

Other films are *Two of a Kind* (1983), *She's Having a Baby* (1988), *It's My Party* (1996), and *Sordid Lives* (2000). She has appeared in nine **television** films and series.

NGOOMBUJARRA, DAVID (1967–). Although not as well known as **David Gulpilil**, David Ngoombujarra is a significant and acclaimed **Aboriginal** actor. A member of the Ngaia Wanga tribe from

Meekatharra in Western Australia, he first appeared in a major role as Davie in *Breaking Loose* (1988). He played a small role in *Young Frankenstein* (1988), before his award-winning role in James Ricketson's *Blackfellas* (also *Day of the Dog*) (1992). He played Pretty-Boy Floyd, a petty criminal who seduces his newly released friend Doug into joining him in crimes of increasing violence and severity. Doug is also in love with Polly, who enjoys shoplifting. The story revolves around Doug's attempts to balance the various claims on his existence, and the final denouement brings some sort of resolution when Floyd sacrifices himself so that Polly and Doug might have some chance of working it out. For this role, Ngoombujarra won the **Australian Film Institute** award as well as the Film Critic's Circle of Australia award for best supporting actor in 1993. The film won the Human Rights and Equal Opportunity Commission Award for a feature film in the same year. A small role in the thriller *The Missing* (1998) followed, and since then, his career as a support actor has blossomed. He played a small part as David in *Crocodile Dundee in Los Angeles* (2001), another as Joseph in the beautifully composed *Serenades* (2001), appearing with David Gulpilil. He was the kangaroo hunter in **Phillip Noyce**'s *Rabbit-Proof Fence* (2002). He again came into the limelight for his role in *Black and White* (2002), where his character, Max Stuart, is sentenced to hang for the brutal rape and murder of a nine-year-old white girl based on a dubious confession. The film is based on the facts of an event that happened in South Australia over 50 years ago. The film was critically acclaimed, but shunned at the box office. However, in 2003 he won his second AFI award for best supporting actor for this film. Since then, he has played Mr. Jimmy in the comedy *Kangaroo Jack* (2003) and a tribesman in the latest *Ned Kelly* (2003).

NOYCE, PHILLIP (1950–). Always a man of cinema, Phillip Noyce's career has shown a remarkable trajectory moving from underground avant-garde, scratching and marking found footage to successfully scaling the heights of **Hollywood** and generating key relationships with such box office draws as Harrison Ford. However, Noyce has by no means turned his back on Australia and has continued to nurse significant personal projects as well as attending to more mainstream commercial fare. He had already begun to make films while a university student, and between 1970 and 1972, was manager of the Sydney Filmmakers' Cooperative and still found time to make a series of short films. These won him a place in the 1973 interim scheme of the newly constituted **Australian Film and Television School**. Over the next five years, his projects gradually became more ambitious, including his **documentary** of the Nimbin Aquarius Festival *Good Afternoon* (1974). In 1977, Noyce directed his first feature-length film *Backroads*, which followed a white and a black man on the run from the law. However, it was his next feature *Newsfront* (1978), a critical and popular success, which threw his career into top gear. *Heatwave* (1982) dealt with the murder and disappearance of environmental journalist Juanita Nelson and it, too, was well received. Altogether, these form a trilogy that establishes Noyce as a trenchant critic of aspects of Australian society while uniting this social concern with a fine feeling for innovation in film form and style.

Noyce's career then took a brief detour when he was lured to **television**, working as director on two miniseries produced by **Kennedy Miller**. These consisted of an episode of *The Dismissal* (1983) and *Cowra Breakout* (1985). He returned to features with an intercultural love story *Echoes of Paradise* (1987). However, the production was an unhappy one with the producer being replaced during the film's making. Nor did it fare any better either at the box office or with critics. Beginning with his next feature, *Dead Calm* (1988), Noyce shifted to more commercially oriented films and a more conventional film style. The film was an elegant narrative of suspense and its small cast included *Sam Neill and Nicole Kidman as a husband and wife threatened by a stranger aboard their yacht. The film's critical and commercial success provided the chance for the director to move to Hollywood. There, Noyce's two films with Harrison Ford—based on the best selling novels by Tom Clancy—*Patriot Games* (1992) and *Clear and Present Danger* (1994) have made him a permanent element of the American industry, where his directorial credits include *Sliver* (1993), *The Saint* (1997), *The Repair Shop* (1998), *The Bone Collector* (1999), and *The Quiet American* (2002).

However, he continues to nurture more personal, Australian projects. Hence, like several others of his generation and before who have established solid directorial careers in Hollywood but have continued to occasionally return to Australia for particular projects, Noyce was back for the compelling drama of the Aboriginal "stolen generation" in *Rabbit-Proof Fence* (2002). *See also* ABORIGINES IN FILM.

– O –

OCKER FILMS. The renaissance in Australian filmmaking involved two quite distinct types of film: the ocker film of the first half of the 1970s and the **art or period** film in the second half of the decade (*see* REVIVAL). Both film styles are unique to the Australian industry. The ocker film cycle began with the semidocumentary *The Naked Bunyip* (1970), followed by *Stork* (1971), *Adventures of Barry McKenzie* (1972), *Alvin Purple* (1973), *Number 96* (1974), *The True Story of Eskimo Nell* (also *Dick Down Under*) (1974), *Petersen* (1974), and *Don's Party* (1976).

The ocker films are quite distinct from the art and period films that followed them, but they are a loose cycle where each film contains a number of characteristics that collectively indicate the style. The films fall in the **genre** of **comedy**. They are set in urban locations, and the characters are motivated not by some psychological cause that the audience is made privy to; rather, the characters act and react in ways that both define and are defined by a particular representation of a social type. That is, the ocker character is comic because, in the nature of comedy, he—never she—stretches situations, language, and cultural mores to some point removed from the normal. Nevertheless, such extrapolation is comic because it is rooted in the real.

The films celebrate the nuances of a particular Australian way of life: working-class (as manifested in Australia) attitudes and contempt for authority, hedonistic beliefs and practices, a culture of beer-drinking (preferably to excess), and a particular form of **masculinity**, which includes loud behavior, a love of watching **sport**, a lack of serious consideration of any issue, and so on. All was excess, "over the top," and confrontational toward those outside the particular culture. Intimately associated with this is the "sending up" of situations and people, just as the character himself is a send-up of all the characteristics of the male. Thus, for example, antipretence is signified by sending up those who are pretentious.

While it might seem that these films released some new element in the Australian character that made them popular, this would deny the presence of similar ocker representations in other media, such as on the TV comedy revue *The Mavis Bramston Show* (1965–1968) and *Aunty Jack* (1971). The popularity of the book and the film *They're a Weird Mob* (1966) was an earlier manifestation of this cultural thread, and on the stage—generally a context averse to such characterizations—plays like *The Legend of King O'Malley* (1970) and *Stork* were popular. It was a time of change, and while grand narratives are rightly suspect, in this case, a certain sense of "throwing off," of discarding old-fashioned and constricting elements of a way of life—a liberation from the conformity of the 1950s—was apparent in cultural products.

That this shedding of certain cultural baggage was popular is shown firstly by the existence of such cultural products, and secondly by their popularity. One reason so many ocker films were made in a short time was that audiences loved them, and they proved that Australian films could return a profit at the box office. Thus they met the criteria of commercial success required by the funding bureaucracies as well as that of exploring the national character, one aspect of it, at least. The new federal funding bureaucracies, the **Australian Film Development Corporation** and the Experimental Film Fund, supported low budget productions that were unashamedly commercial, in an attempt to kick-start the industry.

By the mid-1970s, the ocker films had become a national embarrassment, simply because they not only sent up and parodied certain attitudes and behaviors, but because they lauded and modeled these attitudes and behaviors. Thus, what was once funny caused a new kind of cringe. It was almost as if a golem had been created as a kind of parody, but as that golem assumed a reality, or was perceived as being a reality, then it was no longer welcome. In the absence of other representations of people—representations that were more diverse, for example—then this golem was no longer welcome. As a result of the brouhaha, critics and politicians demanded films that were more artistic, more aesthetic, more uplifting, and of greater sensitivity and sensibility, if they were to be assisted by taxpayer funds. The ocker style died almost overnight. Shadows still remain, however. *Crocodile Dundee* (1986) has traces of the ocker in the character of Mick Dundee and his friends, and traces exist in a less positive way in *Muriel's Wedding* (1994).

OUTBACK. *See* COUNTRY.

– P –

PACIFIC FILM AND TELEVISION COMMISSION (PFTC). The PFTC develops and supports the Queensland film industry, through initiatives that are comparable with those of similar institutions in other states. The commission aims to provide proactive initiatives for writers, producers, and directors, and to support a screen culture in Queensland by financially supporting the Brisbane International Film Festival and by attracting production to Queensland. In the area of development and production, the PFTC aims to increase production opportunities for new and emerging filmmakers; assist filmmakers in enhancing their creative, technical, and business skills so as to further their professional careers; and offer ongoing financial support to experienced filmmakers capable of production. As one would expect from a state-funded body, the PFTC aims to attract interstate and international productions; actively promote the key benefits of basing film production in Queensland and offer a specialist locations service. Finally, the PFTC works to develop screen culture and the exploration of cultural and aesthetic issues by showcasing the best in contemporary world cinema throughout the state, and by offering financial assistance to provide new opportunities for Queensland filmmakers.

The Queensland Government formed the PFTC in 1991 to attract international production to the Gold Coast region of Queensland, in cooperation with **Warner Brothers Movie World Studios**. At the same time, the government created Film Queensland, a funding body for Queensland film projects and, in 1992, Film Events Queensland staged the first Brisbane International Film Festival. In 1997, the operations of Film Queensland and Film Events Queensland were subsumed into the PFTC.

International and Australian films supported by PFTC include *The Phantom* (1996), *Paperback Hero* (1998), *Crocodile Dundee in Los Angeles* (2001), *Scooby-Doo* (2002), *Swimming Upstream* (2003) and the **television** features *South Pacific* (2001) and *Inspector Gadget 2* (2003).

PEARCE, GUY (1967–). Guy Pearce has made a successful transition from the Australian industry to become an international figure. Like many Australian actors, he was born elsewhere: in the United Kingdom, with a New Zealand father and an English mother. The family immigrated to Australia when he was three years old, settling in Geelong, Victoria. Pearce became well known through the long-running **television** soap opera *Neighbours*, playing Mick Young from 1986 to 1990. He debuted on the big screen as Water's rock musician son in *Heaven Tonight* (1990), then played opposite John Savage in the psychological thriller *Hunting* (1991) before gaining international recognition as Adam, the unpleasant but energetic drag queen in ***The Adventures of Priscilla, Queen of the Desert*** (1994). Pearce played the Tasmanian actor **Errol Flynn** in *Flynn* (1996), and in the same year exchanged bodies with **Claudia Karvan** in *Dating the Enemy*. Moving to **Hollywood**, he won acclaim for his characterization of the bitter and ambitious Los Angeles cop Ed Exley—playing opposite **Russell Crowe** and Kevin Spacey—in Curtis Hanson's *L.A. Confidential* (1997). Pearce has taken on and succeeded in a variety of challenging roles, characterized by diversity and intensity. In the thriller *Ravenous* (1999), he was one of the soldiers pursued by a cannibal; in *Memento* (2000), he played the brain-damaged Leonard Shelby; and back in Australia, he played Dale Twentyman, one of three criminal brothers in *The Hard Word* (2002). Grief and a feeling of loss pervade his Australian character, Dr. Sam Franks, in the poorly scripted *Till Human Voices Wake Us* (2002).

Other films include *The Count of Monte Christo* (2002), *The Time Machine* (2002), *Rules of Engagement* (2000) with Tommy Lee Jones and Samuel L. Jackson, *A Slipping Down Life* (1998), *Woundings* (1998), and *Friday on My Mind* (1990). Pearce appears regularly on the stage in Australia, where he lives.

PERIOD FILMS. *See* ART AND PERIOD FILMS.

***PIANO, THE* (1993).** *See entry in New Zealand section.*

***PICNIC AT HANGING ROCK* (1975).** **Peter Weir**'s *Picnic at Hanging Rock* was the first in the **art and period** film **genre** that resulted from the desire of the film industry bureaucracy, such as the **Australian Film Commission**, to support films that had "high" cultural standards—which meant the standards of art or European films—in the Australian industry in the mid 1970s. In the early years of the **revival, ocker** films, which were generally vulgar and painted a sexist view of Australian society, were popular with audiences and therefore with filmmakers, as well as the bureaucracy, because they were profitable. However, *Picnic* heralded a new genre, which had an aesthetic quality that the film bureaucracy now favored, without commercial imperatives.

The source for *Picnic* was a Joan Lindsay novel, where a party of schoolgirls from an upper-middle class private school in 1900 picnic at Hanging Rock, and then disappear. In a European tradition, the resolution is nonexistent, nor is the audience made privy to an understanding of events through some revelations about the psychology of the individuals concerned. That is, there is no dynamic of cause and effect established within the actions of the characters and the movement of the narrative. At the same time, there is no "authentic" interpretation of the film. On the one hand, the film tells about the culture of an age-old land, and the mysteries that lie dormant there. On the other is the unarticulated sexuality and mystery surrounding a group of schoolgirls who attend an institution of rational Western culture, signified by a two-story, stone building apparently stuck in an alien landscape, and by the layers of restrictive clothing worn by the girls.

However the film is interpreted, *Picnic* remains a significant film in the **history** of the Australian industry, and one that was copied often in the next few years.

PORTER, SUSIE. Susie Porter was born and raised in the New South Wales city of Newcastle. She graduated from the National Institute of Dramatic Art in the mid-1990s, debuting on the big screen in **David Caesar**'s *Idiot Box* (1996) and then in the light-hearted *Mr. Reliable* (1996). Porter was quickly recognized as a versatile and promising character actor, and her work rate reflected that. She moved up to play Oggi in **Bruce Beresford**'s uneven story of a group of women imprisoned by the Japanese in Singapore during World War II, *Paradise Road* (1997). Her first real success came with the role of Deirdre in Gregor Jordan's award-winning and popular **crime** film, *Two Hands* (1999), and she followed with the lead role of Vicki in *Feeling Sexy* (1999), where she plays an artist who becomes a mother and wife, and, instead of true happiness, begins to feel that life is less than ideal. The meltdown of her marriage causes her to reassess the situation through the perspective of her artistic creativity. She followed this with the lead of Cin, playing opposite David Wenhan, in the **art film**/romantic comedy *Better Than Sex* (2000), which tells the story of two people falling in love over three days, and for which she was nominated for an **Australian Film Institute** (AFI) best leading actress award. The beauty of this film lies partly in the fact that Porter is not physically beautiful in the classic sense, yet the scenes of nudity and love-making are rich and meaningful. She is not tall, has a round face and pudgy nose, and is covered with freckles, yet is stunning in this role.

Her versatility is further evinced in her next role, that of Jill Fitzpatrick, a lesbian private detective, in the uneven crime thriller *The Monkey's Mask* (2000). Although *Bootmen* was released in the same year, it is obvious that her ability was not recognized in the same way that it was for the other two films. She played Sara, a girlfriend, in this AFI award-winning film. A leading role in Caesar's strange, but also award-winning *Mullet* (2001), followed. As Tully, she negotiates the difficult position of maintaining her marriage to the town policeman when her old lover returns to create emotional havoc throughout the community. In *Teesh and Trude* (2002), she plays Teesh, a study in frustration and alienation, and the film explores the dynamic between two hard and damaged women who exist on the edge and on the sarcasm they have for each other, and a diet of soapies. Yet the human spirit triumphs, as it sometimes does in reality.

Other films include *Welcome to Woo Woop* (1997), *Amy* (1998), *Star Wars: Episode II—Attack of the Clones* (2002), and *Sway* (2002).

PROYAS, ALEX (1963–). Born in Egypt in 1965, Proyas moved to Sydney, Australia, when he was three. After training at the **Australian Film Television and Radio School** (AFTRS), he made video clips for music, and composed the score for **Jane Campion*'s short film *A Girl's Own Story* (1984). His film career has encompassed writing, cinematography, editing, acting and composing, which has given him a complete understanding of the process of filmmaking. Three short films preceded the full-length science fiction, postapocalyptic film, *Spirits of the Air, Gremlins of the Clouds* (1989), set, like **Mad Max** (1979) in the Australian desert. After a break of some years, he directed the **Hollywood**, multigeneric film, *The Crow* (1984), before returning to Australia to write, with Lem

Dobbs and David S. Goyer, and direct the successful, dystopic, science fiction film, *Dark City* (1998), at **Fox Studios** in Sydney. After another break, he directed *Garage Days* (2002), where he again takes the audience into a weird world—this time, that of rock'n'roll.

– R –

RABBIT-PROOF FENCE (2002). After some years of success overseas, **Phillip Noyce** returned to Australia to make this award-winning film, based on a true story of the indomitable courage and spirit of three Aboriginal children. In the not too far distant past, Aboriginal children were removed from their families in a episode of Australian history called the "stolen generations." While the history is too long to be retold here, the program was either, or both of, cruel and unusual, or a rational solution to a complex problem. Thus the film is a monument to the strength of the girls involved, while it romanticizes the reality of the fencing camps, and constructs all non-Aboriginal people as essentially inhuman and driven by religious fundamentalist beliefs. Nevertheless, the reality was that three young girls, taken away from their mothers in the central part of Western Australia and removed to a home for similar children far to the south, escaped from the intolerable conditions in the home. They found the rabbit-proof fence that divides the state from north to south, and followed it the 1,500 miles back to their mothers, through a part of the state that is notoriously dry and that is still difficult for people in vehicles with all the water, food, and fuel they need. The film won the best film award from the **Australian Film Institute**, as well as best original music and best sound, and was nominated in seven other categories. *See also* ABORIGINES AND FILM.

RAFFERTY, CHIPS (1909–1971). Chips Rafferty's film career spanned a low in the **history** of filmmaking in Australia. After an early blossoming in the first 15 years of the century, rationalizations, takeovers, imported film, and the costs of new technology militated against the development of the industry. Nevertheless, some films were successful, especially those that were unashamedly Australian, and Rafferty came to epitomize the Australian character. Tall, rugged, handsome, and suntanned, he was as much at home in urban centers as he was in the bush, the outback. As a practical Australian man, he did not like theory or those who espoused it—most commonly intellectuals—or those who talked a lot. His characters were dry and laconic, easygoing, and unimpressed by authority.

His first film appearances were in *Dad Rudd, M.P.* (1940) and *Ants in His Pants* (1940), followed by a lead in **Charles Chauvel**'s story of the World War I Australian campaign in the Sinai Desert, *40,000 Horsemen* (1941), and then the same director's story of the World War II campaign in Egypt, *The Rats of Tobruk* (1944). Overseas production companies were preeminent in filmmaking in the 1950s. With *Ealing* Studios and director Harry Watt, Rafferty starred in a story about a cattle drive that occurred because of the fear of an invasion of northern Australia in *The Overlanders* (1946), and in a story of the republican movement and rebellion on Australian goldfields, *Eureka Stockade* (1949). With director Ralph Smart, Rafferty starred in two films, the United Kingdom Rank Organisation-produced *Bush Christmas* (1947), and the Ealing Studios-produced *Bitter Springs* (1950). Twentieth Century Fox produced two films in Australia, both with American actors in lead roles, but with strong supporting roles from Rafferty and **Charles Tingwell**: *Kangaroo* (1952) and *The Desert Rats* (1953).

In 1953, Rafferty formed Platypus Productions with writer and director **Lee Robinson**. The company made only one film, *The Phantom Stockman* (1953), but their second company, **Southern International**, made two films. Robinson directed the first—*King of the Coral Sea* (1953)—which starred Rafferty, supported by Tingwell and the young Rod Taylor; the second was one of the first coproductions in Australian film history, between the French Discifilm, the Italian Silver Films, and Southern International. Southern International's next film was also a French coproduction, *Walk into Paradise* (1956) and starred Rafferty, directed by Robinson and Marcello Pagliero.

In his next film, Rafferty returned to an offshore production company to play Sergeant Flaxman in *Smiley* (1956) for London Films. Twentieth Century Fox then produced the sequel, *Smiley Gets a Gun* (1959), with Rafferty in the same character. Roles in other international films, shot in Australia, followed. Warner Bros. made *The Sundowners* (1960); the United Kingdom based Williamson/Powell made *They're a Weird Mob* (1966).

During these years when the Australian industry was at a particularly low ebb, Rafferty moved overseas to play character roles in international films. He played coast watcher Patterson in the Columbia film *The Wackiest Ship in the Army* (1960), with MGM he played the fiddler in *Mutiny on the Bounty* (1962) and Archie Brown in *Double Trouble* (1967). For Universal, he played Father Dillingham in the unexciting *Skullduggery* (1970). One of the significant films leading into the Australian **revival** was *Wake in Fright* (1971). It was an Anglo-Australian coproduction, with a Canadian director, and three British actors in lead roles. However, Rafferty led the strong Australian supporting cast. This film was to be his last, as he died from a heart attack shortly after.

Other films include *The Loves of Joanna Godden* (1947), *The Flaming Sword* (1958), and *Kona Coast* (1968).

RELIGION. While Australia is now a multicultural society, it is difficult to find strong voices for a multiplicity of religious beliefs and perspectives in Australian film. Nevertheless, religion is and was an important element of Australian film. Indeed, a religious group formed the first film production company in Australia; in 1897, the Limelight Department of the Salvation Army, based in Melbourne, began shooting full-length documentaries and films describing its social and religious work. Until 1903, the department shot 80 percent of all film shot in Australia. The Army did not shoot only religious film; various Australian state governments and the New Zealand government commissioned much of its production. For example, the unit produced the official films of Australia's Federation Inauguration Ceremonies and the opening of the first Federal Parliament in 1901. Unfortunately for film production, the new Commissioner Hay, a dour Scotsman, arrived in Australia in 1909 and immediately shut down the film unit, citing a moral laxity in the film business.

Other films have represented the Army, generally sympathetically. Salvationists appear close to the end of *On the Beach* (1959), playing Onward Christian Soldiers and leading prayers under a banner stating, "There is still time, brother." The banner flaps in the breeze in the last scene of the deserted Melbourne streets. The wife of a leader of the strikers in *Strikebound* (1984) is an Army member. Sometimes characters do not match with observed reality and are not plausible, as in *The Sum of Us* (1994), where the grandmother is an Army member and a lesbian. **Rolf de Heer**'s ***Bad Boy Bubby*** (1996) has a young pretty woman from the Salvation Army seducing Bubby just hours after he escapes from his apartment-prison, but viewers are not encouraged to ask how this has occurred, just as the rest of the film's events are analogies rather than actualities. Religious motifs permeate the film's mise-en-scene: icons of Jesus on the cross hang from the apartment-prison walls; Bubby wears a white "dog collar," which he has stolen from his father, a derelict priest; an atheist, who plays the church organ, berates Bubby for his lack of belief; the instrument of his redemption is a woman called Angel. Bubby's mother is excessively religious, instilling in her son a love of Jesus and a fear of the evil world outside of the apartment.

At the time of European settlement, two churches heavily influenced Australian politics and life, the Catholic and the Anglican. (The Anglican Church is equivalent to the Episcopal Church in the United States). Therefore, it might be expected that religion would be a significant element of Australian film, but this is not really the case. As an immigrant to Australia, Nino Culotta is a "wog," not entirely accepted in 1960s Australia (*They're a Weird Mob*, 1966). He gently retaliates, pointing out to his host that the person portrayed in the portrait on the wall is also a wog, the Italian Pope at the time. The socially active priest appears in the Philippines in *Far East* (1982). Many prominent directors, stars, and writers were, and are, Catholics, and many grew up in the 1950s and 1960s when the fracturing of religious tenets was playing its part in the changing cultural web. In the semi-autobiographical ***The Devil's Playground*** (1976), **Fred Schepisi** documented some of the less pleasant practices in a Catholic boarding school, where the subjugation of the flesh, and the humiliation of the young wrongdoer and wrong-thinker was of paramount concern for a religious life. Original sin was rampant.

Filmmakers have not treated the Anglican Church quite so severely. Anglican clergy are minor characters and appear in some form of distress related to their vocation in *The Last Wave* (1977) and *Petersen* (1974). On the other hand, the narrative of two films revolves around issues of religion. In *Sirens* (1993), the Church asks a young clergyman and his wife, recently arrived from England, to visit the home of a controversial painter (based on painter Norman Lindsay) who had outraged civil society by submitting a blasphemous painting in an exhibition. The challenge for the priest was to persuade Norman to withdraw the painting. However, the strictures of religion are no match for the erotic and sensual liberation of the artistic world (with Elle McPherson as one of the liberated artist's models), and the newcomers leave with a changed experience, if not a changed religion.

Orthodox religions appear in more recent films, reflecting the changed immigrant groups after World War II. Greek Orthodox influences are present in some form in *Caddie* (1976), *Kostas* (1979), *Cathy's Child* (1979), *Mull* (1989), *Heartbreak Kid* (1993), and *Only the Brave* (1994). A Greek Orthodox wedding is the denouement in **Death in Brunswick** (1991), while a Russian Orthodox wedding features in *My First Wife* (1984).

Other religions are significant elements in some films since the **revival**. "Kev the Rev" maintains the level of sophistication in *Barry McKenzie Holds His Own* (1974) by delivering a discourse on "Christ and the Orgasm." Fred Schepisi's *A Cry in the Dark* (1988) sensitively handles the Seventh Day Adventist beliefs of Lindy and Michael Chamberlain and the part those beliefs played in the administration of justice and the perceptions of many Australians during the murder trial of the Chamberlains, when their child disappeared in central Australia. In *The Chant of Jimmy Blacksmith* (1978), Schepisi interrogates the inevitability of violent conflict in the juxtaposition of European religions and their attendant beliefs about white society, progress, sin, and salvation, with the frustration of an **Aborigine** who has, to some extent turned his back on his traditional life, and has attempted to become integrated into a religiously molded culture. The film pulls no punches in depicting the violence that such beliefs have on other human beings, and the resulting acts of violence precipitated in this dynamic. Films that focus on the interaction between Aboriginal and white cultures have to acknowledge the immense gulf separating worldviews. Although Western religion is based on notions of sin, including original sin, soul/body duality, a vengeful and/or merciful God, the defilement of the flesh, the possibility of redemption, and so on, Aboriginal culture was based on an oral tradition that bore no resemblance to Western traditions. Thus, in **Charles Chauvel's** *Jedda* (1955), we see the tragic outcome of an Aborigine caught in the grinding of the tectonic plates of juxtaposed cultures. The destruction of the integrity of Aboriginal culture is the subject of **Phillip Noyce**'s *Backroads* (1977), and his *Rabbit-Proof Fence* (2002) interrogates the resilience of that culture in the face of a Western self-righteousness.

Judaism in Australian films is notable for its absence. The comic character Mo in *Strike Me Lucky* (1934) is one of the few examples of a Jewish character, yet not of Judaism. Similarly, few filmmakers have approached Eastern religions. However, *****Jane Campion** approaches the subject of cult deprogramming in *Holy Smoke* (1998). Harvey Keitel successfully exits Kate Winslet from a cult based on Hindu philosophies and rites, but at the cost of falling in love with her.

As one of the fundamental belief structures, and therefore one of the causes of human action, religion has been a significant element in Australian film, either as the subject of the narrative, as a causal agent in the narrative, or as a foundational aspect of character.

REVIVAL. This is one of several terms that were used initially to designate the beginning or restarting of a film industry, that occurred in Australia in the early 1970s. Australia had been the site of film production, undertaken by both local and visiting producers and directors, since the last years of the 19th century (*see* HISTORY). However, by the 1960s, such an initiative had all but run out of financial steam. Hence, the Australian federal government in 1969 decided to offer support to a would-be film industry. Various individuals have lain claim to have been responsible for this government decision. In fact, though, the point was that in the long postwar era of affluence, full employment, and bulging treasury coffers, a government such as that of Australia could be persuaded by both the apparently imminent decay of **Hollywood** and the rise of the European art cinema to undertake a seeding of feature film production. Broadly, the intention was both commercial and cultural. Some films to be produced under a regime of government subsidy would be commercial thus helping to consolidate a film industry which **television** had already helped into existence. However, the intention was not necessarily to make film entrepreneurs rich at the taxpayers' expense.

Hence, some of the other films or even some of the same films should also function as cultural legitimators of state support, winning international recognition for Australia, functioning—in effect—as cultural ambassadors, embodiments of an Australian identity in the making. Two film cycles soon fulfilled these expectations. The first—the **ocker** film of the early 1970s, beginning with *The Adventures of Barry McKenzie* (1972) and *Alvin Purple* (1973)—fulfilled the commercial mandate and proved to be highly popular both at home and, more occasionally, elsewhere such as the United Kingdom. However, critics and bureaucrats were happier with the advent of the **art and period** film—beginning with *Picnic at Hanging Rock* (1975) and *Sunday Too Far Away* (1975)—which were critical successes as well as making money at the box office. The particular history and agencies of government support for feature film production since 1970 are traced in detail elsewhere. Suffice to say here that the twin circumstances of the revival have remained with the industry down to the present. Having both a commercial and a cultural mandate has been both a curse and a blessing: a curse when films do not make money or get good critical notice but a blessing because they frequently manage to do one if not both. Over and above the feature film support, other elements of the revival deserve mention. One was the argument in the founding moment of 1969 for a training school that, in due course, saw the birth of the **Australian Film Television and Radio School**. If the latter helps supply the industry with a steady stream of trained personnel, the advent of an informed film intelligentsia was equally important for purposes of audience and advocacy. Here, a groundbreaking event was the publication in 1981 of Andrew Pike and Ross Cooper's *Australian Film 1901–1978*. As part of the further cultural legitimation of the revival, this book established a definitive canon of Australian feature films stretching from the turn of the century down to the recent present. Thus, by retrospectively claiming an unbroken continuity between the past and the present, champions of Australian film legitimated the start-up as a "revival," a "renaissance," rather than a new start, a birth.

Finally, the effectiveness of these rhetorical moves is further attested by the uncertainty of the period of time that is covered by the term. Should "revival" be confined to the early 1970s and the ocker film cycle? Does it apply up to the early 1980s and the end of the art and period film cycle? Or does it continue down to the present? Given the longevity of the various institutional arrangements that were put in place in the late 1960s and the very early 1970s and ignoring the appearance and disappearance of this or that particular agency and arrangement, it seems most useful and relevant to continue to use the term revival, a practice adopted in this work.

RICHARDSON, DAMIEN. Since his graduation from the Victorian College of the Arts in 1991, Richardson has become an accomplished theater actor and writer. However, his film career has recently germinated and he has appeared in *Horseplay* (2002), *Mallboy* (1999), *Redball* (1999), and *Every Night, Every Night* (1993). He played a successful lead as the naïve and affable robber and butcher, Mal Twentyman in *The Hard Word* (2002) opposite **Guy Pearce** and **Joel Edgerton**. Other films are *A Telephone Call for Genevieve Snow* (2000) and *Blabbermouth and Stickybeak* (1998).

ROBERTS, SCOTT. Scott Roberts studied architecture at Sydney University, worked in various jobs in Asia, Africa, and Britain, and returned to Sydney in 1981. He worked on design projects in the theater, where he wrote his first film treatments. He then worked as a journalist and disc jockey in Rome for a year, before returning to London where he wrote his first screenplay, *The American Way* (1988), which starred Dennis Hopper and Michael J. Pollard. Roberts spent the next 10 years alternating between London and Los Angeles, writing screenplays and participating in all aspects of the production of music videos and film, including *K2* (1991) and *Shadow of the Cobra* (1998). He returned to live in Sydney in 1998, where he wrote and directed *The Hard Word* (2002), his feature directing debut.

ROBINSON, LEE (1923–2003). Lee Robinson is an important transitional figure between an older commercial film industry and the government-supported production sector in place since the **revival**. Born in 1923 of Mormon parents, Robinson in wartime found his way into short story and other writing and this enabled him to get a job with the newly expanded National Film Board's production arm, the Film Division, in 1946 (*see also* COMMONWEALTH FILM UNIT). Central Australia became a liberating place for him and he scripted and directed the documentaries *Namatjira the Painter* (1947)? *Outback Patrol* (1947), and *The Crocodile Hunters* (1949). Meanwhile, for the Department of Information, he also scripted and directed *The*

Pearlers (1949), filmed in Broome, Western Australia. Visiting British director Harry Watt, in Australia for a second time to shoot the feature *Eureka Stockade* (1949) in Sydney, became Robinson's mentor. Not surprisingly, Robinson now moved to follow Watt from **documentary** to features. Teaming up with well-known Australian film actor **"Chips" Rafferty**, he formed Platypus Pictures in 1952. The moment was not auspicious for developing feature films: the local industry was dormant and government had made it very difficult to raise production finance. Consequently, the two were unable to finance a **crime** thriller that Robinson had written. Instead, this script finally was made by Watt's studio **Ealing** in 1958 as *The Siege of Pinchgut*. Nevertheless, the two managed to keep going thanks to some work coming from the Film Board, most especially a splendid series of documentaries to do with different aspects of the Snowy Mountains hydroelectric scheme.

Meanwhile, the company's first feature, *The Phantom Stockman* (1953), was a perfect fulfillment of Robinson's belief that audiences would respond to material that was familiar but also different. The film was an Australian Western set in Central Australia that included an appearance of famous **Aboriginal** painter, Albert Namatjira. Its success at both the local box office and also in overseas distribution caused the duo to form a new company, **Southern International**. Its first feature was *King of the Coral Sea* whose more lavish budget allowed extensive location shooting in North Queensland in 1954. An adventure melodrama, involving illegal immigrants and a kidnapping with Rafferty as hero, the film was commercially successful. The company's next venture was *Walk into Paradise* (1956), which again followed the adventure melodrama structure and was shot in New Guinea as a coproduction. Again the film was highly successful at the box office. However, the company's luck now changed. Two subsequent coproductions, *The Stowaway* (1958) and *The Restless and the Damned* (1959), turned in indifferent performances at the box office, as did *Dust in the Sun* (1958). Although Robinson and Rafferty kept going with documentaries and the **television** *High Adventure* programs for the American television producer/compere Lowell Thomas, Southern International's days were numbered.

Surviving the early 1960s, Robinson worked on *They're a Weird Mob* (1966) as production supervisor. He then formed a partnership with Australian-born actor John MacCallum and at first the two looked to produce a television situation comedy based on *Weird Mob*. However, they were dissuaded from this and instead settled on the happy choice of a children's series for television. Based on such Hollywood forerunners as *Lassie* and *Flipper*, but achieving difference by employing an Australian mammal, a kangaroo, in the central role, the two came up with *Skippy*. Although they achieved an immediate sale to the TCN Channel 9 in Sydney, nevertheless Fauna Productions took a major financial gamble by deficit financing its production in color on film. However, the gamble succeeded enormously well with the series achieving sales in over 120 different markets, most especially the United States, where Kellogg's licensed its brand name. In succession, over the next 15 years appeared *Barrier Reef*, *Boney*, *Shannon's Mob*, and *Bailey's Bird*. The first two did very well, although the last two were less successful. In any case, Robinson was also able to continue with feature films. These included a spin-off from *Skippy*, *The Intruders* (1969), *Nickel Queen* (1971), which he directed, and *Attack Force Z* (1982) and *Southern Cross* (1982), which he produced. He also produced and wrote *Highest Honor* (1982), based on the true story of Australian and British troops staging a daring raid on Japanese-occupied Singapore Harbor during World War II. A remarkable figure in his sheer capacity to keep going in the face of adversity, Robinson's output deserves much more consideration and careful assessment than he has so far been accorded. He died after a lengthy illness in 2003.

ROMPER STOMPER (1992). Written and directed by Geoffrey Wright, *Romper Stomper* explores the world of skinheads in Melbourne. They had become concerned about the changing makeup of their neighborhood, specifically through the influx of Vietnamese people who the skinheads see as threatening the racial purity of the area. (Of course, Melbourne has never been a racially pure **city** since the gold rushes in the mid-19th century.) Later in the film, the Vietnamese take on the skinheads and beat them at their own game. The action is fast and extremely violent, with the fascist, illiterate, and unemployed skinheads led by the muscular, but disturbed, Hando (**Russell Crowe**) taking their frustrations and bitterness out on the Vietnamese in a particularly brutal fashion. Until they retaliate. The film's violence meant that it was originally banned in South Korea and Canada. Funded in part by the **Australian Film Commission** and Film Victoria, *Stomper* repaid this investment in awards. Crowe won the Film Critics Circle of Australia award for best actor, and the film was nominated for six **Australian Film Institute** awards, including best director, and won three awards, including best actor (Crowe). In terms of its subject matter, the film marks a departure for the industry—moving into similar territory as *Reservoir Dogs* (1992)—with an uncompromising approach to the underbelly of contemporary society and culture. *See also BAD BOY BUBBY.*

RONIN FILMS. Ronin Films has two operational directions. First, it was and is an independent exhibition and distribution company, with some forays into production. It was founded in 1974, and has distributed feature films made outside the United States, such as the United Kingdom, Russia, France, and Germany, but also focusing on Asia, distributing features from Thailand, Japan, China, and other Southeast Asian countries, including New Zealand. The company has supported the work of independent Australian producers and directors, through maintaining relationships with filmmakers from their first short films through to their later, internationally successful features. Ronin distributed the early work of directors *****Jane Campion**, *****Vincent Ward**, **David Caesar**, **Baz Luhrmann**, **Scott Hicks**, and Tracey Moffatt. The company provided distribution guarantees for ***Strictly Ballroom*** (1992) in Australia, New Zealand, and Japan, as well as *Waiting* (1991), *Aya* (1990), and *Holidays on the River Yarra* (1990). The company picked up ***Shine*** (1996) at the script stage, and went on to distribute that film. It also released the **comedy** *Road to Nhill* (1997). Since 1998, the company has wound back its involvement in features distribution. Second, the company has distributed **documentaries** throughout Australia, especially to the "nontheatrical" market such as educational institutions. The founder of the company, Andrew Pike, selects the documentaries according to their intrinsic quality and educational interest. The company is interested less in instructional films than in documentaries that explore issues of community interest in a creative and stimulating way. The collection as a whole represents a remarkable cross-section of Australian life in the 1980s and 1990s. In addition to its distribution work, Ronin runs an art house cinema in Canberra—the popular Electric Shadows Cinema.

RUSH, GEOFFREY (1951–). Born in Toowoomba in the state of Queensland, Geoffrey Rush earned his BA at the University of Queensland, studied acting in Paris, and joined the Queensland Theatre Company on his return to Australia. He gained wide experience in classical and modern theater, and he claimed early on that his career has actually been in theater, with "spits and coughs in bits and pieces of films." At 30 years of age, he made his first film appearance as a detective in *Hoodwink* (1981), which starred **Judy Davis**. Fifteen years passed before he played her long-suffering husband, Zachary Welch, in the vastly underrated, Peter Duncan-directed **comedy**, *Children of the Revolution* (1996). He played Dad's son, Dave, in *Dad and Dave: On Our Selection* (1996), and although he played the part of the fool Dave well, there was little audience response to the film. Offers to play roles then began to pour into his agent's office.

The outstanding role of this early period of his film career was the adult David Helfgott in Scott Hick's *Shine* (1996). Rush played the part of the obsessive-compulsive, constantly energized and chain-smoking piano-playing prodigy David Helfgott with such passion and empathy that audiences and critics alike were effusive in their praise, and people flocked to the real Helfgott's concerts with a new understanding and respect for his ability in the face of enormous challenges. Awards for Rush were many including, for best actor, a Screen Actors Guild Award, a British Academy for the Film and Television Arts (BAFTA) award, an **Australian Film Institute** (AFI) award, a Golden Globe, and an Academy Award. He narrated **Gillian Armstrong**'s *Oscar and Lucinda* (1997), based on the book of the same name by Peter Carey, before teaming up again with director Duncan in the lead role of Godfrey Usher for the uneven *A Little Bit of Soul* (1998), for which he nevertheless was nominated for a best supporting actor prize by the AFI.

By this time, he was of obvious interest to international filmmakers, and he went on to play Inspector Javert in *Les Misérables* (1998). His Shakespearean training came into play in this film, as well as the next two: as Sir Francis Walsingham, the aide of the Queen (**Cate Blanchett**) in *Elizabeth* (1998) and Philip Henslowe in *Shakespeare in Love* (1998). For the latter he was nominated for a Golden Globe award, a BAFTA award—he was nominated for a BAFTA award for *Elizabeth* as well—and another Oscar. A further outstanding performance followed as the degenerate but brilliant and irrepressible

Marquis de Sade in *Quills* (2000), for which he was again nominated for a BAFTA award, a Golden Globe, and an Oscar.

While an actor of international stature, Rush returns to Australia for various projects. He was the voice of Bunyip Bluegum in the Australian children's animation of a perennial favorite, *The Magic Pudding* (2000), then John Knox in the award-winning, but convoluted and unconvincing mystery drama, **Lantana** (2001). Another AFI nomination for best leading actor followed for the role of the father Harold Fingleton in *Swimming Upstream* (2003), where he constructs the 1950s father whose love for his children is conditional on their sporting prowess. Always a supporter of the Australian industry, he was the voice of the narrator, in Adam Elliot's animation *Harvie Krumpet* (2003), winner of the 2004 Academy Award and the 2003 AFI award for best short animation. He played Francis Hare in the most recent incarnation of the Ned Kelly story, Gregor Jordan's *Ned Kelly* (2003). In recognition of his talent and contribution to film, the AFI awarded Rush a global achievement award in 2003. He has continued to play strong roles in international productions, making his mark as one of the most versatile and talented actors across a range of **genres** to have started in Australia.

Other films are *Starstruck* (1982), *Twelfth Night* (1987), *Call Me Sal* (1996), *Mystery Men* (1999), *House on Haunted Hill* (1999), *The Tailor of Panama* (2001), *Frida* (2002), *The Banger Sisters* (2002), *Finding Nemo* (2003), *Pirates of the Caribbean: The Curse of the Black Pearl* (2003), and *Intolerable Cruelty* (2003).

– S –

SCHEPISI, FRED (1939–). Fred Schepisi was part of the first wave of feature film directors in the early years of the Australian **revival**. Born in Victoria in 1939, he received a Catholic education and worked initially in advertising. Benefiting from the boom in the making of filmed commercials for **television** triggered by a 1960 government requirement that these be shot in Australia, he joined **Cinesound** in Melbourne in 1963 as its manager and bought the facility in 1966, renaming it The Film House. From there, he continued to make film TV commercials as well as producing and directing a string of sponsored **documentaries**.

By 1972, he was ready to direct feature films and got his chance with "The Priest" episode in the four-part film *Libido*. Written by novelist Thomas Keneally, the episode charts the tormented course of a doomed relationship between a priest (Arthur Dignam) and a nun (Robyn Nevin). Keneally continued to be important for Schepisi in his next film, **The Devil's Playground** (1976), where he played the role of a jolly, hellfire-preaching visiting priest in the Catholic seminary that is the location of the story. Schepisi, as director and scriptwriter, drew substantially on recollections of his own Catholic upbringing for this film, which portrays the growing conflict between young Tom Allen (Simon Burke) and the rigid disciplines of the order, an incompatibility that is mirrored in the experiences of some of the Brothers running the institution. Meanwhile, the relationship with Thomas Kenneally continued into Schepisi's next feature *The Chant of Jimmy Blacksmith* (1978). The film is based on a true turn of the century story about a black man, Jimmy Governor, who eventually turns against white society and is hunted down and savagely killed. Although this film, like its predecessor, won critical acclaim (even to the point of being invited into competition at the Cannes Film Festival), nevertheless, they both did poorly at the box office.

Disappointed at the lack of continuity of work in Australia, Schepisi decided to pursue his directorial career in **Hollywood**. Over the next eight years, he made four films there including the Western *Barbarosa* (1982), the film version of David Hare's play *Plenty* (1985), and the box-office success *Roxanne* (1987), an updating of the play *Cyrano de Bergerac*. Finally, however, he was tempted to return to Australia for a film based on the true-life Lindy Chamberlain case. The story of the latter's child Azaria being taken by a dingo at Uluru (Ayer's Rock) and the mother being wrongfully tried, convicted, and imprisoned for her alleged murder had been written up in the book *Evil Angels* and this became the basis of Schepisi's screenplay (*see EVIL ANGELS*). The director had already worked with actress Meryl Streep on *Plenty* and she played the key role of Lindy. The film did moderately well both critically and commercially, being released in the United States under the title *Cry in the Dark* (1988). However, despite its narrative and its setting, the film was essentially an international production, underlying the fact that although this gifted and stylish director might have had his beginnings in Australia, he was now part of the Hollywood film industry.

Schepisi then directed Sean Connery and Michelle Pfeiffer in the thriller *Russia House* (1990) and Tom Selleck in the romantic comedy *Mr. Baseball* (1992), a film that portrays the vicissitudes of the life of a foreigner in Japan, and the molding that occurs when the "semiospheres" of people of different cultures come into contact. *Six Degrees of Separation* (1993) followed, in a film that set the mantle of stardom on Will Smith, and told an absorbing story of self-realization and self-evaluation, marked by strong performances. *Fierce Creatures* (1997) tried to capitalize on the previous success of the comedy team of John Cleese, Jamie Lee Curtis, and Kevin Kline in *A Fish Called Wanda* (1988), but it was not as successful. The United Kingdom film *Last Orders* (2001) based on a Booker prize winning novel by Graham Swift, told the story of the impact of death of one of a group of friends who met in a British pub. Moving back to the United States, he made *It Runs in the Family* (2003), about a dysfunctional family played by Michael Douglas, Kirk Douglas, and other members of the Douglas clan.

Other films include the romantic comedy *I.Q.* (1994) with Tim Robbins, Meg Ryan, and Walter Matthau.

SCREENSOUND AUSTRALIA. On 11 December 1935, the Federal Cabinet established the National Historical Film and Speaking Record Library as part of the Commonwealth National Library. In recognition that film and sound were different types of historical record from written material, the library became a separate institution with a Board and a new name, the National Film and Sound Archive, in 1984. In 1999, the name changed again to reflect the emergence of digital multimedia productions, to the National Screen and Sound Archive, shortened to ScreenSound Australia. In 2003, after a review of all cultural agencies, the federal government reduced the stature of ScreenSound in giving the responsibility for it to the *Australian Film Commission*, an organization that has no mandate to archive the audiovisual history and culture of Australia.

As the name suggests, the archive was created to keep a record of Australian history and culture through its screen and sound products. It now plays a key role in documenting and interpreting the Australian experience and actively contributing to the development of Australia's audiovisual industry. It collects, stores, preserves, and makes available screen and sound material relevant to Australia's culture, and it complements **documentary** heritage collections. The archive collects, preserves, and shares Australia's moving images and sound recordings from the country's first film images to modern classic films like *Strictly Ballroom* (1992) and *Shine* (1996), from radio and **television** serials like *Blue Hills* to *Blue Heelers*, the songs of Peter Dawson and top-40 hits. When finances permit, the archive makes this collection available through exhibitions, screenings, the ScreenSound website, traveling shows, video and audio productions, live presentations, education programs, and television and radio productions.

The archive now includes more than one million items. In addition to discs, films, videos, audio tapes, phonograph cylinders, and wire recordings, the collection includes supporting documents and artifacts, such as photographic stills, transparencies, posters, lobby cards, publicity, scripts, costumes, props, memorabilia and sound, video and film equipment. In addition, the archive has developed preservation practices to assist with the process of restoring and saving old films. Organizations and individuals access these materials through an online database. Although the archive is significant in developing the cultural memory of Australia, it remains to be seen whether it will be able to continue in that role.

SCREENWEST. ScreenWest is Western Australia's film funding and development agency dedicated to the growth and promotion of film and **television** activity in the state. Its mandate is to provide leadership, support, and services in order to advance Western Australia as an internationally recognized center for screen production. It was founded as the West Australian Film Council in 1978, but this council itself arose from the Producers' Guild of Western Australia, established to support the efforts of local filmmakers in attracting government funding and support. In 1994, after an external review the Council changed its name and some functions (such as the inclusion of television in its ambit). Like similar agencies in other states, it supports activities relating to screen culture, such as assistance to priority projects like telemovies, low-budget feature films, **documentaries**, and animations. ScreenWest brings together external filmmakers and local expertise in cooperative ventures, and advertises local expertise, production facilities, and locations in overseas gatherings.

Specifically, ScreenWest provides financial support for projects with market potential that have a strong likelihood of being produced, but does not fund new media productions. Through marketing grants, it supports the marketing of films made by Western Australia production companies. Production funding exists as loans and direct funding for productions undertaken in Western Australia, but these funds are not meant to be the only finance for a production. Instead, filmmakers have to find other financiers, either governmental, such as the **Film Finance Corporation**, or private, to support the project. Other funds are provided to support the projects of new filmmakers (producers and directors) and writers. In addition, funds are available to support screen culture activities like courses and workshops, industry events, and screen activities, such as festivals.

The documentary *Exile and the Kingdom* (1994) was supported by ScreenWest, and was voted best documentary at the **Australian Film Institute** (AFI) awards in 1994. The feature *Blackfellas* (1993) won the AFI best screenplay and best supporting actor award, but is significant in any case because it was the first film about urban **Aborigines**, and Aborigines played a role in many aspects of the production.

Funding for ScreenWest comes from part of the revenue from the state Lottery Commission. *See also* AUSTRALIAN CENTRE FOR THE MOVING IMAGE; NEW SOUTH WALES FILM AND TELEVISION OFFICE; PACIFIC FILM AND TELEVISION COMMISSION; SOUTH AUSTRALIAN FILM CORPORATION.

SEMLER, DEAN (1943–). Born in Renmark, a **country** town in South Australia, Dean Semler inauspiciously began a career that was to lead to an Oscar and international acclaim, by leaving school at 16 years of age to work as a camera operator in Adelaide. He further honed his cinematographic skills through working at **Film Australia** for nine years. His first films as cinematographer were the unremarkable *Moving On* (1974) and *Let the Balloon Go* (1976), yet his skills are apparent in the stunning *Hoodwink* (1981). He also made the **documentary** about steam trains, *Steam Train Passes* (1974). International attention followed his photography of the dystopic wastelands and action scenes in **Dr. George Miller**'s *Mad Max 2: The Road Warrior* (1981), and he was the logical choice to shoot similar scenes in *Mad Max Beyond Thunderdome* (1985) (*see MAD MAX*

TRILOGY). He shot three other films in between these: Donald Crombie's *Kitty and the Bagman* (1982), *Undercover* (1983), and *Razorback* (1984). **Simon Wincer**'s *The Lighthorsemen* (1987) followed, and **Philip Noyce** chose Semler to evoke fear and tension on the high seas in *Dead Calm* (1989).

By this time he had been offered work in **Hollywood** by the New Zealand-trained director **Roger Donaldson* in the light-hearted *Cocktail* (1988) and *Young Guns* (1988). After further acclaim with John Milius' *Farewell to the King* (1989), Kevin Costner hired him for *Dances with Wolves* (1990). Perhaps Semler's childhood in the big-sky country around Renmark had given him a sense of panorama and color, but whatever the seed, his talent blossomed in this film, winning an Academy Award for best cinematography in 1991, as well as an American Society of Cinematographers' award. Awards were not new to Semler, although an Oscar was. He had been nominated for **Australian Film Institute** (AFI) awards for cinematography for *Mad Max 2: The Road Warrior*, *Undercover*, *The Coca-Cola Kid* (1985), and *The Lighthorsemen*. He won two AFI awards for cinematography for *My First Wife* (1984) and *Dead Calm*, and an Australian Cinematographers Society award for *Razorback* (1984).

Since that time, Semler's Hollywood career has continued unabated, and he has worked on many significant productions, including *City Slickers* (1991), *The Power of One* (1992), *Waterworld* (1995), *The Bone Collector* (1999), *We Were Soldiers* (2002), and *Bruce Almighty* (2003). However, his work does not seem to have achieved the same quality that he did for *Dances with Wolves* and earlier work.

Other films include the Australian productions *Going Sane* (1986) and *Bullseye* (1987). In Hollywood, he has shot *K-9* (1989), *Impulse* (1990), *Young Guns II* (1990), *Super Mario Bros.* (1993), *Last Action Hero* (1993), *The Three Musketeers* (1993), *The Cowboy Way* (1994), *Gone Fishin'* (1997), *The Trojan War* (1997), *Nutty Professor II: The Klumps* (2000), *Heartbreakers* (2001), *D-Tox* (2002), *Dragonfly* (2002), and *XXX* (2002). In addition, Semler has shot **television** miniseries and films for television in Australia, including *Do I Have to Kill My Child* (1976), the story of the government dismissed by the Queen's representative, *The Dismissal* (1983), *Bodyline: It's Not Just Cricket* (1984), *Return to Eden* (1985), *Passion Flower* (1986), *Melba* (1987), and *The Clean Machine* (1988).

SERIOUS, YAHOO (1953–). Yahoo Serious has been involved in only two films, *Young Einstein* (1988) and *Reckless Kelly* (1993). Serious (which is his real name, changed from Greg Pead), is an outrageous character, both as an actor in the films, but also because he cowrote, coproduced, directed, and starred in both films. His **comedies** can only be described as zany, outrageous, and historically inaccurate, but which use these inaccuracies in history as a source of the comedy. Yet he clearly understands Australian humor, as *Young Einstein* was the 10th most popular film at the Australian box office. While *Young Einstein* suggested that Albert Einstein was born in Tasmania, inventing the bubbles in beer as well as rock 'n'roll, *Reckless Kelly* retold the Robin Hood myth of the Kelly gang, within a context of corrupt commerce, green principles, Hollywood illusions, and the Australian Republican movement.

SHINE **(1996).** Directed by **Scott Hicks** from an original screenplay by Jan Sardi, *Shine* is based on the true story of Australian pianist David Helfgott, the musical prodigy who grew up in a poor family whose only certainty in life was the piano. The young Helfgott was affected in some way by his father, but in real life, he never criticizes his father. In the film, Helfgott wins a scholarship to London, where he has a breakdown. Years later, he is rescued from a hospital by Gillian, who encourages him to play again, which he does to acclaim that was mirrored in his real-life comeback. Although now slowing down, Helfgott still attracts thousands to his concerts, which are deeply moving affairs.

Geoffrey Rush plays the part of the obsessive-compulsive Helfgott with incomparable skill and empathy, while **Noah Taylor** plays the young pianist and his developing illness with great sensitivity. The film won nine **Australian Film Institute** awards, including best film, best director, best actor (Rush), best supporting actor (Armin Mueller-Stahl), best cinematography (Geoffrey Simpson), and best original screenplay (Jan Sardi). Rush won an Academy Award for this role as well, and the film was nominated in another six categories. *Shine* has become one of the most popular and critically acclaimed films in Australia. Without a doubt it is one of the most moving.

SHIRALEE, THE **(1957).** One of the films made by **Ealing** and directed by Leslie Norman, *The Shiralee* tells the story of the itinerant rural worker Macauley (**Peter Finch**)—sometimes described as a "swagman" or "swaggie"—who suddenly finds himself taking responsibility for his child. Having returned from "walkabout," he finds his wife entwined in the arms of another, and so he takes the daughter, Buster, with him. In these days, such an action might be labeled "kidnapping." The child is the "shiralee," an Aboriginal world meaning "burden." In their time together, father and daughter explore new depths of understanding and bonding. The barren landscapes of the outback provided both a backdrop to the richness of the relationship, as well as explaining the swagman's love for the **country**. Although Australians **Charles Tingwell**, Bill Kerr, and Ed Devereaux played in supporting roles, the film is really a British film made in Australia, rather than an Australian film.

SILVER CITY **(1984).** This film is included here because it identifies threads in Australian culture and politics about immigration and xenophobic attitudes to immigration. These resurfaced in the late 1990s and early 2000s, with supposedly "illegal" immigrants forced into detention centers, which, some claimed, were little better than concentration camps. These recent incidents are the result of government policy. In *Silver City*, post-World War II immigrants arrive in Australia and are initially settled in corrugated iron huts, before being processed and moved to the cities. The romantic theme did not excite audiences; however, the attitude that some Australians had toward "new" Australians is shown in all its xenophobia, along with the actions of corrupt bureaucrats, and young men who are molesters and rapists. In fact, most of the Australian men exhibit one or more of these characteristics; Australian women are dealt with less harshly by director Sophia Turkiewicz. These postwar immigrants were legal immigrants into Australia, and their time in substandard accommodation (by Australian standards) was limited, unlike the later "illegal" immigrants. The xenophobia that has been remobilized in recent years recycles that of the 1950s.

SITCH, ROB (1962–). Rob Sitch came to film prominence thanks to his ensemble **television** comedy work on *The Late Show*, *The Panel*, and *Frontline* mounted by the production company the D-Generation. Out of the ashes of this group developed Working Dog, a collaboration between Santo Cilauro, Jane Kennedy, Tom Gleisner, and Sitch.

The foursome work as a cohesive team, and there is little focus on individuals. Thus, although Sitch both writes and directs, nevertheless, his work is an outcome of this linkage. Sitch and company won the attention of Australians with *The Castle* in 1997 and followed up its immense box office and critical success with the television film *Degenocide* and the series *A River Somewhere* that same year. In 2000, there was a sequel of sorts to *The Castle* in the shape of *The Dish*, which, although lacking the wit and sparkle of its predecessor, explored new territory in Australian filmmaking. Finally, and most recently, there has been the television send-up of Aussie Tarzan-type nature TV hosts in *Russell Coight's All Aussie Adventure* (2001).

SOCIAL REALISM. Arguably, this **genre** is of central importance in Australian feature cinema since the **revival**, not least because it can accommodate conflicting demands for significance and relevance, budgetary considerations, and dramatic expectations. Everywhere recognized but usually left undefined, social realist feature films narrativize and dramatize social issues and problems, the intention being to inform and educate rather than to simply entertain. Such films aim to be representative, so that over and above their particular dramatization, they are also concerned with a larger social issue or problem whose universality or pervasiveness is implied. Thus, the project of a modernist social realism in Australian cinema can be seen to have been initiated in *Mike and Stefani* (1952). The latter feature, exemplary of this genre in Australian cinema, was concerned with the plight of European refugees in the period immediately after 1945. Taking the two actual figures of the title as its focus of narrative interest, the film thus aimed at exploring not only their particular story and situation but, by extension, that of many others. Filmed on location, using nonprofessional figures in all the story's roles, the film draws on both conventions of **documentary** as well as those of narrative cinema, the latter filtered through the spare, restrained, even detached, style of Italian neorealism.

Further, this film, like others in the genre, tended to be contemporary in terms of timeframe and gravitated toward a mise-en-scene of the familiar, the everyday, even the seedy and the down-at-heel. However, it is important to delimit the Australian social realist film. Simply being concerned with society is insufficient to justify the claims of any film to be part of the genre. After all, on this basis Australian films in other genres, such as *Mad Max* (1979) and *Crocodile Dundee* (1986), would have claims to be bracketed alongside a host of others from *Cathy's Child* (1978) to *Blackrock* (1997). Additionally, social realist films are also implicitly advocative—the problem or issue in question must be socially solvable. Thus, alienation as represented in *Two Thousand Weeks* (1969) is not a social problem or issue, being too abstract and metaphysical. Yet, another problem of identification is the fact that what may seem like realism to one generation may subsequently seem more artificial to later viewers. Hence, several films of the 1970s including *Between Wars* (1974), *Sunday Too Far Away* (1975), and *Newsfront* (1978), acclaimed in their time as social realist, nowadays would probably be bracketed as historical or period films. On the other hand, *You Can't See Round Corners* (1969), a far less prestigious vehicle based on a popular novel and TV series, would qualify both because it is concerned with a particular social issue (conscription) and because of its contemporary working-class milieu and situation.

It is only toward the end of the long boom in Australia from around the mid-1970s onward, that social realism as a genre in the Australian cinema begins to hit its straps. Thus, films such as *Jack and Jill: A Postscript* (1970), *27A* (1974), *The FJ Holden* (1977), and *Mouth to Mouth* (1978), which were neither **ocker** comedies nor **art/period** films, hint at the successive waves of social realism that were to come. All four were contemporary in setting and concerned with the working class. Indeed, in *Mouth to Mouth*, the specific issue pursued was unemployment and the ravages it wreaks on young lives. Social deprivation and lack of emotional security lead one of the four main characters to drift into prostitution while another returns to the institution from which she emerged early in the film.

Over the past 25 years, deterioration in social conditions has turned the perception of Australia into that of the Unlucky Country. This together with the increasing diversity of the social fabric has proved to be fertile ground for filmmakers with an inclination toward social realism. There has been a noticeable pull in this general direction on the part of both individual films and filmmakers. Indeed, a list of representative titles would run from *Three to Go* (1971), *Hard Knocks* (1980), *Annie's Coming Out* (1984), *Return Home* (1989),

Angel Baby (1995), *Bad Boy Bubby* (1993), and *Metal Skin* (1994). Such films tend to concentrate on different geographies of the Australian **city** and the living of city life whether on the streets or elsewhere. The vision of city life in many of these features is nasty, brutish, and short. Other recent representations of this dystopian vision are *Romper Stomper* (1992), *Idiot Box* (1996), *The Boys* (1997), and *Blackrock*. Indeed, the persistence of this kind of film has enabled audience, producers, and critics to claim a distinctive tradition of urban social realism. Such a cycle includes *Queensland* (1976), *Mouth to Mouth, Lover Boy* (1988), *Romper Stomper, Metal Skin, The Boys,* and *Blackrock*. Set in the working-class Melbourne western suburbs, these films follow tough, hard-edged stories that concern males with no way out from nihilistic futures. The protagonists are caught in the dislocations of unemployment, alienation, violence, racism, and psychological breakdown.

Finally, it is worth noting another recent cycle inside the genre of social realism that appears to challenge if not violate rules of sober cinematography, mise-en-scene, soundtrack, editing, and subject matter. This concerns the introduction within the social realist framework of other elements variously called "suburban surrealism" or "magical realism." Early anticipations of this tendency include *Dalmas* (1973) and *Surrender in Paradise* (1976). In turn, some of the more contemporary inheritors of this tendency have included *Strictly Ballroom* (1992), *Muriel's Wedding* (1994), *The Adventures of Priscilla, Queen of the Desert* (1994), and *Bad Boy Bubby*. Other critics, however, would argue that these deviations from a mode dominated by a desire for naturalism has been mostly at the surface level of setting, performance, and situation and does not signify either a shift in dramatic structure or generic innovation. Nevertheless, these modifications do serve to highlight the ongoing relevance and centrality of the social realist genre in Australian cinema.

SOUTH AUSTRALIAN FILM CORPORATION (SAFC). The creation of the South Australian Film Corporation was, in its day, a revolutionary act by Labor Premier Don Dunstan, in that it was an initiative designed to generate revenue and jobs from a new industry, a cultural industry, as well as to make a significant contribution to the cultural identity of the state. This was a pioneering initiative in Australia, and its creation proved to be both popular and culturally significant. In the next eight years, most other Australian states founded similar corporations. Established under *The South Australian Film Corporation Act*, the corporation began operations in 1972 with **Gil Brealey** as chairman and director, and moved quickly to work on films that heralded a renaissance in the film industry and history. The films ranged from the **socially realist** *Sunday Too Far Away* (1975), through the mystifying *Picnic at Hanging Rock* (1975), the child adventure *Storm Boy* (1976), and the historical war film *Breaker Morant* (1980). These films were unashamedly Australian in content and theme, used Australians as cast and crew, and, apart from *Breaker Morant*, catapulted the Australian landscape into the narrative. Even *Breaker Morant*, set in South Africa, was shot in and around Burra, originally a copper-mining town in South Australia.

This period of intense creativity did not continue with subsequent governments and changes in the leadership of the corporation. It moved into **television** production, and after a review in 1993, the SAFC ceased to be a producer and became South Australia's film development agency, providing investment, development programs, and training support for film, television, and new media production in South Australia. The SAFC now operates production and post-production facilities, and offers a locations service and other assistance to producers intending to shoot in South Australia.

The SAFC has supported the production of many interesting and arresting films over its 30-year life, and many films have addressed and interrogated social issues, such as those surrounding the juxtaposition of Aboriginal and other Australian cultures. Significant films supported by the SAFC include *Travelling Light* (2003), **Rolf de Heer**'s *Alexandra's Project* (2002), Craig Lahiff's *Black and White* (2002) and *Heaven's Burning* (1997), **Phillip Noyce**'s *Rabbit-Proof Fence* (2000), John Polson's *Siam Sunset* (1998), **Scott Hicks'** *Shine* (1996), *The Adventures of Priscilla, Queen of the Desert* (1993), **Simon Wincer**'s *The Lighthorsemen* (1987), and **Peter Weir**'s *Gallipoli* (1980).

SOUTHERN INTERNATIONAL. Southern International was formed in 1953 by **Chips Rafferty** and the **documentary** filmmaker **Lee Robinson**, after an earlier company, Platypus Pictures, showed that filmmaking could by profitable. Its first feature, the Australian Western

The Phantom Stockman (1953) was directed by Robinson, starred Rafferty and proved successful both in Australia and overseas, as the company drew on the popular Western **genre**, laced with the motif of the damsel-in-distress who is saved by the mysterious stranger. It was followed by the more financially ambitious *King of the Coral Sea* (1954), starring Rafferty, **Charles "Bud" Tingwell**, and Rod Taylor. *King of the Coral Sea* was an adventure melodrama set in the Torres Strait. It continued Southern International's run of financial success in Australia and in the overseas **television** market, and led to the filming of *Walk into Paradise* (1955), an adventure melodrama filmed in New Guinea. Like its predecessors, this was successful, partly because of the exotic location. Unlike the other films, however, it was codirected by the Frenchman Marcel Paglieri, who had been brought in to direct the dialogue of its French stars, the film being a coproduction between Southern International and Discifilm, the production company of French producer Paul-Edmond Decharme.

Walk into Paradise was Southern International's most ambitious production. Filmed in the New Guinea Highlands in color and at a cost of UK£65,000, it established a relationship between the Australian and French producers that was to see them make the less successful *The Stowaway* (1958) and *The Restless and the Damned* (1959). *Walk into Paradise* attracted the attention of the American Joseph E. Levine. His company, Embassy Films, bought the American rights for US$60,000, changed the title to *Walk into Hell*, added some extra scenes, and marketed it successfully to American audiences. It was this success that had helped prompt the making of the less fortunate *The Stowaway* and *The Restless and the Damned.* The Northern Territory-filmed *Dust in the Sun* (1958) was likewise unable to restore Southern International's fortunes, and the company ceased production. The coproduction system used to make films has been a successful formula for other filmmakers in later years.

SPENCE, BRUCE (1945–). Bruce Spence was born in Auckland, New Zealand, but moved to Australia at an early age and became involved in two influential and experimental theater groups in 1960s Melbourne: La Mama and the Pram Factory. He can be identified immediately in any film through his six feet seven height, and thin and gangly physique. His career began with a bang in the early years of the **revival**, and has continued consistently since that time. Although not often in a leading role, his characters always strengthen the plot and viewer interest in any film in which he plays. In addition, he has played in many **television** films and series, and straight-to-video films, in his long career.

His first film was also the first film of the **ocker** cycle of the Australian **revival**, **Tim Burstall**'s *Stork* (1971), where he starred as the six-foot, blue collar, deranged Marxist revolutionary, exploding on the screen in a film that is still talked about for its influence on Australian filmmaking and culture. Strangely, since that time he has had few lead roles, although his supporting roles have often been memorable, such as the gyro captain in *Mad Max 2: The Road Warrior* (1981) and Jedediah the pilot in *Mad Max Beyond Thunderdome* (1985) (*see MAD MAX* TRILOGY). He played the lead of geologist Lance Hackett in the obscure Werner Herzog film that did not live up to its potential, *Wo die grünen Ameisen träumen* (*Where the Green Ants Dream*) (1984). He has appeared in many other significant films since the revival: **Peter Weir**'s *The Cars That Ate Paris* (1974), *Mad Dog Morgan* (1976), **Phillip Noyce**'s *Newsfront* (1978), John Duigan's films *Dimboola* (1979) and *The Year My Voice Broke* (1987), and **Alex Proyas**'s *Dark City* (1998).

Recently, Spence's career has seemed to take a second wind. He broke into the **Hollywood** industry in a small way with the part of Gahjii in *Ace Ventura: When Nature Calls* (1995), and followed this up with Khayman in the vampire film *Queen of the Damned* (2002). He was the voice of Chum in *Finding Nemo* (2003), played the Trainman in *The Matrix Revolutions* (2003), and Cookson in Australian director **P.J. Hogan**'s *Peter Pan* (2003).

Other films are *The Firm Man* (1975), *The Great McCarthy* (1975), *Oz* (1976), *Let the Balloon Go* (1976), *Eliza Fraser* (1976), *Double Deal* (1981), *The Return of Captain Invincible* (1983), *Midnight Spares* (1983), *Buddies* (1983), *Pallet on the Floor* (1984) (a New Zealand film), *Bullseye* (1987), *Bachelor Girl* (1988), *Ricky and Pete* (1988), *The Shrimp on the Barbie* (1990), . . . *Almost* (1990), *Sweet Talker* (1991), and *Hercules Returns* (1993).

SPORT. Although sport is often said to be of central importance to the Australian nation and character and an abiding passion particularly for its male half, this interest barely shows up in feature films of the

revival period. Quite remarkably, there is no evidence of interest on the part of filmmakers in most codes of football (with the exception of home grown Australian Rules), nor in cricket, the two seasonal sports. Equally there is also little evidence of interest in gambling and horse racing in these later years. On the other hand, prowess in the water and in swimming related events does seem to continue to attract attention. Coincidentally, this is an area in which gender finds particularly sharp expression and representation.

Each of these propositions can be examined in more detail. First is the nonrepresentation of football and particularly the code of Australian Rules. The latter game is unique to Australia and it is not surprising that various filmmakers, concerned to infuse elements of Australian cultural identity in their films, have often turned to this code. Hence, for example, early **television** series and films of the revival, including *And the Big Men Fly* (1974), *The Great McCarthy* (1975), and *The Club* (1980) have all concerned themselves with the game of Australian Rules both on and off the field. All were set in Melbourne and football became a means of interrogating other aspects of contemporary life, most especially the various ways in which men related both to **women** and to other men. However, this particular interest was short-lived and soon petered out. Two more recent features have again returned to football as a means of offering broader insights into the society at large. *Kick* (1999) breaks rank, concentrating on a private school in Sydney where the code is Rugby Union. The team's star player secretly nurses a desire to be a ballet dancer so that the film is concerned to explore what constitutes **masculinity** in the present. However, *Kick* also lacks a good deal of credibility so far as its hero is concerned in that he is in a position to choose between the two careers, thereby unconsciously suggesting that he already belongs to an upper-class elite. By contrast *Australian Rules* (2002) is set in a depressed coastal **country** town in South Australia and concerns people given much less in the way of life choices. The film marks the coming to consciousness of the central figure, who is white. However, his best friend is an **Aboriginal** boy who, although a better footballer, is unable to withstand the social pressures that surround him, and which finally destroy him.

Horse racing has thrown up a number of films. The sport was one of the first to be exhibited in theaters in the early period of Australian cinema. One of the first *actualités* was the shooting of the 1886 Melbourne Cup, repeated in 1897. In 1936, **Ken G. Hall** made *Thoroughbred*, a film starring Helen Twelvetrees, and one of a cycle of Australian-made films that Hall hoped would attract international audiences using international themes. **Simon Wincer**'s *Phar Lap* (1983) concerned a champion horse that won everything before it in Australia in the 1930s. However, when the horse went to America, it soon died either because of an illness or poisoning. The film that celebrated the horse suffers from two attendant weaknesses. First, the fact that its Australian audience knows the outcome tends to weaken its story and its drama. Moreover, by depicting a failure and hinting at wicked doings, the film tends to seem like a whine, an excuse for failure, which raises the question as to why the film was made in the first place. The horse-racing industry is now in a process of transition. While on-track attendance has been declining, gambling on races continues to grow and the on-track decline is more than matched by the growing audience for cable racing channels, whether at home, in hotels, or in recognized betting locations. Thus, the overall lack of filmic interest is puzzling, given the importance of racing in the early years of cinema.

The third area of sport has to do with swimming. Because swimming is a solo sport, the films in this short cycle—*Dawn!* (1979), *The Coolangatta Gold* (1984), *The Surfer* (1986), and *Swimming Upstream* (2003)—lay a heavy stress on the gender of the central character. The first is concerned with women while the second focuses on a father's obsession with a favorite son winning a beach swimming event when it is the neglected son who is the real champion. Finally, father and son learn to come to grips with this and with themselves. Meanwhile, *The Surfer* drifts away from its central interest in water in favor of **crime** melodrama, while *Swimming Upstream* is a story of a father who disliked his son to an extent that is difficult to rationalize.

Altogether, then, sport has failed to ignite the passion of filmmakers although, as was evinced by the 2000 Olympic games held in Sydney, sport itself continues to capture the popular imagination.

STONE **(1974).** *Stone* involves two stories. One comprises the plot and narrative of the film. The other is the story of the film and the **Australian Film Commission** (AFC) and reveals both the nature of film

production in Australia at the time, and the tight grip that the bureaucracy had on the nature of the emerging industry. The film is unique
in that it is a decidedly serious film, at a time—the early years of the
revival—when the prevailing style of filmmaking was the **ocker**
style, involving satire and the send-up of anything vaguely serious.
Stone is about a mythical Sydney biker gang, the Gravediggers, which
is both a name and a play on the term "digger," or Australian soldier.
The Gravediggers are all veterans, most from Vietnam, but some from
Korea. (The "patch" worn by the Gravediggers is a skull wearing the
slouch hat of the Australian digger. A real motorcycle club, the Vietnam Veterans, has now appropriated the patch as their own.) Many of
the cast and crew, such as Director **Sandy Harbutt**—who also produced and played the lead role of "Undertaker"—and Ken Shorter,
were from the theater, with training, experience, and acclaim in that
field. Some, such as Helen Morse and **Rebecca Gilling**, went on to
television and film careers. Significantly for a later film about bikers,
one of the major characters had the name of "Bad Max."

A characteristic of the ocker films was the so-called working-class
disregard for the sensibilities and mores of people and institutions
that were not working class. These sensibilities and mores were parodied and made objects of comedy, and the general theme of the films
was "anti": antipretentiousness, anti-intellectual, and so on. But the
sensibilities and mores were surface features. On the other hand,
Stone questioned fundamental elements of culture: justice, war, social justice, and so on, in a decidedly caustic critique.

The story of the film's marketing is an interesting saga. Made for
$192,000 with backing from the **Australian Film Development
Corporation**, the film was never going to be a blockbuster. It was severely panned by critics and the tabloid press at its premiere, but as-
tounded the critics, and the film's backers as well by breaking box office records wherever it was screened. Although there was a cult
element of bikers who attended the film, only about 400 existed in
Sydney at the time, and the film ran for 15 weeks there, suggesting a
wider audience.

The film was to be released internationally, which meant exposure
at Cannes. The Film Development Corporation had been absorbed by
the Australian Film Commission, which then held the rights to the
film, so Harbutt and AFC bureaucrats flew to Cannes to promote

Stone along with other films. For whatever reason, the AFC did not promote *Stone* at Cannes or at the Australian exhibition at the London Film Festival, nor in AFC promotional material. The film did not fit in with what the AFC considered Australian films have as their subjects. After the five-year distribution rights ran out, Harbutt re-edited the film and took it to Cannes independently in 1980, where he sold it to Japan, Greece, and Germany, for example.

While the AFC tried to bury the film through ignoring it, it has gone from strength to strength, and has remained one of the most-viewed films from the 1970s. In 1993, the Stone Anniversary Run took place, from Sydney to Newcastle, to mark the 25th anniversary of the funeral run depicted in the film. Some 30,000 bikers and recreational riders attended. The film remains popular and will remain an icon both as a film that resisted the contemporary ocker style, and as a warning about the power and nature of film bureaucracies.

Harbutt never worked again in the film industry, not by choice, but because he was never offered any further work either as director or actor.

STORM BOY (1976). Essentially a children's film, *Storm Boy* is based on a novel by Colin Thiele and expresses the love of people and landscape that marked contemporary South Australian filmmaking. Filmed in the beautiful Coorong region of South Australia, the film tells the story of the young Mike and his developing friendship with Fingerbone Bill (**David Gulpilil** in an early role), an outcast from the local **Aborigine** tribe. Together, they raise three orphan pelican chicks. Marginalization, alienation, friendship, and respect for people and the environment are themes interwoven into an allegory that diverged from the contemporary preoccupations with the **ocker** and **art and period** films of the **revival**.

For Geoff Burton, the film won the 1978 cinematographer of the year award from the Australian Cinematographers Society. In the previous year, the film had been nominated for six **Australian Film Institute** (AFI) awards including best director (Henri Safran), best lead actor (Gulpilil), best screenplay, and won the best film award.

STRICTLY BALLROOM (1992). *Strictly Ballroom* is the fifth most successful film at the Australian Box Office, grossing $21.8 million.

Prefiguring the success of director **Baz Luhrmann**'s later film, ***Moulin Rouge!*** (2001), *Strictly Ballroom* won many awards in Australia and overseas. In Australia, the film won eight **Australian Film Institute** awards—including best film, best director, best screenplay, best supporting actor, and best supporting actress—and was nominated for another five awards. The film was nominated for three British Academy for the Film and Television Arts (BAFTA) awards, including best costume design and best production design, and was nominated for five others. At Cannes, it won the Award of the Youth for a foreign film. Other prizes included the London Critics Circle Film Award, a Golden Globes nomination, and numerous film festival awards.

The film revolves around the clash of old, befuddled tradition with the energy and spontaneity of youth. The young and talented dancer Scott Hastings (**Paul Mercurio**) wants to introduce new steps into a routine for the Pan-Pacific Grand Prix, promoted under the auspices and rules of the Australian Dance Federation, as interpreted and judged by the by-the-book adjudicator, Barry Fife (**Bill Hunter**). To accompany him in his routine, Scott chooses the frumpy, bespectacled Fran (Tara Morice) as his training partner, as the glamorous and spunky Liz Holt (Gia Caridis) has abandoned him for another partner. The pair win the contest controversially and by public acclaim through their rendition of the *pasa doble*, taught to them by Fran's Spanish father and grandmother. Critics have generally welcomed the film as a return to the exuberance and energy of traditional Hollywood **musicals**, using the film technology, costuming, and fantastic themes of contemporary filmmaking.

SUNDAY TOO FAR AWAY **(1975).** A product of the new **South Australian Film Corporation**, *Sunday* launched the Australian film industry into an era of new directions that challenged dominant **Hollywood** themes and narratives, and successfully so. The film is a realistic examination of the "**mateship**" that, in part, originated in the outback of Australia among those who worked with sheep and cattle. Such people were the foundation of the Australian union movement, and were pivotal in the formation of the Australian Labor Party, which first became an entity in outback Queensland. The outback plays a compelling part in the narrative, separating the family life of men from their working environment, and forcing them to band together in order to maintain a standard of living, in contrast with the cocky, the owner of the sheep station.

Foley (**Jack Thompson**) is a gun shearer (a gun shearer is the person who can shear the most number of sheep in one day), and is, by virtue of his skill, the leader of the men. The competition is fierce, the battle to be the best rages, and the isolation intensifies conflict within the group and with the cocky.

– T –

TAYLOR, NOAH (1969–). The characters Noah Taylor has played in some Australian films have in common a disassociation from all that goes on around them, displayed particularly effectively by his unemotional, hang-dog expression, surveying the absurdity of existence. His first appearances were in **coming-of-age** films, where his portrayal of unrealized alienation and internal conflict marked his characters: as the youth Danny Embling coming to terms with his burgeoning sexuality in John Duigan's *The Year My Voice Broke* (1987), Duigan's sequel, *Flirting* (1991), and *The Nostradamus Kid* (1993). Critics and colleagues applauded his role as the adolescent David Helfgott in *Shine* (1996), resulting in the Screen Actors Guild nominating him for the outstanding supporting actor award, and the Fort Lauderdale International Film Festival awarded him the best actor award. He played the lead role of Danny, the writer suffering extended and terminal writer's block, in the Italian-Australian coproduction of **Richard Lowenstein**'s *He Died with a Felafel in his Hand* (1999). He had appeared briefly as a David Bowie fan in the earlier Lowenstein film *Dogs in Space* (1987), about several young people who shared a house in Melbourne. Taylor has appeared in less successful Australian films like Geoffrey Wright's *Lover Boy* (1988), *The Prisoner of St. Petersburg* (1990), *Dead to the World* (1991), *One Crazy Night* (1993), *Dad and Dave: On Our Selection* (1995)— where he worked again with **Geoffrey Rush**—the short *Down Rusty Down* (1996), and *True Love and Chaos* (1997).

Taylor has made a successful transition to the international screen. In Europe, he played the journalist in the United Kingdom-produced

Woundings (1998), the lead of Simon in the US/British film *Simon Magus* (1999), then in the French production *Mauvaise passé* (1999) followed by a small part in the United Kingdom/German production of *The Nine Lives of Thomas Katz* (2000). The American industry has recognized his talents for playing unusual parts: he appeared in the poorly received *There's No Fish Food in Heaven* (1998), as Dick Roswell in *Almost Famous* (2000), in *Lara Croft: Tomb Raider* (2001), *Lara Croft and the Cradle of Life: Tomb Raider 2* (2003), and *Vanilla Sky* (2001), and he played Adolf Hitler in the controversial *Max* (2002), and *The Sleeping Dictionary* (2002).

TAYLOR, ROBERT. Robert Taylor is an emerging talent, graduating from the Western Australia Academy of Performing Arts in 1986. He had a successful career in **television** productions, and his first feature film was as Agent Jones in ***The Matrix*** (1999). Subsequently, he appeared in the black comedy *Muggers* (2000) and the thriller *Vertical Limit* (2000), before playing the lead role of Jack Behring in the less-than-successful *After the Rain* (2000). However, he followed this with the significant role of the crooked lawyer Frank Malone in *A Hard Word* (2002) and Sherritt Trooper in *Ned Kelly* (2003).

TELEVISION. The broadcasting institution is so completely a shadow, a part, a forerunner, and a base to the film industry that it is surprising how often this truth is forgotten. Indeed, it is only perhaps because of the cultural cache that terms such as "film" and "cinema" have—as opposed to the term "television"—that it is possible to be forever forgetful. Rather, what always should be borne in mind is the way that film and television are Siamese twins, forever joined at a metaphorical hip even if they often wish to be free of each other. In the case of Australia, three television stations (two private and commercial and one public service) began broadcasting in 1956 in Sydney and Melbourne. By the early 1960s, up to 80 percent of the population fell within a broadcast signal. Early hopes that the institution would provide plenty of job opportunities for Australians, both before and behind the camera, came to naught because of the high quantity of imported programs, especially those then coming from Hollywood, the new home of US network television fiction series. To counter this, lobbyists prevailed upon a reluctant federal government to inquire into the state of the film requirements for the new industry, an investigation that initially seemed to fall on deaf ears but later led to decisive government action in establishing a feature film production industry. Television, too, gained in this new regime. For example, by the early 1970s, television producers—like their siblings in feature films—could apply for production subsidies. Equally, too, a new film school soon expanded its name to include training for both the small as well as the big screen.

Put another way, if Australia did not have a thriving television industry in the mid to late 1960s, it is doubtful whether government would have taken the steps necessary to establish a feature production industry together with a battery of ancillary agencies that served both sectors. Broadly speaking, at that time and since, film and television have existed alongside each other, distinct yet intertwined in a myriad of different ways. To mark these broad connections, five specific links can be indicated here. Take, for example, the situation of screen actors. As a craft notoriously inclined toward very high levels of unemployment, it is certainly the case that many would-be film actors would have long abandoned the business had it not been possible for them to gain often constant and lengthy periods of employment on long-running television series. However, this important point is cultural as well as economic. Australian television is in the business of generating and maintaining a kind of star system that feature film is incapable of providing in its own right—even though it has often gathered the fruits of the former's labor. Instead, television has made available a veritable galaxy of faces and bodies in innumerable series' episodes with the better, more intriguing, and more visually interesting rising to the surface of viewer attention. Who, for example, could doubt that an actor such as John Woods is, rightly, better remembered for his sterling role in the long-running television series, *Blue Heelers*, than in the forgotten feature *The Office Picnic* (1972). Equally, when **Crocodile Dundee** (1986) made **Paul Hogan** an international star, he had already attained Australian stardom through his long apprenticeship in television.

Another point of connection between the two institutions has to do with the way that screen narratives can spin off from one medium to the other. Hence, many Australian feature films have been based on popular television series from *Country Town* (*Bellbird*), *Number 96*, and *The Box* down to *Police Rescue* and *Pizza*. Mentioning the two markets also highlights that particular hybrid, the telemovie. The first telemovie appeared around 1975 at a time when Australian television even briefly played with the two-hour episode series such as *Case for the Defence*. However, *Case* is long forgotten, although telemovies continue to be produced and broadcast right down to the present. Given the attention often lavished on obscure areas of film production, such as the avant garde and experimental film, it is surely time for a systematic appraisal of this particular output.

A fourth point of overlap between film and television has to do with different production companies and individual producers who have frequently shuttled back and forward between the two areas. Television stations, including the Nine Network and the Seven Network, have been regular investors in feature films, a move that makes economic sense both in terms of taking cultural gambles that may pay off at the box office and in terms of securing broadcast rights over new feature films. Meanwhile, such companies as **Hoyts** and **Village Roadshow**, long associated with film distribution and exhibition, have also been involved in the startup of particular television series. Although this kind of criss-crossing has been a long-term trend, it is also worth noticing here a particular historical congruence between film and television. This has to do with the successive cycles of historical (**art and period**) films produced in Australia in the period 1975 to 1982 and the burgeoning in the historical television miniseries under a regime of "quality" between around 1980 and 1987. Here, there would seem to be a very strong link. Not only did several writers, producers, and directors move from feature film to television drama but, arguably, the television miniseries enabled further elaboration of the regimes of narrative and mise-en-scene that had already been deployed in the Australian feature film a little time earlier.

Clearly, then, since the 1960s down to the present, the fate of Australian film has been inextricably mixed with the trajectory of Australian television in a variety of different ways that have only been hinted at here. In addition, more arguably, the economic and cultural health of the latter is at least a precondition if not a guarantee of the well-being of the former. *See also* AUSTRALIAN CHILDREN'S TELEVISION FUND.

THOMPSON, JACK (1940–). Jack Thompson was born in Sydney, New South Wales, where Sydney actor John Thompson adopted him at the age of eight. Thompson worked as a jackaroo, joined the army for six years, then continued his education at the University of Queensland, where he began acting. His film career started in 1970, with a small part in *That Lady from Peking*, and he benefited from the **revival** in film in Australia in the 1970s, especially the interest in and exploration of the archetypal Australian character. In *Wake in Fright* (1971), he was the drunken, loud-mouthed larrikin (verging in this film on the loutish). As the gun-shearer in **Sunday Too Far Away** (1975) he shows that, underneath the brash, tough, wiry, working-class hero is a person concerned about the surfacing pointlessness of the direction of his life. He expands on the larrikin identity in the character of the SP ("starting-price"; that is, illegal) bookmaker's lair in *Caddie* (1976). In *The Club* (1980), he is a coach of a losing football team, and is in the throes of being replaced. In *The Chant of Jimmy Blacksmith* (1978), he played the minister who tried, to the limits of his blinkered understanding, to help Jimmy live as a part-aboriginal in the white world. In **Breaker Morant** (1980), as the lawyer from New South Wales, he grows in moral indignation while coming to an understanding of the Machiavellian machinations of the British military, in his fight to save the Australian soldiers from the firing squad. This role won him the **Australian Film Institute** (AFI) best actor award, as well as the Cannes award for best supporting actor (which indicates the lack of uniformity in determining "lead" and "supporting" roles). He played the wise, high-country bushman Clancy in **The Man from Snowy River** (1982). His roles seemed to fill out and solidify the changing representations of the Australian male, and in *The Sum of Us* (1994), he plays the archetypal working-class father, coming to terms with the revelation that his son is gay. In his later work he has moved beyond these representations of Australian **masculinity**.

Thompson's repertoire of films and **television** programs is, by Australian standards, impressive. It includes *Libido* (1973), *Petersen* (1974), *Scobie Malone* (1975), *Mad Dog Morgan* (1976), *The Journalist* (1979), *The Earthling* (1980), *Bad Blood* (1981), *Flesh and Blood* (1985), *Burke and Wills* (1985), *Short Circuit* (1986), *Ground Zero* (1987), *Turtle Beach* (1991), *Wind* (1992),

Resistance (1992), *A Far-Off Place* (1993), *Ruby Cairo* (1993), *Flug der Albatros* (1995), *Broken Arrow* (1996), *Last Dance* (1996), *Excess Baggage* (1997), *Under the Lighthouse Dancing* (1997), *The Magic Pudding* (2000), *Yolngu Boy* (2001), and *Original Sin* (2001). He has played in other, more popular, films outside Australia: in *Merry Christmas, Mr. Lawrence* (1983), lawyer Sonny Seiler in *Midnight in the Garden of Good and Evil* (1997), and Cliegg Lars in *Star Wars: Episode II—Attack of the Clones* (2002).

In 1994, the AFI conferred on Thompson the **Raymond Longford** Award, in honor of his significant contribution to Australian filmmaking. In 1998, the Film Critics Circle of Australia granted him the Special Achievement Award for his corpus of work and his contribution to Australian cinema.

THORNTON, SIGRID (1959–). Sigrid Thornton was born in Canberra. She first played in a **television** series, and she was well placed to take a leading role in the films of the **revival**, beginning with a part in *The FJ Holden* (Michael Thornhill, 1977) and in the same year, a bitchy schoolgirl in the period film, **Bruce Beresford**'s *The Getting of Wisdom*. Her first leading role was as Angela in the Simon Wincer thriller, *Snapshot* (1979), for which she was nominated for an **Australian Film Institute** best actress award. In 1982, she starred as the tough, yet spunky no-nonsense young woman Jessica Harrison in *The Man from Snowy River* and its sequel, *The Man from Snowy River II* (1988), where she falls in love with the young man whom the film is named after (**Tom Burlinson**). She played a supporting role in Wincer's *The Lighthorsemen* (1987), and has played in many films since then that have not been successful at the box office, such as the U.S.-made science fiction thriller *Trapped in Space* (1994), *Whipping Boy* (1996), and *Love in Ambush* (1997). More significantly, she plays Mayor Wilson in the Disney film *Inspector Gadget 2* (2003).

THRING, FRANK SR. (1883–1936). Father of the actor Frank Thring, Frank Thring Sr. was born in Tasmania in 1888. There he gained a foothold in the newly emerging film industry as a traveling exhibitor. By 1915, he was in Melbourne where he became part owner of a chain of theaters, Electric Theatres. Three years later, he was managing director of the distribution company, J.C. Williamson Films and by 1926 had become joint managing director of the newly established **Hoyts** Theatres Ltd. However, more interested in the filmmaking end of things, he sold his interests in 1930 and established **Efftee Productions**. Over the next six years, he produced and directed a string of seven features: *Diggers* (1931), *The Sentimental Bloke* (1932), *His Royal Highness* (1932), *Harmony Row* (1933), *A Ticket in Tatts* (1934), *Clara Gibbings* (1934), and *The Streets of London* (1934).

Meanwhile, he continued to be active as a businessman acting as managing director of Efftee Productions. Like Sir Hugh Dennison in Sydney, he also became a kind of media mogul of the time. In 1933, he branched into theatrical promotion, planning to establish a Hollywood-like star system with celebrities who could move between stage, screen, and even radio. To that end, he bought Melbourne station 3XY in 1935. However, as a film businessman, he found increasing difficulty in having his features released and this persuaded him to become a passionate advocate of protection of the local production industry. Encouraged by the legislative backing that the New South Wales government had given to producers, he moved Efftee Films to Sydney in 1935. Here he set up links with the Mastercraft Film Corporation and began work on another feature, *Collitt's Inn*. Ironically, given the difficulties that **Hollywood** was causing Australian producers such as himself at the box office, he died in 1936 shortly after returning from a business trip to the United States.

TINGWELL, CHARLES "BUD" (1923–). To follow Charles Tingwell's career as an actor is to follow the development of the Australian cinema industry. If it can be said that a person is born for a performing career, then it can be said for Tingwell. He began work as a professional actor while he was at school in 1940, then he joined the Royal Australian Air Force from 1941 to 1945. The first stage in his career was in Australia in the decade from 1946 to 1956, a time when a career in the film industry meant a precarious existence. He was noticed in a small role in **Ken G. Hall**'s *Smithy* (1946), and then played the lead of a young naval officer in the melodramatic war story *Always Another Dawn* (1947), and then the less than heroic lead in yet another Australian racing story, *Into the Straight* (1949). The British studio **Ealing** had set up a production facility in Australia, and Tingwell acted the son of a pioneer family in the third of their features, *Bitter*

Springs (1950). He played supporting roles in two films made by Twentieth Century Fox, the generic Western set in Australia, *Kangaroo* (1952)—with Peter Lawford and Maureen O'Hara—and the war drama, *The Desert Rats* (1953). Turning down a contract offered by Fox, Tingwell worked with **Cecil Holmes** on his feature directorial debut, *Captain Thunderbolt* (1953), and with director **Lee Robinson** as the star of *King of the Coral Sea* (1954).

Given the generally depressed state of the Australian industry after 1950, it was clear to Tingwell that he might develop his career if he traveled overseas. Doubtless his work with Ealing and Fox gave him confidence that he would be able to succeed. In this second stage of his career, he worked in the United Kingdom in film and **television** from the late 1950s. He worked for Hammer, Rank, and MGM-British, where he successfully played the role of Inspector Craddock in the four Miss Marple mysteries, beginning with *Murder, She Said* (1961). He played in many films, including the thriller *Nobody Runs Forever* (1968) with another expatriate Australian, Rod Taylor, and worked in television.

However, in the early 1970s the Australian government was beginning to support the film industry, and Tingwell returned to Australia in 1972 for the third stage of an already flourishing career, in an industry that was also beginning to grow. He worked initially in television, and his first film role in this stage was in **Tim Burstall**'s *Petersen* (1974), in which he played the clergyman father of Petersen (**Jack Thompson**). Since then he has appeared most often in strong supporting roles in many films, including *End Play* (1975), ***Breaker Morant*** (1980), *A Cry in the Dark* (also known as ***Evil Angels***) (1988), ***The Castle*** (1997), *Wog Boy* (2000), ***The Dish*** (2000), and *Ned Kelly* (2003). In addition, he has played in many television series, and has directed at least 14 of these. He is the quintessential character actor, bringing narrative power to both likeable and villainous characters.

His contribution to the Australian film industry was recognized when the **Australian Film Institute** presented him with the **Raymond Longford** Award in 1998. Now over 80 years of age, he is one of the elder statesmen of the industry, and is widely respected for his sense of humanity and integrity.

Other films include *The Glenrowan Affair* (1951), *Smiley* (1956), ***The Shiralee*** (1957), *Life in Emergency Ward 10* (1959), *Bobbikins* (1960), *Tarzan the Magnificent* (1960), *Cone of Silence* (1961), *Mur-*

der at the Gallop (1963), *Murder Ahoy* (1964), *Murder Most Foul* (1964), *Secret of Blood Island* (1965), *Dracula: Prince of Darkness* (1966), *Thunderbirds Are GO* (1966) (voice), *Eliza Fraser* (1976), *Summerfield* (1977), *Money Movers* (1979), *The Journalist* (1979), *Puberty Blues* (1981), *Freedom* (1982), *My First Wife* (1984), *A Test of Love* (1984), *Malcolm* (1986), *Windrider* (1986), *Shotgun Wedding* (1993), *Amy* (1998), *Tulip* (1998), *The Craic* (1999), *Innocence* (2000), *Will Full* (2001), and *The Inside Story* (2002).

***TWO HANDS* (1999).** Gregor Jordan's film is included here as it was a **crime** thriller in the mold—Australianized for domestic consumption—of Quentin Tarantino's *Reservoir Dogs* (1992) and Guy Ritchie's *Lock Stock and Two Smoking Barrels* (1998). Starring Heath Ledger, **Bryan Brown**, Rose Byrne, and **Susie Porter**, it tells multiple stories that become interconnected in various ways, and establish a fleeting coherence. Pando (Bryan Brown) is the leader of a small gang of sometimes incompetent criminals. He moves easily from discussing the finer points of origami with his young son to shooting those with whom he disagrees. Jimmy (Heath Ledger) loses money that belongs to Pando, and then Pando has to show that such incompetence can be redeemed only through Jimmy's death. In the process, however, the gang kills a street kid—who has the lost money—and the streetkid's partner becomes the agent of karma.

The film changed the crime **genre** by moving away from depictions of the Chandleresque private detective who ended up delivering justice in a world-weary way to depictions of a corrupt society where the law was essentially irrelevant and inconsequential. Any justice that might have occurred happened as a result of some kind of rebalancing of the forces of good and evil in the world, rather than through any human intervention. *Two Hands* won the **Australian Film Institute** award for best film in 1999. *See also* GENRE *and* CRIME.

– V –

VILLAGE ROADSHOW. The youngest of Australia's national distribution/exhibition chains, this group found its way into the industry after World War II. Australia continued to enjoy a cinema-

254 • VILLAGE ROADSHOW

going boom in this period and this persuaded a Melbourne businessman, Roc Kirby, to open a series of hard-top cinemas in that city's suburbs. Recognizing the need to diversify into other forms of outlet and collaborating with two other entrepreneurs, the Kirby group became Village Theatres, which opened its first drive-in in an outer Melbourne suburb in 1954. Shortly, Village had other drive-ins in other suburbs, in **country** Victoria and in Tasmania. Soon, however, **television** began to have devastating effects on cinema attendance and the company was forced to close some of its outlets. Despite this, it pressed ahead and partnered **Greater Union** in a new drive-in in Geelong, leading to the latter buying a one third interest in the company.

Thanks to holding lucrative reissue rights to the film **South Pacific** (1958) and the judicious management of both its hard-tops and drive-ins, Village now moved into both production and distribution. Hexagon Productions became its filmmaking arm and the group was particularly associated with the **ocker** cycle of the early 1970s with *Alvin Purple* (1973) in particular proving to be a big hit. Meanwhile, Roadshow Distributors was formed in 1968, one-third owned by Village. Securing the Australian franchise for American International Pictures put the company well on the way to being a major force in the industry. Nor did Village neglect its core business, pouring money into cinema building, especially targeting the inner city. In the late 1970s, it opened car-racing tracks in Sydney and Village Family Entertainment Centres in Melbourne. Greater Union Film Distributors merged with Village Roadshow Distributors in 1987 to form Roadshow Film Distributors.

The last 20 years has seen this expansion continue. In the early 1980s, Village Roadshow entered television in conjunction with Matt Carroll and Greg Coote and produced a range of drama series aimed at both the domestic and the international markets. Among its several hits was *GP* and *Paradise Beach*. Meanwhile, in 1985, Village opened Cinema City in the heart of Melbourne. Two years later, it entered a joint venture agreement with Greater Union to build multiplexes in the larger shopping complexes in most Australian states. In 1989, it was involved in building Movieworld theme park on the Gold Coast and this was followed six years later with a film studio owned in conjunction with Warners (*see* WARNER BROTHERS

MOVIE WORLD STUDIOS). Nothing succeeds like success and the 1990s has seen Village Roadshow expand its exhibition interests into the United Kingdom, the United States, Europe, and Asia. Meanwhile, the company followed the lead of American majors into other areas of the leisure industry including owning and operating the Daydream Island resort, running radio stations in Malaysia while continuing to nurture and expand its core businesses. By the end of the millennium, Roadshow claimed to be the largest film distributor in Australia while Village claimed to be the largest exhibition chain in the world.

– W –

WARNER BROTHERS MOVIE WORLD STUDIOS. The American company Warner Brothers Studios is a subsidiary of AOL Time Warner Inc. Since 1971, the Australian company **Village Roadshow** Limited has had an exclusive film distribution deal with Warner Brothers Studios. Since 1992, the two companies have held a two-thirds majority share in Sea World Property Trust; together these three companies own the theme park Warner Brothers Movie World, located next to the studios at Queensland's Gold Coast.

The studio facilities include sound stages, casting production offices, water tanks, editing suites, wardrobe, make-up, construction workshops, a preview theaterette, visual effects studio, film processing, post production, travel, and freight services. In 2002, Warner Roadshow announced that in addition to building new production offices and construction workshops on the site, it was expanding the number of soundstages from six to eight. This represents a 50 percent increase in the total soundstage area. Queensland's **Pacific Film and Television Commission** provided an $8 million loan for the expansion project, which went ahead after the Federal Government introduced a 12.5 percent tax rebate in 2001 for qualifying Australian expenditure in big-budget productions.

The studio credits include the features *Scooby-Doo* (2002), *Ghost Ship* (2002), *The Great Raid* (2004), *Peter Pan* (2003), and *Crocodile Dundee in Los Angeles* (2001); and numerous **television** series. *See also* FOX STUDIOS AUSTRALIA.

WATTS, NAOMI (1968–). Naomi Watts was born in England, and, after the death of her father when she was 10, immigrated to Australia with her mother at the age of 14. Her first role was in *For Love Alone* (1986), which starred *Sam Neill and **Hugo Weaving**. After different jobs in the fashion industry, including as a model, she returned to the screen in *Flirting* (1991), alongside her friend **Nicole Kidman** and Thandie Newton, followed by an equally small role in John Duigan's *Wide Sargasso Sea* (1993). Her first lead was in **George Miller**'s *Gross Misconduct* (1993), playing the seducer of Justin Thorne (Jimmy Smits). In the same year, she played in John Dingwall's *The Custodian* (1993), again with Hugo Weaving and **Anthony LaPaglia**.

The most that can be said about her roles in these films was that she learned a great deal from them, as the films were not spectacularly successful, nor were her parts. She opted to go to **Hollywood**, where she established herself as an actress at the second tier, in films like *Tank Girl* (1995), *Persons Unknown* (1996), *Under the Lighthouse Dancing* (1997), and *A House Divided* (1998). She established an international reputation for the role of aspiring actress in David Lynch's thriller *Mulholland Drive* (2001), where she emerged as an actress of great ability and presence. Critics applauded that role, and she was awarded many prizes at international film festivals. Since then her career has blossomed, with starring roles in *The Ring* (2002), *Ned Kelly* (2003), and *21 Grams* (2003).

Other films include *Matinee* (1993), *Dangerous Beauty* (1998), *Strange Planet* (1999), *Ellie Parker* (2001), *Down* (also, *The Shaft*) (2001), *Plots with a View* (2002), *Rabbits* (2002), *Le Divorce* (2003), and *We Don't Live Here Anymore* (2004).

WEAVING, HUGO (1960–). Born in Nigeria, Hugo Weaving spent his early life and teens in South Africa and England, finally arriving in Australia in 1976. He graduated from the National Institute of Dramatic Art in 1981 and, since that time, has been one of the most prolific and versatile of Australian actors. He has won two **Australian Film Institute** awards for best lead actor—in 1991 for the blind photographer in *Proof* (1991) and in 1998 for *The Interview* (1998)—and he was nominated in 1994 for the same award for his role in *The Adventures of Priscilla, Queen of the Desert* (1994). The Blockbuster

Entertainment Awards nominated him for favorite villain in 2000 for his role as Agent Smith in *The Matrix* (1999) and the Montreal World Festival awarded him the best actor prize for his role in *The Interview*. The Screen Actors Guild nominated him as a member of the cast for each of the two **Lord of the Rings* films released up to November 2003, for outstanding performances. In 1998, he won the Australian Star of the Year award.

His career began with a walk-on role as a student in *Maybe This Time* (1980), which did little to impress as he did not appear again until 1983 in the low-budget *The City's Edge*, and then as the dour romantic lead in *For Love Alone* (1986). He followed this with the lead in the English period melodrama *The Right Hand Man* (1987), playing the cad, and in . . . *Almost* (1990) (also known as *Wendy Cracked a Walnut*), he played the perfect lover, Jake, for Wendy (Rosanna Arquette). *Proof* (1991), directed by Jocelyn Moorhouse, cemented his reputation as a highly skilled character actor. He played Martin the blind photographer, who is so paranoid that he believes that people lie when they describe the world to him, so he takes photos, which he then asks other people to describe, to corroborate the initial description. He then played the amoral capitalist Sir John in **Yahoo Serious'** offbeat, successful **comedy** *Reckless Kelly* (1993). He could do little with the role of the husband Jonathon in Stephan Elliott's *Frauds* (1993), but fitted well into the role of the corrupt Detective Church in *The Custodian* (1993), perhaps prefiguring his later role as Agent Smith. In 1995, Elliott cast him as the drag queen in *Priscilla*. Weaving followed this with the unlikely voice of Rex the Sheepdog in the animal fantasy *Babe* (1995) and the sequel *Babe: Pig in the City* (1998), that of Bill Barnacle in *The Magic Pudding* (2000), and the narrator in *Horseplay* (2003).

Although his success could have meant an easy transition to Hollywood, Weaving stayed with the Australian industry, or offbeat productions elsewhere. He played a rocker stuck in a time warp when he tried to negotiate with some petty criminals in the quirky road movie *True Love and Chaos* (1997). His second AFI award came from the role of petty thief under police interrogation in the thriller *The Interview* (1998). With **David Wenham** and **Sacha Horler**, he attempted to resuscitate a difficult narrative in *Russian Doll* (2001), which was not entirely successful.

Weaving has played in two of the most successful film series in Australian and New Zealand film **history**. In the Wachowski brothers' Matrix series—*The Matrix* (1999), *The Matrix Reloaded* (2003), *The Matrix Revolutions* (2003)—he played the leader of the agents, Agent Smith, which are computers that take on human form to prevent humans from realizing their true condition, to prevent them from perceiving the illusion of the Matrix. In *****Peter Jackson**'s ****Lord of the Rings** trilogy—*The Fellowship of the Ring* (2001), *The Two Towers* (2002), and *The Return of the King* (2003)—he plays the serious, introspective Elrond half-Elven, one of the lords of the elves, and finally leaves Middle Earth to travel over the sea. This last trilogy has cemented his name as one of the great actors of contemporary cinema.

Weaving has played in some 12 **television** films, short films, and miniseries. His other feature films include *Exile* (1994), *What's Going On, Frank?* (1994), *Bedrooms and Hallways* (1998), *Strange Planet* (1999), **Rolf de Heer**'s *The Old Man Who Read Love Stories* (2001), and *Peaches* (2003).

WEIR, PETER (1944–). Peter Weir studied arts and law at Sydney University, followed by TV work where he learned the techniques of cinematography and editing. His first internationally distributed film was *The Cars That Ate Paris* (1974). While that was a horror film, **Picnic at Hanging Rock** (1975) entered the realm of the mystical, when a group of private-school girls wander off and are never seen again. This was the first film of the **revival** that shied away from the **ocker** cycle that had been so successful up to this time. *The Last Wave* (1977) documents the conflict a barrister undergoes when his world, his tectonic plate, grinds against that of **Aboriginal** mythology. He followed this with the *The Plumber* (1980), which is one of his few unsuccessful films, although it was made strictly for **television**. In *Gallipoli* (1981), Weir directed and shared writing credits. He juxtaposes the apparent stupidity and class-consciousness of British officers with the egalitarianism of Australian soldiers in the carnage of the World War I trenches in the Dardenelles. In *The Year of Living Dangerously* (1983), Weir weaves a story about a journalist in Indonesia at the time of the 1965 revolution, causing sometimes difficult change, a process mirrored in the choices facing the journalist. In these films, Weir developed what has become his trademark:

the juxtaposition of cultures that causes fracturing in the fabric of one or both. At the same time, that process allows for human characteristics that transcend the difference of culture.

In *Witness* (1985), Weir had two firsts: his first "Hollywood" film and his first film that moved outside the geography and culture of Australia. A young Amish boy witnesses a murder and a policeman is charged with ensuring his safety, while he lives in the Amish community. In a sensitive and sometimes comic way, the story relates the changes in and developments that occur in this juxtaposition. *The Mosquito Coast* (1986) was less successful commercially, and showed the inability of two cultures to easily jigsaw together, when a missionary attempts to transpose religious culture into an apparently innocent jungle. *Dead Poets Society* (1989) tells of the life-changing, liberating effect that comes from challenging the status quo in a **coming-of-age** story. *Green Card* (1990) was a less successful comedy, but *Fearless* (1993) was a powerful examination of a man and the life changes that occur after he miraculously survives an airline disaster. *The Truman Show* (1998) followed, examining the constructed nature of reality and the vicarious existence that people live through television. In 2003, he directed *Master and Commander: The Far Side of the World*, a historical adventure at the time of the Napoleonic Wars.

WENHAM, DAVID (1965–). David Wenham is one of the rising stars of the Australian film industry. A graduate of the University of Western Australia, which has a nationally renowned theater school, he played first in the **television** series *Sons and Daughters* (1982) before roles in two television films: *The Heroes* (1988) and *Come in Spinner* (1990). Three films were to change his status from almost unknown to award winning. He appeared in a small part in *Greenkeeping* (1992), then earned critical praise for his depiction of a pyromaniac in *Cosi* (1996), then played the part of the sociopath Brett Sprague, an ex-convict who returns home to unpleasant consequences in *The Boys* (1997). The part was not new to Wenham; he had played in the stage play of the same name. This role brought him wide critical recognition. He was nominated for a Film Critics Circle of Australia award and an **Australian Film Institute** (AFI) award for best male actor, in 1998. A major role as "Diver Dan" in the popular television series *Sea Change* (1998–1999) added to his acting credentials.

Wenham then played the lead role of Father Damien in Paul Cox's moving retelling of the real story, *Molokai: The Story of Father Damien* (1999), for which the AFI again nominated him as best actor in a leading role (in 2002). In this film, Wenham starred with others of the caliber of Kris Kristofferson, Peter O'Toole, Derek Jacobi, **Leo McKern**, and *Sam Neill. Jonathan Teplitzky's **art film** *Better Than Sex* (2000) followed, with Wenham playing Josh, a photographer who over a three-day period falls in love with a mutually falling Cin, played by **Susie Porter**. Both Porter and Wenham put in compelling performances, and both were nominated for best leading actor and actress awards by the AFI. His career picked up momentum, and in 2001 he played in *Russian Doll*, *Moulin Rouge!* and the lead role of the bank-destroying Jim Doyle in **Robert Connolly**'s thriller about banking, corruption, and the revenge of the ordinary person, *The Bank*. The AFI again nominated him for best actor in a lead role. He played the noble Faramir, brother of Boromir, in *Peter Jackson**'s stunning *Lord of the Rings: The Two Towers* (2002) and *Lord of the Rings: The Return of the King* (2003) (see also *LORD OF THE RINGS*). Teplitzky's second film, the comedy *Gettin' Square* (2003), was not well received, but Wenham's character, Joe Spitieri, has been applauded, winning him an Australian Comedy Award for outstanding comic performance in a feature film, and finally, after four nominations, the AFI award for best leading actor. Few characters have the courage to play such antiheroic roles after the success of a noble character like Faramir. Wenham is established as a world-class actor, with a portfolio of a versatile range of roles across a range of **genres**. He has an imposing screen presence, whether he plays a vaguely innocent lover, a dedicated hacker, or a noble human.

Other films include *Seeing Red* (1992), *No Escape* (1994), *Gino* (1994), *Idiot Box* (1996), *Dark City* (1998), *A Little Bit of Soul* (1998), *Russian Doll* (2001), *Dust* (2001), *The Crocodile Hunter: Collision Course* (2002), *Pure* (2002), and *Basilisk Stare* (2003).

WILLIAMSON, DAVID (1942–). David Williamson was born in Melbourne, Victoria, and graduated from Monash University in 1964 with a degree in mechanical engineering, whereupon he worked for General Motors Holden before returning to academia as a lecturer in social psychology and thermodynamics at Swinburne Institute of

Technology from 1966 to 1972. However, his interest in writing was not to be denied, and as a student he wrote scripts for revues, and in 1968, wrote his first play, *The Indecent Exposure of Anthony East*, which established his trajectory into scriptwriting. His ascendancy coincided with a renaissance in artistic creativity in Australia, fostered by the policies of the newly elected Labor Government in 1972. Williamson was the writer for some of the seminal films of the **revival**, beginning with the **ocker** films *Stork* (1971) and *Petersen* (1974)—both directed by **Tim Burstall**—and then moving to the more complex and analytical *Don's Party* (1976) and *The Club* (1980)—both directed by **Bruce Beresford**. In terms of critical and popular acclaim, the highlight of this early period was the Beresford-directed *Gallipoli* (1981), although, in the previous decade, critics had applauded *The Club* and *Don's Party*, and the public had enjoyed the characters that *Stork* and *Petersen* threw up on the screen. For *The Year of Living Dangerously* (1982), Williamson worked with **Peter Weir** to sculpt a screenplay out of C.J. Koch's novel. Other scripts and screenplays followed—such as *Travelling North* (1987)—but few achieved the filmic success of his earlier work. Williamson has won, and has been nominated for a number of **Australian Film Institute** awards. He has won best screenplay awards for *Don's Party*, *Gallipoli*, and *Travelling North*, and was nominated for the award for *The Club*, *Phar Lap* (1983), *The Year of Living Dangerously*, *Emerald City* (1988), and *Sanctuary* (1995).

Scripts for films are only one element of Williamson's work, and he is an accomplished and widely appreciated writer of plays and **television** films and miniseries. Although his work has sometimes been met with charges of superficiality and commercialism, these are made by those who seek to denigrate genuine creative ability in deference to some "higher" order of things. He has been one of the commanding figures of the Australian film revival.

Other credits include *Libido* (1973), *The Removalists* (1975), *Eliza Fraser* (1976), *Duet for Four* (1982), *The Perfectionist* (1987), and *Brilliant Lies* (1996).

WINCER, SIMON (1943–). Born in Sydney in 1943, Wincer joined the Australian Broadcasting Commission (ABC) before working for three years as a stage manager and director in British **television**. In turn, this allowed him to return in 1970 to Crawford Productions in Melbourne. There he worked on the police series, *Matlock Police*, and the company's first soap opera, *The Box*. In 1979, Wincer was ready to direct his first feature, the thriller *Snapshot*, following this the next year with a political thriller/fantasy *Harlequin*, for which he was nominated for best director by the **Australian Film Institute** (AFI). Both were squarely aimed not at an Australian art cinema audience but were instead pitched at an international market. (The latter even recycled such figures as Robert Powell, Broderick Crawford, and David Hemmings).

Wincer then proceeded to change film **genres**, his next project being the 1983 feature *Phar Lap*, a project deemed to have strong appeal for an Australian audience attracted to period films, and which won him a second AFI nomination for best director. However, *Phar Lap* always ran the risk of an ending that was still well known (the horse died in mysterious circumstances in America). Hence, despite an interesting script by **David Williamson**, the film did only moderately well in Australia and sunk without trace in international outlets. Thereafter, Wincer has mostly worked as director in **Hollywood** films although local contacts and the exigencies of international film have occasionally drawn him back to Australia. Much of this American work has been concerned with mainstream genres such as the sci-fi comedy *D.A.R.Y.L.* (1985) and the children's *Free Willy* (1993). Meanwhile back in Australia he made the spectacular but vacuous *The Lighthorsemen* (1987) and *Quigley* (1990), an outback adventure with television's *Magnum PI* star Tom Selleck. More recent offerings have been the unfunny Western comedy *Lightning Jack* (1994) for **Paul Hogan** and *The Phantom* (1996), based on the famous action comic strip and shot mostly in Queensland. Like many other directors and others who have emerged in the period of the **revival**, Wincer's productive career is otherwise undistinguished, although merely continuing to exercise his craft in the United States and Australia is a sufficient triumph in itself.

Other films include *Harley Davidson and the Marlboro Man* (1991), *Operation Dumbo Drop* (1995), *Crocodile Dundee in Los Angeles* (2001), *The Young Black Stallion* (2003), *NASCAR 3D: The IMAX Experience* (2004).

WOMEN. The subject of women and Australian film is a hub with a number of spokes. These include broad questions of women in the film industry and women in representation. Although these issues overlap, nevertheless, they can also be taken in turn. Thus, the matter of women in the industry has to do with questions of diversity and equity which in turn raises other issues including matters of recruitment, training, funding access, career advancement, and the gender impacts of new technologies. To further articulate, promote, and network, an industry body—Women in Film and Television (WIFT)— came into existence in 1982. Primarily functioning as a networking organization, WIFT facilitates the exchange of information between members working in film, **television**, video, and new media. Additionally, as part of encouraging a diverse screen culture, it also seeks to improve the status and representation of women on the screen. Historically, women have tended to have more of a space before the camera rather than behind it. However, the 1945 reorganization of the Australian government **documentary** production unit, later **Film Australia**, created job opportunities for both Judy Gollan and Joan Long which, in turn, was to allow the latter to move into writing, directing, and producing. Meanwhile, in the 1950s, Norma Disher worked in a production triumvirate with Keith Gow and Jock Levy at the Waterside Worker's Film Unit.

In general though, it was not until the **revival** that increased opportunities for women began to occur in the Australian film industry. Here, there are some obvious and not so obvious patterns to do with general gender inequalities in the wider society. First, the film industry, for the most part, is dominated by men. Equally, too, there are many stories of women carving successful careers in particular sectors of the industry. Thus, for example, Liz Mullinar is a top casting person while Natalie Miller is an important figure in distribution. Given its obvious continuities with such areas as fiction writing and publishing, it is not surprising to find women figuring prominently in the area of writing. Among notable screenwriters are several women recruited from television including Sonia Borg, Anne Brooksbank, and Eleanor Whitcombe. When women have sought to move into other areas of the industry, they have often found it hard going. Hence, only a handful of notable cinematographers including Mandy Walker and Sally Bongers are at work in the Australian production industry. Women have frequently benefited from partnerships with males. Among such notable duos in the Australian film industry in the past and the recent present have been director **Raymond Long-ford** and actress Lottie Lyell, director/producer **Charles Chauvel** and actress turned writer Elsa Chauvel, documentary makers Bob Connolly and Robyn Anderson, and director/producer Nadia Tass and David Parker. Nevertheless, in this period, there have been other avenues into particular parts of the industry. Film directing has been one of these destinations and a significant number of women directors work or have worked in Australia. These include **Gillian Armstrong**, Jane Ballantyne, *****Jane Campion**, Joy Cavill, Glenda Hamblyn, Jackie McKimmon, **Sue Milliken**, Jocelyn Moorehouse, and Nadia Tass. Women producers have not been so common although notable examples include Jan Chapman, Maggie Fink, Sandra Levy, Joan Long, and Pat Lovell.

Shifting from the subject of women behind the camera to women before the camera, the matter of representation is central. One of the most recurring roles for women actors in feature fiction is that of the mother figure. Thus, the woman is represented as mother to children and wife to husband in a stream of Australian films that include *Jedda* (1955), *The Getting of Wisdom* (1977), *Newsfront* (1978), *My Brilliant Career* (1979), *Evil Angels* (1988), *Little Women* (1995), and *The Castle* (1998). Equally, though, images of maternity are called into question in other films including *Monkey Grip* (1982), *Fran* (1985), *High Tide* (1987), *****The Piano** (1993), *Muriel's Wedding* (1994), and *Lillian's Story* (1996). In this latter group, the increasing presence of a daughter and her accession into adulthood calls into question the familial and sexual identity of the older woman figure. The films then trace the consequent negotiation of gender identity the younger woman undertakes. Meanwhile, a more conservative subject of the formation of women as romantic heterosexual partner has recurred in films as different as *The Best of Friends* (1982), *Lonely Hearts* (1982), *Norman Loves Rose* (1982) *The Big Steal* (1991), and *Green Card* (1991). However, the very recent incursion of women into the production industry as writers, directors, and producers has witnessed a surge of feminist films that subtly subvert heterosexuality and mock images of Australian **masculinity**, most especially within the **genre** of the romantic **comedy**. Such a cycle of comically satirical films include Jane Campion's *Sweetie* (1989), Shirley Barrett's *Love Serenade* (1996),

Emma-Kate Croghan's *Love and Other Catastrophes* (1996), Megan Simpson-Huberman's *Dating the Enemy* (1996), Clara Law's *Floating Life* (1996), Cherie Nowlan's *Thank God He Met Lizzie* (1997), Sue Brook's *Road to Nhill* (1997), and Monica Pellizari's *A Fistful of Flies* (1997).

Turning from the heterosexual woman to the lesbian, there are fewer examples of a lesbian cinema within the marquee of Australian film. Although there are hints of lesbianism in **Picnic at Hanging Rock** (1976), *Journey among Women* (1977), and *The Getting of Wisdom* (1977), it has mostly been short independent films that have taken up issues relating to lesbianism. However, it has also been at the center or close to the center of three recent features. *The Sum of Us* (1994) is principally concerned with a heterosexual father coming to grips with his son's sexuality. However, the grandmother was lesbian and the film uses this as a means of constructing a more inclusive sexual liberalism. *Love and Other Catastrophes* (1996), a satirical comedy, focuses on two groups of lovers, the one heterosexual and the other lesbian. Finally, *Dallas Doll* (1994) is another satirical comedy in which the young woman visitor seduces all members of the same family. Overall, then, it is clear that the project of a women's cinema has helped strengthen and diversify the range of possibilities within Australian film both behind and before the camera.

– Y –

YOUNG EINSTEIN (1988). Surprisingly, this little-known film is the 10th most popular at the Australian box office, taking $13.4 million. It won an **Australian Film Institute** award for its music, and was nominated for cinematography, sound, and screenplay. In the United States, Serious won the Celebrated Filmmaker Award from Harvard University's Hasty Pudding Club. While popular in Australia, the film did not travel well to international markets, where many critics did not comprehend the ability of the star, writer, and director, **Yahoo Serious**, to spoof himself. Humor is often culturally specific, and *Einstein* was very successful within Australian culture, although some United States critics stated that their children enjoyed the film.

The film is set in a parallel universe of the island state of Tasmania, where Einstein is the son of apple farmers, and invents bubbles for beer, "roll'n'rock" by transforming a viola into a guitar, and the first surfboard. Not surprisingly, he finds Marie Curie also in this remote part of the world, and with her saves the world from nuclear disaster. The film hints at the world-shattering implications of these discoveries, and hence the genius of those who made them.

Illustrations

Graeme Blundall Alvin Purple.

Holly Hunter and Anna Paquin in The Piano. *(Photograph Courtesy Jan Chapman)*

From left: Miranda (Anne Lambert), Marion (Jane Vallis), Edith (Christine Schuler), and Irma (Karen Robson) in Picnic at Hanging Rock. *(Photograph Courtesy Peter Weir)*

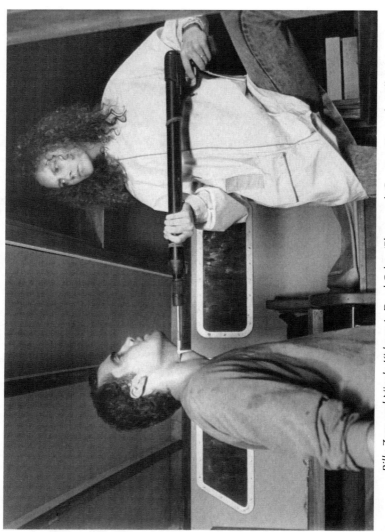

Billy Zane and Nicole Kidman in Dead Calm. (Photograph Courtesy Kennedy Miller)

Anthony LaPaglia and Kerry Armstrong in Lantana. (Photograph Courtesy Jan Chapman)

Mel Gibson with the Feral Kid (Emil Minty) in Mad Max 2. (Photograph Courtesy of Kennedy Miller)

Molly (Everlyn Sami) and Daisy (Tianna Sansbury) in Rabbit-Proof Fence. (Photograph Courtesy of the Australian Film Finance Corporation, the Premium Movie Partnership, South Australian Film Corporation, and Jabal Pty. Ltd.)

Geoffrey Rush as pianist David Helfgott in Shine. (Photograph courtesy Jane Scott)

NEW ZEALAND

Acronyms and Abbreviations

AFTA	Academy of Film and Television Arts
ANZAC	Australia and New Zealand Army Corps
BCNZ	Broadcasting Corporation of New Zealand
EC	European Community
EEC	European Economic Community
LOTR	*Lord of the Rings*
NFU	National Film Unit
NZBC	New Zealand Broadcasting Corporation
NZFA	New Zealand Film Archive
NZFC	New Zealand Film Commission
SPADA	Screen Producers and Directors Association
TVNZ	Television New Zealand
UK	United Kingdom
US	United States
UVF	Ulster Volunteer Forces

Chronology

1895   A.H. Whitehouse used Thomas Edison's Kinetoscope to exhibit New Zealand's first motion pictures. **29 November:** The *New Zealand Herald* carried the first advertisement for a motion picture.

1896   13 October: Charles Godfrey's Vaudeville Company included the first screening of a motion picture as part of the show, at the Opera House, Auckland. **14 October:** New Zealand's first film review appeared in the *New Zealand Herald.*

1898–1900   Alfred Whitehouse was the first filmmaker in New Zealand, making 10 films in this period, and he was the first person to publicly screen a New Zealand film. His film *The Departure of the Second Contingent for the Boer War* (1900) is the oldest surviving film from New Zealand. **1 December:** Whitehouse filmed the opening of the Auckland Exhibition. **26 December:** Filming race days was a favorite occupation of early Australian and New Zealand filmmakers. Whitehouse filmed the Ellerslie race day in Auckland.

1901   The Salvation Army Limelight Department was commissioned by the government to film the visit by the Duke and Duchess of York.

1902   The Salvation Army's Biorama Company began touring New Zealand to make films.

1904   British showman Thomas J. West showed films as part of a tour by the musical group The Brescians, then immigrated to Australia.

1905 During their filmmaking tours, Biorama developed a "real-time" method of filmmaking, where shots of the local community and locations were developed overnight, then exhibited within that community the next day.

1906 The importation of United States culture began with the exhibition of the film *America at Work* in Auckland. At 10,000 feet in length, requiring two projectors and two operators, it was a testimony to the technological mastery of the United States film industry. An amendment to the *Offensive Publications Act 1892* allowed for the searching of premises for indecent material.

1907 *Ned Kelly*, the Australian bushranger feature, screened in New Zealand. It stands in stark contrast in every way to *America at Work*.

1908 New Zealand's first building converted for permanent cinema use was His Majesty's Theatre in Wellington. At the same time, the Hayward family bought the Royal Albert Hall in Auckland as a permanent cinema.

1910 The legislation that was to govern censorship in New Zealand until 1954, the *Indecent Publications Act*, became law. The first purpose-built cinema, the King's Theatre in Wellington, was built.

1911 Suburban cinemas were built. **25 November:** The Queens, in Auckland, was the first New Zealand cinema to screen continuously for 12 hours from 11:00 A.M.

1912 George Méliès brother, Gaston, arrived in New Zealand. He shot five travel films and three narratives, which were *Hinemoa, How Chief Te Ponga Won His Bride* (both 1,000 feet), and a short feature, *Loved by a Maori Chieftess* (2,000 feet).

1913 The first distribution company, New Zealand Picture Supplies, was incorporated by Fuller and the Haywards. **14 March:** Méliès' film, *Loved by a Maori Chieftess*, screened.

1914 **1 August:** George Tarr produced a short feature, also called *Hinemoa*, telling the story of the separation of Maori lovers. At 2,500 feet, it is, arguably, the first New Zealand feature film. It was shot and edited in eight days, and opened on **17 August**.

1916 The government passed the *Cinematograph-film Censorship Act*, which established the office of the censor to maintain public decency in films. It was illegal to exhibit films that the censor had not approved.

1919 James McDonald toured New Zealand and made four ethnographic films that documented the traditional life of the Maori.

1920 Rudall Hayward was the production assistant on Australian director Beaumont Smith's *The Betrayer in Rotorua*. Later, Hayward was assistant director of *The Birth of New Zealand*.

1921 Rudall Hayward's first feature, *The Bloke from Freeman's Bay*, was so bad that his uncle bought it from Rudall for 150 pounds, then burned it.

1922 Rudall Hayward directed *My Lady of the Cave*. It was the first time a New Zealand novel had been transformed into a film. He subsequently directed at least three other feature films—*Rewi's Last Stand* (1925), *The Te Kooti Trail* (1927), and *The Bush Cinderella* (1928).

1923 The censor demanded that 900 feet of the first feature film, *The Romance of Sleepy Hollow*, be cut.

1926 Ted Coubray established New Zealand Radio Films Ltd. He made a series of short documentaries for industry, including *Bottled Health* (1926) and *Magic Collar Box* (1927).

1927 Rudall Hayward made the first of the community comedies, *A Takapuna Scandal*. Ted Coubray made the horse-racing feature *Carbine's Heritage*, which attracted capacity audiences in Auckland.

1928 Michael and Joe Moodabe formed Amalgamated Theatres, which grew to a chain of 32 theaters by 1932, despite, or perhaps because of, the Depression.

1929 Edwin Coubray conducted the first sound tests for New Zealand Radio Films. Rudall and Hilda Hayward filmed and exhibited another seven community comedies. **20 December:** The 3,500-seat picture palace, The Civic Theatre, opened in Auckland with the screening of the talkie *Three Live Ghosts.*

1930 The first New Zealand-made talkie was Ted Coubray's first edition of *Coubray Tone News.* The film of Remarque's *All Quiet on the Western Front* was temporarily banned.

1931 Rudall Hayward was Australia Cinesound's reporter in New Zealand, and filmed the aftermath of the Napier earthquake.

1934 Because of some public dissatisfaction with the judgments of the censor, the parliament amended the Cinematographic Films Act so that the minister of internal affairs could appeal the censor's ruling. A new classification was established to allow films to be screened without cuts at Film Society events.

1937 Reflecting a cultural fascination with horse racing, Rudall Hayward located cameras around the Ellerslie racecourse in order to capture greater realism in horse race filming.

1938 In order to make films that focused on Maori and other historical issues, Jim Manley incorporated the company Eppics.

1940 In an effort to generate a film industry in New Zealand, a group led by Gordon Mirams successfully lobbied the Labor government to establish a film production unit, particularly to film documentaries and travelogues. It came to fruition a year later.

1940–1970 Only three feature films were made during this period, all by John O'Shea.

1941 The National Film Unit began making films as the government's principal film producer until 1990. Stanhope Andrews led the unit, and Rudall Hayward became a photographer.

1942 Recognizing the pedagogical value of films, the government established the National Film Library as a lending institution for schools to access.

1945 Gordon Mirams' *Speaking Candidly* was the first book on the New Zealand film industry. With 133 cinemas in Australia and New Zealand, Robert Kerridge's Odeon chain became the largest in the region.

1946 Rudall Hayward immigrated to the United Kingdom.

1947 Roger Mirams and Alun Falconer became freelance reporters for Fox Movietone.

1948 Falconer (director) and Mirams (cameraman) left the National Film Unit to form the Pacific Film Unit, which specialized in making short sponsored documentary films. New Zealand actor Bathie Stuart, who starred in Beaumont Smith's Australian-made *The Adventures of Algy* (1925), presented film lectures in the United States.

1949 After working as a newsreel editor and director with the National Film Unit, Cecil Holmes immigrated to Australia. The government amended the censorship legislation so that films would be rated according to broad audience age groups, rather than being simply cut.

1950 The National Film Unit magazine-film *Weekly Review* ceased production after 459 issues since 1941. John O'Shea joined the Pacific Film Unit, which changed its name to Pacific Film Productions when Falconer left.

1952 The National Film Unit began producing the monthly magazine-film *Pictorial Parade*. The first feature since World War II, John O'Shea's *Broken Barrier*, was released by Pacific Films. Rudall Hayward returned to New Zealand to make documentaries.

1954 *The Wild One* was banned.

1954–1957 Pacific Films produced *Pacific Magazine*, a magazine format newsreel intended to accompany features.

1955 *Rebel without a Cause* was allowed into the country after an appeal.

1957 Roger Mirams left Pacific Films, and the name John O'Shea became synonymous with Pacific Films. Rudall and Ramai Hayward traveled to China to make documentaries at the invitation of the Chinese government.

1960 By June, television was accessible throughout New Zealand, and cinema attendances dropped.

1964 John O'Shea's *Runaway* was released by Pacific Films.

1966 Pacific Films released John O'Shea's *Don't Let It Get You.*

1967 Believing that the dialogue would cause embarrassment in mixed company, the censor stipulated that *Ulysses* must be shown only to segregated audiences.

1969 Pacific Films employed 22 permanent staff and television commercials accounted for three-quarters of its revenue.

1970 The short film *This is New Zealand*, made for the World Expo in 1970, was released to huge audience acclaim within the country. The first New Zealand feature film to be broadcast on New Zealand television was *Rewi's Last Stand*. A film analysis course was introduced at Victoria University. This and other related events mark an upsurge of interest in films as cultural artifacts. **February:** The first color television signals were transmitted.

1972 The first Wellington Film Festival comprised a program of 17 films. **December:** The journal *Alternative Cinema* began publication of articles about New Zealand film culture.

1975 Auckland University offered a graduate course in film studies.

1977 *Sleeping Dogs*, directed by Roger Donaldson and introducing Sam Neill, was the first New Zealand film to be released in the United States. **November:** The Interim Film Commission met to advise the government on policy to establish and develop a film industry.

1978 As in Australia, the New Zealand government became concerned to develop and define "national identity" and culture. The Broadcasting Corporation of New Zealand offered grants to film and television producers for programs that articulated these aims. **November:** The New Zealand Film Commission was formed to support and encourage New Zealand filmmakers through financing the development and production of feature films, with the broader brief of making New Zealand culture available to overseas markets through film.

1979–1991 With the upturn in the film industry, Pacific Films released six features: *Sons for the Return Home* (1979), *Pictures* (1981), *Among the Cinders* (1984), *Leave All Fair* (1985), *Ngati* (1987), and *Te Rua* (1991).

1980 Tax lawyers saw film production as a way of reducing company and individual taxes. Feature film production increased each year up to 1984, when 14 films were made. The tax laws were then changed. Color television was present in 67 percent of New Zealand homes. The New Zealand Film Commission took films to Cannes for exhibition.

1981 **9 March:** The New Zealand Film Archive was founded, with enthusiast Jonathan Dennis as first director.

1982 Sam Pillsbury's *The Scarecrow* was chosen for screening during the Director's fortnight at Cannes, the first New Zealand feature to be honored in this way.

1983 Roger Donaldson was the first New Zealand director to move to California to live and work, successfully making the transition in films like *The Bounty* (1984) and *No Way Out* (1987). Merata Mita was the first woman to direct a feature-length film, *Patu!* Jim Booth was the second appointment to the directorship of the New Zealand Film Commission. During his five-year term, 27 features were produced and the short film fund was established.

1984 This year marked the summit of film production with 14 films made. The government gradually closed loopholes in the taxation laws, severely restricting the flow of finance into film production, resulting in only four features being produced by 1986.

1985 Lawyer David Gascoigne replaced founding chairman Bill Sheat at the Film Commission.

1987 Concerned about the growth in sales and rentals of prerecorded videos, the parliament passed the Video Recordings Act, which established the Video Recordings Authority to censor and classify videos. The Guild of Film and Television Artists presented the Rudall Hayward Memorial Award to John O'Shea for "exceptional contributions to the industry." Barry Barclay's feature *Ngati* was chosen for the critics' week at Cannes; it was the first film written and directed by Maori. Peter Jackson's second film as director, *Bad Taste*, was released.

1988 Merata Mita was the first Maori woman to write and direct a feature fiction film, *Mauri*. In the United States, the home video market generated greater revenue than the cinema. The implications of this are still being realized, as investors and filmmakers realize that local productions have a market, which, in turn, generates greater activity in the film industry.

1990 The potential market for films had increased enormously through the penetration of color television and video players into homes, creating the market alluded to previously. Ownership of household video recorders increased from nil in 1980 to 68 percent by the end of the decade. Ninety-six percent of households owned at least one color television. John O'Shea was awarded the Order of the British Empire (OBE), an award of the British Commonwealth, for services to the film industry. Jane Campion's *An Angel at My Table* won seven awards at the Venice Film Festival. It was the first New Zealand film to compete in this festival.

1992 The Film Commission presented John O'Shea with the first Lifetime Achievement Award for services to film. The New Zealand Film Archive launched the Last Film Search in an attempt to find and archive films. Seven thousand films were found.

1993 Jane Campion won the first New Zealand Oscar for best original screenplay for *The Piano* at the Academy Awards. Anna Paquin was the first New Zealander to win an Oscar for best supporting actress for the same film. Censorship legislation was combined in the Films, Videos and Publications Classifications Act.

1994   The Office of Film and Literature Classification was established under the Classifications Act. Lee Tamahori's *Once Were Warriors* established a record by taking more than NZ$6 million at the box office.

1995   Actor Bruno Lawrence died suddenly. *Cinema of Unease*, Sam Neill's iteration of the history of cinema in New Zealand, was released for the British Film Institute's Century of Cinema series.

1996   New Zealand celebrated the Centenary of Cinema, and indicators of new interest in films continued to manifest. The Asia-Pacific Film Festival was held in Auckland, Waikato University held a New Zealand film conference, and the Moving Image Centre joined with the Film and Television Centre at Auckland University to host a conference on documentary film. *Planet Man* won the best short film award at the Cannes Film Festival Critics' Week.

1997   Peter Jackson and Costa Botes released *Forgotten Silver*, a documentary about Colin Mackenzie, a New Zealand film pioneer who invented all kinds of film techniques, and who left the evidence in a lost city in New Zealand. The film was a total hoax, and resulted in the coining of the term "mockumentary" to describe such films.

1998   **December:** Centenary of filmmaking in New Zealand celebrated.

1999   *What Becomes of the Broken Hearted* won 11 prizes at the New Zealand Film Awards, including best director, best actor, best supporting actor, and best screenplay. **December:** The Last Film Search, the seven-year nation-wide search for films, ended.

2000   The Bank of New Zealand Traveling Film Show projected more than 90 free screenings of sound and silent films from the New Zealand Film Archive in the first five-month tour. Tours continued up to the present. **30 November–3 December:** The New Zealand Film Archive and the Victoria University of Wellington hosted the 10th Conference of the History and Film Association of Australia and New Zealand.

2001   March: The New Zealand Film Archive announced plans to produce and circulate VHS video programs of films for use in schools to explore New Zealand history and heritage. **July:** Filmmaker John O'Shea died. **November:** The Rosier Fund was launched, dedicated to preserving early New Zealand film, particularly nitrate film.

2001-2003   December: The first film of Peter Jackson's *Lord of the Rings* trilogy, *The Fellowship of the Ring*, was released. The sequels were released in December in 2002 and 2003. The films won huge international audiences and critical acclaim, and once again focused the world's attention on New Zealand, especially as a tourist destination, but also as the country that successfully attempted one of the most ambitious projects in film history.

2002   January: The first director of the National Film Archive and film industry activist Jonathan Dennis died.

2003   *Whale Rider* blitzed the New Zealand Film Awards with nine prizes, including best feature film, best director, best actress, best supporting actor, and best supporting actress. The film won 13 awards internationally, including the humanities award and the cinema audience award at the Sundance Festival.

Introduction

New Zealand has a relatively small population of four million. Thus, in the environment of a global village, successful filmmakers and actors often have been headhunted, or they otherwise have moved to the greener pastures of more lucrative and challenging projects elsewhere, from Australia to Hollywood. Sometimes they have returned with even more challenging projects. Peter Jackson's *Lord of the Rings* trilogy (2000–2003) was one of the most ambitious projects in the history of filmmaking. Yet the film raises questions that require exploration, if not answers, in any discussion of New Zealand film.

DEFINING NEW ZEALAND FILM

In these days of globalized networks of studios, corporations, distribution chains, actors, crew, and so on, how does one define a New Zealand film? For the sake of this discussion, the *Lord of the Rings* trilogy is regarded as a single film, a justifiable claim since the three films are not sequels or prequels, but part of a single narrative. Director Peter Jackson is from New Zealand and established a reputation based on films made entirely in New Zealand. Screenwriter Frances Walsh was born in Wellington, New Zealand, and has collaborated with Jackson on other films. The film was shot in New Zealand, and most of the special effects were manufactured there by the New Zealand companies, Weta Digital, and Weta Workshop. Production companies were WingNut Films from New Zealand and New Line Cinema from the United States. Jackson stated that he was indebted to crew members from Australia, and stated that the film was really a coproduction. Some major cast members were Australian—Cate Blanchett (Galadriel), Hugo Weaving (Elrond) and David Wenham (Faramir)—and some of the cast and crew were New

Zealanders—Sala Baker (Sauron) and Marton Csokas (Celeborn). According to these criteria, the film is a product of New Zealand.

Many other elements of the film are from outside New Zealand. The narrative is not located in any one country, but New Zealand has now assumed Middle Earth as its own. The story is not specific to a particular culture, nor are the characteristics of the narrative culturally located. The trappings of any particular culture are not apparent; that is, consumer items do not identify the culture as "Western consumer," "New Zealand," or anything else. In a general sense though, the film is obviously a product of United States–European culture, rather than Arabic or Asian. Hence, "global" and "international" here mean "Western." In summary, the film is international in its narrative, made with an international cast and crew, garnering international recognition and audiences, but with New Zealand credits.

As a result of these kinds of circumstances, defining a New Zealand film is becoming increasingly more difficult, as the industry becomes more international and globalized. Hollywood stars are not only from the United States, but also from almost anywhere, including New Zealand. Local film stars may be also stars outside the country of their birth or adoption. Similar statements apply to the various members of the crew, and for production companies. On the other hand, although Hollywood genres are infiltrating every corner of the world where films are screened, so too are the local variations on those genres significant. Such local variations might include specific locations, specific themes peculiar to a country, narratives that are specific to the history and culture of a country, language nuances, habits, and different understandings of particular genres; for example, what is comic in one culture might not be in another.

Thus, when critics and others talk about it—the entity called New Zealand film—as though it were a given, they are speaking within an outmoded paradigm. The *Lord of the Rings* is an example of the problems of definition, but there are many others. This was not always the case. A New Zealand film was identifiable because it was made in New Zealand, with New Zealand cast and crew, with narratives that were identifiable as from New Zealand, and audiences that were generally limited to New Zealand. The case of Australia has shown that, even in the earliest days of filmmaking, such clear-cut definitions were sometimes problematic, and similar conclusions can be drawn in relation to the New Zealand industry, although to a lesser extent. Nowadays though, the globalization of the industry has led to a blurring of definitions about what comprises a New Zealand film.

As with its Australian counterpart, the 1978 *Film Commission Act* defined a New Zealand film, for the purpose of funding, as one with significant New Zealand content in terms of the film's creators, production team, cast, financiers, copyright holder, equipment, and technical facilities. In its determinations, the Commission has regard for the subject of the film, the locations where the film would be made, the nationalities and places of residence of the production crew and the cast, as well as the owners of the companies investing in the film, and those who are to own the copyright. In addition, the sources of funding, the location of the production and postproduction facilities has to be considered. In reality, such classifications have become increasingly difficult.

Another element in the equation is that of international films that are made locally, drawing on the expertise of the local industry, with no elements that identify local settings being apparent. *The Last Samurai* (2003), for example, was made in New Zealand, but set in Asia. The currency exchange rate and available expertise make it possible for films to be made in New Zealand cheaper than elsewhere, without loss of quality.

New technologies have affected the making of films in New Zealand because these technologies make possible wider distribution of film. For example, in the days before television, New Zealand film was accessible only to those people who went to a screening. This meant a large proportion of the population. Outside New Zealand, such film was more difficult to screen simply because of the problems of printing new copies, distributing them, and generating an audience sufficient for a theater owner to make a profit. This changed slightly with the advent of television, and cable and satellite television, which opened up a new market for such films. Video and DVD sales and hire are now a significant element in the revenue calculations of film producers. Such sales and hire open new and international markets to New Zealand films.

HISTORY OF FILMMAKING IN NEW ZEALAND

Until recently, the history of the industry in New Zealand was one of boom and bust, to an even greater extent than Australia's. New Zealanders embraced film from the first screening in 1895, and in 1906 began their love affair with United States films with *America at Work*, and permanent cinemas were built in 1908. People such as the Hayward family and Michael and Joe Moodabe dominated distribution and exhibition through theater chains that were susceptible to United States economic pressures to screen U.S. product. Thus in 1925, 95 percent of the films shown in New Zealand came from the United States and New Zealanders became avid fans of this imported fare. Nevertheless, the local industry began early when, in 1914, Frenchman Gaston Méliès drew on a Maori legend to make *Hinemoa*, New Zealand's first feature film.

Paralleling the influx of American product was the emergence of the work of Rudall Hayward, who was to become one of the pioneers of an indigenous film industry. He completed his first feature, *The Bloke from Freeman's Bay*, in 1921. He made a number of films, but *Rewi's Last Stand* remains his best. Filmed in 1925, it was remade with sound and released in 1940. Another filmmaker, Edwin Coubray, pioneered the used of sound, but the expensive technology resulted in fewer films being made in New Zealand for the small local market. From the 1930s, non-New Zealand directors, using outside finance, made a small number of films for overseas audiences, which drew on the "exotic" elements of Maori culture (Simmons 1999: 39–49). Many of these films misrepresented that culture.

By 1945, New Zealanders were among the most frequent cinema attendees in the Western world, averaging 20 excursions each year. Their film diet was almost pure Hollywood in this pretelevision era, with some exotic dishes from Great Britain and Australia. Between 1940 and 1970, only three feature films were made in New Zealand for the New Zealand market. Outside of the film industry, the other strong cultural influence on New Zealand was Britain, as the center of the British Empire of which New Zealand was a distant outpost. Migration established a relationship that was cemented through wartime allegiances. The ANZAC (Australia and New Zealand Army Corps) contributions at Gallipoli and the Western Front in World War I, and in the European and Asian theaters in World War II—where 20,000 New Zealanders died—strengthened the binary. The King/Queen of England was and is the King/Queen of New Zealand, and the Privy Council in Britain was the highest court of appeal for the nation. Economic ties were also strong. From the 1920s and following the development of refrigeration, a significant portion of New Zealand income came from the export of dairy products—mainly butter and cheese—and mutton to the United Kingdom. British culture was imported into New Zealand. The real/reel thing came from overseas.

However, New Zealanders were able to see themselves reflected—perhaps through a glass darkly—in the documentaries that were made by the National Film Unit, commencing in 1941, and the weekly newsreels that were made to accompany the screening of the one or two feature films that comprised a normal cinema program. Private companies, such as Pacific Films Ltd., were established to produce, primarily, documentaries for and about industry, but also for public screenings. In 1970, the National Film Unit made the documentary *This is New Zealand*, a film about the splendor of the country, which people queued to see.

The success of such a documentary—in the first year of the significant decade of the 1970s—suggests a new and emerging national consciousness, a focusing on New Zealand as a place of beauty in its own right, distinct from either the United States or the United Kingdom. The first television screening of a New Zealand feature film supports this argument. At the same time that *This is New Zealand* was released, Rudall Hayward's *Rewi's Last Stand* was broadcast on television. It is significant that this first film should address Maori issues. Other events attest to an emerging viewpoint that films, especially domestic productions, were a legitimate mode of storytelling, depicting and recycling issues, identities, and national culture set in familiar biospheres and semiospheres, with actors speaking a familiar language. For example, universities introduced film analysis courses and cities established film festivals. A further step in the legitimation of film culture was the establishment of the New Zealand Film Archive in 1981, designed to collect earliest examples of film of all types and to archive these as significant elements in the national history. Color television, introduced in 1970, reinvigorated the possibility of screen culture, through providing a new medium for the viewing of films.

Economic fissuring contributed to a reassessment of national consciousness of "New Zealand." By the mid-1970s, economic changes in the United Kingdom confronted New Zealanders with the need to reassess the national economy. Up to this time, New Zealand had been content to supply the United Kingdom with all the dairy products, mutton, and other primary produce that her inhabitants could consume. In

1973, Great Britain joined the Common Market, the precursor to the European Economic Community and the European Community, which meant that most of the products New Zealand had supplied were now supplied by European countries, leaving New Zealand abandoned on the world market. More importantly, the idea that Great Britain was the spiritual and economic home was overturned. This sense of dislocation was profound, but the upside was that some New Zealanders began to explore and value their own stories and experiences, even though this work was often much less romantically ideal, and more socially realistic or suburban surreal, than the world of *This is New Zealand*. This dislocation, paralleling other changes mentioned above, resulted in a need to fill the vacuum, and in the realm of storytelling, was met in part through government recognition of the industry, manifesting in the establishment of grants to films that might develop and define national culture and identity. In 1978, the New Zealand Film Commission was formed to financially support and encourage New Zealand filmmaking. In addition, tax lawyers discovered that significant write-offs were available to companies investing in film production, meaning that funds became available to filmmakers that allowed them to make mistakes in their work; that is, companies would receive a tax benefit whether films were successful or not. The possibility was that some films would be successful on the international market. Roger Donaldson's *Sleeping Dogs* was the first New Zealand film to be released in the United States, and while not spectacularly successful, showed that the quality of production was equivalent to that of Hollywood.

As a result of these economic and cultural changes, in the following decades feature film production blossomed, throwing up many forgettable films in the process of establishing the skills and filmmaking abilities of some fine actors, directors, and crew, resulting in films of stature that have won international critical acclaim. As a result, these people easily cross from the world of New Zealand filmmaking into that of international filmmaking. Although it is accurate to say that New Zealand filmmaking loses something in that process, it is just as accurate to say that international filmmaking is enriched. When international films are, in turn, created in New Zealand, the skill base within the country is both enhanced and showcased. As the *Lord of the Rings* trilogy has shown, the benefits for New Zealand can be enormous. It is not so much the case that *Lord of the Rings* has showcased New Zealand; rather, *LOTR* has created the Middle Earth identity for New Zealand. The film has created a persona for the country, on which that country has capitalized.

THE NARRATIVES OF NEW ZEALAND FILM

It is difficult to generalize about the narratives and themes of New Zealand film. In the documentary made for the British Film Institute's *Century of Cinema* series, Sam Neill characterized New Zealand cinema as the "cinema of unease" (Neill 1995). It was the cinema of unease, not because of its self-consciousness, but because it explored the darker sides of New Zealand culture. He saw the road as a central signifier of New Zealand film, lonely, leading to isolated spaces, and evoking restlessness and darkness. One element of that unease was the relationship between Maori and *pakeha*, or non-Maori New Zealanders, at least in later films. That these relationships have been of significance for New Zealand filmmakers reflects the significance the relationships have for New Zealand culture in general. The first three films made in New Zealand—by Gaston Méliès in the second decade of the new century—focused on Maori. In the last decade, the most arresting and confronting film, because of its raw violence, was Lee Tamahori's *Once Were Warriors* (1994), which traces the dissolution of a dysfunctional Maori family. Whether consciously or not, filmmakers have used the medium to articulate the dynamics surrounding the juxtaposition of cultures. Yet, the unease Neill discusses is apparent not only in relations between Maori and pakeha, but in the examples thrown up by the new wave of filmmakers of the late 1970s. At the beginning of the decade, the National Film Unit's *This Is New Zealand* had portrayed the countryside and its people in the best possible light, with shots of majestic landscapes and invigorated, positive inhabitants. However, the directors of the late 1970s imagined a different New Zealand. Geoff Murphy's irreverent and illogical *Wild Man* (1977)—a New Zealand version of Barry Humphries—demonstrated the anarchic and roughly hewn attitudes and skills that marked the early work of these filmmakers. Rejecting classical Hollywood cause and effect relationships, new director Paul Maunder's *Landfall* (1977) investigated the joys of communal living, in a somewhat self-conscious and now-dated fashion. Roger Donaldson's *Sleeping Dogs* (1977) was a kind of transposition of Vietnam to New Zealand. These films proved that New Zealand audiences wanted to see their own diverse stories negotiated in a familiar language in familiar locations. However, *Sleeping Dogs* also showed that a market for New Zealand film existed in the United States; that New Zealand film had world-class potential. These early films proved that directors like Donaldson, Maunder, Murphy, John Laing, and others had the ability and filmic sense to weave stories in a way that was attractive for New Zealand and, sometimes, international audiences.

Although these films varied in subject, some filmmakers turned their attention to the darker sources of New Zealand history for their stories, creating a narrative space of unease. John Laing's *Beyond Reasonable Doubt* (1980) revealed the police corruption and deceit in the true story of the investigation and trial of a farmer accused, tried, and convicted of murder, but who was later pardoned. Michael Black's *Pictures* (1981) painted a chilling picture of documented pakeha violence and brutality, as does *Utu* (1983). People from other countries in the South Pacific populate New Zealand and their fate has often paralleled that of Maori. Martyn Sanderson's *Flying Fox in a Freedom Tree* (1990) told a bitter story about the effects of colonization on Western Samoa, causing the eventual suicide of a despairing man who had lost his cultural identity. British Director Mike Newell's *Bad Blood* (1982) retold a tragedy of violence in a rural community caused through ostracism, alienation, and paranoia in a west coast community of the South Island. Although these films were set in rural settings, the city was no enlightened site of "ease" either. Urban Auckland was the setting for John Laing's *Other Halves* (1984), a reconstruction from Sue McCauley's autobiographical novel, where class and race conflicts were promoted in part through a corrupt and racist police force, and where men were all potential womanizers. In his fourth film, *Heavenly Creatures* (1994), Peter Jackson recreated the famous Parker-Hulme story about two high school girls who cold-bloodedly plotted and then murdered one of their mothers with a brick in a Christchurch park in 1954.

Other films did not draw on real events, but were nevertheless evidence of Neill's unease thesis. Jane Campion's *The Piano* (1993) was a bleak film about, on one level, suppressed sexuality as the cornerstone of Western civilization. Derided by some, the film has won critical acclaim around the world, manifesting in numerous awards. The film added another level to the corpus of international successes generated from the New Zealand industry. Campion's earlier film, *An Angel at My Table* (1990), was more triumphant, although it told a bleak story. It was based on the autobiographies of the late Janet Frame, a writer and poet, who spent much of her life in institutions, wrongly diagnosed as schizophrenic, and made to endure 200 instances of electric shock therapy. This film won many awards at home and internationally. Other women have become significant filmmakers since 1977. For example, Gaylene Preston was production designer for *Middle Age Spread* (1979), then director for *Mr. Wrong* (1985), *Ruby and Rata* (1990), *Bread and Roses* (1993), and the documentary about and by women in war, *War Stories: Our Mother Never Told Us* (1995). More recently, she produced and directed the strange *Perfect Strangers* (2003). Alison Maclean directed the award-winning *Crush* (1992), while more recently, Gillian Ashurst wrote and directed the uneven *Snakeskin* (2001) and Christine Jeffs wrote the screenplay and directed *Rain* (2001). She went on to direct the film about the life of Sylvia Plath, *Sylvia* (2003). Niki Caro wrote and directed the award-winning story about the transformation of Maori lore, *Whale Rider* (2002), while Merata Mita is a powerful directorial voice for Maori people.

Even in this brief discussion it is evident that every genre is present in New Zealand film, and while there are elements of unease, there are other and equally legitimate characteristics. Some examples of those genres point to the international stature of the industry. Geoff Murphy's road movie comedy *Goodbye Pork Pie* (1980) was not one of those, but it is significant because it was a huge box office success and was the first film to cover costs purely from the domestic market, and which was a milestone and a turning point in the industry. It was evidence that New Zealand audiences enjoyed films about New Zealand life. Vincent Ward's *The Navigators: A Medieval Odyssey* (1988) was a complex thriller with political overtones, juxtaposing medieval life with contemporary New Zealand urban existence. Of a similar genre was Murphy's *The Quiet Earth* (1985), a science fiction film about the last survivors on Earth. The film met with enthusiastic reviews both in New Zealand and overseas. Although not set in medieval times or the future, *Desperate Remedies* (1993) was a 19th-century melodrama about love and passion, but also about liberation from the chains of convention. Peter Jackson's early fantasy/comedies—*Bad Taste* (1986), *Meet the Feebles* (1990), and *Braindead* (1992)—have been dubbed "splatstick" for their excessive depiction of the act of murder, and have become cult films. Other comedy films include Ian Mune's *Came a Hot Friday* (1984) and Harry Sinclair's *Topless Women Talk about Their Lives* (1997).

Children's films have been successful for New Zealand filmmakers, in part for their topicality. For example, *The Whole of the Moon* (1996) told the story of the highs and lows of children in a cancer ward, united—regardless of race or class—in their battle against cancer. *Bonjour Timothy* (1995) has the underdog winning the affection of the girl against all odds, in a film about coming-of-age anxieties of sex and love. Ian Mune's *The End of the Golden Weather* (1991) retold the story of playwright Bruce Mason's childhood, and was received enthusiastically by audiences in New Zealand. At the other end of the spectrum, war films are significant in the industry. John Reid's *The Last Tattoo* (1994) explored the tensions that festered in the early 1940s when U.S. soldiers were rotated through Wellington on rest and recreation leave. John Laing's *Absent without Leave* (1993) told the stories of young people, whose lives were interrupted and changed by war, learning about love, trust, and responsibility. Of course, the New Zealand film industry would be incomplete without a film about the previously all-conquering All Blacks Rugby Union team. Alan Clayton's *Old Scores* (1991) provided that piece of the jigsaw.

THE FUTURE

If the road is still a central signifier of New Zealand film, then it is clear that the nature of the road has changed. Although still leading to new and interesting places, the road is both built by experts and traveled by people for whom the road is no longer uncertain. That it leads to new territories is clear; that those new territories can be explored with confidence is also clear. Thus the cinema of unease has given way to the cinema of confidence, the confidence that filmmakers need in order to undertake audacious projects like the *Lord of the Rings* trilogy, the minimalist essay on the possibilities arising from boredom in Christine Jeff's *Rain* (2001), or the understated lyricism of *Whale Rider* (2002).

Despite the success of the films of Aotearoa, such as *The Lord of the Rings*, some fragility still haunts the industry. Reasons for this fragility include the value of the dollar (which affects the profitability of filmmaking in New Zealand in comparison with other places), the interests of the public, and the loss of cast and crew to more ambitious projects that may be mounted overseas more successfully. On the other hand, many changes have occurred since 1977 that have provided a firm foundation for a thriving industry. Filmmakers, cast and crew have shown that they are equal to the world's best in making films with international themes, while other films have shown that the world is interested in New Zealand narratives and settings. Additionally, the New Zealand government has seen the economic benefits of a viable film industry, and has broadened its support through the establishment of the Screen Council of New Zealand, whose aim is to double the size of the screen production industry in five years. Given this level of government encouragement of the already-proven ability of the industry, the future appears secure, and such support continues.

This dictionary has neglected any discussion of adult films. Little is known about their significance to the industry. Doubtless, their sale and viewing, if not their manufacture, are a significant and arguably legitimate element of the broader New Zealand film industry, but research is almost nonexistent.

The Dictionary

– A –

ACADEMY OF FILM AND TELEVISION ARTS (AFTA). The Academy of Film and Television Arts is an industry-wide organization comprising the full memberships of many groups, all of whom are represented on the AFTA board: the Screen Producers and Directors Association (SPADA), New Zealand Directors Guild, New Zealand Film and Video Technicians Guild, Nga Aho Whakaari, Women in Film and Television (WIFT), Actors Equity, and the New Zealand Writers Guild. The Academy organizes the Nokia New Zealand Film Awards (*see* NEW ZEALAND FILM AND TELEVISION AWARDS). Although the academy receives support from many industry groups, and although it organizes the film and television awards, it plays an otherwise low-profile role in the industry.

– B –

BAILEY, BERT. *See entry in Australian section.*

BOLLINGER, ALUN (1948–). Alun Bollinger has worked as camera operator, cinematographer, and director of photography on many films since the resurgence in filmmaking in the late 1970s, and has the reputation of being one of New Zealand's leading cinematographers. Certainly, he has worked with many significant filmmakers. He began as cinematographer for **Geoff Murphy**'s *Wild Man* (1977), then Murphy and **John Clarke**'s *Dagg Day Afternoon* (1977), then teamed up with Murphy again for ***Goodbye Pork Pie*** (1980). Bollinger was cinematographer for *Middle Age Spread* (1979) and later renewed the association with **Gaylene Preston** as camera operator for *Mr. Wrong* (1985) and *Bread and Roses* (1994), and again as cinematographer for *War Stories* (1995) and *Perfect Strangers* (2003). With Paul Maunder, he was cinematographer for *Sons for the Return Home* (1979), and also for **John Laing**'s *Beyond Reasonable Doubt* (1980).

Bollinger was cinematographer for **Vincent Ward**'s *Vigil* (1984), and **Ian Mune**'s *Came a Hot Friday* (1985) and *The End of the Golden Weather* (1991), and was camera operator for *What Becomes of the Broken-Hearted* (1999). He was the New Zealand director of photography for **Roger Donaldson**'s *No Way Out* (1987), and camera operator for **Jane Campion**'s *The Piano* (1993). Bollinger worked as cinematographer with **Peter Jackson** on *Heavenly Creatures* (1994), the mockumentary *Forgotten Silver* (1995), and *The Frighteners* (1996), and continued this association as director of photography for the second unit of both *Lord of the Rings: The Fellowship of the Ring* (2001) and *Lord of the Rings: The Return of the King* (2003) (*see* LORD OF THE RINGS TRILOGY).

Other camera operator credits include *Heart of the Stag* (1984), and cinematographer credits include *For Love Alone* (1986), *A Soldier's Tale* (1988), *Cinema of Unease: A Personal Journey by Sam Neill* (1995), and *Woundings* (1998).

– C –

CAMPION, JANE (1954–). Internationally acclaimed director Jane Campion was born in Wellington, New Zealand, in 1954; however, she now makes her home in Sydney, Australia. She attended the *Australian Film Television and Radio School,** which introduced her to the craft, and she has already directed at least 14 feature films, produced three features, and been credited as writer for eight. In addition, she has worked as an actress, cinematographer, editor, casting director, and camera operator between 1982 and 1989. At the 1986 Cannes Film Festival, her first short film *Peel* (1982) won the Palme D'Or; other awards followed for the short films *Passionless Moments* (1983) and *Girl's Own Story* (1984). Her feature film directorial debut was for *Sweetie* (1989), which won major international awards, including the Georges Sadoul Prize in 1989 for best foreign film, the Los Angeles Film Critics' New Generation Award in 1990, the American Independent Spirit Award for best foreign feature, and the Australian Critics' Awards for best film, best director, and best actress.

In 1990, Campion directed *An Angel at My Table*, a dramatized autobiography of Janet Frame, which won the best director prize at the **New Zealand Film and Television Awards**. In 1993, she won a Golden Palm at Cannes for *The Piano* paralleled by a best director award from the ***Australian Film Institute**. That film won her an Oscar for best screenplay in 1994. Since then, she has been less successful. *The Portrait of a Lady* (1996), based on the Henry James' novel of the same name and starring ***Nicole Kidman**, John Malkovich, and Barbara Hershey, was not well received by critics and filmgoers. The quirky and erotic *Holy Smoke* (1999), starring Harvey Keitel and Kate Winslet, quickly reduces to the man-versus-woman battle that dominates Campion's oeuvre. In this case, the man is a complete fool, even dancing around the Australian desert in a dress and lipstick, like some spawn from *__Priscilla__*, while Winslet's character dominates him. *In the Cut* (2003) is a move into the erotic thriller *__genre__ based on Susanna Moore's bestseller, at least on the surface, but it has not been well received either.

CLARKE, JOHN (1948–). Now living in Melbourne, Australia, New Zealand-born John Clarke is famous for his *__comedy__ and political satire, and is regarded as one of the best humorists in the region. His **television** political satire serves up some of the immortal moments in comedy. He has worked in many fields within the film and television industry: as an actor, writer, crew member, director, composer, and producer. He has 23 acting appearances and 17 film writing credits, as well as credits for writing and directing programs and films for television. Writing credits include *Dagg Day Afternoon* (1977)—he also composed the songs—*__Lonely Hearts__* (1982), *Man and Boy* (1986), *Lust and Revenge* (1996), and *The Man Who Sued God* (2001), starring comedian Billy Connolly.

The rise of Clarke's personal star matches that of the *__revival__ in the Australian and New Zealand industry. His first film appearance was as the expatriate in *The Adventures of Barry McKenzie* (1972). He subsequently returned to New Zealand to play Dr. Daggenheimer

304 • CROWE, RUSSELL

in **Geoff Murphy**'s *Wild Man* (1977) and later starred in and directed (with Murphy again) *Dagg Day Afternoon* (1977). As Fred Dagg, he wore a black singlet, crumpled hat, shorts and gumboots, and satirized post-pioneering "blokes" and "blokesses" in a way that made the character an instant icon. Clarke was nominated for an *Australian Film Institute** best screenplay award in 1982 for *Lonely Hearts*, which was shared with Paul Cox, and the film won the best film award. *Lonely Hearts* is a drama about two older people who begin to have feelings for each other, told with compassion and humor, and full of real characters who surround and complicate everyday lives. In 1986, he was the voice of the farmer Wal, in the animated story of farmer and dog, *Footrot Flats: The Dog's Tale*. He played Sheedy, alongside other luminaries of the Australian industry like *Bryan Brown** and **Russell Crowe**, in Stephen Wallace's *Prisoners of the Sun* (also *Blood Oath*) (1990), which told the story of the court-martial of murderous Japanese soldiers on the island of Ambon after World War II. Clarke then played in the Australian black comedy *Death in Brunswick** (1991), as the gravedigger Dave, best friend of Carl Fitzgerald (**Sam Neill**), and his best friend is committed to help him overcome his travails. As the shifty poker machine licensee Bernie Fowler in the Australian comedy *Crackerjack* (2002), he stands opposite those who want to maintain the genteel lifestyle of a poker-machine free club, but are faced with dwindling membership and financial resources.

Clarke's other film appearances include the self-directed *Man and Boy* (1986), *George Miller**'s *Les Patterson Saves the World* (1987), *Those Dear Departed* (1987), *Never Say Die* (1988), and *The Alive Tribe* (1997).

CROWE, RUSSELL. *See entry in Australian section.*

– D –

DONALDSON, ROGER (1945–). Roger Donaldson was born in Ballarat in Victoria, Australia, in 1945 and reversed the normal pattern by immigrating to New Zealand in 1965. He was cofounder of the **New Zealand Film Commission** and worked as a director, producer, writer, and art director. He directed the feature film *Sleeping Dogs* (1977), the first film made in New Zealand in 15 years, and starting the revival in New Zealand filmmaking. Arguably, it was the first New Zealand film exhibited in American theaters. Starring **Sam Neill**, it is set in a totalitarian state, reflecting aspects of Prime Minister Robert Muldoon's National Government. Since then, he has directed many films in New Zealand, but has also won acceptance in the global industry with directing work in the United Kingdom and *****Hollywood**. *Nutcase* (1980) was made in New Zealand, and is a little-known but remarkably tight gangster parody. *Smash Palace* (1981)—which he also wrote and produced—is a well-constructed drama interrogating the issue of divorce and its effects on those it involves.

The American and United Kingdom production of the story of Captain Bligh—*The Bounty*, 1984—followed and starred *****Mel Gibson**, Laurence Olivier, and Anthony Hopkins—among other Hollywood stars—and had modest box-office success. *Marie* (1985) was less successful, but Donaldson followed this with *No Way Out* (1987), a thriller starring Kevin Costner, Gene Hackman, and Sean Young, which was well received by critics and at the box office. *Cocktail* (1988) was a light-hearted drama starring Tom Cruise and *****Bryan Brown**, about life in the bars of New York. Stars like working with him, and in the remake of Sam Peckinpah's 1972 film *The Getaway* (1994), Alex Baldwin and Kim Basinger replace Steve McQueen and Ali MacGraw in a film where all the characters are vile, and have no redeeming features. Donaldson then tackled science fiction. *Species* (1985) is the story of an alien female who metamorphoses into successively more powerful forms, and for whom human life is to be crushed as humans would a cockroach. He then turned his hand to disaster movies in the form of *Dante's Peak* (1997) with Pierce Brosnan and Linda Hamilton, but the *****genre** had been overworked by this time, and this film brought nothing new to the frame. His two latest films, *Thirteen Days* (2000) and *The Recruit* (2003), are closer to his American home with the former retelling the drama of the Cuban missile crises in 1962 and the latter weaving a web of treachery in the Central Intelligence Agency (CIA). Other films include *Cadillac Man* (1990), starring Robin Williams and *White Sands* (1992).

Donaldson was nominated at the 1989 Razzie Awards for Worst Director for *Cocktail*, and at the Cannes Film Festival was nominated for the Golden Palm Award for *The Bounty*. He is doubtless one of the most successful of the filmmakers to have both received their grounding in the industry in New Zealand and contributed significantly to the strength of that industry.

DUFF, ALAN (1950–). Alan Duff wrote the novel on which the popular *Once Were Warriors* (1994) was based. He was only slightly involved in the production of the film, and seeing its commercial success, attempted to float a company to produce a film of his second novel, *One Night Out Stealing* (1992). This was unsuccessful, but Duff reworked his 1997 Montana Fiction Book Award novel, *What Becomes of the Broken-Hearted* (1999), into a film script with the same title. Although not as successful as *Once Were Warriors*, it ranks as the second most popular film, after *Warriors*, in New Zealand.

– E –

EVISON, PAT (1924–). Pat Evison began her acting career in 1975 on **television**, and her feature film career began with a Paul Maunder film, *Landfall* in 1977. This drama/thriller costarred Denise Maunder, John Anderson, **Sam Neill,** and Gael Anderson, and tells of two men and two women who live a kind of urban hippie existence, but the ideal relationships gradually disintegrate. Evison then appeared in Donald Crombie's Australian film *Caddie* (1976) as Mrs. Norris, alongside Helen Morse, Takis Emmanuel, **Jack Thompson*, and Jacki Weaver. Her next feature film was *Tim* (1979), starring **Mel Gibson*, Alwyn Kurts, and Piper Laurie, and was adapted from Colleen McCullough's novel of the same name, which tells the story of the developing relationship between an intellectually handicapped young man and a middle-aged American woman who both teaches him to write and is attracted to him. In 1983, Evison was nominated for an **Australian Film Institute* award for best supporting actress for *The Clinic* (1982), a David Stevens' *comedy about the comings and goings in one day of a venereal disease clinic. She also appeared in *My Grandfather Is a Vampire* (1991) playing Leah. Also called *Grampire*, this David Blyth film is a children's comedy about an 11-year-old Lonny who discovers that his nice, friendly grandfather might be a vampire. Evison's failing eyesight forced her to retire from the stage and screen soon after. She has been an effective character actor who focused her film activity in Australia and New Zealand.

Other films include *The Earthling* (1980), *Bad Blood* (1981), *Starstruck* (1982), *The Silent One* (1984), *A Street to Die* (1985), and *What the Moon Saw* (1990).

– F –

FOX, KERRY (1966–). Kerry Fox is one of New Zealand's foremost actors with an international career. After completing drama school, she starred as Janet Frame in the **Jane Campion** film *Angel at My Table* (1990). Fox won the 1990 award for best female performance at the **New Zealand Film and Television Awards** for this film. *Angel at My Table* is a drama based on the true story of the author Janet Frame, and also stars **Martyn Sanderson** and Alexia Keogh. She later moved to Australia to play the emotionally needy young sister Vicki in ***Gillian Armstrong**'s *The Last Days of Chez Nous* (1992). Returning to New Zealand, she played Andrea Joyce in *The Rainbow Warrior* (1992). She subsequently appeared as the radical white South African in *Friends* (1993), a film about three women and the effects of apartheid in South Africa. She followed this with the lead role as a greedy medical student in Danny Boyle's British-produced drama/thriller *Shallow Grave* (1994), which had unanticipated international success.

Back in New Zealand, Fox's next role was Kelly Towne in John Reid's *The Last Tattoo* (1994), which told the story of American servicemen and their relationship with New Zealand women in World War II. She was nominated for the ***Australian Film Institute** (AFI) award for best leading actress for her role of sheep farmer Sally Voysey in Michael Blackmore's *Country Life* (1994) with **Sam Neill**, a version of Anton Chekhov's *Country Life* set in the Australian outback. In David Attwood's unnoticed—perhaps because the subject is almost taboo—*Saigon Baby* (1995), she played Kate Cooper, an infertile British woman who was prepared to buy a baby in Southeast Asia, with John Hurt as the middleman in the deal. Moving to

308 • GIBNEY, REBECCA (1964–)

Canada, Fox was nominated for the Genie Award for best supporting actress for her role as the bride-to-be awaiting the return of her gay brother, in the film *The Hanging Garden* (1997). Fox returned to Australia to play the lead role of Sonja Buloh in Richard Flanagan's *The Sound of One Hand Clapping* (1998), a story of a postwar migrant father and, predominantly, his daughter, and their struggles in a work camp on the rugged west coast of Tasmania.

In the Canadian production of the documentary-style *To Walk with Lions* (1999), Fox played Lucy Jackson. She has never neglected the New Zealand film industry, and returned to play the policewoman in Brita McVeigh's little-known short drama, *Thinking about Sleep* (1999). In the same year, she played in the British *comedy *Fanny and Elvis* (1999), as a woman in her thirties desperate to conceive a child. Still on a sexuality theme, she played in the much more significant *Intimacy* (2000)—directed by Patrice Chereau—as an actress who engages in a sexual relationship with a stranger, and they find common ground only through making love. In 2001, Fox won the best actress award at the Berlin International Film Festival for this role, and the film was acclaimed at the Sundance Festival. In the Australian production of Craig Lahiff's *Black and White* (2002), she plays Helen Devaney, one of two legal aid lawyers—Robert Carlyle is the other—who try to represent the case for a half-Aboriginal fair worker who is accused, and found guilty of, murder. The film is based on a true story from South Australia in the 1950s. Fox was less successful as the lead in the thriller in the mould of *The Sixth Sense*, *The Gathering* (2002). Again in Australia, in the short film directed by Jessica Hobbs, *So Close to Home* (2003), she plays Maggie, a woman who meets a mysterious teenage girl on a train, and the story then develops into an investigation into the lives of refugees and critiques their treatment in Australia.

Other films include *Welcome to Sarajevo* (1997), *The Wisdom of Crocodiles* (1998), *The Darkest Light* (1999), and *The Point Men* (2001).

– G –

GIBNEY, REBECCA (1964–). One of Australia and New Zealand's most recognized actors, Rebecca Gibney was born in New Zealand in

1964. Her film career began in 1983 in New Zealand with the film produced and written by **John O'Shea**, *Among the Cinders* in which she played Sally. The film tells a *coming-of-age story of a young teenage runaway and his grandfather. She followed this with a part in **Gaylene Preston**'s *Mr. Wrong* (1985). She then moved to Australia to play the bleeding-heart, middle-class social worker Jill Harkness involved in a system where the state believes it can do a better job than parents at caring for children, in Paul Maloney's *social realist film, *I Live with Me Dad* (1985). After playing in many **television** series, she then starred in the thriller *Jigsaw* (1990), trying to unravel her husband's secret life. In the romantic *comedy *Lucky Break* (1995), she played Gloria Wrightman, the jealous fiancé of Eddie (*Anthony LaPaglia), who is becoming attracted to the disabled writer, Sofie (Gia Carides). Gibney played Penny Macgregor in the family adventure *Joey* (1997). Since then, she has appeared in many television series and television films, and has been nominated for awards in these roles.

GOODBYE PORK PIE (1980). Geoff Murphy and **Ian Mune** wrote the screenplay for this film, which Murphy subsequently directed. The film is significant for two reasons. It was the first to recover its costs from the domestic market. It proved to skeptics, especially those in the distribution and exhibition chains, that New Zealanders were appreciative of narratives about themselves, rather than those about people in other countries that had populated the silver screen for 30 years. Second, it was the first New Zealand feature screened at Cannes.

The film resembles in some ways the *ocker comedy films of the same period in Australian filmmaking, in that it is about young men who lead unproductive lives with anarchic abandon, causing good-natured mayhem for those in their wake. Violence is not a feature of their activities as they traverse New Zealand in a yellow Mini Minor, so they maintain the empathy of the audience. Indeed, one audience gave the film a standing ovation.

– H –

HANNA, PAT (1888–1973). Born in Whitianga, Pat Hanna's career began in entertaining troops in World War I on the Western Front. He toured Australia with his *comedy troupe, "Diggers," in the 1920s, and he took the character of the lanky digger, Chic Williams, into three films about the Australian Infantry Forces (AIF). The first, *Diggers* (1931), was made by *Efftee Productions, and was a series of three sketches cohering through their common soldier characters. The first two sketches are comedies, while the third is a sentimental version of a popular song. Disagreeing with *Frank Thring Sr.'s direction of *Diggers*, Hanna set up his own company to produce the second and third films—*Diggers in Blighty* (1933) and *Waltzing Matilda* (1933). Both films are comedies, but the final film was dismally received, and Hanna could not draw out further the wartime character of Chic Williams. As was the nature of the contemporary industry, Hanna worked as a writer, actor, director, and producer.

HAYWARD, RUDALL (1900–1974). Rudall Hayward was one of the founders of the New Zealand film industry. He was one of the earliest directors whose talent as a storyteller revealed an understanding of the visual medium of film. In addition, his films showed the respect that he had for **Maori** people and culture. Beginning his film career as production assistant on *The Betrayer in Rotorua* (1921), he was the assistant director of *The Birth of New Zealand* (1922). In between he made his first feature, *The Bloke from Freeman Bay*, which was alleged to have been so bad that an uncle bought and burned it. If that film is discounted, he went on to make his directorial debut with *My Lady of the Cave* (1925). Based on a serial that appeared in the *New Zealand Herald* in 1921, the film tells the story of a shipwrecked clerk who is saved, initially, by another survivor of a Maori attack, a white girl Beryl and her faithful guard Rau. Finally, the clerk and Beryl marry. She is the ideal pioneer woman in contemporary terms, and the film shows something of a growing respect Hayward developed for Maori culture.

Hayward followed this with *Rewi's Last Stand*, originally made in 1925 but remade as a sound feature in the late 1930s. Based on events during the New Zealand Wars of the 1860s, the story revolves around the clash of cultures and the response of individuals—as distinct from the response of identifiable interest groups—to situations. Once again, his balanced portrayal of both Maori and the British-led army is notable. The young British soldier forms a relationship with a

Maori woman of rank, establishing a situation that is unusual in contemporary films about different races. Unusual, too, is the Maori perspective on the events related by the soldier. Hayward's next film was *The Tee Kooti Trail* (1927), which was an early attempt at docudrama rather than fiction. He used actual locations where events occurred, and, as far as possible, closely followed the sequence of events surrounding a Maori attack against invading settlers. Although he was an apologist for the rationale of British settlement, the film took pains to present a Maori culture of integrity and honesty. In 1972, he co-directed with his second wife, Ramai, his last feature film, *To Love a Maori*, which explored the problems faced by young Maori when they left their rural communities for the urban centers. Once again, it showed their respect for Maori culture and their involvement with it. It was his first color feature, and the first made by a New Zealander in New Zealand.

Hayward was not only a director of feature films. He made a number of short comedies, beginning with *A Takapuna Scandal* (1927). These films were shot in a local community and subsequently screened in that same community. In 1931, he was appointed New Zealand reporter for the Australian newsreel company, *****Cinesound**. In the 1950s, the Chinese government invited him and Ramai to China to make documentaries.

His contribution to the industry is noted and honored in the Rudall Hayward Memorial Award, established by the Guild of Film and Television Artists and awarded for exceptional contributions to the industry.

Other films include *The Bush Cinderella* (1928) and, as director of photography, *On the Friendly Road* (1936).

HOLMES, CECIL. *See entry in Australian section.*

– J –

JACKSON, PETER (1961–). Through his ambitious inspiration to film J.R.R Tolkien's masterpiece, Peter Jackson has achieved international recognition and acclaim, and is recognized as one of the best directors in the history of cinema. In addition to directing, he wrote the screenplay and produced the *Lord of the Rings: The Fellowship of the Ring* (2001), *Lord of the Rings: The Two Towers* (2002), and *Lord of the Rings: The Return of the King* (2003) (*see LORD OF THE RINGS TRILOGY*). Jackson learned his craft over a long apprenticeship from 1976, working in almost every creative and technical element of the industry. These include working as producer, director, writer, actor, as well as on special effects and visual effects, as editor, in the make-up department, as a cinematographer, and as costume designer.

Jackson saw the release of his first film as a director, *Bad Taste*, in 1987. Taking four years to complete, the film became a horror/ science fiction cult classic, and eventually won acclaim and prizes at the Cannes Film Festival. He then cowrote and directed the animated musical *comedy, *Meet the Feebles* (1989). He came to national and international attention through the award-winning *Heavenly Creatures* (1994), based on the story of two teenage girls who brutally murdered one of their mothers with a brick in 1952. The insight in the story is that two people can perform criminal acts that one of them would not be able to commit. In 1995, he codirected and cowrote *Forgotten Silver*, which is presented as a *documentary about pioneering New Zealand filmmaker Colin McKenzie, whose work with mechanized camera and color film preceded the reality by decades. The film is a first-class parody that highlights the director's knowledge and love of early cinema. The effect of the film, in the sense that it has been taken as real, has been likened to Orson Welles' broadcast of *War of the Worlds*.

Jackson was by this time recognized as an emerging talent by the international community and made *The Frighteners* (1966) for Universal Pictures with an international cast including Michael J. Fox and Trini Alvarado. This comedy/horror film was released to mixed critical reception, partly because the computer-generated special effects went nowhere. In his next films—*The Lord of the Rings* trilogy— his use of computer animations was much more effective and restrained. The three films were shot at the same time (that is, the shooting was completed before the first film was released), and then released at intervals of 12 months, on each Boxing Day. If he was not internationally acclaimed before these films, he certainly was afterward. Jackson won British Academy of Film and Television Arts (BAFTA) prizes for direction and film for both *The Two Towers* and

The Fellowship of the Ring and the ***Australian Film Institute** awarded best foreign film awards for the two films. The Academy of Science Fiction, Fantasy, and Horror Films voted a Saturn Award for *The Fellowship of the Ring* in 2002, and the American Film Institute voted *The Fellowship of the Ring* Movie of the Year in 2002. *The Fellowship of the Ring* was nominated for Oscars for Best Picture, Best Director, and Best Screenplay in 2002, while *The Two Towers* was nominated for an Oscar for Best Motion Picture of the Year in 2003. *The Return of the King* scooped the Academy Awards in 2004, winning 11 Oscars, including best achievement in directing and best motion picture of the year. The British Academy for Film and Television Arts (BAFTA) awarded the film four prizes in the same year, including best film. His next feature is *King Kong*.

Other films Jackson directed include *The Valley* (1976) and *Braindead* (1992), in which he acted.

– L –

LAING, JOHN (1948–). John Laing began work with the New Zealand Film Unit, with which he has made many films, and his career with them has been solid, without being extraordinary. His first film, *Beyond Reasonable Doubt* (1980), was based on the true story of a miscarriage of justice involving two young people who went missing and whose bodies were found three months later in the Waikato River. Local farmer Arthur Thomas was tried and later pardoned for the crime, his conviction resting on a contrived case constructed by dissembling police. The film won the 1982 Grand Prix award at the Cognac Festival de Film Policier. In 1983, he won the International Critics' Jury prize for *The Lost Tribe* (1983) at the Catalonian International Film Festival. Laing also wrote and produced this thriller, which has been widely criticized for its lack of character motivation and poor narration, traits that are often forgiven in European filmmaking—it won two other prizes at film festivals in France—but not in those in the ***Hollywood** classical style. However, the cinematography is excellent. *Dangerous Orphans* (1985) followed, a *Boy's Own*-style film about the drugs, thieves, and gangsters, and the private detective. Laing's next film, *Absent without*

Leave (1992), is also based on the true story of Ed, a young soldier in 1942 who goes AWOL when he finds out his 16-year-old girlfriend, Daisy, is pregnant. He eventually finds himself sentenced to 60 days in prison. The subtext is the development of love and trust; the path from naiveté to wisdom. This film was nominated for the Golden St. George Award at the 1993 Moscow International Film Festival. Laing then worked on **television** productions until 2001, when he directed *No One Can Hear You* (2001), a slasher film made in the United States about the lives of an apparently sedate suburban family, when the crazed house guest arrives.

LAWRENCE, BRUNO (1941–1995). A man of many talents as actor, writer, composer, crew member, producer, British-born Bruno Lawrence's first acting appearance was in a United Kingdom television series. In New Zealand in 1980, he starred as Pat in **John Laing**'s *Beyond Reasonable Doubt*, a drama and thriller based on a true story about a miscarriage of justice involving murder, trials, sentencing, and a subsequent pardon. Bruno Lawrence was a very complex actor who was capable of strange, tense, and intriguing performances. He is credited as actor in 24 feature films, including the important **Roger Donaldson** film *Smash Palace* (1981), Mark Joffe's thriller *Grievous Bodily Harm* (1988), and *Spotswood* (1992). In addition, he played a part in writing four feature films, including *Smash Palace* and the significant science fiction film, *The Quiet Earth* (1985), sharing writing credits here with Bill Baer and **Sam Pillsbury**. He was very popular with audiences in both Australia and New Zealand, yet he did not venture outside that market.

Lawrence won the 1987 **New Zealand Film and Television Award** for best male lead performance for his role in *The Quiet Earth*, as well as best screenplay. He also won the 1995 **Rudall Hayward** Award for a special contribution to the New Zealand film industry. At the Italian Fantafestival he won the 1986 best actor award for *The Quiet Earth*, and the 1988 best actor award for *As Time Goes By*. Also in 1988, Lawrence was nominated for the *Australian Film Institute** award for best supporting actor for *Grievous Bodily Harm*.

Lawrence died in 1995 within months of being diagnosed with lung cancer.

LORD OF THE RINGS TRILOGY (2001–2003). Peter Jackson's *Lord of the Rings* trilogy comprises the three films *Lord of the Rings: The Fellowship of the Ring* (2001), *Lord of the Rings: The Two Towers* (2002), and *The Lord of the Rings: The Return of the King* (2003). In the history of cinema, this trilogy will be known as one of the most ambitious projects ever attempted, as well as through the success it achieved and the acclaim it received. The trilogy exemplifies the high standard New Zealand filmmaking can achieve, in cooperation with other expertise. J.R.R. Tolkien's narrative of the rings of Middle Earth had long been waiting for retelling on the silver screen, but many problems prevented this. The story-line is complex and has many parallel interwoven plots, making it difficult for any scriptwriter to ensure that an audience will be able to follow the multiple plot lines, yet still bring some kind of coherence to a project that would overwhelm a normal film timeline through its complexity. Few of the settings are in similar environments, meaning that a filmmaker has to find a vast range of landscapes to cover the various environments in the epic story. Specialized animation techniques to film everything from individual beings from hell to vast armies, with other special effects to bring to life the multitude of environments, were necessary. In order to provide continuity, the whole project had to be shot before the first film was edited, meaning that funds had to be provided for the shooting of three films before any returns could be expected, if such returns were possible in any case. Jackson's triumph is that he successfully went where no man had previously considered venturing, to bring to the screen a story that deviated only slightly from Tolkien's original, unlike earlier attempts (an animated version of 132 minutes, covering the first two books, was made in 1978). In so doing, he expressed initiative, innovation, courage, and belief in his ability and that of the team of artists and craftsmen who worked with him. New Line studio deserves mention since the studio had faith in Jackson for funding three films without any prospect of a return during filming.

Of course, weaknesses in the films are apparent, and are evident simply because the films are so close to the novels that any deviation from Tolkien's narrative is prominent. For example, the character of Gimli is turned into something of a comic figure, when he was, in fact (or fiction), a noble and courageous warrior and leader of a nation.

All three films have been enormously successful at the box office. For example, the last in the trilogy, *The Return of the King*, had a budget of US$94 million. In the first six weeks of its release, it made US$337,817,998 in the United States and UK£54,366,487 in the United Kingdom.

The trilogy's significance for the New Zealand industry is that the films were made by a New Zealand director, in New Zealand, using New Zealand production facilities (such as special effects factories), and with a cast and other crew that included New Zealanders. Yet the film was an international film by any criteria. It is clear that the wheel has turned. Initially, New Zealand filmmakers made films about New Zealand for New Zealand audiences, some of which were screened overseas to good responses. Then some of those filmmakers and cast went to international sites, most notably **Hollywood*, to make films generally regarded as international, that were successful on the international market, but whose narratives and production were not related to New Zealand. Peter Jackson has shown that the site for international filmmaking has changed, and now successful, international films can be made in New Zealand with a cast and crew that are international in composition. For the New Zealand film industry, *Lord of the Rings* clearly marks not only its coming-of-age, but its superiority in some respects to more established filmmaking sites, such as Hollywood. To some extent, proof of this claim is found in the 11 Academy Awards won by *Lord of the Rings: The Return of the King* in 2004, and the four prizes voted by the British Academy for Film and Television Arts (BAFTA). The Oscars included best motion picture, best director, best adapted screenplay, best make-up, best sound mixing, best art direction, best costume design, best visual effects, best original score, best film editing, and best original song.

– M –

MAORI IN FILM. Maori have played a significant role in New Zealand film, at many different levels. Arriving in New Zealand in 1912, Gaston Méliès produced three films of Maori stories in 1913: *Hinemoa*, *How Chief Te Ponga Won His Bride*, and *Loved by a Maori Chieftess*. Later overseas filmmakers made films about the Maori to satisfy an overseas demand for depictions of "exotic" cultures, for example, *Green Dolphin Street* (1947), *The Seekers* (1954), *Until They Sail* (1957), and *In Search of the Castaways* (1962). Apart from those voyeuristic examples, many filmmakers have interrogated the juxtaposition of the tectonic plates of cultures, with the consequent grinding, crushing, and reforming. **Rudall Hayward**'s *The Te Kooti Trail* (1927) is based on a true story of the war of the warrior Te Kooti against spreading European settlements. Set in the same era, the 1860s, but released in 1940, Hayward's *Rewi's Last Stand* is a narrative of intercultural love where the ties of culture bound more tightly than those of love. Hayward was interested in the tensions of such love, but it is indicative of the sometimes begrudging respect between these cultures that such love was understood to be both real and not taboo. In other countries at this time, love of this nature might have been practiced, but with the threat of certain death for one or both of the participants. For example, the Australian film *****Charles Chauvel**'s ***Jedda** (1955) springs to mind, although here the death of both is a result of the impossibility of either culture accepting their love.

Hayward's second wife, Ramai te Miha, codirected his last feature—which was also the first color feature made by a New Zealander in New Zealand—*To Love a Maori* (1972). This film focused on the problems of children—specifically, Maori teenagers—when they move from supportive, small, rural communities to larger, anonymous cities, where they establish new relationships, including those with *pakeha*. (*Pakeha* refers to New Zealanders of Caucasian descent. Maori sometimes use the term in a negative way, although not always, and there is nothing implicitly negative in the term.) The *****coming-of-age** essay articulates and explores the different rites of passage—and the justice of them—that young people were subjected to. The innocence and natural egalitarianism of younger children is the subject of a film contemporaneous with Hayward's. Michael Forlong's *Rangi's Catch* (1973) is a children's film set in an idyllic rural valley, far from the alienating, corrupt, and unnatural influences of the *****city**. In such a semiosphere, among similarly innocent children, there are no barriers. A young Temuera Morrison plays Rangi, a character who is the antithesis of Morrison's later character, Jake Heke in *Once Were Warriors* (1994). Similar in some respects to Hayward's *To Love a Maori*—in that its subject is the problems that some young people have—Mike Walker's *Kingpin* (1985) is set in a child welfare training center established for young Maori and Polynesian miscreants. Although bullying and intimidation are rife, the presence of many in such a place is intimately connected to the reality of homes and lives destroyed by alcohol and violence. The film is quite didactic: society's systems are not working.

For **Pacific Films**, **John O'Shea** and Roger Mirams made *Broken Barriers* (1952), mapping the differences between cultures and the love that can nevertheless develop. This time, the resolution was positive. Similarly, *Arriving Tuesday* (1986) is a light-hearted look at couples, where the harmony and warmth of a Maori couple is contrasted with the bickering and abrasiveness of the *pakeha* couple.

More recent films explore the violence and death resulting from the juxtaposition of cultures and the apparent impossibility of a peaceful resolution. Michael Black's *Pictures* (1981) is set in the New Zealand Land Wars of the second half of the 19th century. Its slant is less positive. Things were never what they seemed in the Victorian era and the veneer of Victorian formality and colonial achievement, celebrated in the metropolitan center, was premised on a regime of violence and brutality in the distant colonies. In this case, the juxtaposition of cultures is marked by forced labor in building the signifier of colonial power and conquest, the railroad, and the summary execution of the powerless, who dared to object to the brutal regime. **Geoff Murphy**'s *Utu* (1983) is set in the same time, with a similar theme of violence and revenge, death and tragedy. **Lee Tamahori**'s *Once Were Warriors* interrogates the destruction of the nobility and integrity of the Maori warrior through the depiction of a dysfunctional Maori family in a dysfunctional Maori urban culture, and evolving responses to that.

Some other films are worthy of mention. **Jane Campion**'s *The Piano* (1993) presents a surprisingly stereotyped image of Maori, as people who were focused on sex and spoke in sexual innuendos, complementing their simple and naïve actions. Alexander Markey's *Hei Tiki* (1935) is different in that it does not depict relationships between *pakeha* and Maori, but intertribal conflict in Maori. Paul Maunder's *Sons for the Return Home* (1979) takes a slightly different look at the juxtaposition of cultures and the human tragedy that sometimes results. A Western Samoan family moves to New Zealand when the son is four. Later, when he attends university, he falls in love with a white girl, but the romance is marred by overtones of racism and fear in all groups. Finally, Merata Mita's *Mauri* (1988) is a powerful film about identity and Maori birthright. *Mauri* is the first film made by a Maori woman and the first made from an entirely Maori perspective.

MUNE, IAN (1941–). Born in Auckland, Mune's successful career has included work as an actor, director, writer, crew member, second unit director, assistant director, producer, and art director. His debut as director was in **television**. He then moved to film beginning with *Came a Hot Friday* (1985), a *comedy of conmen, horse racing, gambling, fast cars, and loose women set in the 1940s, where Friday night excitement was a visit to the boozer for a pie and chips (going to a hotel/bar to drink and eat a meat pie and French fries). He wrote the screenplay from Ronald Morrieson's novel, and the film was a Kiwi classic and was enthusiastically reviewed. Mune won best director and best screenplay prizes at the 1986 **New Zealand Film and Television Awards** for this film. With Bill Bauer, he wrote the script for and directed *Bridge to Nowhere* (1986), which capitalizes on the fantasies—or perhaps the reality—that children have about people who live alone. *The Grasscutter* (1990) was made in New Zealand for a United Kingdom company, and explored the life of a supergrass after he had left the Loyalist UVF in Belfast to live in New Zealand, where his past catches up to him.

For his next film—which he wrote with Bruce Mason—*End of the Golden Weather* (1991), Mune won best director and best film at the New Zealand Film and Television Awards in 1992. This *action/ adventure film is set in the 1930s and tells of 11-year-old Geoff's dreams and romantic adventures, and the understanding of those dreams that comes with his developing friendship with Firpo, who dreams of competing in the Olympic Games. *Whole of the Moon* (1997) tells the story of Kirk, a teenage boy diagnosed with bone cancer, and Marty, a street-wise kid suffering from low self-esteem. It is a film about the triumph of the human spirit, and Mune won the best screenplay prize in the 1996 New Zealand Film and Television Awards and a Golden Gryphon at the Giffoni Film Festival. He contributed to the writing of this screenplay. Mune followed this with

What Becomes of the Broken Hearted? (1999), a sequel to *Once Were Warriors* (1994), which relates the subsequent life and redemption of Jake, the deeply flawed and violent husband in *Warriors*. The film won many prizes at the New Zealand Film and Television Awards in 1999, including best director, best screenplay, best actor, and best actress. In 2000, Mune won the **Rudall Hayward** Award for his contribution to the film industry in New Zealand. Most recently, Mune has worked as second unit director on **Peter Jackson**'s *Lord of the Rings: Fellowship of the Ring* (2001).

Mune's writing credits—sometimes with others—include **Roger Donaldson**'s *Sleeping Dogs* (1977) and *Nutcase* (1980), *Goodbye Pork Pie* (1980) with director **Geoff Murphy**, and the screenplay for *The Silent One* (1984). His abilities do not end there, and he often appears in small parts. Credits include Bullen in *Sleeping Dogs*, the U-boat commander in *Nutcase*, Barry Gordon in *Shaker Run* (1985), Hanna in *Dangerous Orphans* (1985), *Backstage* (1988), the Reverend in *The Piano* (1993), the Judge in *Once Were Warriors*, *Topless Women Talk about Their Lives* (1997), *Nightmare Man* (1999), *Savage Honeymoon* (2000), and Bounder in *Lord of the Rings: The Fellowship of the Ring* (2001). His contribution to the industry in New Zealand has been immense.

MURPHY, GEOFF (1946–). Geoff Murphy was a teacher and published author before moving into the film industry. His first credit was in special effects for the political adventure *Sleeping Dogs* (1977), but then he worked on the scripts and directed both the New Zealand incarnation of the Australian *ocker film *Wild Man* (1977) and, with **John Clarke**, the *comedy *Dagg Day Afternoon* (1977). He followed this with *Goodbye Pork Pie* (1980), a film with rowdy and crude characters that audiences loved. Success here meant that his next task was the ambitious production of *Utu* (1982), the most expensive film made in New Zealand up to that time. It is a play about revenge (*utu*), first on the part of the **Maori** warrior whose village was pillaged, and then on the part of the settler whose wife is killed. His interest in Maori *history is evinced in his production of Merata Mita's *Patu!* (1983), and consulting and acting in Mita's psychodrama *Mauri* (1988). Murphy directed *The Quiet Earth* (1985), starring **Bruno Lawrence**, an intriguing science fiction/horror film, which won awards for best direction at the Fantafestival in 1986 and the best direction prize at the **New Zealand Film and Television Awards** in 1987. The story evolves from an experiment gone wrong, and all living creatures have disappeared from the Earth. Murphy wrote and directed *Never Say Die* (1988), a comedy/thriller about international business and political intrigue complete with explosions and car chases. Its production suffered from financing problems, and while trying to draw on many *genres, does not succeed in any.

Murphy then moved to *Hollywood, where he has directed solid genre fare without achieving the distinction he did in New Zealand. The reason might be that he was a director in Hollywood, whereas in New Zealand he could engage his vast ability in writing, producing, consulting, as well as directing. Directorial credits in Hollywood began with *Young Guns II* (1990), a sequel with a hackneyed storyline, and continued with *Freejack* (1990), a second-rate science fiction/thriller. The next was the sequel *Under Siege 2: Dark Territory* (1995), and the last was the science fiction/*action sequel *Fortress 2* (1999).

Murphy returned to New Zealand to direct the *documentary *Berta Revisited* (2001), and then the international banking conspiracy thriller *Spooked* (2004). Meanwhile, he was the second unit director on all three films of **Peter Jackson**'s *Lord of the Rings* trilogy.

– N –

NEILL, SAM (1947–). Sam Neill's career has been long and remarkably varied. He is capable of playing across varying national and international *genres, with consistency in his ability to become widely differing characters: from loveable action heroes, psychotic authoritarians, damaged everymen, and even a libertine painter who was regarded as something of an antichrist.

Although he is attributed sometimes with a New Zealand birth, Neill was born in Northern Ireland to army parents, moving to New Zealand in 1954, where he studied for a BA in Literature. After working with theater groups, he became a scriptwriter, editor, and director with the New Zealand National Film Unit, where he directed six documentaries between 1974 and 1978. He appeared in two films in this time, *Landfall* (1975)—following the collapse of a back-to-mother Earth commune—and *Ashes* (1975)—where he played a priest whose faith is wavering in a remake of T.S. Eliot's *Ash Wednesday*. In 1977, *Sleeping Dogs* offered him his first major feature film role. Directed by **Roger Donaldson**, this film was a drama/thriller and told the story of a loner caught in a political turmoil between the forces of a repressive government and guerrillas in the resistance movement. Neill migrated to Australia on its release, and he was cast as the young grazier Harry Beachem in *Gillian Armstrong's *My Brilliant Career* (1979), where he played opposite the self-tortured character of Sybylla Melvyn (*Judy Davis). Three more roles in Australian films quickly followed: *Just Out of Reach* (1979), where he again played the poet opposite the tortured young woman; the *comedy *The Journalist* (1979); and *Lucinda Brayford* (1980).

Based on his success in these roles, Neill then played the starring role of the antichrist Damien Thorn in the third of the *Omen* series— *The Final Conflict* (1981), made in the United States—then the cuckolded husband Mark in the French production *Possession* (1981). He followed this with the role of Marian in the Polish/Italian film about Pope John Paul II, *From a Far Country* (1981). He returned to Australia to play Sergeant Costello in *Tim Burstall's *Attack Force Z* (1982) before returning to the United Kingdom to star in *Ivanhoe* (1982) and the British/French spy film *Enigma* (1983). He played Lazar in *Fred Schepisi's romantic drama *Plenty* (1985)—with Meryl Streep, Charles Dance, Tracey Ullman, and John Gielgud— and returned to Australia to play Captain Starlight in *Robbery Under Arms* (1985). Then, he played James Quick, the dashing but arrogant teacher who forms a relationship with a poor young woman in 1930s Australia in *For Love Alone* (1986), and this was followed with another film set in 1930s Australia, *The Good Wife* (1987). Here, Neill plays Neville Gifford, the stranger who comes into town and forms a romantic liaison with Marge Hills (Rachel Ward), who is married to Sonny (*Bryan Brown). Later, he starred as Lindy Chamberlain's husband Michael in Fred Schepisi's *A Cry in the Dark* (also *Evil Angels*) (1988). Neill's international stature was ensured after he played opposite *Nicole Kidman in *Philip Noyce's *Dead Calm* (1989), as the distraught middle-aged husband threatened by the interloper Billy Zane. In the Australian comedy *Death in Brunswick

(1991), he played the unkempt cook in a scruffy restaurant, who becomes involved with criminals.

Neill returned to New Zealand to film for the first time in 14 years, first as the New Zealand police chief Alan Galbraith, playing opposite John Voight in the American and New Zealand coproduction of *The Rainbow Warrior* (1992), which told the true story of the sinking of that vessel by French agents. He then played the unsympathetic husband of Holly Hunter in **Jane Campion**'s award-winning *The Piano* (1993). Back in Australia, he played the Australian libertine painter Norman Lindsay opposite Hugh Grant and Elle Macpherson in *Sirens* (1994), where priest Anthony Campion (Grant) and his wife (Tara Fitzgerald) are dispatched on a mission to convince Lindsay to withdraw an allegedly blasphemous painting from a show.

In 1996, Neill again returned to Australia to play David Hoyle (Agent Nine) in the comedy/drama *Children of the Revolution*, which relates the story of Stalin spending his last night with an Australian woman who subsequently raised their love-child, who was to bring Australia to the brink of civil war. He played Professor Mortlock in the Australian-made *My Mother Frank* (2000), which received mixed responses, unlike those for **Rob Sitch*'s **The Dish* (2000), where Neill played the inoffensive, saddened character of Cliff Buxton, leader of the satellite dish team in rural Australia that communicated vision and sound of the first moon landing. He was the voice of Sam Sawnoff in *The Magic Pudding* (2000), and the narrator for the animated cartoon film *Leunig Animated* (2002). A role in **David Caesar*'s **crime*/comedy *Dirty Deeds* (2002) followed, which told of the United States mafia's attempt to colonize Australian operations. He returned to New Zealand to play The Man in **Gaylene Preston**'s thriller *Perfect Strangers* (2003), which interrogates the nature of reality in a bizarre reweaving of the "mating game" theme.

Neill has also played in many other American and European productions. As Captain Vasily Borodin, the commander of the Russian submarine in *The Hunt for Red October* (1990), he cemented his reputation for playing international characters. Others films include *Le Sang des autres* (1984), *Bis ans Ende der Welt* (1991), *Memoirs of an Invisible Man* (1992), *Jurassic Park* (1993), *Hostage* (1994), *The Jungle Book* (1994), *Country Life* (1994), John Carpenter's *In the Mouth of Madness* (1995), *Restoration* (1995), *Victory* (1995), *Snow*

White: A Tale of Terror (1997), *Event Horizon* (1997), *The Horse Whisperer* (1998), *The Revenger's Comedies* (1998), *Molokai: The Story of Father Damien* (1999), *Bicentennial Man* (1999), *Jurassic Park III* (2001), and *The Zookeeper* (2001). Other films are in production, and Neill has recently turned to directing.

Although he has played in numerous films, in character roles that have been challenging and diverse, Neill has had little critical acclaim manifesting as awards. After winning the 1989 **Australian Film Institute* award for best actor in a lead role for *A Cry in the Dark*, he was nominated for best lead actor in 1991 for *Death in Brunswick*, in 1993 for best supporting actor for *The Piano*, and in 2000 for best supporting actor for *My Mother Frank*.

His ***documentary** on the New Zealand Film Industry, *Cinema of Unease: A Personal Journey by Sam Neill* (1995), was commissioned by the British Film Institute as part of the *Century of Cinema* series and remains one of the best introductions to New Zealand cinema.

NEW ZEALAND ACADEMY OF FILM AND TELEVISION ARTS. *See* ACADEMY OF FILM AND TELEVISION ARTS.

NEW ZEALAND FILM AND TELEVISION AWARDS. The New Zealand Film and Television Awards were established by the **Academy of Film and Television Arts** of New Zealand (AFTA) in 1986. The awards are supported by the New Zealand Film Commission, New Zealand Trade and Enterprise, and various other organizations and corporations. In 1999, the awards presentation was split into two events—for **television** and films—and the new name for the film awards is the Nokia New Zealand Film Awards, reflecting the sponsorship of the awards. This sponsorship is reflected in the range of individual awards, from the Village Force Cinemas best film to the Henderson Rental Cars best performance in a short film. The awards generate interest in and support for the film industry in New Zealand, and contribute to the principle that support for performance arts is the province of business, as well as government, and that the market is not the only arbiter of such activity.

NEW ZEALAND FILM ARCHIVE. For many years, friends and colleagues of the film critic, enthusiast, and historian Jonathan Dennis had been pressing the government to set up a film archive that would restore and preserve significant film and **television** material from New Zealand's *history. Although such an archive would have been unsupported in earlier times—which saw film as a light medium of entertainment—by the 1980s, the importance of film as a record of the history and culture of a nation had become apparent. As a result, in 1981, the Film Archive was established under the direction of Jonathan Dennis. Unlike its sister organization in Australia—*Screensound Australia*—the Archive plays an active part in developing the consciousness of history and culture, as told in film for New Zealanders. To this end, the Archive has a film show touring New Zealand almost continuously, showing segments of the total collection to enthusiastic audiences around the country. Another initiative the Archive mounted was the Last Film Search. Because nitrate film base has an unstable life, many films taken in the early years of New Zealand's history were being lost. The aim of the Search was to find these films and to restore them for future generations as a record of history and culture. Seven thousand significant films and film segments were collected, both in New Zealand and overseas.

NEW ZEALAND FILM COMMISSION (NZFC). The New Zealand government established the New Zealand Film Commission as part of a general thrust to develop and define *national identity* and culture in the late 1970s. In November 1977, the Interim Film Commission met to advise the government on the policies that would be needed to establish and support a film industry. In November 1978, the NZFC replaced the Interim Commission, with the brief of supporting and encouraging filmmakers through financing the development and production of feature films, and then of exporting New Zealand culture through film. In its own words, the Commission's purpose is "to contribute to the creation of cultural capital in New Zealand through audience-targeted feature films in a sustainable screen industry." In 1980, the Commission began this task partly by taking films to Cannes. The Commission now provides finance by way of equity investment, but also provides loans against presales, sales advances, or distribution guarantees. Before requesting Commission support, projects require evidence of market attractiveness at both domestic and international levels; that is, the Commission is not in the business of providing funds for arthouse films. In addition, the Commission encourages projects to obtain private sector financing. Like its counterpart in Australia, the Commission will also fund co-productions, if the writer or director is either a New Zealander or a resident. In 2002, the Commission moved into writing development through financing the first Screenwriter's Laboratory. The depth of the Commission's support is shown in its investment in seven new features in 2002, with development finance for another 63 projects on its books.

NOKIA NEW ZEALAND FILM AWARDS. *See* NEW ZEALAND FILM AND TELEVISION AWARDS.

– O –

ONCE WERE WARRIORS **(1994).** Few films have the courage to trace elements of violence when that violence occurs within a family or to take an uncompromising, unromantic position regarding race. Yet this film—based on a novel by **Alan Duff**—shows as well the strengths of **Maori** culture, in the diverse paths Maori have taken to rediscover and redefine that culture. At the same time, director **Lee Tamahori** does not turn away from exploring the dark side of Maori culture. No one viewing the film could hide from the obvious implication that the dark side, the world of excess alcohol and violence, exists within their culture—whether Maori or something else—unless they never read the newspaper, watched the news, or went out. Although the film sometimes opines that the violence is perpetrated by the husband, Jake, because of some kind of psychological addiction to being a wage slave, and the frustration that brings, it is less than clear about the dynamic of violence established by Jake and Beth.

Her attraction to him seems purely sexual, and she enjoys the sexuality that is part of his syndrome of violence. In this sense, the film holds a bigger mirror up to Western culture: it is not just the violence dynamic that occurs in some instances in Maori culture, but the violence that occurs in many cultures. Tamahori is brave enough to suggest possible paths to breaking the cycle of violence: paths comprising a return to some form of traditional culture and the respect that lay within that culture; gaining a respect and identity through suffering brutal initiation into the urban tribe, complete with the external badges of identity; or learning the internal strengths of the traditional culture and recovering identity and respect through that process.

O'SHEA, JOHN (1920–2001). John O'Shea rightfully holds the title of founder of the New Zealand film industry. He made the only three feature films between 1940 and 1970, and he would have liked to make more, as he deplored what he saw as the Americanization of the world (*see* PACIFIC FILMS). Like many contemporary filmmakers then and now—in Australia, for example—he saw films as essential elements of culture, a means of storytelling that molded and reinforced notions of identity. He there directed three feature films—the only feature films made in New Zealand between 1940 and 1970—*Broken Barrier* (1952), *Runaway* (1964), and *Don't Let It Get You* (1966). After 1966, he moved from directing to producing. He was concerned about what he considered the unique feature of New Zealand, the European culture and consciousness juxtaposed with a **Maori** culture and consciousness. This grinding of cultures finds a means of articulation, if not a solution, in his films. For O'Shea, films were a means of shaping a cultural revolution and influencing opinion. His lobbying carried a significant weight in the decision of the government to establish the **New Zealand Film Commission** in 1978. Recognizing the value of film as an historical artifact—again partly through O'Shea's lobbying—the government also established the **New Zealand Film Archive** to ensure that the cultural heritage of New Zealand was saved. He was a founding Board member in 1981 and remained until 1999. In 1990, O'Shea was awarded the Order of the British Empire (OBE)—an award given by the Queen of England in an antiquated system of recognition—for his services to film, and the Film Commission awarded him a Lifetime Achievement Award in 1992. In 2001, his name was given to an annual film fellowship for young filmmakers.

– P –

PACIFIC FILMS (PACIFIC FILM UNIT). "Pacific Films" and "**John O'Shea**" are an inseparable and an integral element in the genesis of the New Zealand film industry. Originally established in 1948 by Alun Falconer, the Pacific Film Unit was planned to create an independent filmmaking company. Its first film was a short *doc-umentary, *The Story of a Store*, made for the Hays Department Store in 1949. By 1950, Alun Falconer had left to follow a career in China, and John O'Shea joined the company. Between 1940 and 1970, only three feature films were made in New Zealand, all by O'Shea: *Broken Barrier* in 1952, *Runaway* in 1964, and *Don't Let It Get You* in 1966. During these years, Pacific Films continued to grow and pros-per by making road safety films, industry-sponsored documentaries, and by covering sporting events, such as the All Blacks rugby union test matches. As the company grew, more staff were recruited and the permanent staff increased to 28. However, by the 1970s government cutbacks had reduced the staffing level to just six.

Film schools in New Zealand were non-existent at the time, and Pacific Films was positioned to fill a much-needed avenue for the new, aspiring filmmakers. For example, Jonathan Dennis, the first di-rector of the **New Zealand Film Archive**, who worked closely with O'Shea, described Pacific Film's position in the film industry as a creative area, combining the practical and academic, with invigorat-ing and inspiring discussions in the informal workplaces. O'Shea's six-part **television** series, *Tangata Whenua* in 1974, opened the door for **Maori** to begin telling their stories on film. In addition, O'Shea had a determination and drive to ensure New Zealand had its own film industry, an industry that would tell and retell the stories of New Zealand culture and identity.

In 1978, after continued lobbying by O'Shea for funding, the gov-ernment established the **New Zealand Film Commission** and he be-came part of the Film Archives Group. All the films and production records for Pacific Films were entered into the Film Archive in 1992, becoming a tangible record of New Zealand. John O'Shea died in Wellington in July 2001.

***PIANO, THE* (1993).** Written and directed by **Jane Campion**, *The Pi-ano* tells the story of people trying to maintain the conventions and the polite, repressed traditions of a civilization that is at the opposite end of the Earth, when faced with another geography of wild and des-olate landscapes, another climate of rain and mud, another people of primal innocence and lack of repression. An illiterate New Zealand bachelor, Stewart (**Sam Neill**), has somehow arranged to marry a mute widow Ada (Holly Hunter), who communicates with the world through her piano and a sign language interpreted by her daughter Flora (Anna Paquin). Stewart refuses to accept the piano, which is left crated at the high tide mark, but another local, Baines (Harvey Keitel), becomes interested in it, and in its power to help him seduce Ada. She is no walkover, however.

This brief synopsis cannot do justice to the film. The actors play multilayered parts; no character is the way he or she seems at first, and all have lives marked by fear and hesitation. The camerawork is superb. Attesting to its significance and acclaim at an international level, the film has won a plethora of awards. For example, at Cannes in 1993, Holly Hunter won the best actress, and Jane Campion the Golden Palm awards. In the same year, the *Australian Film Institute** nominated the film in 13 categories, and it won an unparalleled 11 awards, including best film, best director, best leading actor (Keitel), best leading actress (Hunter), and best cinematography. At the British Academy of Film and Television Awards (BAFTA) the next year, the film was nominated in seven categories—including best film—and won the best leading actress award (Hunter), the best costume design, and best production design awards. At the Academy Awards, it was nominated in five categories, and won Oscars for best leading actress, best supporting actress (Paquin), and best screenplay written directly for the screen (Campion).

The Piano was the 14th most popular film at the Australian box office with receipts in excess of $11 million, and has taken over US$40 million in the United States—a significant feat. It remains one of the most important in the corpus of New Zealand films.

PILLSBURY, SAM (1946–). Born in New York, Sam Pillsbury has worked in the film and **television** industry as director, writer, producer, and second-unit director since 1981. He was first assistant director on **Geoff Murphy**'s *Goodbye Pork Pie* (1981). His directing debut came in *The Scarecrow* (1982), a thriller/horror film based on a Ronald Morrieson novel, full of sexual deviance, corruption, and degenerate characters in a small, 1950s New Zealand town. The film was nominated for best film at the 1982 Italian Mystfest festival.

Pillsbury then cowrote and produced *The Quiet Earth* (1985). In 1987, the film won the best film and best screenplay prizes at the **New Zealand Film and Television Awards**. He then directed the historical drama *Starlight Hotel* (1987), a road movie set in Depression-era New Zealand telling of the renewal of a hardened old man in the face of the innocence and love of a young girl; in part, a retelling of the myth that feminine beauty and innocence can redeem fallen *masculinity.

Pillsbury returned to the United States to direct the erotic thriller *Zandalee* (1991), starring Nicolas Cage, Judge Reinhold, and Erika Anderson. He then directed some 11 television films and programs, before *Free Willy 3: The Rescue* (1997) and the drama *Morgan's Ferry* (1999). Returning to New Zealand, he directed *Crooked Earth* (2001), an *action and drama film about **Maori** and white contact that has had mixed reviews. Back in the United States, Pillsbury took over the direction of *Where the Red Fern Grows* (2003).

PRESTON, GAYLENE (1947–). Gaylene Preston has been involved in filmmaking since the renaissance in filmmaking in the late 1970s. Her career began as production designer in John Reid's *Middle Age Spread* (1979), and she has had experience in writing, directing and producing. In 1984, she teamed up with Robin Laing to form Preston–Laing Productions, which produced two of the films they collaborated on. Together they made four films. Preston directed and Laing produced *Mr. Wrong* (1984), a thriller that draws on noir lighting conventions and a well-crafted production design to build tension and terror. The film was the first made by a female director and producer duo, and was not well accepted by cinema chains. Their second film, *Ruby and Rata* (1990), was a *comedy that celebrated the little machinations that people use to get by in life, but which often lead to greater comic situations. The film won awards for best editing, best soundtrack, best film score, and best male performance at the 1990 **New Zealand Film and Television Awards**.

In 1994, Preston and Laing combined again to make *Bread and Roses* (1994). Preston turned the autobiography of Sonja Davies — who was an independent socialist, a nurse during World War II, and one of the first members of the *women's movement that led to a career in politics — into the screenplay for the film, which she also directed. The two collaborated for *War Stories* (1995) (also *War Stories Our Mother Never Told Us*), a film about the real experiences of seven women—played by the women themselves—during World War II, and the consequences of that war for them. *War Stories* won the best film prize at the 1995 New Zealand **Film and Television Awards**. Preston wrote the screenplay for and directed *Perfect Strangers* (2003), which Laing once again coproduced. About the apparent kidnapping of a woman by a man who seems to declare his love faster than they can remove their clothes, the film has not been successful at the box office, and has had mixed reviews.

Preston's films are marked by a compassion and understanding of real life and real people, and her films have a distinctive flavor, combined with humor and warmth. She has also made award-winning documentaries and commercials. For her contribution to the film industry, she was awarded the Officer of New Zealand Order of Merit.

– Q –

***QUIET EARTH, THE* (1985).** This film is one of the most significant films to have come from New Zealand, and is even more noteworthy as it is a science fiction/horror film. Directed by **Geoff Murphy**, *The Quiet Earth* tells the story of a scientist—played by **Bruno Lawrence**—and an experiment gone wrong; it is a time when all living creatures have disappeared from the Earth. After meeting two other remaining people, the group begins to realize the devastating consequences of what happened to them and to the Earth, and their relationships gradually collapse. The film was based on the novel by Craig Harrison, and was adapted for the screen by Lawrence, Bill Baer, and **Sam Pillsbury**. It won the best screenplay—adaptation in the 1987 **New Zealand Film and Television Awards**.

– R –

***RAIN* (2001).** This was the first film that Christine Jeffs directed, although she was assistant editor for *Crush* (1992) and *Absent Without Leave* (1992). She wrote the screenplay for *Rain* from a novel by

Kirsty Gunn. The film explores one of the significant situations in the late 20th- and early 21st-century Western culture, which is not just the disintegration of the family unit, but the specific traits that lead to such disintegration. The tragedy unfolds while a family holidays in a seaside cottage in 1971. The alcoholic mother flirts with a photographer neighbor, the teenage daughter manipulates her sexuality into that situation, and the father and brother are caught somewhere in the middle. There is a darkness, a sense of unease, that permeates the narrative amidst the sensuality and debauchery. The film might be a manual for how a family should not be. Jeffs later directed the international *Sylvia* (2002), about the life of Sylvia Plath.

– S –

SANDERSON, MARTYN (1938–). Actor and writer Martyn Sanderson has had a long and extensive career in New Zealand film. He first appeared playing Fitzpatrick in Tony Richardson's *Ned Kelly* (1970), which starred Mick Jagger. In 1977, Sanderson wrote—with **Bruno Lawrence**—and acted in the *comedy *Wild Man*, and followed this with similar scripting and acting roles in the poorly made drama/ romance *Solo* (1978). He moved to Australia for a small part in *The Journalist* (1979), and then returned to New Zealand for another small part in *Squeeze* (1980) before playing a major role as Detective John Hughes in **John Laing**'s *Beyond Reasonable Doubt* (1980). Another role in a factual drama about a murder followed in *Bad Blood* (1981), a disturbing study of small-town alienation. Later, he played the vicar in *Utu* (1983), a film about conflict with **Maori** tribes in the 1860s, and followed this with the role of Inspector Gulland in the factual story of *Sylvia* (1985), about her pioneering work teaching Maori children to read in the 1940s, and the institutional hurdles she had to leap. He played the father of a boy coming to the realization that he might be gay in *My First Suit* (1985). Sanderson won the 1990 **New Zealand Film and Television Award** for best supporting actor for the role of Frank Sargeson in the **Jane Campion**-directed *Angel at My Table* (1990). He played Henry in Alan Lindsay's well-received *Savage Play* (1995), a series of moving stories about the juxtaposition of cultures in New Zealand. A leading role (Bryce Tilfer) in

Grant Lahood's *Chicken* (1996) followed, an underrated film about a pop icon reduced to making fried chicken commercials. More recently, Sanderson appeared in ***The Lord of the Rings: The Fellowship of the Ring*** (2001), playing the gatekeeper of Bree.

Other films include John Laing's *The Lost Tribe* (1983), *Wild Horses* (1983), *Trial Run* (1984), *The Tale of Ruby Rose* (1988), *Never Say Die* (1988), *Old Scores* (1991), *The Rainbow Warrior* (1992), *Desperate Remedies* (1993), *The Last Tattoo* (1994), and *Cow* (2001).

SLEEPING DOGS **(1977).** *Sleeping Dogs* launched the careers of **Sam Neill** and director **Roger Donaldson**, but more importantly was, arguably, the film that heralded the renaissance of filmmaking in New Zealand. The narrative is multilayered, with the breakup of the marriage of an ordinary man, Smith, occurring within a context of the collapse of a totalitarian society, in which revolutionary guerilla groups do battle with government special forces. Smith is inexorably drawn into this battle, and his anguish over the loss of his family is articulated only through his defiant lack of concern for his own well-being. That such a scenario could be relevant to people at the time is a comment on the right-wing leanings of the contemporary New Zealand government, as well as a belief that the United States, following Vietnam, would send military forces into a country to protect a status quo that was sympathetic to its own totalitarianism. The film showed first, that audiences would respond to New Zealand–made films, with narratives drawn from that culture, set among familiar landmarks, with actors who spoke with familiar characteristics of language. Second, the film proved that New Zealand films were able to find a market in the United States, and could win critical approval. The success of this film led directly to the hurried establishment of the Interim Film Commission in November 1977, and then the **New Zealand Film Commission** in the following year, as the New Zealand government recognized the potential of this new type of industry—a cultural industry with the potential to develop cultural capital.

SMASH PALACE **(1981). Roger Donaldson** shared the writing credits for this film, which he also directed. It is a common 20th-century story of a souring relationship, and the destructive effect it has on those who were once in love, as well as those who are drawn into the vortex of hate, most importantly the child, Georgie (Greer Robson). Al (**Bruno Lawrence**) and Jacqui Shaw (Anna Jemison) own a car wrecking yard, which Al sees as his domain and his life, but whose rusting wrecks signify their corroding relationship. Unfortunately, Jacqui sees the yard only as a springboard to another life. Unhappy, she has an affair with a police officer neighbor, Ray, and from there events slide rapidly into the abyss of breaking relationships, with the child in the center of the cyclone of twisted emotions. Domestic violence orders, threats of death, violence, fear, and revenge all play a part. The film was successful at home and abroad, signifying the common experiences that it highlights. Indeed, the *New York Times* listed it as one of the ten best films of the year.

SPENCE, BRUCE. *See entry in Australian section.*

– T –

TAMAHORI, LEE (1950–). Lee Tamahori is of **Maori** and British lineage and began his career in the film industry in 1970, after working as a commercial artist and photographer. Since then he has worked as director, second unit director, assistant director, in the sound department, and as an actor. He worked as assistant or second unit director on the Australian-made *Merry Christmas Mr. Lawrence* (1983), the American and New Zealand coproduction *Nate and Hayes* (1983), and the New Zealand productions *Wild Horses* (1983), *Utu* (1983), *Among the Cinders* (1983), *The Silent One* (1984), **The Quiet Earth** (1985), *Came a Hot Friday* (1985), and *Bridge to Nowhere* (1986). His long apprenticeship comprised eight films as a boom operator and a further nine films as second unit or assistant director before he was given the chance to direct. This apprenticeship included directing about 100 **television** commercials in the late 1980s, and he was acclaimed for his storytelling style.

Tamahori made his directorial debut in the television series *The Ray Bradbury Theatre* (1985), and followed this with the rarely seen *Thunderbox* (1989). His next film cemented his reputation though. Based on the novel by **Alan Duff**, *Once Were Warriors* (1994) exploded onto cinema screens with an unrelenting intensity and power that highlighted problems of domestic violence, specifically in one Maori family. In contrast to the novel, the film removes women from partial responsibility for the dynamic of violence that the novel articulated. The film won many awards, including best director at the 1994 **New Zealand Film and Television Awards**, the 1994 Grand Prix des Amériques, the prize of the ecumenical jury and the public prize at the Montreal World Film Festival, and the 1995 audience award at the Rotterdam International Film Festival.

Based on this success, Tamahori moved to ***Hollywood** and directed the uneven *crime thriller *Mulholland Falls* (1996), followed by the more successful survival thriller *The Edge* (1997), which combined a man-against-the-elements narrative with Tamahori's visual *mise-en-scene*. The crime thriller *Along Came a Spider* (2001) followed, which returned a greater profit at the box office but was not as complex as the previous film. The challenge of his next film was to attempt to reinvigorate an icon and a ***genre** whose star might have waned, and Tamahori rose to the challenge with the successful 20th installment in the James Bond 007 franchise, *Die Another Day* (2002).

TELEVISION. New Zealand's first official television transmission was broadcast at 7:30 P.M. on Wednesday, 1 June 1960. The staid New Zealand government of the time had set up a committee to examine the feasibility of television broadcasting in 1949, some ten years after NBC began broadcasting in the United States. Initially, broadcasting was limited to Auckland, then to Christchurch and Wellington in 1961. Broadcasting began in Dunedin in 1962 and subsequently around the rest of the country. Television infrastructure and programming was funded by a television licensing system, introduced in August 1960, and by 1965, more than 300,000 licenses had been issued. This year was significant, as it heralded the beginning of television advertising. At this early time, national networks did not exist, and programs were shown in one part of the country, then shipped to another for subsequent rebroadcast. Similarly, no network for news programs existed until 1969 when the first network news bulletin was transmitted simultaneously around the country.

The isolation of New Zealand was made clear in 1968, when tape of the Apollo 11 moon-landing had to be flown from Australia to New Zealand for subsequent broadcast. New Zealand gained entry into the simultaneous news world of the global village in 1971, when the Wakworth satellite station was opened, and the first live international broadcast was the royal wedding of Princess Anne and Captain Mark Phillips in 1973. The global village has interests outside news, enjoying the romance of fairy tales. Until 1974, television broadcasting was in black and white, and in the 1980s, videotape replaced film.

The making of programs was an ad hoc affair. Many of the early shows were studio based, broadcast live in Auckland and then sent on tape to other centers for rebroadcast. These early years saw the birth of long-running series, such as *Country Calendar*, a 15-minute rural news magazine program that is still running in a 30-minute format. New Zealand television drama began in 1963 (*All Earth to Love*) and continued with programs like *Shortland Street* in 1992, which enjoyed considerable overseas success. Talent shows were also popular, using formats that had been successful overseas, such as *New Faces*, beginning in 1974. Entertainment programs covered pop music (*Let's Go* in 1963, *C'mon* in 1966), opera and music hall, although Graham Kerr hosted the first cooking show before migrating to Australia to repeat the success. Game shows, also with a cross-national format, were consistently popular, including *It's in the Bag* (1973), *Mastermind* (1979), the perennial favorite *Sale of the Century* (1989), and *The Chair* (2002). Children's television was also popular, with shows like *Spot On* from 1974. More recently, *What Now?* has played since 1981. Comedy has been one of the strengths of New Zealand television, and **John Clarke**'s 1973 spawning of Fred Dagg proved immensely and immediately popular, and exportable. Ginette McDonald brought Lynn of Tawa into life in 1979, although satire emerged in 1977 with *A Week of It* and, in 1980, with *McPhail and Gadsby*. Introduced by Billy T. James, Maori comedy made its mark in the early 1980s.

Television broadcasting was regulated by the New Zealand Broadcasting Corporation (NZBC), which operated from 1962. In 1975, a second government-owned network was put on air, when the NZBC was dissolved and replaced by Television One and Television Two. However, this was deemed inappropriate and wasteful of resources, so in 1980, the television channels were merged into the Broadcasting Corporation of New Zealand (BCNZ). In an era of economic rationalism, this structure was clearly inappropriate, so the BCNZ was disestablished in 1988 and the state-owned, autonomous commercial television company, Television New Zealand, was formed, with a purely commercial focus. A year later, deregulation allowed for the sale of UHF television frequencies to private enterprise, and the third television network began broadcasting in 1989, with a fourth beginning in 1997. Pay television entered the market in 1990, and digital satellite broadcasting began in 1998, allowing access to 40 channels.

From 1 March 2003, legislation once again changed the structure of television broadcasting. The TVNZ bill divided the old Television New Zealand into a transmission company and a television company (TVNZ). Legislation requires the television company to balance commercial considerations with public broadcasting imperatives, set out in its charter. As in Australia, television has provided a parallel employment track and training ground for cast and crew working intermittently in the film industry.

TILLY, GRANT. Grant Tilly has played in many support roles, and some leading roles, but has not yet excited critics or audiences. He began his career with Geoffrey Steven's film, *Skin Deep* (1978), playing the character Phil Barrett. A drama/thriller, it tells the story of a masseuse from the *city who has expectations of a quieter life in a *country town. However, behind the facade of small-town respectability and the attempt to harness progress, she finds familiar double standards. Tilly subsequently appeared in **John Laing**'s drama/thriller *Beyond Reasonable Doubt* (1980), playing David Morris. Based on an actual incident, the film tells the chilling story of an injustice involving a local farmer Arthur Thomas. Harvey and Jeanette Crewe went missing and were found three months later in the Waikato River. Police and the prosecutors ignored evidence pointing to a particular person, and Thomas was tried and convicted. After nine years imprisonment and the collapse of his marriage, he was pardoned.

Later in 1981, Tilly appeared in *Race for the Yankee Zephyr*, playing Collector. Directed by David Hemmings, this is an *action/ adventure film that also starred Ken Wahl, Lesley Ann Warren, Donald Pleasence, and George Peppard. The film relates the story of a man who finds the wreckage of a DC3, the Yankee Zephyr, in a remote lake in the Southern Alps of New Zealand. The fact that $50 million in gold from World War II is in the plane opens up the possibility that other, less honest, people might want to salvage the plane. Working again with director John Reid, Tilly played the lead role of Arthur Donovan in *Carry Me Back* (1982), followed by a support role to Tommy Lee Jones in the adventure story *Nat and Hayes* (1983).

Tilley later moved to Australia to appear in Bob Ellis's quirky *Warm Nights on a Slow Moving Train* (1988), playing the politician who is one of a number of people seduced on the Melbourne to Sydney train by a part-time prostitute (Wendy Hughes). He followed with a role in Megan Simpson's Australian–New Zealand production of *Alex* (1993), a rite-of-passage story that tells of a Kiwi girl whose dream is to win the 100-meter freestyle event at the Rome Olympics. In 1998, he appeared in the Richard Franklin-directed *Brilliant Lies* (1996), an interesting story about sexual activities in families and outside them. Since then, he has appeared in two **television** films.

Other films include *Middle Age Spread* (1979), John Laing's *Other Halves* (1984) and *Dangerous Orphans* (1985), and *The Returning* (1990).

– U –

***UTU* (1983). Geoff Murphy** drew on the Western *genre for this film set during the Land Wars of the 1870s. The British-led colonial army sacks the village to which one of their scouts, Te Wheke, belongs. He vows *utu* (revenge), as do the *pakeha* whose families and properties are destroyed in his subsequent rampage. As in *The Chant of Jimmy Blacksmith* (1978), the apparently excessive violence is the result of not only revenge for misdeeds, but also revenge for making it impossible for a peaceable bicultural existence. The only conclusion is that tragedy accompanies the encounter of cultures whose interests are irreconcilable.

The **New Zealand Film Commission** supported the making of *Utu*, and much effort was expended in authenticating choreography and costume. The film received mixed critical response, but nevertheless attracted large audiences, making it for a time the second-highest-grossing film in New Zealand. Re-edited for overseas release, critics in the United States applauded *Utu* as providing both adventure and accurate historical information, a case once again where a fictional account becomes authenticated as a factual event.

– W –

WARD, VINCENT (1956–). Working as a director, writer, actor, producer, and art director, Vincent Ward has become one of New Zealand's most accomplished filmmakers, in part through his ability to create arresting visual narratives. Doubtless, his training as a painter and his two-year experience living in an isolated **Maori** community has played some part in this. He cowrote and directed his first short film, *A State of Sedge*, while still a student. His second film was a *documentary that explored the relationship between a middle-aged schizophrenic man and his Maori mother, *In Spring One Plants Alone*. His feature directorial debut, *Vigil* (1984), established his reputation as a writer and filmmaker of power and poetry. Shot at the foot of Mount Messenger, the *coming-of-age film is visually stunning and narratively uneven and received mixed reviews. However, as New Zealand's first entry in competition at Cannes in 1984, it received a standing ovation and Ward was nominated for the Golden Palm. Back in New Zealand, Ward—with cowriter Graeme Tetley—won the best original screenplay prize at the 1986 **New Zealand Film and Television Awards**, and the film also won best cinematography and best production design.

Ward then directed the Australian/New Zealand coproduction *The Navigator: A Medieval Odyssey* (1988), for which he had the original idea and was one of the writers. The story involves a young boy who digs a hole in medieval England and arrives in present-day New Zealand, but the film cannot be paraphrased so easily. Suffice to say that Ward received a five-minute standing ovation at Cannes in 1988, and he was nominated again for the Golden Palm. The film won 11 prizes at the 1989 New Zealand Film and Television Awards, including best director, best film, best cinematography, and best original screenplay. At the 1988 *Australian Film Institute** ceremony, it won six awards, including best film and best director, and was nominated for another two. It also won other international awards.

Moving into the international industry, Ward coproduced, directed, and created the story for the drama/romance *Map of the Human Heart* (1993), financed by international backers including the **Australian Film Finance Corporation*, Vincent Ward films, as well as French, English, and American companies. The story of the love between a half-Eskimo boy, Avik, and a half-Cree Indian girl, Albertine, won critical acclaim in part because of the realism imparted when cast and crew flew in helicopters to Arctic ice floes in order to shoot the film. *What Dreams May Come* (1998) tells the story of the search of deceased painter Chris Williams (Robin Williams) for his widow, Annie (Annabella Sciorra), who has committed suicide in grief and has gone to a different place. Ward envisions the afterlife as a painted world, a filmic world of new technologies.

Ward wrote the story for *Alien 3* (1992), and acted as one of the businessmen in the brilliant Mike Figgis-directed *Leaving Las Vegas* (1995). He played Smith in the American comedy *The Shot* (1996) and Nathan in another Mike Figgis film, *One Night Stand* (1997). He was executive producer for Edwin Zwick's *The Last Samurai* (2003). Although he has moved into the international industry, his contribution may be to enrich the stories of other cultures and times in the same way that he has for New Zealand.

WATKIN, IAN (1940–). In terms of numbers of films, Ian Watkin is one of the most-filmed actors in the New Zealand film industry. Predominantly known as an actor, Watkin was also a writer—with **Bruno Lawrence**, **Martyn Sanderson**, and **Geoff Murphy**—of *Wild Man* (1977). Directed by Murphy, this **comedy* stars Lawrence, Tony Barry, and Sanderson, in a story about two conmen who operated in the semi-lawless goldfields of the west coast of the South Island in the latter half of the 19th century. He then played Dudley in **Roger Donaldson**'s *Sleeping Dogs* (1977)—which starred **Sam Neill**, a fiction about revolutionaries in a right-wing state, and the practice of "ahimsa," or nonviolence. Although not widely seen, Donaldson's *Nutcase* (1980) is an amusing parody of the gangster **genre*, with Watkin as Godzilla. He then played Kevin Ryan in **John Laing**'s *Beyond Reasonable Doubt* (1980), the story of a much-publicized murder trial and retrial, conviction, and subsequent pardon of an innocent man.

The role of Mears in Laing's *The Lost Tribe* (1983) followed, an adventure/thriller about an anthropologist who disappears while looking for a lost tribe. In *Utu* (1983), Watkin plays the Doorman in a film about the **Maori** wars of the 1860s. He followed this with the part of Bill in *Death Warmed Up* (1985), a horror/thriller about a young boy seeking revenge on a scientist who caused him to kill his parents. As Father Vincent in the excruciating *My Grandfather Is a Vampire* (1991), he was practicing for his next role as Uncle Les in **Peter Jackson**'s splatter film *Braindead* (1992). This is a hilarious and sometimes gross horror film about Lionel and his girlfriend, watched over by his mother, who is bitten by a Rat Monkey and begins acting very strangely indeed. A long time passed before his next film role, in Mark Beesley's *Savage Honeymoon* (2000), a comedy about sex, rock 'n' roll, motorbikes, and alcohol.

Other films include *Middle Age Spread* (1979), ***Goodbye Pork Pie*** (1980), *Bad Blood* (1981), *Carry Me Back* (1982), *Pallet on the Floor* (1984), *Send a Gorilla* (1988), and *Just Me and Mario* (1988).

WHALE RIDER (TE KAIEKE TOHORA)* (2002).** Niki Caro directed one short film in 1994 and a feature in 1997 before adapting the screenplay for *Whale Rider* from a novel by Sir Witi Ihimaera. While **Peter Jackson** made New Zealand a household term for the ***Lord of the Rings trilogy, Niki Caro emerged from relative obscurity to international significance through the creation of a story of the overcoming of cultural and personal limitations by a young **Maori** girl, Paikea—played by Keisha Castle-Hughes in a role that won international critical acclaim. The story itself is modeled on the contemporary favorite of a young girl overcoming barriers to achieve, in what is portrayed as a patriarchal system of tribal leadership. The power of the story lies in its recreation as a tale of beauty and sense of triumph, rather than its ideological content. Pai is effectively an orphan, brought up by grandparents in a tribe that will become leaderless after the male grandparent dies. Through her mastery of the initiation processes, Pai proves to herself and the tribe that limitations are meant to be broken, and are simply social constructions in most instances.

Whale Rider scooped the pool at the 2003 **New Zealand Film and Television Awards**—being nominated for four prizes including best actor and best supporting actor—and winning nine prizes, including best film, best screenplay, best director, and best actress. It was nominated for and won many awards internationally: the film won a British Academy of Film and Television Arts children's award, and was nominated for both an ***Australian Film Institute** award for best foreign film and an Academy Award for best actress in a leading role.

Bibliography

As can be seen in these pages, both Australia and New Zealand have a history of involvement with motion pictures that extends back to the 1890s and 1900s. Sheltered by distance, the white populations of these neighbors on either side of the Tasman have shared a common thirst for entertainment. This, in turn, soon saw the establishment of thriving local production industries and vigorous distribution organizations, looking after exhibitors' demands for local films and the increasingly glamorous products of the United States and other countries. However, despite these promising beginnings and some of the more prominent films made in the first half of the 20th century, the development of cinema in Australia and New Zealand has not been continuous.

Instead, from around 1912 onward, foreign dominance of distribution and exhibition, and competition from overseas—notably both Hollywood and the United Kingdom—led to the almost complete drying up of feature production by the 1950s and 1960s. Kristen Thompson's 1985 study of international distribution, *Exporting Entertainment*, provides an excellent background to the larger forces operating on Australian and New Zealand film in this period. However, inspired by the Canadian example, governments first in Australia and then in New Zealand decided to develop state-subsidized film production industries. These are now almost-permanent parts of the cultural and business landscapes in both countries. Very many of the essays and books that are cited deal with this grand subject.

Nonetheless, the track records of the two industries are mixed. First, the two have produced only a small number of feature films that have won critical and commercial recognition at home and abroad. Second, they have also produced film industry personnel including directors, actors, cameramen, and others who have moved to join a world feature-film production industry based in Hollywood. As a string of items testify—beginning with Stuart Cunningham ("Hollywood Genres, Australian Movies"), Peter Hamilton and Sue Mathews (*American Dreams: Australian Movies*), and Glen Lewis (*Australian Movies and the American Dream*) and running down to Laurence Simmons ("Distance Looks Our Way"), and Brian McDonnell ("Postwar Hollywood Representations of New Zealand")—this love–hate relationship is a perennial feature of film culture, including film writing, in the two places. However, on the other side of the ledger, many of the features produced under various systems of subsidization sponsored by the two governments have produced indifferent performances at both the commercial and critical box office. In turn, as will be seen below, this has been particularly valuable and useful to the film scholar and student, triggering as they have recurring inquiries, debates, and controversy about the ongoing viability of such arrangements. However, rather than making incidental references to the bibliography that follows, it is worth providing a more systematic set of introductory remarks.

The best single reference guide to the subject of Australian film is the book-length bibliography published by Brian Reis, *Australian Film*. As well as this, the guide compiled by Brian McFarlane, Geoff Mayer, and Ina Bertrand, *The Oxford Companion to Australian Film*, is an excellent reference source, offering entries covering most of the important subjects. Unfortunately, the guide has no bibliography or any reference to the work of Reis. Similarly, there is as yet no single bibliography on the subject of New Zealand film. However, Geoffrey Churchman and Ian Conrich's *Celluloid Dreams* can function as a useful substitute. In addition, the collections by Jonathan Dennis and Jan Bieringa (*Film in Aotearoa New Zealand*) and the more recent book by Helen Martin and Sam Edwards (*New Zealand Film 1912–1996*) frequently provide useful background and contexts that serve as substitutes of sorts. One other landmark in the field of reference works and the bibliography of Australian cinema is also worth mention; namely, the two volumes by Andrew Pike and Ross Cooper (*Australian Film 1900–1977*), and Scott Murray (*Australian Film 1978–1994*), respectively. Published by Oxford University Press, these two volumes collectively cover the years from 1901 to 1994 as far as the output of feature films in Australia is concerned. Constituting a kind of canonical guide, the two form part of what will clearly be a series and provide excellent coverage, as far as production credits, synopsis, production and reception history, and critical evaluation are concerned. Again, there is nothing yet comparable available in relation to feature films in New Zealand, although the Martin and Edwards' 1997 study, also published by Oxford, serves as a substitute of sorts. As a footnote to this subject area, it is also worth mentioning the volume *Twin Peeks* edited by Deb Verhoeven. In the first volume to be devoted to the twin subject of film in the two countries of Australia and New Zealand, this book has a number of interesting essays, as well as a most useful filmography of all feature films produced in the two places up to the time of its publication in 1999.

Marking the still recent infancy of writing about film in the two countries, there are few major biographical studies of individual filmmakers. This is most glaringly the case in Australia, where, given the number of good film historians at work, one might have expected that there would be solid biographies of important figures, such as Raymond Longford, Ken Hall, and Lee Robinson, yet no such studies exist. Instead, the only full study is Cunningham's monograph, *Featuring Australian: The Cinema of Charles Chauvel*, although it is finally more concerned with his films rather than his biography. On the other hand, in the case of New Zealand, Roger Horrock's biography of Len Lye is a major work on this international avant-garde film artist. Other than these, the student must search out shorter biographical entries and profiles in other volumes. Besides the human subjects, there are also a number of interesting studies of particular films. Despite international interest in the two cinemas, only a small handful of feature films have attained classic status such that the interested student will find critical discussion of these in international journals and anthologies. Chief among these films have been *Mad Max*, *The Piano,* and *Lord of the Rings*, which have been explored in a number of international publications.

A focus on films and their investigation prompts mention here of Australian and New Zealand writers whose written work have given them international reputations. Three such figures stand out. In New Zealand, Roger Horrocks has been an important figure in the development of film study in higher education and he has been a prolific writer. In Australia, Adrian Martin has bestridden the divide between film reviewing and film criticism with a grace and imagination that is fast reaching an international audience. Meanwhile, Tom O'Regan's 1997 book, *Australian National Cinema*, has been hailed as both a thorough and compelling study of Australian cinema, as well as a highly imaginative and cogent theorization of the more general subject of national cinema.

In the realms of policy and economics concerning the production industries, one looks to reports and other documents produced by government bodies and other agencies such as the Australian Film Commission
and the New Zealand Film Commission. However, the two-volume
study of Australian government film policy, funding, and film output
published in 1987 and 1988 by Susan Dermody and Elizabeth Jacka,
The Screening of Australia, has become an internationally acclaimed
classic in the field. Again, there is no comparable study in New Zealand,
although those interested will be able to glean much comparable information and insight from both Dennis and Bieringa, and Martin and Edwards. These last-mentioned works are obviously of great significance
for this expansive subject. However, government and film intertwine in
a number of different ways as sketched and explored by Bertrand and
Diane Collins in *Government and Film in Australia*. One of these particular themes is that of censorship. Film censorship has often operated
with a heavy hand in the two places, most especially Australia, which
has a history of illiberality second only to that of the Republic of Ireland. Solid, detailed accounts of censorship in Australia can be found in
Bertrand's *Film Censorship in Australia*, and in Bertrand and Collins.
Similarly, for a study of this institution in New Zealand, one should turn
to Paul Christoffel's *Censored: A Short History of Censorship in New
Zealand*, and, more recently, Chris Watson and Roy Shuker's *In the
Public Good? Censorship in New Zealand*.

The development of state support for a feature film production industry in Australia and New Zealand coincided with the emergence of the
women's movement so that it comes as no surprise to find several reports
and books that deal with the intersection of women and film. Julie Bailey's 1999 report, *Reel Women*, published by the Australian Film, Television and Radio School, is a typical example of the first, concentrating as
it does on matters to do with industry, economics, employment, and policy. Meanwhile, Annette Blonski, Barbara Creed, and Freda Freiberg's
Don't Shoot Darling and Deborah Shepard's recent *Reframing Women*
examine the subject in Australia and New Zealand by concentrating on
screen subjects and matters of reception. It is also worth mentioning Jocelyn Robinson and Beverley Zalcock's 1997 volume *Girls' Own Stories*,
which takes up the subject in relation to the two industries.

There are yet two other major areas of interest within Australia and
New Zealand's film culture. These are those sectors having to do with in-

digenous film on the one hand and the avant-garde, experimental, under-ground, or amateur film on the other. Regarding the first, mention must be made of the study of Maori film in New Zealand by Martin Blythe, *Naming the Other*, because of its ready availability in libraries overseas. Nothing of this magnitude has been published in Australia concerning Aborigines and film, although one should consult Karen Jennings 1993 monograph, *Sites of Difference*. Also relevant is a third volume published the same year in the United Kingdom, Peter Loizos' *Innovation in Ethnographic Film*, which concerns indigenous cinema both in Oceania and elsewhere. Meanwhile, the major source for avant-garde film is *Cantrills' Film Notes*, published from Australia for over 30 years but an excellent introduction to the field there and across the Tasman.

So far as exhibition is concerned, various studies of cinemas and their history as sites of reception do exist. However, except for the 1982 study by Dianne Collins, "The 1920s Picture Palace," there is nothing on how the film-going experience was mediated in cinemas in Australia or New Zealand in their heyday. Instead, what does exist has been written by scholars more interested in architecture of buildings than in the patrons that filled them.

Several periodicals provide information about and analysis of the film industry. *Media International Australia* is devoted to matters of policy, economics, and industry, not only in film but also in other areas of the media industries. Hence, to the extent to which film overlaps its domain of interest, the journal often carries useful and valuable material relating to Australian cinema, and, less frequently, to that of New Zealand. Until its recent demise, *Cinema Papers* was almost the indispensable guide to current happenings in Australian film. Modeling itself on a magazine such as *Sight and Sound,* although veering in the direction of popular accessibility, it covered the production and reviewing of recent feature films with less coverage of other kinds of film. In addition, from time to time, it also featured supplements to do with New Zealand. Meanwhile, across the Tasman, *On Film* is the best single equivalent. Again, too, more essays that are critical can be found in the journal *Illusion*.

Finally, websites maintained by various Australian and New Zealand institutions, organizations, and periodicals provide a rich source of information and analysis. The websites of government and semigovernment authorities, for example, are noteworthy for their meticulous collection of information, which is one of the side benefits of a state-supported industry. For example, the Australian Film Commission site (www.afc .gov.au) contains detailed statistics about the industry, as well as information about films supported by the commission. The sites of similar organizations—such as the Film Finance Corporation (www.afc.gov.au), Film Australia (www.filmaust.com.au), and Screensound (www.screen sound.gov.au)—provide detailed information about their roles and work. Across the Tasman Sea (or "The Ditch" as it is known in the vernacular), the New Zealand Film Commission site (www.nzfilm.co.nz) and other sites, such as the New Zealand Film Archive (www.filmarchive.org.nz), provide similar information about the New Zealand industry. The Australian Film Institute (www.afi.org.au) oversees the annual film award judging, as does the Academy of Film and Television Arts of New Zealand (AFTA), which does not have an official website but its awards are listed on a website hosted by an individual (http://www.lonely.geek.nz/ nzawardsindex.html). Censorship in each country is the responsibility of the benign-sounding Office of Film and Literature Classification (www.oflc.gov.au/splash.html and www.censorship.govt.nz), and the sites explain the role and classification system each organization uses.

In Australia, each state has set up a corporation to support and encourage filmmaking within its borders. The South Australian Film Corporation (www.safilm.com.au) is the oldest. Although New Zealand does not have states, it does have similarly oriented organizations to promote filmmaking, such as Film New Zealand (www.filmnz.com/home/ index.html) and Film South New Zealand (www.filmsouth.com). Websites also allow easy access to electronic journals and other periodicals. The two most significant are *Screening the Past* (www.latrobe.edu.au/ screeningthepast) and *Senses of Cinema* (www.sensesofcinema.com), while the early, digital editions of *Continuum* provide a wealth of detail and analysis (wwwmcc.murdoch.edu.au/ReadingRoom/continuum2 .html). *Inside Film* (www.if.com.au) is an essential reference for people working in the industry. Of course, details of most Australian and New Zealand films appear on the Internet Movie Database (www.imdb.com). Other websites listed deal with almost every aspect of cinema in Australia.

Film research in each country begins with the relevant film commission; that is, the Australian Film Commission (AFC) and the New Zealand Film Commission. Filmmakers who receive assistance from the AFC are required to file a copy of the finished product with the commission; however, this requirement is sometimes not met. Both countries have film archives—the New Zealand Film Archive (which is very active in screen education) and Screensound Australia, which is now the responsibility of the AFC. Each of the Australian state film authorities has detailed records of the films that have been produced with the assistance of that body. Notable among these are Film Victoria, the South Australian Film Corporation, and the New South Wales Film and Television Office, followed by the Western Australia Film and Television Corporation, the Pacific Film and Television Corporation, and Screen Tasmania. In Victoria as well, film collections are in the Australian Centre for the Moving Image, and detailed information about films is available at the Australian Film Institute. The Australian National Library in Canberra is the best source of publications about Australian film, and in both Australia and New Zealand, university libraries have quite extensive research collections, depending on the size of the university and its particular focus. In Australia though, some universities have moved student focus away from the study of films toward the production of films—although the contraction in the industry makes such initiatives questionable.

BIBLIOGRAPHY—CONTENTS

REFERENCE WORKS

Addis, Erika, and Miriana Marusic. "Foxtrot Tango: A National Directory of Women Freelancing in Film." Chippendale, NSW: E. Addis, 1986.

Allard, Andrea. *Australian Feature Films: 1930–1939: A Critical Bibliography.* Melbourne: Australian Film Institute Research and Information, 1983.

Allender, Robert. "Disordered Cinema." *Landfall* V, no. 4 (December 1951).

———. "The National Film Unit." *Landfall* II, no. 4 (December 1948).

Andrews, Stanhope. "Shadow Catching: Some Thoughts on Documentary Films in New Zealand." In *Year Book of the Australian Film Commission 50 Films*, ed. Howard Wadman. Sydney: Australian Film Commission, 1978.

Australian Feature Films [CD-ROM]. Royal Melbourne Institute of Technology, 1994.

Australian Feature Films 1970+: Stills, Posters, Lobby Cards. Canberra: National Film Archive, National Library of Australia, 1981.

Australian Film and Television Reading List. Canberra: National Film Archive, National Library of Australia, 1981.

Australian Films for Children: A Comprehensive List of Films Produced in Australia for Children, prepared by the Australian Council for Children's

Films and Television, with assistance from the Australian Film Commission, Australian Council for Children's Films and Television, East Melbourne, 1983.

The Australian Image: A Journey Through Australia's Image and Sound Heritage. 3 vols. [VHS videorecording]. Hosted by Bill Hunter. Canberra: Australian Capital Television and The National Film and Sound Archive, 1989.

Auty, M. *"Patu!" Monthly Film Bulletin* 606 (July 1984).

Barclay, Barry. *Our Own Image.* Auckland: Longman Paul, 1990.

Bartlett, P.J. "His Majesty's Theatre and Arcade." Auckland: University of Auckland, School of Architecture, 1980.

Barton, Christina, and Deborah Lawler-Dormer, eds. "After/Image: Feminism and Representation in New Zealand Art 1973–1993." Wellington: City Gallery, 1993.

Baxter, B. "New Zealand Cinema." *Films and Filming* 369 (June 1985).

Baxter, John. *The Australian Cinema.* Sydney: Angus and Robertson, 1970.

———. "Filmstruck: Australia at the Movies." Sydney: Australian Broadcasting Corporation, 1986.

Beilby, Peter, ed. *Australian Motion Picture Yearbook 1980.* North Melbourne: Cinema Papers in association with New South Wales Film Corporation, 1980.

———. *Australian Motion Picture Yearbook 1981/82.* North Melbourne: Cinema Papers in association with New South Wales Film Corporation, 1981.

Beilby, Peter and Ross Lansell, eds. *Australian Motion Picture Yearbook 1983.* North Melbourne: 4 Seasons in association with Cinema Papers, 1982.

Bell, Richard A. "Cultural Exchange in Two Wendt Films: *Sons for the Return Home* and *Flying Fox in a Freedom Tree.*" Thesis (MA), University of Auckland, 1997–1998.

Benjamin, Julie. "Film Pioneers: Margaret Thomson and Kathleen O'Brien." *OnFilm* 7, no. 4 (1990).

———. "Film Pioneer: Stanhope Andrews." *OnFilm* 7, no. 3 (1990).

Berryman, Ken. *The Australian Film Industry and Key Films of the 1970s: An Annotated Bibliography.* Carlton South, Vic.: George Lugg Film Information and Research Centre, Australian Film Institute, 1980.

Beth, Stephanie. "Stephanie Beth." *Alternative Cinema* (Summer 1983–1984).

Bilbrough, Milo. "Car Crash View: Alison Maclean's *Crush.*" *Illusions* 20 (1992)

———. "In Spring One Plants Alone: Telling the Story." *Illusions* 7 (1988).

———. "A Taste of Kiwi: Moving Images from Aotearoa." *Illusions* 20 (1992).

Blythe, Martin. "From Maoriland to Aotearoa: Images of the Maori in New Zealand Film and Television." Thesis (PhD), UCLA, 1988.

———. *Naming the Other: Images of the Maori in New Zealand Film and Television.* Metuchen, NJ: Scarecrow Press, 1994.

Boland, Michaela, and Michael Boddy. *Aussieworld: Australia's Leading Actors and Directors Tell How They Conquered Hollywood*. Sydney: Allen and Unwin, 2004.

Bordwell, David. "The Art Cinema as a Mode of Film Practice." *Film Criticism* 4, no. 1 (1979) 56–64.

Bordwell, David, and Kristin Thompson. *Film Art: An Introduction*. 7th ed. Boston: McGraw-Hill, 2001.

Brand, Simon. *The Australian Film Book: 1930–Today*. Sydney: Dreamweaver Books, 1985.

Broadley, C., and J. Jones. *Nambassa: A New Direction*. New Zealand: A.H. & A.W. Reed, 1979.

Broatch, Mark. "Moviegoing." *Quote Unquote* (December 1995).

Bromby, R. "New Zealand." *Sight and Sound* XLVII, no. 2 (Spring 1978).

Bruzi, Stella. "Tempestuous Petticoats: Costume and Desire in The Piano." *Screen* 36, no. 3 (Autumn 1995).

Cairns, Barbara, and Helen Martin. *Shadows on the Wall: A Study of Seven New Zealand Feature Films*. Auckland: Longman Paul, 1994.

Calder, Peter. "Lord Leads Biz." *Variety* (19–25 October 1998).

Campbell, Russell. "Dismembering the Kiwi Bloke: Representation of Masculinity in *Braindead*, *Desperate Remedies* and *The Piano*." *Illusions* 24 (1995).

———. "The Discourse of Documentary: Narrational Strategies in *Bastion Point Day 507*, *Wildcat*, *The Bridge* and *Patu!*" *Illusions* 4 (1987).

———. "Feature Film-Making in New Zealand—It All Seems Reasonably Obvious." *Working Culture* (May 1999).

———. "The New Right and Documentary Film in New Zealand: Someone Else's Country and Revolution." *Illusions* 29 (1999).

———. "Plain Hard Hazardous Work: Cecil Holmes at the NFU." *Illusions* 7 (1988).

———. "Smith & Co.: The Cinematic Redefinition of Pakeha Male Identity." *Illusions* 7 (1988).

Cantrill, Arthur, and Corinne Cantrill, (comps.) *Index to Cantrill's Filmnotes: Issues 1 to 51152 (1971–1986)*. Melbourne: Arthur and Corinne Cantrill, 1987.

Caputo, Raffaele, and Geoff Burton, eds. *Second Take: Australian Film-Makers Talk*. Sydney: Allen & Unwin, 1999.

———. *Third Take: Australian Film-Makers Talk*. Sydney: Allen & Unwin, 2002.

Carbutt, John. "Gay Films Made in New Zealand: Politics and Aesthetics." Thesis (MA), University of Auckland, 1987.

Chen Chui-Lee, "An Offshore Producer's Adventures in Maoriland." *Alternative Cinema* (Winter/Spring 1983).

Christoffel, P. *Censored: A Short History of Censorship in New Zealand*. Wellington: Department of Internal Affairs, 1989.

Churchman, Geoffrey B., ed. *Celluloid Dreams: A Century of Film in New Zealand.* Wellington: IPL Books, 1997.

Cinema Papers, New Zealand Issue (May–June 1980).

Cinema Papers, 20th Anniversary Issue 1997–1998 (April 1994).

Clark, Al, ed. *The Film Yearbook. Vol. 1.* Melbourne: Currey O'Neil Ross, 1984.

Clarke McKenna, N. *Angel in God's Office: My Wartime Diaries.* Birkenhead, N.Z.: Tandem Press, 1996.

Cleave, Peter. "Old New Zealand/New New Zealand: Representation of Pakeha–Maori in *The Piano.*" *Illusions* 24 (1995).

Cochran, Christoper. "St. James Theatre, Courtenay Place, Wellington;" cultural heritage assessment New Zealand Historic Places Trust/Pouhere Taonga [Wellington, N.Z.]: The Trust, [1993]

Collins, Felicity, and Therese Davis. *Australian Cinema after Mabo.* Sydney: Cambridge University Press, 2004.

Conrich, Ian. *Views from the Edge of the World: New Zealand Film.* London: Kakapo Books, 1997.

Cooke, Susan, Sue Larcombe, and Marian MacGowan, eds. *The Production Book 1991.* Sydney: B.P. Publishing, 1991.

Cultural Ministers Council (Australia). Statistical Advisory Group. The Australian Cultural Industry: Available Data and Sources. 2nd ed. Canberra: Australian Government Publishing Service, 1990.

Cunningham, Stuart. *Framing Culture: Criticism and Policy in Australia.* Sydney: Allen & Unwin, 1992.

Cunningham, Stuart, and Graeme Turner, eds. *Media in Australia: Industries, Texts, Audiences.* Sydney: Allen & Unwin, 1993.

Curnow, Wystan, and Roger Horrocks, eds. *Figures of Motion: Selected Writings.* Auckland: Auckland University Press, 1984.

Currie, Cathy. "Hidden Treasures: Documenting an Exhibition of Prisoners' Art." *Illusions* 13 (1990).

Curtis, Rosemary, and Shelley Spriggs, eds. *Get the Picture: Essential Data on Australian Film, Television and Video.* 3rd ed. Sydney: Australian Film Commission, 1994.

Davis, Catherine. "Tainui Stephens—Four Documentaries: The Challenge of Biculturalism." Thesis (MA), University of Auckland, 1997.

Davis, Susan, Alison Maclean, and Helen Todd. "She Through He: Images of Women in New Zealand Feature Films." *Alternative Cinema* (Summer 1983–1984).

Dawson, Johnathon, and Bruce Molloy, eds. *Queensland Images in Film and Television.* Brisbane: University of Queensland Press, 1990.

Day, P. *The Radio Years: A History of Broadcasting in New Zealand.* Auckland: Auckland University Press, 1994.

Dennis, Jonathan, ed. *Aotearoa and the Sentimental Strine: Making Films in Australia and New Zealand in the Silent Period*. Wellington: Moa Films, 1993.

———. *Moving Images from Aotearoa/New Zealand*. Sydney: Museum of Contemporary Art, 1992.

———. *Te Maori Film Season. He Pito Whakaatu a Nga Iwi Maori: Films of the Tangata Whenua*. Auckland: New Zealand Film Archive, 1987.

Dennis, Jonathan, and Jan Bieringa, eds. *Film in Aotearoa New Zealand*. 2nd ed. Wellington: Victoria University Press, 1996.

Dennis, Jonathan, and Clive Sowry. *The Tin Shed: The Origins of the National Film Unit*. Wellington: New Zealand Film Archive, 1981.

Dennis, Jonathan, and Sergio Toffetti, eds. *Te Ao Marama: Il Mondo Della Luce*. Torino: Le Nuove Muse, 1989.

Department of Internal Affairs. *The Dictionary of New Zealand Biography*. Vol.1. Wellington: Allen & Unwin and the Department of Internal Affairs, 1990.

Dowling, David. "War and Peace: *On the Beach* with Bruce and Maurice." *Illusions* 20 (1992).

Downey, P.J. "Documentary Film in New Zealand." *Landfall* IX, no. 4 (December 1955).

Downie, John. "A Milestone of Fabulous Digitalisation—Lord of the Rings." *Illusions* 34 (Winter 2002).

———. *The Navigator: A Mediaeval Odyssey*. Trowbridge, Wiltshire: Flick Books, 2000.

———. "Seeing Is Not Believing: Vincent Ward's Map of the Human Heart." *Illusions* 21/21 (1993).

Dunne, Linda. "The 1930s as a Distinct Period in the History of Film-making in New Zealand." Research essay, Wellington: Victoria University Press, 1980.

Dyson, Linda. "The Return of the Repressed? Whiteness, Femininity and Colonialism in *The Piano*." *Screen* 36, no. 3 (Autumn 1995).

Edwards, Denis. "Get It in Writing." *Quote Unquote* (April 1996).

Edwards, Sam. "Cinematic Imperialism and Maori Cultural Identity." *Illusions* 10 (1989).

———. "Docudrama from the Twenties: Rudall Hayward, Whakatane, and *The Te Kooti Trail*." *Whakatane Historical Review* 41, no. 2 (1993).

Eggleton, David. "Grimm Fairytale of the South Seas: *The Piano*." *Illusions* 23 (1994).

The Encore Directory 1986. Chekeven, Manly, NSW, 1986– (annual).

Film Weekly Motion Picture Directory. Film Weekly Pty. Ltd., Sydney, 1936/37–1969/70(?) (annual).

Fraser, Bryce, ed. *The Macquarie Book of Events*. Sydney, NSW: Macquarie University, 1983.

Frow, John, and Meaghan Morris, eds. *Australian Cultural Studies: A Reader.* Sydney: Allen & Unwin, 1993.

Fyfe, Judith. *War Stories Our Mothers Never Told Us*, Auckland: Penguin Books, 1995.

Gerstner, David, and Sarah Greenlees. "Cinema by Fits and Starts: New Zealand Film Practices in the Twentieth Century." *Cineaction* 51 (2000).

Gillett, Sue. "Lips and Fingers: Jane Campion's *The Piano*." *Screen* 36, no. 3 (Autumn 1995).

Goldson, Annie. "Getting the Picture." *Women's Studies Journal* 11, no. 1–2 (August 1995).

———. "Piano Recital." *Screen* 38, no. 3 (Autumn 1997).

Grant, Barry K. *A Cultural Assault: The New Zealand Films of Peter Jackson.* Nottingham [England]: Kakapo Books in association with Nottingham Trent University, Centre for Asia-Pacific Studies, 1999.

Guttenbeil, 'Ofa-Ki-Levuka Louise. "Knock, Knock: Is Anybody Out There?—NZ Film: Is There Interest in Pacific Island Stories?" Thesis (MA), University of Auckland, 1999.

Halliwell, William K. *The Filmgoer's Guide to Australian Films*. Sydney: Angus & Robertson, 1985.

Hardy, Ann. "Heavenly Creatures and Transcendental Style." *Illusions* 26 (1997).

———. "The Last Patriarch: *The Piano*." *Illusions* 23 (1994).

———. "Tales of Ordinary Goodness." *Illusions* 12 (1989).

———. "Worldwars in Suburbia: A Reconsideration of *Ruby and Rata*." *Illusions* 20 (1992).

Harrison, Tony. *The Australian Film and Television Companion*. East Roseville, NSW: Simon & Schuster Australia, 1994.

Harwood, Elizabeth H. "A Brick in a Stocking: Abject Desires in *Heavenly Creatures*." Thesis (MA), University of Auckland, 1995.

Hayward, B.W., and S.P. Hayward. *Cinemas of Auckland: 1896–1979*. Auckland: Auckland Lodestar Press, 1979.

Henry, Ella. "Mana Waka." *OnFilm* 7, no. 2 (1990).

Herrick, Linda. "The Kiwi Kid in Hollywood." *Sunday Star-Times*, 21 January 1996.

Hight, Craig, and Jane Roscoe. "Forgotten Silver: An Exercise in Deconstructing Documentaries." *Metro* 112 (1997).

Hillyer, Minette. "We Calmly and Adventurously Go Travelling: New Zealand Film, 1925–1935." Thesis (MA English), University of Auckland, 1997.

Horrocks, Roger. *Composing Motion: Len Lye and Experimental Filmmaking*. Wellington: National Art Gallery, 1991.

———. *Len Lye: A Biography*. Auckland: Auckland University Press, 2001.

———. "New Zealand Cinema: Cultures, Policies, Films." 129–37 in *Twin Peeks: Australian and New Zealand Feature Films*, edited by Deb Verhoeven. Melbourne: Damned Publishing, 1999.

———. "New Zealand Documentary: Aims and Styles." *Alternative Cinema* (December 1976–January 1977).

———. "New Zealand Film History." *Alternative Cinema* (October 1977).

———. *New Zealand Film Makers at the Auckland City Art Gallery*. Auckland: Auckland City Art Gallery, 1985.

———. "*Patu!*: Interview with Merata Mita." *Alternative Cinema* (Winter/Spring 1983).

Horrocks, Roger, and W. Curnow eds. *Composing Motion: Len Lye and Experimental Film-Making*. Auckland: Auckland University Press, 1984.

Horrocks, Roger, and Karl Mutch. "Political Films in New Zealand: From 'Liberal' to 'Radical'." *Alternative Cinema* (Autumn/Winter 1982).

Horrocks, Roger, and P. Tremewan. *On Film 11*. Auckland: Heinemann, 1989.

Ingham, G. *Everyone's Gone to the Movies: The Sixty Cinemas of Auckland . . . And Some Others*. Auckland: Cyclostyle, 1973.

I Love Australian Movies—the Best: Australian Films 1984/85. Sydney: Australian Film Commission, 1984.

"Interview with Geoff Steven (on Gung Ho: Rewi Alley of China and The Humble Force)." *Alternative Cinema* (December 1980).

James-Bailey, Julie. *Index to the Transcripts of Public Hearings to the Tariff Board on the Motion Picture Industry and Television Programs 1973 (monograph no. 3)*. Australian Film and Television School, North Ryde, NSW: n.d.

Jeffery, Tom, ed. *Film Business: A Handbook for Producers*. Sydney: Australian Film Television and Radio School, and Allen & Unwin, 1989.

Jesson, Bruce. "*Patu!*: A Review." *Alternative Cinema* (Winter/Spring 1983).

Jones, Stan. "'Ecstasies in the Mossy Land': New Zealand Film in Germany." 151–70 in *Twin Peeks: Australian and New Zealand Feature Films*, edited by Deb Verhoeven. Melbourne: Damned Publishing, 1999.

Joseph, M.K. "Documentary Film in New Zealand." In *Arts Year Book 6*, edited by Eric Lee-Johnson. Wellington: Wingfield Press, 1950.

King, Michael. *New Zealanders at War*. Auckland: Heinemann Reed, 1981.

———. "Tangata Whenua: Origins and Conclusions." *Landfall* 121 (March 1977).

Knewstubb Theatres. CINEMAS: Dunedin and districts, Dunedin: 1974.

Lang, Rachel. "Making History (Niuklia Fri Pasifik)." *OnFilm* 6, no. 2 (1989).

Lascelles, David. *Eighty Turbulent Years: The Paramount Theatre Wellington 1917–1997*, Wellington: Millwood Press, 1997.

Lennox, B. *Film and Fiction: Studies of New Zealand Fiction and Film Adaptations*. Auckland: Longman Paul, 1985.

Lightman, H.A. "The New Zealand National Film Unit." *American Cinematographer* LX (March 1979).

Long, Martin. "Whose Voice Is It Anyway?—Six Films About Trade Unions." *Sites* 16 (Autumn 1988).

Lovell, Patricia. "Australian Film, the Fragile Industry." Melbourne: Australian Institute of International Affairs, 33rd Roy Milner Memorial Lecture, 1983.

Maclean, Alison, et al. "Irene 59." (Interview with Shereen Maloney), *Alternative Cinema* (Summer 1983–1984).

Maloney, Shereen. "Doc." *Alternative Cinema* (Autumn/Winter 1984).

Marno, Larissa. "Stubborn Passions: An Interrogation of the Gender Imbalance in the New Zealand Film Industry." Thesis (MA), University of Auckland, 1997.

Martin, Helen. "Bread and Roses." *Illusions* 23 (1994).

———. "In Spring One Plants Alone: A Matter of Seeing It." *Alternative Cinema* (Spring/Summer 1984–1985).

Martin, Helen, and Sam Edwards. *New Zealand Film 1912–1996*. Auckland: Oxford University Press, 1997.

Maunder, Paul. "Time of Transition (*The Widows and the Generals*, *Street Rights*, *No Spy Waihopai*, *Standing Together*, *Kanaky au Pouvoir*)." *Illusions* 9 (1988).

McClinchy, Aimee. "Kiwis Share in Production Bonanza Down Under." *The National Business Review*, 30 April 1999.

McDonald, Lawrence. "Alice in Yonderland: Snakeskin's Uneasy Ride Down the Two-Land Blacktop." *Illusions* 34 (Winter 2002).

———. "Critique of the Judgement of *Bad Taste*, or Beyond *Braindead* Criticism." *Illusions* 21/22 (1993).

———. "Film as a Battleground: The Construction of Social Space, Gender Conflict and Other Issues in *Once Were Warriors*." *Illusions* 24 (1995).

———. "Guardians of an Absent Meaning: Gaylene Preston's War Stories." *Illusions* 25 (1996).

———. "A Road to Erewhon: A Consideration of Cinema of Unease." *Illusions* 25 (1996).

McDonnell, Brian. *Fresh Approaches to Film*. Auckland: Longman, 1998.

———. "Images of Aotearoa: Rural and Urban Settings in NZ Films." *Alternative Cinema* (Spring/Summer 1984–1985): 5–7.

———. "Postwar Hollywood Representations of New Zealand." *Film Criticism* 25, no. 3 (Spring 2001): 6–21.

———. "The Translation of New Zealand Fiction into Film." Thesis (PhD), University of Auckland, 1986.

McFarlane, Brian, ed. *Literature/Film Quarterly*: *The Australian Cinema* 21, no. 2 (1993), published as a book by Salisbury State University.

——. *New Australian Cinema: Sources and Parallels in American and British Cinema*. Melbourne: Cambridge University Press, 1992.

McFarlane, Brian, Geoff Mayer, and Ina Bertrand, eds. *The Oxford Companion to Australian Film*. South Melbourne: Oxford University Press, 1999.

McGill, David. *Full Circle: The History of the St. James Theatre*. Wellington: Phantom House, 1998.

Meares, B. "New Zealand." *Sight and Sound* LIV, no. 4 (Autumn 1985).

Mikalsen, Ron. "Nine Years: Themes and Ideas." *OnFilm* 3, no. 3 (1986).

Ministry of Culture and Heritage (NZ). *Cultural Policy in New Zealand, 1998*.

——. "Review of Government Screen Funding Arrangements." Discussion Paper, 2004.

Mirams, G. *Speaking Candidly*. Hamilton: Paul's Book Arcade, 1945.

Moran, Albert. Film Education and Training: Performance and Policy. Brisbane: Griffith University, 1992.

——. *Film Policy: An Australian Reader*. Brisbane: Institute for Cultural Policy Studies, Griffith University, 1994.

Moran, Albert, and Tom O'Regan, eds. *An Australian Film Reader*. Sydney: Currency Press, 1989.

——, eds. *The Australian Screen*. Melbourne: Penguin, 1989.

Morris, Meaghan, and John Frow, eds. *Australian Cultural Studies: A Reader*. St. Leonards, N.S.W.: Allen and Unwin, 1993.

Mune, Ian. *Big Brother, Little Sister*. Wellington [N.Z.]: Dept. of Education, 1977.

Murphy, Kathleen. "Totems and Taboos: Civilization and Its Discontents According to Lee Tamahori." *Film Comment* (September–October 1997).

Murray, Scott, ed. *Australian Cinema*. Sydney: Allen & Unwin, 1994.

——, ed. *Australian Film 1978–1994: A Survey of Theatrical Features*. 2nd ed. Melbourne, Vic.: Oxford University Press with Cinema Papers and the Australian Film Commission, 1995.

——. *Back of Beyond: Discovering Australian Film and Television*. Sydney: The Australian Film Commission, 1988.

——. *The New Australian Cinema*. Melbourne: Thomas Nelson Australia with Cinema Papers, 1980.

——. "A Short History of New Zealand Film: 1977–1994." *Cinema Papers* 97, no. 8, (January 1994): New Zealand Supplement.

Murray, Scott, and Robert Le Tet. "*Beyond Reasonable Doubt*: John Barnett: Producer." *Cinema Papers* (New Zealand Supplement) 27 (May–June 1980): 38.

Mustafa, Aysen, ed. *Bitumen, Dirt Tracks and Lost Highways: Australian Road Movies—A Select Bibliography and Filmography*. South Melbourne, Vic.: Australian Film Institute, 2002.

National Centre for Australian Studies. "The Big Picture: Documentary Film-Making in Australia." Clayton, Vic.: National Centre for Australian Studies, Monash University, 1993.

National Research Bureau. Office of Film and Literature Classification New Zealand. "Public and Professional Views Concerning the Classification and Rating of Films and Videos: Qualitative Research Report." Auckland: 2000.

Neill, Sam. "Cinema of Unease: A Personal Journey." Documentary film in the series *Celebrating the Moving Image,* edited by Sam Neill and Judy Rymer, 1995.

Newman, David B. "The Image of New Zealand as Portrayed in the Films of the Government Publicity Office 1922–1930." A Research Paper. Wellington: Victoria University Press, 1984.

New Zealand Film Archive. *He Pito Whakaatu a Nga Iwi Maori: Films of the Tangata Whenua.* (Catalogue, 1987).

———. *Maori & Pacific Films from New Zealand/Des Films Maoris & Pacifiques de la Nouvelle-Zealande, 1901–1984.* (Catalogue, 1984).

New Zealand Film Commission. "Focus on Expansion: New Zealand Film and Television Conference 1992." Wellington: Onfilm, 1992.

———. *1987–1988, 48 Feature Films, New Zealand.* Wellington: New Zealand Film Commission, 1987.

New Zealand Institute of Economic Research. "Creative Industries in New Zealand: Economic Contribution." *Industry New Zealand,* 2002.

New Zealand Trade and Enterprise. "Taking on the World, the Report of the Screen Production Industry Taskforce, 2003."

Norgrove, Aaron. "But Is It Music? The Crisis of Identity in *The Piano.*" *Race & Class* 40, no. 1 (1998).

O'Brien, Bernadette. *An Annotated Bibliography of the Australian Film Industry: 1980–1982.* Melbourne: Australian Film Institute, 1985.

O'Connor, Mary Ellen. "Film and Myth: A Study of the Feature Films of Rudall Hayward, 1922–1940." Research essay, University of Auckland, 1979.

O'Regan, Tom, *Australian National Cinema.* London: Routledge, 1996.

O'Shea, John. *Documentary and National Identity.* Auckland: Centre for Film, Television and Media Studies, University of Auckland, 1997.

———. *Don't Let It Get You: Memories-Documents.* Wellington: Victoria University Press, 2001.

———. "Ethnographic Films Made on the Maori Minority in New Zealand (a Report to UNESCO, 1966)." In *Don't Let It Get You,* 2001.

Palmer, S. *A Who's Who of Australian and New Zealand Film Actors: The Sound Era.* Metuchen, New Jersey: Scarecrow Press, 1988.

Parker, Dean. "Scoundrel Times at the Film Unit." *Illusions* 7 (1988).

Peeters, Theo. *Peter Weir and His Films: A Critical Bibliography.* Melbourne: Australian Film Institute Research and Information, 1983.

Performing Arts Yearbook of Australia 1977–1981, Showcast Publications, Mosman, NSW, annual.

Perkins, Reid. "Imagining Our Past Part 1: Colonial New Zealand on Film from *The Birth of New Zealand* to *The Piano*." *Illusions* 25 (1996).

———. "Imagining our Past Part 2: Colonial New Zealand on Film from *The Birth of New Zealand* to *The Piano*." *Illusions* 22 (1997).

Pike, Andrew, and Ross Cooper. *Australian Film 1900–1977: A Guide to Feature Film Production.* Melbourne: Oxford University Press in association with the Australian Film Institute, 1980.

———. *Reference Guide to Australian Films 1906–1969.* Canberra: National Film Archive, National Library of Australia, 1981.

Pinflicks Communications and New Zealand Institute of Economic Research. "The New Zealand Screen Production Industry: Capability Study." Industry New Zealand, 2003.

Porter, Hal. *Stars of Australian Stage and Screen.* Adelaide: Rigby, 1965.

Pradhan, Tara. "The Politics of Identity: Shereen Maloney, Feminist Film Maker." Thesis (MA), University of Auckland, 1991.

Price, S. *New Zealand's First Talkies: Early Film-Making in Otago and Southland 1896–1939.* Dunedin: Otago Heritage Books, 1996.

Puttnam, David. "Film Industry Will Need Helping Hand." *New Zealand Herald*, 27 November 1996.

Queensland Production Directory 1994. Brisbane: Film Queensland, c1994.

Quinby, Rohan G.H. "Parallel Worlds: New Zealand and Film Incentives." *Scoop Media* (July 2003)

Rattigan, Neil. *Images of Australia: 100 Films of the New Australian Cinema.* Dallas: Southern Methodist University Press, 1991.

Rayner, Jonathan. *Cinema Journeys of the Man Alone: The New Zealand and American Films of Geoff Murphy.* Nottingham, England: Kakapo Books in association with Nottingham Trent University, Centre of Asia-Pacific Studies, 1999.

———. *Contemporary Australian Cinema: An Introduction.* Manchester: Manchester University Press, 2000.

Read, Lynette. "Rain Woman—Christine Jeffs." *Illusions 33* (Autumn 2002).

———. "*Rain* and the Tradition of Art Cinema in New Zealand." *Illusions 34* (Winter 2002).

Reid, John Howard, ed. *Some Aspects of Film Production in New Zealand.* Wellington: Queen Elizabeth II Arts Council, 1972.

———. *Sons of Cinemascope.* Wyong, NSW: Reid's Film Index Publishing, 1999.

Reid, Nicholas. *A Decade of New Zealand Film:* Sleeping Dogs *to* Came a Hot Friday. Dunedin: John McIndoe, 1986.

Reis, Brian. *Australian Film: A Bibliography.* London: Mansell Publishing, 1997.

Reynolds, S., ed. *Australian Film 1978–1994.* Melbourne: Oxford University Press, 1995.

Ridley, Suzanne, comp. "Archives Index: Index to a Guide to Material on Film, Broadcasting and Television Held in the Australian Archives (monograph no. 12)." Australian Film and Television School, North Ryde, NSW, 1979.

Roberts, Hugh. "Standing Upright Here." *New Zealand Books* 5, no. 4 (October 1995).

Robinson, Rebecca. "Authenticity, Mimicry, Industry: *The Frighteners* as Cultural Palimpsest." *Illusions* 28 (1999).

Roddick, Nick, ed. *Cinema Papers Yearbook.* Shepperton, UK: B. L. Kay Publishing Co., 1986.

———. "Long White Cloud over New Zealand Film in the Eighties." *Cinema Papers* 53 (September 1985).

Rorke, J. "A.H. Whitehouse: An Early Film Pioneer." *Whakatane Historical Review* 32, no. 1 (1984).

Roscoe, Jane, and Craig Hight. "Silver Magic: Generic Transformation and Forgotten Silver." *Illusions* 25 (1996).

Samu, Lina-Jodie Vaine. "Framed in Reference: Tangata Whenua Represented in Documentary Film From 1971 to 1983." Thesis (MA), University of Auckland, 1995.

Sanderson, Martyn. "Some Notes Struck by *Patu!*" *Alternative Cinema* (Winter/Spring 1983).

Sayer-Jones. *Law Brief: The Australian Film and Television Industry in the Nineties, a Film Lawyer's Guide for Non-Lawyers.* Sydney: Trade News Corporation, 1992.

Sayle, Jane. "The Gendered Sublime in *Memory and Desire.*" *Illusions* 28 (1999).

Schmidt, Johanna. "Mother, Monster or Mate: The Representation of Women in the Films of Four New Zealand Directors." Thesis (MA), University of Auckland, 1997.

Selwyn, Gabrielle. "Evoking Memory, Truth and Testimony in the New Documentary." Thesis (MA), University of Auckland, 2002.

Seton, Jo. "We're Taking This Car to Invercargill or The Male Must Get Through." *Alternative Cinema* (Summer 1983–1984).

Shadbolt, Tim. *Utu: The Story of the Film.* Auckland: Huia, 1982.

Shelton, Lindsay. "The Film Culture." *Cinema Papers Special Issue* (May–June 1980).

Sheppard, Deborah. *Reframing Women: A History of New Zealand Film.* Auckland: HarperCollins, 2001.

——. "Reframing Women: a History of Women and Film in New Zealand." Thesis (PhD), University of Auckland, 1999.

——. "Writing a Woman Filmmaker's Life and Work: a Bio-filmography of Gaylene Preston." Thesis (MA), University of Auckland, 1992.

Sherran, Garry. "Cinema Industry Brings Home Bacon." *Sunday Star-Times*, 21 January 1996.

Shirley, Graham, and Brian Adams. *Australian Cinema: The First 80 Years.* Sydney: Angus and Robertson and Currency Press, 1983.

Sigley, Simon. *User Friendly: The Cinema of New Zealand: A Short Survey.* Nancy, France: Maitrise Cinema et Audio-Visuel, 1990.

Simmons, Laurence. "Casting Aside Old Nets: John O'Shea's First Fight Against Racism." *Illusions* 33 (Autumn 2002).

——. "Distance Looks Our Way: Imagining New Zealand on Film." 39–49 in *Twin Peeks: Australia and New Zealand Feature Films*, edited by Deb Verhoeven. Melbourne: Damned Publishing, 1999.

——. "Language and Magical Realism in Broken English." *Illusions* 26 (1997).

——. "A Little Clunky and Manic . . ." *Midwest* 10 (1996).

Sklar, Robert. "Social Realism with Style: An Interview with Lee Tamahori." *Cineaste* 21, no. 3 (1995).

Sluka, Jeff. "Punitive Damage." *Illusions* 29 (1999).

Smith, Jane. "Knocked About in New Zealand: Postcolonialism Goes to the Movies." In *Mythologies of Violence in Postmodern Media,* edited by Christopher Sharrett. Detroit: Wayne State University Press, 1999.

Sowry, Clive. *Film Making in New Zealand: A Brief Historical Survey.* Wellington: New Zealand Film Archive, 1984.

Stevens, R.J. *Public Policy and the New Zealand Feature Film Industry: An Economic Appraisal.* Wellington: New Zealand Film Commission, 1984.

Stewart, John, *An Encyclopaedia of Australian Film*, Sydney: Reed Books, 1984.

Tapp, Peter, and James Sabine, eds. *Australian Feature Films* [CD-ROM]. Melbourne: Informit, Royal Melbourne Institute of Technology and The Australian Catalogue of New Films & Videos Ltd., 1995.

Te Manu Aute. "Te Manu Aute." *OnFilm* 4, no. 1 (1986).

Treole, Victoria, ed. *Australian Independent Film.* Sydney: Australian Film Commission, 1982.

Turner, Stephen. "Cinema of Justice: The Feathers of Peace." *Illusions* 33 (Autumn 2002).

Verhoeven, Deb, ed. *Twin Peeks: Australian and New Zealand Feature Films.* Melbourne: Damned Publishing, 1999.

Wakefield, Philip. "Strangely Normal (Opera in the Outback)." *OnFilm* 6, no. 3 (1989).

Ward, Russell. *The Australian Legend*. 2nd ed. Sydney: Oxford University Press, 1966.

Ward, Vincent, Alison Carter, Geoff Chapple, and Louis Nowra. *Edge of the Earth: Stories and Images from the Antipodes*. Auckland: Heinemann Reed, 1990.

Watson, Chris. "Sex, Angst and Deviance: Adolescent Film—A Genre—and New Zealand." *Illusions* 13 (1990): 12–18.

Watson, Chris, and Roy Shuker. *In the Public Good? Censorship in New Zealand*. Palmerston North: Dunmore Press, 1998.

Webb-Pullman, Julie. "People to People: The Widows and the Generals and Kanaky au Pouvoir." *Illusions* 6 (1987).

Wells, Peter. "Documentary Cinema in the Making." *Art New Zealand* 32 (1984).

Williams, Bridget Books and the Department of Internal Affairs. *The Dictionary of New Zealand Biography, Volume Two 1870–1900*. Wellington, 1993.

Willis, H. "New Zealand Report." *Cinema Papers* 14 (October 1977).

Zubrycki, Tom. *Archival Resources for the Filmmaker*. Sydney: Australian Film and Television School, 1982.

Zwartz, Sally. "Getting an Idea off the Ground: *Flight of Fancy*." *OnFilm* 4, no. 2 (1987).

———. "Making of The Mighty Civic." *OnFilm* 5, no. 6 (1988): 29.

HISTORY

General

Aquilia, Pieter. "Wog Drama and White Multiculturalists: The Role of Non Anglo-Australian Film and Television Drama in Shaping a National Identity." *Journal of Australian Studies* (March 2001).

The Australian Image: A Journey through Australia's Image and Sound Heritage. 3 vols. [VHS videorecording]. Hosted by Bill Hunter. Canberra: Australian Capital Television and The National Film and Sound Archive, 1989.

Baxter, John. *The Australian Cinema*. Sydney: Angus & Robertson, 1970.

Bilbrough, Milo. "A Taste of Kiwi: Moving Images from Aotearoa." *Illusions* 20 (1992).

Brand, Simon. *The Australian Film Book: 1930–Today*. Sydney: Dreamweaver Books, 1985.

———. *Australia's Film Industry* (Australian Knowledge, no. 10). Sydney: Australian Knowledge, 1987.

Churchman, Geoffrey B., ed. *Celluloid Dreams: A Century of Film in New Zealand*. Wellington: IPL Books, 1997.

Collins, Diane. *Hollywood Down Under: Australians at the Movies, 1896 to the Present Day.* North Ryde, NSW: Angus & Robertson, 1987.

Day, P. *The Radio Years: A History of Broadcasting in New Zealand.* Auckland: Auckland University Press, 1994.

Dennis, Jonathan, and Jan Bieringa, eds. *Film in Aotearoa New Zealand.* 2nd ed. Wellington: Victoria University Press, 1996.

Dennis, Jonathan, and Clive Sowry. *The Tin Shed: The Origins of the National Film Unit.* Wellington: New Zealand Film Archive, 1981.

Gerstner, David, and Sarah Greenlees. "Cinema by Fits and Starts: New Zealand Film Practices in the Twentieth Century." *Cineaction* 51 (2000).

Gibson, Ross. "On the Back of Beyond—An Interview with Tom O'Regan, Brian Shoesmith and Albert Moran." *Continuum: The Australian Journal of Media and Culture* 1, no. 1 (1987): 3.

——. *South of the West.* Bloomington: Indiana University Press, 1992.

Goldsmith, Ben. "The Comfort Lies in All the Things You Can Do: The Australian Drive-in—Cinema of Distraction." *Journal of Popular Culture* 33, no. 1 (1999): 153–64.

Hall, Sandra. *Australian Film Index: A Guide to Australian Feature Film since 1900.* Melbourne: Thorpe, 1992.

——. *Critical Business: The New Australian Cinema in Review.* Adelaide: Rigby Publishers, 1985.

Hayward, B.W., and S.P. Hayward. *Cinemas of Auckland: 1896–1979.* Auckland: Auckland Lodestar Press, 1979.

Herd, Nick. *Independent Filmmaking in Australia 1960–1980.* Sydney: Australian Film and Television School, 1983.

Hindle, John. *Complete Guide to Australian Films* (Little Australian Library), 4 vols. Melbourne: Dynamo Press, 1984.

Hodsdon, Barrett. *Straight Roads and Crossed Lines: The Quest for Film Culture in Australia from the 1960s.* Shenton Park, WA: Burnt Porridge Group, 2001.

Horrocks, Roger. "N.Z. Film History." *Alternative Cinema* (October 1977).

Lawson, Sylvia. "Good Taste at Hanging Rock: Some Notes on the Death, Rebirth and Stillbirth of Australian Feature Film-Making." 201–12 in *Conflict and Control in the Cinema: A Reader in Film and Society*, edited by John Tulloch. Melbourne: Macmillan, 1977.

Martin, Adrian. "No Flowers for the Cinephile: The Fates of Cultural Populism 1960–1988." 117–38 in *Island in the Stream*, edited by Paul Foss. Sydney: Pluto Press, 1988.

Martin, Helen, and Sam Edwards. *New Zealand Film 1912–1996.* Auckland: Oxford University Press, 1997.

McClinchy, Aimee. "Kiwis Share in Production Bonanza Down Under." *The National Business Review*, 30 April 1999.

McDonnell, Brian. "Postwar Hollywood Representations of New Zealand." *Film Criticism* 25, no. 3 (Spring 2001): 6–21.

McDonald, Lawrence. "A Road to Erewhon: A Consideration of *Cinema of Unease*." *Illusions* 25 (1996).

Meares, B. "New Zealand." *Sight and Sound* LIV, no. 4 (Autumn 1985).

Mikalsen, Ron. "Nine Years: Themes and Ideas." *OnFilm* 3, no. 3 (1986).

Miller, George. *White Fellas Dreaming: A Century of Australian Cinema*. [Documentary film] edited by George Miller, 1996.

Moran, Albert. *Projecting Australia: Government Film since 1945*. Sydney: Currency Press, 1991.

Moran, Albert, and Tom O'Regan, eds. *An Australian Film Reader* (Australian Screen Series). Sydney: Currency Press, 1985.

New Zealand Film Archive. *He Pito Whakaatu a Nga Iwi Maori: Films of the Tangata Whenua*. (Catalogue, 1987).

————. *Maori & Pacific Films from New Zealand/Des Films Maoris & Pacifiques de la Nouvelle-Zélande, 1901–1984*.

O'Regan, Tom, and Brian Shoesmith, eds. *The Moving Image: Film and Television in Western Australia 1896–1985*. History and Film Association of Western Australia, 1985.

Paterson, Barbara. *Renegades: Australia's First Film School*. Melbourne: Helicon Press, 1996.

Perkins, Reid. "Imagining Our Past Part 1: Colonial New Zealand on Film from *The Birth of New Zealand* to *The Piano*." *Illusions* 25 (1996).

————. "Imagining Our Past Part 2: Colonial New Zealand on Film from *The Birth of New Zealand* to *The Piano*." *Illusions* 22 (1997).

Reade, Eric. *The Australian Screen: A Pictorial History of Australian Film Making*. Melbourne: Lansdowne Press, 1975.

————. *History and Heartburn: The Saga of Australian Film 1896–1978*. Sydney: Harper & Row, 1979.

Simmons, Laurence. "Distance Looks Our Way: Imagining New Zealand on Film." 39–49 in *Twin Peeks: Australia and New Zealand Feature Films*, edited by Deb Verhoeven. Melbourne: Damned Publishing, 1999.

Sowry, Clive. *Film Making in New Zealand: A Brief Historical Survey*. Wellington: New Zealand Film Archive, 1984.

Sunshine and Shadows: 70 Years of Australian Cinema. Produced and directed by Brian Adams; scripted by David Stratton. (Motion picture: 16mm; sd; col; 93 min.) Sydney: Australian Broadcasting Commission, 1976.

Sydney Film Festival. *40 Years of Film: An Oral History of the Sydney Film Festival*. Sydney: Sydney Film Festival, 1992.

Thoms, Albie. *Surfmovies: The History of the Surf Film in Australia*. Sydney: Shorething Publishing, 2000.

Tulloch, John, and the Australian Film Institute. *Legends on the Screen: The Australian Narrative Cinema 1919–1929*. Sydney: Currency Press and Carlton South: Australian Film Institute, 1981.
Willis, H. "New Zealand Report." *Cinema Papers* 14 (October 1977).

Pre–1970

The Australian Image: A Journey through Australia's Image and Sound Heritage. 3 vols. [VHS videorecording]. Hosted by Bill Hunter. Canberra: Australian Capital Television and The National Film and Sound Archive, 1989.
Barr, Charles. *Ealing Studios*. London: Cameron and Tayleur, 1977.
Berryman, Ken, ed. *Screening the Past: Aspects of Early Australian Film*. Canberra: National Film and Sound Archive, 1995.
Collins, Diane. "Cinema and Society in Australia, 1920–1939." Thesis (PhD), University of Sydney, 1975.
———. "The Movie Octopus." 102–20 in *Australian Popular Culture*, edited by Peter Spearritt and David Walker. Sydney: Allen & Unwin, 1987.
Cooper, Ross Francis. "And the Villain Still Pursued Her: Origins of Film in Australia; 1896–1913." Thesis (MA), Australian National University, 1971.
———. "A History of the Australian Film Industry 1896–1930." Thesis (BA Hons), Monash University, 1965.
Day, P. *The Radio Years: A History of Broadcasting in New Zealand*. Auckland: Auckland University Dennis, Jonathan, ed. *Aotearoa and the Sentimental Strine: Making Films in Australia and New Zealand in the Silent Period.* Wellington: Moa Films, 1993.
Dennis, Jonathan, ed. *Aotearoa and the Sentimental Strine: Making Films in Australia and New Zealand in the Silent Period.* Wellington: Moa Films, 1993.
———, ed. *Moving Images from Aotearoa/New Zealand*. Sydney: Museum of Contemporary Art, 1992.
———, ed. *Te Maori Film Season. He Pito Whakaatu a Nga Iwi Maori: Films of the Tangata Whenua*. Auckland: New Zealand Film Archive, 1987.
———, ed. *The Tin Shed: The Origins of the National Film Unit*. Wellington: The New Zealand Film Archive, 1981.
Dennis, Jonathan, and Sergio Toffetti, eds. *Te Ao Marama: Il Mondo Della Luce*. Torino: Le Nuove Muse, 1989.
Dermody, Susan. "Rugged Individualists or Neocolonial Boys?: The Early Sound Period in Australian Film, 1931/2." (Media Papers, no. 12), Faculty of Humanities and Social Sciences, NSW Institute of Technology, Broadway, NSW, 1981.
———. "Two Remakes: Ideologies of Film Production I) 1919–32." 33–59 in *Nellie Melba, Ginger Meggs and Friends: Essays in Australian Cultural His-*

tory, edited by Susan Dermody, John Docker, and Di-Lisilla Modjeska. Malmsbury, Vic.: Kibble Books, 1982.

Dunne, Linda. "The 1930s as a Distinct Period in the History of Film-Making in New Zealand." Research essay. Wellington: Victoria University Press, 1980.

Edwards, S.R. "Docudrama from the Twenties: Rudall Hayward, Whakatane, and *The Te Kooti Trail*." *Whakatane Historical Review* 41, no. 2 (1993).

Edmondson, R., and Andrew Pike. *Australia's Lost Films: The Loss and Rescue of Australia's Silent Cinema*. Canberra: National Library of Australia, 1982.

Forgotten Cinema. Produced and directed by Anthony Buckley. (Motion picture: 16mm; sd; b&-rw; 59 min.) Ajax Films, Sydney, 1967.

Harris, James. "New Zealand Newsreels." *Sight and Sound* 13, no. 50 (July 1944): 38–39.

Headon, David. "Significant Silents: Sporting Australian on Film, 1896–1930." *Journal of Popular Culture* 33, no. 1 (1999): 115.

Hillyer, Minette. "We Calmly and Adventurously Go Travelling: New Zealand Film, 1925–35." Thesis (MA), University of Auckland, 1997.

Long, Joan, and Martin Long. *The Pictures That Moved: A Picture History of the Australian Cinema 1896–1929*. Richmond, Vic.: Hutchinson, 1982.

McDonnell, Brian. "Postwar Hollywood Representations of New Zealand." *Film Criticism* 25, no. 3 (Spring 2001).

Mirams, G. *Speaking Candidly*. Hamilton: Paul's Book Arcade, 1945.

Newman, David B. "The Image of New Zealand as Portrayed in the Films of the Government Publicity Office 1922–1930." Research paper. Wellington: Victoria University Press, 1984.

Newsfront. Directed and scripted by Phil Noyce. (Motion picture: 35mm; sd; col; 110 min.) Palm Beach Pictures Pty. Ltd., Sydney, 1978.

Now You're Talking. Produced by Anthony Buckley, directed and scripted by Keith Gow. (Motion picture: 16mm; sd; b&w; 47 min.) Sydney: Film Australia, 1979.

O'Connor, Mary Ellen. "Film and Myth: A Study of the Feature Films of Rudall Hayward, 1922–1940." Research essay, University of Auckland, 1979.

O'Regan, Tom, ed. "Australian Film in the 1950s." *Continuum* 1, no. 1 (1987).

Paech, Paul. "Cinema in Adelaide to 1945." Thesis (BA Hons), University of Adelaide, 1975.

The Passionate Industry. Produced by Frank Bagnall, directed and scripted by Joan Long. (Motion picture: 16mm; b&-rw; sd; 59 min.) Sydney: Australian Commonwealth Film Unit, 1973.

Perry, George. *Forever Ealing: A Celebration of the Great British Film Studio*. London: Pavilion Books, 1981.

The Pictures That Moved. Produced by Frank Bagnall and directed by Alan Anderson. (Motion picture: 16mm; sd; b&w; 46 min.) Sydney: Australian Commonwealth Film Unit, 1968.

Price, S. *New Zealand's First Talkies: Early Film-Making in Otago and Southland 1896–1939.* Dunedin: Otago Heritage Books, 1996.

Reade, Eric. *Australian Silent Films: A Pictorial History of Silent Films from 1896 to 1929.* Melbourne: Lansdowne Press, 1970.

———. *The Talkies Era: A Pictorial History of Australian Sound Film Making 1930–1960.* Melbourne: Lansdowne Press, 1972.

Reid, Russel. "New Zealand's Film Production." *Films in Review* 2 (October 1951): 36–37.

Shirley, Graham, and Brian Adams. *Australian Cinema: The First Eighty Years.* Angus & Robertson and Currency Press, Sydney, 1983.

Sydney Film Festival, 22nd. *Salute to Australian Film: Australian Feature Film Retrospective 1911–1971.* Sydney: Film Festival, 1975.

Tulloch, John. *Australian Cinema: Industry, Narrative and Meaning* (Studies in Society, 1). Sydney: Allen & Unwin, 1982.

———. *Legends on the Screen: The Australian Narrative Cinema 1919–1929* (Australian Screen series). Sydney: Currency Press and Australian Film Institute, 1981.

Union Theatres Ltd. *Ten Years' Progress in the Motion Picture Industry of Australia.* Sydney: Union Theatres Ltd., 1921.

Walker, Dylan. *Adelaide's Silent Nights: A Pictorial History of Adelaide's Picture Theatres During the Silent Era.* National Film and Sound Archive, undated.

———. "The Rise of a Popular Culture: Adelaide Cinema, 1896–1913." In *From Colonel Light into the Footlights: The Performing Arts in South Australia from 1836 to the Present,* edited by Andrew D. McCredie. Adelaide: Page 1 Books, 1988.

Wasson, Mervyn. *The Beginnings of Film in Australia.* Melbourne: Australian Film Institute, 1964.

Post–1970

Abbey, Ruth, and Jo Crawford. "Crocodile Dundee or Davy Crockett: What *Crocodile Dundee* Doesn't Say about Australia." M*eanjin* 46, no. 2 (June 1987): 145–152.

The Australian Image: A Journey through Australia's Image and Sound Heritage. 3 vols. [VHS videorecording]. Hosted by Bill Hunter. Canberra: Australian Capital Television and The National Film and Sound Archive, 1989.

Bachmann, Gideon. "Films in Australia." *Sight and Sound* 46, no. 1 (1976–1977): 32–36.

Berryman, Ken. *The Australian Film Industry and Key Films of the 1970s: An Annotated Bibliography*. Melbourne: Australian Film Institute, 1980.

Bilbrough, Milo. "A Taste of Kiwi: Moving Images from Aotearoa." *Illusions* 20 (1992).

Bromby, Robin. "In the Picture: Australia." *Sight and Sound* 48, no. 4 (1979): 230–31.

———. "Test for Australia." *Sight and Sound* 48, no. 2 (1979): 85–98.

Campbell, Russell. "Feature Film-Making in New Zealand—It All Seems Reasonably Obvious." *Working Culture* (May 1999).

Canova, Gianni and Fabio Malagnini. *Australia 'New-wave'*. Milan: Gammalibri, 1984.

Clancy, Jack. "Film: The Renaissance of the Seventies." 168–79 in *Intruders in the Bush: The Australian Quest for Identity*, edited by John Carroll. Melbourne: Oxford University Press, 1982.

———. "The Search for Form in Australian Cinema." *Island Magazine*, no. 22 (Autumn 1985): 21–25.

Clarke McKenna, N. *Angel in God's Office: My Wartime Diaries*. Birkenhead, N.Z.: Tandem Press, 1996.

Conrich, Ian. *Views from the Edge of the World: New Zealand Film*. London: Kakapo Books, 1997.

Craven, Ian, ed. *Australian Cinema in the 1990s*. Ilford, Essex: Frank Cass, 2000.

Dermody, Susan, and Elizabeth Jacka, eds. *The Imaginary Industry: Australian Film in the Late '80s*. Sydney: Australian Film Television and Radio School Publications, 1988.

———. *The Screening of Australia, Volume 1: Anatomy of a Film Industry*. Sydney: Currency Press, 1987.

———. *The Screening of Australia, Volume 2: Anatomy of a National Cinema*. Sydney: Currency Press, 1988.

Groves, Don, and Michaela Boland. "Oz Studio Space to Grow 70% by 2004." *Variety*, 6–12 May 2002.

Hall, Sandra. "The Themes of the Emerging New Look Australian Cinema." *Bulletin*, 3 September 1985: 118–120.

Hutton, A. B. "Nationalism in Australian Feature Film of the 1970s." Preliminary Thesis (MA), University of Melbourne, 1979.

Jaivin, Linda. "Australia Hits Big Time with a Croc of Gold." *Far Eastern Economic Review* 138, no. 51 (17 December 1987): 54–55.

Mathews, Sue. *35mm Dreams: Conversations with Five Directors about the Australian Film Revival*. Ringwood, Vic.: Penguin, 1984.

McFarlane, Brian. *Australian Cinema 1970–1985*. London: Secker & Warburg, 1987.

McFarlane, Brian, and Geoff Mayer. *New Australian Cinema: Sources and Parallels in American and British Film*. Cambridge: Cambridge University Press, 1992.

Murray, Scott, ed. *The New Australian Cinema*. Melbourne: Nelson, 1980.

O'Regan, Thomas Andrew. "The Enchantment with Cinema: Film in the 1980s." 118–145 in *The Australian Screen*, edited by Albert Moran and Tom O'Regan. Melbourne: Penguin, 1989.

———. "Knowing the Process but Not the Outcome: Australian Cinema Faces the Millennium." In *Culture in Australia*, edited by Tony Bennett and David Carter. Melbourne: Cambridge University Press, 2001.

———. "The Politics of Representation: An Analysis of the Australian Film Revival." Thesis (PhD), Griffith University, 1985.

Reid, Mary Anne. *Long Shots to Favourites: Australian Cinema Successes in the '90s*. North Sydney: Australian Film Commission, 1993.

———. *More Long Shots: Australian Cinema Successes in the '90s*. Sydney and Brisbane: Australian Film Commission and Australian Key Centre for Cultural and Media Policy, 1999.

Reid, Nicholas. *A Decade of New Zealand Film:* Sleeping Dogs *to* Came a Hot Friday. Dunedin: John McIndoe, 1986.

Roddick, N. "Long White Cloud Over New Zealand Film in the Eighties." *Cinema Papers* 53 (September 1985).

Rohdie, Sam. "The Film Industry." 138–55 in *Communications and the Media in Australia*, edited by Ted Wheelwright and Ken Buckley. Sydney: Allen & Unwin, 1987.

Stratton, David. *The Last New Wave: The Australian Film Revival*. Sydney: Angus & Robertson, 1980.

———. "Their Brilliant Careers: 'New Wave' Australian Film Makers." 88–91 in *Movies of the Seventies*, edited by Ann Lloyd. London: Orbis, 1984.

Walsh, Michael. "Building a New Wave: Australian Films and the American Market." *Film Criticism* 25, no. 2 (Winter 2000–2001): 21–39.

"What Has Gone Wrong in Australia?" *World Press Review (NY)* 33, no. 9 (September 1986): 59.

White, David. *Australian Movies to the World: The International Success of Australian Films since 1970*. Sydney: Collins, 1984.

BIOGRAPHY

Collected

Atterton, Margot. *The Illustrated Encyclopaedia of Australian Showbiz*. Brookvale, NSW: Sunshine Books, 1984.

Bridget, Williams Books, and the Department of Internal Affairs. *The Dictionary of New Zealand Biography, Volume Two 1870–1900*. Wellington, 1993.

Cairns, Barbara, and Helen Martin. *Shadows on the Wall: A Study of Seven New Zealand Feature Films*. Auckland: Longman Paul, 1994.

Dennis, Jonathan, and Jan Bieringa, eds. *Film in Aotearoa New Zealand*. 2nd ed. Wellington: Victoria University Press, 1996.

Department of Internal Affairs. *The Dictionary of New Zealand Biography. Volume 1*. Wellington: Allen & Unwin and the Department of Internal Affairs, 1990.

Dugan, Michael. *Film Stars (Famous Australians, 14)*. South Melbourne: Macmillan, 1981.

Horrocks, Roger. *New Zealand Film Makers at the Auckland City Art Gallery*. Auckland: Auckland City Art Gallery, 1985.

Murray, Scott, and Raffaele Caputo. "Dictionary of directors." 318–335 in *Australian Cinema*, edited by Scott Murray. St. Leonards, NSW: Allen & Unwin in association with Australian Film Commission, 1994.

Palmer, Scott. *A Who's Who of Australian and New Zealand Film Actors: The Sound Era*. Metuchen, NJ: Scarecrow Press, 1988.

Piton, Jean-Pierre, and Francis Schall. "De Brilliants Carriers." *La Revue du Cinema: Image et Son*, 387 (October 1983): 73–88.

Porter, Hal. *Stars of Australian Stage and Screen*. Adelaide: Rigby, 1965.

Reid, Nicholas. *A Decade of New Zealand Film: Sleeping Dogs to Came a Hot Friday*. Dunedin: John McIndoe, 1986.

Trengrove, Kim. *Out of Character: Conversations with Australian Actors*. Ringwood, Vic.: Penguin 1991.

White, David. *Australian Movies to the World: The International Success of Australian Films since 1970*. Melbourne: Fontana Australia & Cinema Papers, 1984.

Individual Cast and Crew

Alysen, Barbara. "David Badbury." *Cinema Papers*, no. 31 (March–April 1981).

"Armstrong, Gillian." *Current Biography* 56, no. 8 (1995): 3.

Baxter, John. "A Fistful of Koalas." *Cinema Papers*, no. 57 (May 1986): 26–29.

Bell, Richard A. "Cultural Exchange in Two Wendt Films: *Sons for the Return Home* and *Flying Fox in a Freedom Tree*. Thesis (MA), University of Auckland, 1997–1998.

Berryman, Ken. "Obituaries: Cecil Holmes 1921–1994." *Cinema Papers*, no. 102 (December 1994): 19–21.

Bilbrough, Milo. "Car Crash View: Alison Maclean's *Crush*." *Illusions* 20 (1992).

Brennan, Richard. "Peter Weir: Profile." *Cinema Papers*, no. 1 (1974): 16–17.
———. "Wendy Hughes." *Cinema Papers*, no. 40 (October 1982): 428–432.
Carlsson, Susanne Chauvel. *Charles and Elsa Chauvel: Movie Pioneers*. St. Lucia, Qld.: University of Queensland Press, 1989.
Chauvel, Elsa. *My Life with Charles Chauvel*. Sydney: Shakespeare Head Press, 1973.
"Chips Rafferty: Mrs Goffage's Son Depicts the Cornstalk Australian." *People* (Sydney) 3, no. 16, 8 October 1952: 24–27.
Clune, Frank. "The Debunking of Errol Flynn." *Bulletin*, 13 April 1938: 50.
Delamoir, Jeannette. "Louise Lovely: The Construction of a Star." Thesis (PhD), La Trobe University, 2002.
Downie, John. "A Milestone of Fabulous Digitalisation—Lord of the Rings." *Illusions* 34 (Winter 2002).
———. *The Navigator: A Mediaeval Odyssey*. Trowbridge, Wiltshire: Flick Books, 2000.
———. "Seeing Is Not Believing: Vincent Ward's *Map of the Human Heart*." *Illusions* 21/21 (1993).
Dundy, Elaine. *Finch, Bloody Finch: A Life of Peter Finch*. New York: Holt, Rinehart & Winston; London: Michael Joseph, 1980.
Faulkner, Trader. *Peter Finch: A Biography*. London: Angus & Robertson, 1979.
Finch, Peter. "How I Learned to Laugh at Myself." *Films and Filming* 4, no. 12 (September 1958): 7.
Gillett, Sue. "Lips and Fingers: Jane Campion's *The Piano*." *Screen* 36, no. 3 (Autumn 1995).
Goldson, Annie. "Piano Recital." *Screen* 38, no. 3 (Autumn 1997).
Grant, Barry K. *A Cultural Assault: The New Zealand Films of Peter Jackson*. Nottingham, England: Kakapo Books in association with Nottingham Trent University, Centre for Asia-Pacific Studies, 1999.
Hall, Ken G. *Australian Film: The Inside Story*. Sydney: Summit Books 1980.
———. *Directed by Ken G. Hall: Autobiography of an Australian Film-Maker*. Sydney: Lansdowne Press, 1977.
Hardy, Ann. "Worldwars in Suburbia: A Reconsideration of *Ruby and Rata*." *Illusions* 20 (1992).
———. "The Last Patriarch: *The Piano*." *Illusions* 23 (1994).
———. "*Heavenly Creatures* and Transcendental Style." *Illusions* 26 (1997).
Harris, Max. "Errol Flynn: An Australian Tragedy." *Bulletin*, 23 September 1980: 80–82, 84.
Heathwood, Gail. "Leo McKern Comes Home to Travel North." *Vogue Australia* 31 (March 1987): 206–207.
"He Came from Down Under." *TV Guide* (US) 9, no. 17, 20 April 1961: 17.

Holmes, Cecil. "Lee Robinson." *Sydney Cinema Journal* 3 (Winter 1967): 28–31.

——. *One Man's Way: On the Road with Rebel Reporter, Filmmaker and Adventurer*. Ringwood, Vic.: Penguin, 1986.

Horrocks, Roger. *Len Lye: A Biography*. Auckland: Auckland University Press, 2001.

James, Clive. *Unreliable Memoirs*. New York: Alfred A. Knopf, 1981.

Legg, Frank. *The Eyes of Damien Parer*. Adelaide: Rigby, 1963.

——. *Once More on My Adventure*. Sydney: Ure Smith, 1966.

Lovell, Patricia. *No Picnic: An Autobiography*. Sydney: Macmillan, 1995.

Macdonald, Marion. "Making of the Thompson Image." *Bulletin*, 19 July 1975: 74–75.

Martin, Helen. "Bread and Roses." *Illusions* 23 (1994).

McDonald, Lawrence. "Alice in Yonderland: Snakeskin's Uneasy Ride Down the Two-Land Blacktop." *Illusions* 34 (Winter 2002).

McDonald, Neil. *War Cameraman: The Story of Damien Parer*. Melbourne: Lothian Books, 1994.

Monkman, Noel. *Quest of the Curly-Tailed Horses: An Autobiography*. Sydney: Angus & Robertson, 1962.

Moran, Albert. "King of the Coral Sea: An Interview with Lee Robinson." *Continuum: An Australian Journal of the Media* 1, no. 1 (1987): 100–110.

Murray-Smith, Joanna. "Wayward Haywood." *Cinema Papers*, no. 63 (May 1987): 38–39.

Norgrove, Aaron. "But Is It Music? The Crisis of Identity in *The Piano*." *Race & Class* 40, no. 1 (1998).

Parsons, Fred. *A Man Called Mo*. Melbourne: Heinemann, 1973.

Read, Lynette. "*Rain* and the Tradition of Art Cinema in New Zealand." *Illusions* 34 (Winter 2002).

Rene, Roy. *Mo's Memoirs*. Melbourne: Reed & Harris, 1945.

Rensin, David. "Playboy Interview: Paul Hogan—Candid Conversation." *Playboy*, 35 (July 1988).

Riddell, Elizabeth. "John Hargreaves—Making His Mark." *Theatre Australia* 6, no. 3 (November 1981): 56–57.

Roberts, Margaret. "Ken Hall Reflects on Entertainment and Nationalism." *Australian Film Review* 1, no. 24 (19 January–1 February 1984).

Rorke, J. "A.H. Whitehouse: An Early Film Pioneer." *Whakatane Historical Review* 32, no. 1 (1984).

Sayle, Jane. "The Genered Sublime in Memory and Desire." *Illusions* 28 (1999).

"Sir Robert Helpmann Talks about the Filming of Don Quixote, about Rudolph Nureyev, about Dancing for a Film and about What's Ahead for Him." *Vogue Australia* 17 (February 1973): 60–63.

Sluka, Jeff. "Punitive Damage." *Illusions* 29 (1999).

Starkiewicz, Antoinette. "Two Animators: 1. Yoram Gross." *Cinema Papers*, no. 48 (October–November 1984): 334–338; 380–381.

Turner, Stephen. "Cinema of Justice: The Feathers of Peace." *Illusions* 33 (Autumn 2002).

Walkabout to Hollywood. [Video recording: sd; col; 50m]. Great Britain, British Broadcasting Corporation, 1980.

FILM THEORY AND CRITICISM

General

Australian Film Commission. *From Script to Screen Australian Style: Some Camera and Other Angles*. Sydney: Australian Film Commission, 1979.

Barclay, Barry. *Our Own Image*. Auckland: Longman Paul, 1990.

Bertrand, Ina. *Approaches to Australian Film: Historical Research and The Story of the Kelly Gang*. (Video recording: sd; col with b&w sequences; 30 min.) North Ryde, NSW: Australian Film and Television School, 1981.

Blythe, Martin. *Naming the Other: Images of the Maori in New Zealand Film and Television*. Metuchen, NJ: Scarecrow Press, 1994.

Bordwell, David. "The Art Cinema as a Mode of Film Practice." *Film Criticism* 4, no. 1 (1979): 56–64.

Bruzi, Stella. "Tempestuous Petticoats: Costume and Desire in *The Piano*." *Screen* 36, no. 3 (Autumn 1995).

Butterss, Phil. "Becoming a Man in Australian Film in the Early 1990s." 79–94 in *Australian Cinema in the 1990s*, edited by Ian Craven. Ilford, Essex: Frank Cass, 2000.

———. "From Ned Kelly to Queens in the Desert: Masculinity in Australian Film." 158–71 in *Social Justice: Politics, Technology and Culture for a Better World*, edited by Susan Magarey. Adelaide: Wakefield, 1998.

Campbell, Russell. "Feature Film-Making in New Zealand: It All Seems Reasonably Obvious." *Working Culture* (May 1999).

Carroll, John. "National Identity." 209–25 in *Intruders in the Bush*, edited by John Carroll. Melbourne: Oxford University Press, 1982.

Coyle, Rebecca, ed. *Screen Scores: Studies in Contemporary Australian Film Music*. Sydney: Australian Film, Television and Radio School, 1997.

Cunningham, Stuart. "Hollywood Genres: Australian Movies." In *An Australian Film Reader*, edited by Albert Moran and Tom O'Regan. Sydney: Currency Press, 1983.

Curnow, Wystan, and Roger Horrocks, eds. *Figures of Motion: Selected Writings*. Auckland: Auckland University Press, 1984.

Dennis, Jonathan, ed. *Moving Images from Aotearoa/New Zealand*. Sydney: Museum of Contemporary Art, 1992.

Dermody, Susan, and Elizabeth Jacka. "'Australian-ness' and the Film Industry: Between Rhetorics of Business and National Culture" (Media Papers no. 18), Faculty of Humanities and Social Sciences, Broadway, NSW: NSW Institute of Technology, 1983.

Faulk, Tina. "Images of Asia: Films Reflect Ambivalence Felt by Many." *Far Eastern Economic Review* 155, no. 47 (1992): 44.

Faulkner, Craig. "A Geography of the Screen: Landscape in Australian Narrative Cinema." Thesis (MA), Flinders University, 1984.

Hall, Sandra. *Critical Business: The New Australian Cinema in Review*. Adelaide: Rigby, 1985.

Hamilton, Peter, and Sue Mathews. *American Dreams: Australian Movies*. Sydney: Currency Press, 1986.

Haynes, Roslynn D. *Seeking the Centre: The Australian Desert in Literature, Art and Film*. Port Melbourne: Cambridge University Press, 1999.

Herrick, Linda. "The Kiwi Kid in Hollywood." *Sunday Star-Times*, 21 January 1996.

Hinde, John. *Other People's Pictures*. Sydney: Australian Broadcasting Commission, 1981.

Jones, Stan. "'Ecstasies in the Mossy Land': New Zealand Film in Germany." 151–70 in *Twin Peeks: Australian and New Zealand Feature Films*, edited by Deb Verhoeven. Melbourne: Damned Publishing, 1999.

Lewis, Glen. *Australian Movies and the American Dream* (Media and Society series). New York: Praeger, 1987.

Martin, Adrian, ed. "Film: Matter of Style." *Continuum: The Australian Journal of Media and Culture* 5, no. 2 (1992).

———. "The Offended Critic: Film Reviewing and Social Commentary." *Senses of Cinema 2002*, no. 8 (July–August 2000).

McDonnell, Brian. *Fresh Approaches to Film*. Auckland: Longman, 1998.

McKee, Alan. "Accentuate the 'Negative': Reality and Race in Australian Film Reviewing." *Australian Studies in Journalism 1999*, no. 8 (1999): 139.

Molloy, Bruce. "Before the Interval: An Analysis of Some Aspects of Australian Social Mythology in Selected Australian Feature Films, 1930–1960," 2 vols. Thesis (PhD), Griffith University, 1984.

———. *The Bush Myth*. (Video recording: sd; col; 89 min.) Australian Film and Television School Resources Unit, Sydney, 1982.

Myers, David. "Bleeding Battlers from Ironbark," Capricornia Institute, Rockhampton, Qld., 1987.

O'Regan, Tom. "Cinema Oz: The Ocker Films." 75–98 in *The Australian Screen*, edited by Albert Moran and Tom O'Regan. Ringwood: Penguin Books, 1989.

——. "Writing on Australian Film History: Some Methodological Comments." (Occasional Paper/Local Consumption, 5), Sydney: Local Consumption Publications, 1984.

Roberts, Hugh. "Standing Upright Here." *New Zealand Books* 5, no. 4 (October 1995).

Sharrett, Christopher, ed. *Crisis Cinema: The Apocalyptic Idea in Postmodern Narrative Film*. Washington: Maissonneuve Press, 1993.

Shelton, Lindsay. "The Film Culture." *Cinema Papers Special Issue* (May–June 1980).

Simmons, Laurence. "Distance Looks Our Way: Imagining New Zealand on Film." 39–49 in *Twin Peeks: Australia and New Zealand Feature Films*, edited by Deb Verhoeven. Melbourne: Damned Publishing, 1999.

——. "A Little Clunky and Manic . . ." *Midwest* 10 (1996).

Smith, Jane. "Knocked About in New Zealand: Postcolonialism Goes to the Movies." In *Mythologies of Violence in Postmodern Media*, edited by Christopher Sharrett. Detroit: Wayne State University Press, 1999.

Thoms, Albie. *Polemics for a New Cinema: Writings to Stimulate New Approaches to Film*. Sydney: Wild and Woolley, 1978.

Tulloch, John. *Australian Cinema: Industry, Narrative and Meaning*. Sydney: George Allen and Unwin, 1982.

——, ed. *The Australian Journal of Screen Theory*. Sydney: University of New South Wales, 1979.

Turner, Graeme. "Art Directing History: The Period Film." 99–117 in *The Australian Screen*, edited by Albert Moran and Tom O'Regan. Ringwood, Victoria: Penguin, 1989.

——. "The Genres Are American: Australian Narrative, Australian Film and the Problem of Genre." *Literature-Film Quarterly* 21, no. 2 (1993): 102.

——. *Making It National: Nationalism and Australian Popular Culture*. Sydney: Allen & Unwin, 1994.

——. *National Fictions: Literature, Film and the Construction of Australian Narrative*. 2nd ed. Sydney: Allen and Unwin, 1993.

——. "Whatever Happened to National Identity?" *Metro* 100 (Summer 1994): 32–35.

Ward, Vincent, Alison Carter, Geoff Chapple, and Louis Nowra. *Edge of the Earth: Stories and Images from the Antipodes*. Auckland: Heinemann Reed, 1990.

Studies of Particular Films

Adams, Phillip. "The Dangerous Pornography of Death." *Bulletin* 100, 1 May 1979: 38, 41.

ATOM. Strikebound: *A Study Guide.* Carlton South, Vic.: Australian Teachers of Media, 1984.

Barber, Susan. "*The Adventures of Priscilla, Queen of the Desert.*" *Film Quarterly* 50, no. 2 (1996–1997): 41–45.

Barbour, David H. "Heroism and Redemption in the *Mad Max* Trilogy." *Journal of Popular Film & Television* 273 (Fall 1999): 28–34.

Bertrand, Ina. Splendid Fellows *(1934) and Australian History, Written and Presented by Ina Bertrand.* (Video recording: sd; col; 46 min.) Australian Film and Television School, Sydney, 1983.

"A Better Class of Rambo." *Economist* 302, no. 7487, 28 February 1987: 42.

Blue Fin special issue. *Metro,* no. 45 (1978).

"The Breaker—a Man Who Didn't Get the Breaks." *Bulletin* 101, 2 December 1980: 140.

Broderick, Mick. "Heroic Apocalypse: *Mad Max,* Mythology and the Millennium." In *Crisis Cinema: The Apocalyptic Idea in Postmodern Narrative Film,* edited by Christopher Sharrett. Washington, DC: Maisonneuve Press, 1993.

Brown, Max. "Cecil Holmes' *Three in One.*" *Meanjin* (March 1957): 61–62.

Burt, Jillian. "Ghosts . . . of the Civil Dead." *Cinema Papers* 68 (March 1988): 8–11.

Butterss, Phil. "Representation, Power and Genre in *The Piano.*" 158–71 in *Ex-Tensions: Essays in English Studies from Shakespeare to the Spice Girls,* edited by Sue Hosking and Di Schwerdt. Adelaide: Wakefield, 1999.

———. "When Being a Man Is All You've Got: Masculinity in *Romper Stomper, Blackrock, Idiot Box* and *The Boys.*" *Metro* 117 (1998): 40–46.

Cairns, Barbara, and Helen Martin. *Shadows on the Wall: A Study of Seven New Zealand Feature Films.* Auckland: Longman Paul, 1994.

Calder, Peter. "Lord Leads Biz." *Variety* (19–25 October 1998).

Chauvel, Charles. *In the Wake of the Bounty.* Sydney: Endeavour Press, 1933.

Chauvel, Charles, et al. *Eve in Ebony: The Story of Jedda.* Sydney: Columbia Pictures, 1954.

Chute, David. "The Ayatollah of the Moviola." *Film Comment* 18, no. 4 (July–August 1982): 26–31.

Clark, Al, ed. *Making Priscilla.* Ringwood, Vic.: Penguin, 1994.

Cooper, Ross. "Filmography: Beaumont Smith." *Cinema Papers* 8 (March–April 1976): 333.

———. "The Mcdonagh Sisters." *Cinema Papers* 3 (July 1974): 260–61.

———. "W. Franklyn Barrett: Filmography." *Cinema Papers* 2 (April 1974): 164–65.

Cooper, Ross, and M. T. Wasson. "Raymond Longford: Filmography." *Cinema Papers* 1 (January 1974): 51.

The Crew: On the Set of Storm Boy. (Video recording: sd; col; 21 min.) North Ryde, NSW: Australian Film and Television School, 1979.

Crofts, Stephen. *The Case of* Shame: *Identification, Gender and Genre in Film.* Melbourne: Australian Film Institute, 1993.

———. "*The Coolangatta Gold*: Men and Boys on the Gold Coast." 112–121 in *Queensland Images in Film and Television*, edited by Jonathon Dawson and Bruce Molloy. St. Lucia, Qld.: University of Queensland Press, 1990.

———. "Identification, Gender and Genre in Film: The Case of Shame." *The Moving Image* 2 (1993): 5–60.

Dowling, David. "War and Peace: On the Beach with Bruce and Maurice." *Illusions* 20 (1992).

Dunn, Maxwell. *How They Made Sons of Matthew*. Sydney: Angus & Robertson, 1949.

Dyson, Linda. "The Return of the Repressed? Whiteness, Femininity and Colonialism in *The Piano*." *Screen* 36, no. 3 (Autumn 1995).

Elley, D. "*The Devil's Playground*." *Films and Filming* 24, no. 1 (October 1977): 33–34.

Else, Eric. *The Back of Beyond: A Compilation for Use in Studying John Heyer's Film of Inland Australia.* London: Longmans, 1968.

Fyfe, Judith. *War Stories Our Mothers Never Told Us.* Auckland: Penguin Books, 1995.

Gardner, Susan. "From Murderer to Martyr: The Legend of 'Breaker' Morant." 2–31 in Breaker Morant *(Critical Arts Monograph no. 1)*. Johannesburg: Critical Arts Study Group, 1981.

Gillett, Sue. "Lips and Fingers: Jane Campion's *The Piano*." *Screen* 36, no. 3 (Autumn 1995).

Goldson, Annie. "Piano Recital." *Screen* 38, no. 3 (Autumn 1997).

Hunter, Ian. "Corsetway to Heaven: Looking Back to Hanging Rock." *Arena*, no. 41 (1976): 9–11.

"Jesus Was an Outlaw." *Filmnews* (August 1976): 1.

Kael, Pauline. "The Current Cinema: Trials." *New Yorker* 64, 28 November 1988: 103–108.

Kingston, Claude. "The Term and I." 12–21 in *It Don't Seem a Day Too Much*. Adelaide: Rigby, 1971.

Long, Joan. "The Sentimental Bloke on Celluloid." 115–22 in *The World of the Sentimental Bloke*, edited by Barry Watts. Sydney: Angus & Robertson, 1976.

Lowenstein, Richard, and Peter Thompson. *Richard Lowenstein on the Making of* Strikebound. (Video recording: sd; col; 33 min.) North Ryde, NSW: Australian Film and Television School, 1985.

Loyd, Justine. "The Politics of Dislocation: Airport Tales—*The Castle*." In *Cinema and the City: Film and Urban Societies in a Global Context*, edited by Mark Shiel and Tony Fitzmaurice. Oxford: Blackwell Publishers, 2001.

The Making of Blue Fin: *Post Production.* Executive director, John McGowan. (Video recording: sd; col; 25 min.) North Ryde, NSW: Australian Film and Television School, 1978.

The Making of Sunday. Director, photography, script: Edwin Scragg. (Motion picture: 16mm; col; sd; 25 min.) Adelaide: Scope Films, 1975.

Margolis, Harriet, ed. *Jane Campion's* The Piano. Port Melbourne: Cambridge University Press, 2000.

McDonald, Lawrence. "Adaptations and Sequels: The Limitations of *What Becomes of the Broken-Hearted.*" *Film Criticism* 25, no. 3 (Spring 2001): 37–45.

———. "Critique of the Judgement of Bad Taste or Beyond *Braindead* Criticism." *Illusions* 21/22 (1993).

Merryweather, Louise, Ken Berryman, and Alan Mayberry (comps). *Peter Weir's Film of Gallipoli: Film Study Guide.* Melbourne: Applied Media Resources, Education Dept of Victoria, 1981.

Murray, Scott, and Robert Le Tet. "Beyond Reasonable Doubt: John Barnett: Producer." *Cinema Papers* 27 (May–June 1980), New Zealand Supplement: 38.

Mustafa, Aysen, ed. "AFI Screen Bibliographies. *The Back of Beyond.*" South Melbourne, Vic.: Australian Film Institute, 2002.

———. "AFI Screen Bibliographies. *Head On*: a Select Bibliography." South Melbourne, Vic.: Australian Film Institute, 2002.

———. "AFI Screen Bibliographies. *Jedda.*" South Melbourne, Vic.: Australian Film Institute, 2002.

———. "AFI Screen Bibliographies. *Walkabout.*" South Melbourne, Vic.: Australian Film Institute, 2002.

———. "AFI Screen Bibliographies. *Wrong Side of the Road.*" South Melbourne, Vic.: Australian Film Institute, 2002.

Newman, Kim. "*Death in Brunswick.*" *Sight & Sound* 1, no. 10 (February 1992).

Norgrove, Aaron. "But Is It Music? The Crisis of Identity in *The Piano.*" *Race & Class* 40, no. 1 (1998).

Parker, Dean. "Scoundrel Times at the Film Unit." *Illusions* 7 (1988).

Rayner, Jonathan. *Cinema Journeys of the Man Alone: The New Zealand and American Films of Geoff Murphy.* Nottingham, England: Kakapo Books in association with Nottingham Trent University, Centre of Asia-Pacific Studies, 1999.

Read, Lynette. "Rain Woman—Christine Jeffs." *Illusions* 33 (Autumn 2002).

Reid, Mary Anne. *Long Shots to Favourites: Australian Cinema Successes in the 90s.* North Sydney: Australian Film Commission, c1993.

Sanderson, Martyn. "Some Notes Struck by *Patu!*" *Alternative Cinema* (Winter/Spring 1983).

Shadbolt, Tim. Utu!: *The Story of the film.* Auckland: Huia, 1982.

Silberg, Jon. *"Shame."* *American Film* 13, no. 10 (1988).

Thompson, Christina. "John Duigan's Moral Tales." *Cinema Papers* no. 67 (January 1988): 17–19.

Tomaselli, K.G., S. Gardner, S. Gray, and M. Vaughan. *"Breaker Morant."* *Critical Arts Monograph* 1 (1981).

Townsend, Helen. *Phar Lap: A Pictorial History.* Adapted from the screenplay by David Williamson; photography by David Parker. Sydney: Lansdowne, 1983.

Ward, Vincent, Alison Carter, Geoff Chapple, and Louis Nowra. *Edge of the Earth: Stories and Images from the Antipodes.* Auckland: Heinemann Reed, 1990.

Studies of Particular Filmmakers

Allison, Edmund. *Australian Filmmaker Edmund Allison.* Interview. (Video recording: sd; col; 90 min.) North Ryde, NSW: Australian Film and Television School, 1985.

Amery, Kerryn L. "Lottie Lyell: 1890/1925." 70–89 in *Hidden Women: Locating Information on Significant Australian Women.* Melbourne: Melbourne College of Advanced Education, 1986.

———. "The McDonaghs: Isobel McDonagh, 1899–1979; Phyllis McDonagh, 1900–1978; Paulette McDonagh, 1900–1978." 90–100 in *Hidden Women: Locating Information on Significant Australian Women.* Melbourne: Melbourne College of Advanced Education, 1986.

Armstrong, Gillian, and Michael Carlton. *Australian Filmmaker: Gillian Armstrong.* Interview by Michael Carlton. (Video recording: sd; col; 23 min.) North Ryde, NSW: Australian Film and Television School, 1979.

Armstrong, Gillian, and Peter Thompson. *Filmmaker Interview: Gillian Armstrong.* Interview by Peter Thompson. (Video recording: sd; col; 43 min.) North Ryde, NSW: Australian Film and Television School, 1983.

Australian Film Institute. *AFI Screen Bibliographies: Tracey Moffatt.* South Melbourne: Australian Film Institute, 2001.

Benson, John. *An Annotated and Critical Bibliography on Australian Filmmaker Tim Burstall.* Melbourne: Australian Film Institute, 1983.

Bezjak, Anita. "The McDonagh Sisters 1899–1982:1900–1978; 1901–1978." 228–34 in *Footnote People in Australian History,* edited by Ann Atkinson. Broadway, NSW: The Fairfax Library in Association with Daniel O'Keefe Publishing, 1987.

Bickel, Lennard. *In Search of Frank Hurley.* Melbourne: Macmillan, 1980.

Boland, Michaela, and Michael Boddy. *Aussieworld: Australia's Leading Actors and Directors Tell How They Conquered Hollywood.* Sydney: Allen and Unwin, 2004.

Boyd, Russell, and Graham Shirley. *Cinematographer Russell Boyd.* Interviewed by Graham Shirley. (Video recording: sd; col; 35 min.) Australian Film and Television School, North Ryde, NSW, 1978.

Boyd, Russell, and Peter Thompson. *Feature Film Lighting: Russell Boyd.* Interviewed by Peter Thompson. (Video recording: sd; col; 56 min.) Australian Film and Television School, North Ryde, NSW, 1985.

Bruce Beresford: An Annotated Bibliography. Melbourne: Australian Film Institute Research and Information, 1985.

Buckley, Tony. *Tony Buckley.* (Video recording: sd; col; 20 min.) North Ryde, NSW: Australian Film and Television School, 1986.

Buckley, Tony, and Peter Thompson. *Australian Filmmaker: Tony Buckley* (second interview). Interview by Peter Thompson. (Video recording: sd; col; 30 min.) North Ryde, NSW: Australian Film and Television School, 1985.

Cantrill, Arthur. *Midstream: A Survey/Exhibition of the Filmwork by Arthur and Corinne Cantrill, 1963–79.* Parkville, Vic.: Ewing and George Paton Galleries, Melbourne University Union, 1979.

Cargill, R. "'Make It Australian': The Films of Charles Chauvel." Thesis (BA Hons), Monash University, 1976.

Charles Chauvel—The Action Director. (Motion picture: 16mm: sd; col with b&-rw; 112 min.) United Cinema, 1972.

Coleman, Peter. *Bruce Beresford: Instincts of the Heart.* Sydney: Angus & Robertson, 1992.

Collins, Felicity. *The Films of Gillian Armstrong.* St. Kilda, Vic.: Australian Teachers of Media, 1999.

Cowan, Tom. *Australian Filmmaker: Tom Cowan.* Interview. (Video recording: sd; col; 35 min.) North Ryde, NSW: Australian Film and Television School, 1979.

Cunningham, Stuart. *Featuring Australian: The Cinema of Charles Chauvel.* Sydney: Allen & Unwin, 1991.

Curtis, Keryn Michelle. "Australian Television and Film: A Case Study of Kennedy Miller." Thesis (BA Hons), Griffith University, 1985.

Deling, Bert, and Allan Hogan. *Australian Filmmaker: Bert Deling.* Interview by Allan Hogan. (Video recording: sd; col; 35 min.) North Ryde, NSW: Australian Film and Television School, 1978.

Front Line (Video recording sponsored by the Australian Film Commission, the Tasmanian Film Corporation and the Australian War Memorial: sd; col with b&-rw; 56 min.) Sydney: David Bradbury, 1979.

Gooley, Bill, and Graham Shirley. *Australian Filmmaker: Bill Gooley.* Interview by Graham Shirley. (Video recording: sd; col; 29 min.) North Ryde, NSW: Australian Film and Television School, 1984.

Grant, Barry K. *A Cultural Assault: The New Zealand Films of Peter Jackson.* Nottingham, England: Kakapo Books in association with Nottingham Trent University, Centre for Asia-Pacific Studies, 1999.

Hannam, Ken, and Allan Hogan. *Australian Filmmaker: Ken Hannam*. Interview by Allan Hogan. (Video recording: sd; col; 44 min.) North Ryde, NSW: Australian Film and Television School, 1978.

Herrick, Linda. "The Kiwi Kid in Hollywood." *Sunday Star-Times*, 21 January 1996.

Hetherington, John. "The Immortal Cameraman: Damien Parer." 162–8 in *Australians—Nine Profiles*. Melbourne: Cheshire, 1960.

Holmes, Cecil, and Allan Hogan. *Australian Filmmaker: Cecil Holmes*. Interview by Allan Hogan. (Video recording: sd; col; 30 min.) Sydney: Australian Film and Television School, 1978.

Jeffrey, Tom, and Allan Hogan. *Australian Filmmaker: Tom Jeffrey*. Interview by Allan Hogan. (Video recording: sd; col; 30 min.) Sydney: Australian Film and Television School, 1978.

Kathner, Rupe W. *Let's Make a Movie: A Story of Picture Production in Australia*. Sydney: Currawong Publishing Co., 1945?

Larkins, Bob. *Chips: The Life and Films of Chips Rafferty*. South Melbourne: Macmillan, 1986.

Lawson, Sylvia. "Cecil Holmes." *Sydney Cinema Journal* 3 (Winter 1967): 31–33.

Lowenstein, Richard, and Peter Thompson. *Australian Filmmaker: Richard Lowenstein*. Interview by Peter Thompson. (Video recording: sd; col; 33 min.) North Ryde, NSW: Australian Film and Television School, n.d.

Lyle, Valda, Tom Politis, and Ross Stell. *Stanley Hawes: Documentary Film-Maker (monograph no. 2)*. Sydney: WEA Film Study Group, 1980.

Murphy, Kathleen. "Totems and Taboos: Civilization and Its Discontents According to Lee Tamahori." *Film Comment* (Sept/Oct 1997).

Mustafa, Aysen, ed. "AFI Screen Bibliographies. Baz Luhrmann Bibliography." South Melbourne, Vic.: Australian Film Institute, 2002.

———. "AFI Screen Bibliographies. Catherine Martin." South Melbourne, Vic.: Australian Film Institute, 2002.

———. "AFI Screen Bibliographies. Cecil Holmes (1921–1994)." South Melbourne, Vic.: Australian Film Institute, 2002.

———. "AFI Screen Bibliographies. Charles "Bud" Tingwell." South Melbourne, Vic.: Australian Film Institute, 2002.

———. "AFI Screen Bibliographies. Damien Parer (1912–1944)." South Melbourne, Vic.: Australian Film Institute, 2002.

———. "AFI Screen Bibliographies. Francis Birtles (1881–1941)." South Melbourne, Vic.: Australian Film Institute, 2002.

———, ed. "AFI Screen Bibliographies. Frank Hurley (1885–1962)." South Melbourne, Vic.: Australian Film Institute, 2002.

Noyce, Phil, and Michael Carlton. *Australian Filmmaker: Phil Noyce*. Interview by Michael Carlton. (Video recording: sd; col; 45 min.) North Ryde, NSW: Australian Film and Television School, 1978.

Pate, Michael and Bryon Quigley. *Michael Pate*. Interview by Bryon Quigley. (Video recording: sd; col; 33 min.) North Ryde, NSW: Australian Film and Television School, 1981.

Peeters, Theo. *Peter Weir and His Films*. Melbourne: Australian Film Institute, 1983.

Pike, Andrew. "Ken G. Hall: Filmography." *Cinema Papers* 1, January 1974: 89–91.

Rayner, Jonathan. *Cinema Journeys of the Man Alone: The New Zealand and American Films of Geoff Murphy*. Nottingham, England: Kakapo Books in association with Nottingham Trent University, Centre of Asia-Pacific Studies, 1999.

Robinson, Lee, and Graham Shirley. *Australian Filmmaker: Lee Robinson*. Interview by Graham Shirley. (Video recording: sd; col; 90 min.) North Ryde, NSW: Australian Film and Television School, 1987.

Routt, Bill. *The Cinema of Charles Chauvel*. (Video recording: sd; col with b&w sequences; 64 min.) North Ryde, NSW: Australian Film and Television School, 1982.

Schepisi, Fred. *Australian Filmmaker: Fred Schepisi*. Interview. (Video recording: sd; col; 40 min.) North Ryde, NSW: Australian Film and Television School, 1984.

———. "Fred Schepisi." 136–71 in *The Stump Jumpers: A New Breed of Australians*, edited by Neil Lawrence and Steve Bunk. Sydney: Hale & Iremonger, 1985.

Sheppard, Deborah. "Writing a Woman Film-maker's Life and Work: A Biofilmography of Gaylene Preston." Thesis (MA), University of Auckland, 1992.

Simmons, Laurence. "Casting Aside Old Nets: John O'Shea's First Fight against Racism." *Illusions* 33 (Autumn 2002).

Sklar, Robert. "Social Realism with Style: An Interview with Lee Tamahori." *Cineaste* 21, no. 3 (1995).

Snow, Sand and Savages. (Motion picture: sd; b&w; 47 min.) Sydney: Anthony Buckley Productions, 1972.

Spark, C. "Reading *Radiance*: The Politics of a Good Story." *Australian Screen Education* no. 32 (Spring 2003): 100–104.

Tait, Viola. *A Family of Brothers: The Taits and J. C. Williamson; A Theatre History*. Melbourne: Heinemann, 1970.

Thoms, Albie, and Stephen Maclean. *Albie Thoms Talks with Stephen Maclean*. (Video recording: sd; col; 30 min.) North Ryde, NSW: Australian Film and Television School, 1979.

Thornhill, Michael, and Allan Hogan. *Australian Filmmaker: Michael Thornhill*. Interview by Allan Hogan. (Video recording: sd; col; 38 min.) North Ryde, NSW: Australian Film and Television School, 1978.

Weir, Peter, and Peter Thompson. *Peter Weir Interview*. Interview by Peter Thompson. (Video recording: sd; col; 45 min.) North Ryde, NSW: Australian Film and Television School, 1983.

Weis, Bob, and Karin Altmann. *Australian Filmmaker: Bob Weis*. Interview by Karin Altmann. (Video recording: sd; col; 34 min.) North Ryde, NSW: Australian Film and Television School, 1986.

INDUSTRY STRUCTURE, ECONOMICS, AND DISTRIBUTION

Adams, Phillip, and Antony Ginnane. *The Australian Film Industry: Homegrown or Foreign-Owned?* (Counterpointforum), Perth: Murdoch University Press, 1983.

Allen, John, ed, *Entertainment Arts in Australia* Sydney: Paul Hamlyn, 1968.

Andrews, E.S. "Movie-Making in the Public Service." *Journal of Public Administration* 9, no. 2 (March 1947).

Australian Film Commission. "Australian Film and Television Finance and Investment." North Sydney: Australian Film Commission, 1985.

Barnett, John. "Cutting It Fine." *OnFilm* 1, no. 4 (1984).

———. "The Size and Structure of the New Zealand Film Industry." *Cinema Papers Special Issue*. (May–June 1980).

Baxter, B. "New Zealand Cinema." *Films and Filming* 369 (June 1985).

Bowie, John. "Tax Laws: Any Incentive?" *OnFilm* 1, no. 2 (February 1984).

Broadley, C., and J. Jones. *Nambassa: A New Direction*. New Zealand: A.H. & A.W. Reed, 1979.

Bureau of Industry Economics. "Audiovisual Industries in Australia: A Discussion Paper." Canberra: Bureau of Industry Economics, 1994.

Calder, Peter. "Lord Leads Biz." *Variety*, 19–25 October 1998.

Campbell, Russell. "Feature Film-Making in New Zealand: It All Seems Reasonably Obvious." *Working Culture* (May 1999).

Campling, John T., and Grant Michelson. "A Strategic Choice-Resource Dependence Analysis of Union Mergers in the British and Australian Broadcasting and Film Industries." *Journal of Management Studies* 35, no. 5 (1998): 579ff.

Cinema Papers. "The New Zealand Film Commission." *Cinema Papers Special Issue* (May–June 1980).

Course Materials for the Seminar. Australian Film Investment, Sheraton Wentworth Hotel, Sydney, 21 April 1983, presented by the Australian Film Commission, Australian Society of Accountants, Institute of Chartered Accountants in Australia. North Sydney: Australian Film Commission, 1983.

De Chiera, Frank. *Foreign Language Film Exhibition and Distribution in Australia (Research and Survey Unit monograph no. 13)*. Sydney: Australian Film and Television School, 1980.

Entertainment Is Big Business: Let's Invest in It. Double Bay, NSW: Producers and Directors Guild of Australia, 1976.

Film Expo 80. Cinema Papers, Melbourne, 1981.

Financing Australian Films, the Wentworth Hotel, Melbourne, 2 December 1982, seminar presented by the Australian Film Commission, the institute of Chartered Accountants in Australia and the Australian Society of Accountants. Sydney: Australian Film Commission, 1982.

Flint, Michael. "International Film Financing: Transcript of a Seminar with Michael Flint." Sydney: Australian Film and Television School, 1979.

Gerstner, David, and Sarah Greenlees. "Cinema by Fits and Starts: New Zealand Film Practices in the Twentieth Century." *Cineaction* 51 (2000).

Ginnane, Antony. "Pictures for Profit." *OnFilm* 1, no. 5 (1984).

Gunter, Fiona. "Guild Guide." *OnFilm* 7, no. 2 (1990).

Harrison, P.A. "The Motion Picture Industry in N.Z. 1896–1930." Thesis (MA), Auckland University, 1974.

Hodsdon, John Barrett. "The Australian Film Industry: A Case Study." Thesis (MEcon), Macquarie University, 1974.

———. *Minor Exhibition and Distribution in Australia.* Sydney: Sydney Filmmakers Co-op, 1978.

———. *A Study of the Secondary Film Market. Report to the Film, Radio and Television Board of the Australia Council.* 1976.

How Should a Federal or State Government or Merchant Bank Assess the Viability of a Planned Feature Film Project. Balmain, NSW: Film and Television Production Association of Australia, 1978.

Investing in Australian Films: Course Materials for the Seminar, Parmelia Hilton Hotel, Mill St., Perth, 28 April 1983, presented by the Western Australian Film Council, the Australian Film Commission, and the Law Society of Western Australia. Subiaco, WA: Western Australian Film Council, 1983.

Jesson, Bruce. "Chainbusters to the Rescue?" *OnFilm* 3, no. 1 (1985).

———. "Commission with a New (Bank) Role." *OnFilm* 2, no. 5 (1985).

———. "Equity: Rules for Roles." *OnFilm* 1, no. 5 (1984).

———. "Home Market, Home Truths." *OnFilm* 2, no. 3 (1985).

———. "Money Talks." *OnFilm* 1, no. 4 (1984).

———. "A Nebulous Business." *OnFilm* (April–May 1984).

———. "Taking the Cake." *OnFilm* 2, no. 4 (1985).

Jones, Ross. "Film Exhibition and Distribution." 47–54 in *Australian Microeconomics: Policies and Industry Cases*, edited by Chris Terry. Sydney: Prentice-Hall, 1980.

———. "The Film Industry in Australia: The Effects of Oligopoly, Vertical Integration and Foreign Control." Thesis (BComm.), University of Newcastle, 1977.

Kearney, Brian. "An Appraisal of the Financing of the Modern Australian Feature Film Industry, the Role of the Australian Film Commission and the Development of Private Enterprise." Thesis (MGenStud), University of New South Wales, 1986.

Kedgley, Sue. "Dealing Out the Details." *OnFilm* (July 1986) [Special Issue].

Lang, Rachel. "Cash Flow Criteria." *OnFilm* 6, no. 6 (1989).

Martin, Peter. *Investment and Distribution Contracts: What Do They Do and How Do You Handle Them?* Sydney: Australian Film and Television School, 1980.

————. *A Miscellany of Cute Investment Structures: Non-Recourse Loans and Other Animals.* Sydney: Australian Film and Television School, 1980.

————. *Some Aspects of Film Production and Investment.* Sydney: Australian Film and Television School, 1980.

May, Sue. "Gascoigne: He Has Ways." *OnFilm* 2, no. 6 (1985).

————. "A Guilt-Edged Investment." *OnFilm* 2, no. 3 (1985).

Maynard, John. "Putting Your Gucci in Your Mouth." *OnFilm* 1, no. 6 (1984).

McCluskey, Margaret, et al. *Getting an A.F.C. Grant.* Bryon Quigley interviews Margaret McCluskey, Murray Brown and Vicki Molloy. (Video recording: sd; col; 41 min.) North Ryde, NSW: Australian Film and Television School, 1983.

Meares, Belinda. "Tracking Down the Treaties." *OnFilm* (July 1986).

*Ministry of Culture and Heritage. Review of Government Screen Funding Arrangements, Discussion Paper, 2004.

Molloy, Simon, and Barry Burgan. *The Economics of Film and Television in Australia.* Sydney: Australian Film Commission, 1993.

Murphy, Geoff. "Distributing a NZ Film in NZ." *Alternative Cinema* (Winter/Spring 1983).

Mustafa, Aysen, ed. *AFI Screen Bibliographies. Independent Exhibition and Distribution in Australia: Natalie Miller—A Case Study.* South Melbourne, Vic.: Australian Film Institute, 2002.

Newman, David. "The Independent New Zealand Motion Picture Industry: 1960–1986." Thesis (MA), Victoria University of Wellington, 1987.

New Zealand Film Commission. "Focus on expansion: New Zealand Film and Television Conference 1992." Wellington: *OnFilm*, 1992.

————. *1987–1988, 48 Feature Films, New Zealand.* Wellington: New Zealand Film Commission, 1987.

New Zealand Film Institute. "The 1982 Budget: Questions and Answers." *Alternative Cinema* (Spring 1982).

New Zealand Institute of Economic Research. *Creative Industries in New Zealand: Economic Contribution.* Industry New Zealand, 2002.

New Zealand Trade and Enterprise. *Taking on the World.* The Report of the Screen Production Industry Taskforce, 2003.

Nicolaidi, Mike. "Labour: Which Formula?" *OnFilm* 1, no. 5 (1984).

O'Shea, John. "Lessons in Survival." *OnFilm* 2, no. 3 (1985).

Pinflicks Communications and New Zealand Institute of Economic Research. *The New Zealand Screen Production Industry: Capability Study.* Industry New Zealand, 2003.

Reid, John, ed. "Shelton: A Delicate Balance." *OnFilm* (April–May 1984).

———. *Some Aspects of Film Production in New Zealand.* Wellington: Queen Elizabeth II Arts Council, 1972.

Roddick, N. "Long White Cloud over New Zealand Film in the Eighties." *Cinema Papers* 53 (September 1985).

Romig, Darrell Lynn. "Investment in Australian Films under Division 10BA." Thesis (MBA), University of Queensland, 1987.

Schou, Kirsten. *The Structure and Operation of the Film Industry in Australia.* North Ryde, NSW: Australian Film and Television School, 1982.

Schultz, Leo. "Reality Hits Mirage." *OnFilm* 5, no. 5 (1988).

Sherran, Garry. "Cinema Industry Brings Home Bacon." *Sunday Star-Times*, 21 January 1996.

Short, Erica. "Television and the NZ Film Industry." *Cinema Papers* (March–April 1981).

Sinclair, Penelope, et al. "Industry Access Scheme?" *OnFilm* 7, no. 3 (1990).

Smyth, Mervyn. "The Economics of the Australian Film Industry." Thesis (MEcon), University of New South Wales, 1976.

———. "The Economics of the Australian Film Industry" (Media Centre paper no. 13). Centre for the Study of Educational Communication and Media, School of Education, La Trobe University, 1980.

Stratton, David. *The Avocado Plantation: Boom and Bust in the Australian Film Industry.* Sydney: Macmillan, 1990.

Thompson, Kristin. *Exporting Entertainment: America in the World Film Market 1912–1934.* London: BFI, 1985.

Tossman, David. "Five Ways Forward." *OnFilm* 1, no.1 (December 1983): 5–7.

Towards a Western Australian Film and Television Industry: Seminar 22nd–24th June, 1984, Fremantle, WA: Film and Television Institute, 1984.

United States Department of Commerce, Bureau of Foreign and Domestic Commerce, Motion Picture Section, "Motion Pictures in Australia and New Zealand," compiled by Eugene Irving Way. (Trade Information Bulletin no. 608.) Washington: U.S. Government Printing Office, 1929.

Williams, Mark. "Bad Movies Always Make Them Cry." *New Outlook* (March–April 1985).

STUDIES OF NONGOVERNMENT FILM ORGANIZATIONS

Bertrand, Ina. "Australian Film Studies: Efftee Productions" (Media Centre Papers no. 7), Centre for the Study of Educational Communications and Media, La Trobe University, 1977.

Coopers, and Lybrand. "The Queensland Film, Television and Video Industry—the Facts: A Report on Research into the Training Needs of the Queensland Film, Television and Video Industry." North Quay, Qld.: Arts Training Queensland, 1992.

Curtis, Keryn Michelle. "Australian Television and Film: A Case Study of Kennedy Miller." Thesis (BA Honours), Griffith University, 1985,

Dawson, Jan. *A Report on Information Resources, Publications and Distribution and Exhibition Services.* Carlton, Vic.: Australian Film Institute, 1976.

Filmwork. Produced and directed by John Hughes. (Motion picture: 16mm; sd; col; 44 min.) Sydney: Waterside Workers Federation Film Unit, 1979.

O'Brien, Terry. *The Greater Union Story 1910–1985: 75 Years of Cinema in Australia.* Sydney: The Greater Union Organisation, 1985.

Pike, Andrew. "The History of an Australian Film Production Company: Cinesound 1932–1970." Thesis (MA), Australian National University, 1972.

"60th Anniversary Hoyts Corporation." *Variety* 324, no. 3 (August 1986): 60–90. (Special section).

Willis, Joy. "National Studios: The Last Colonial Dream." Thesis (BA Honours), Griffith University, 1985.

GOVERNMENT AND FILM

Cultural Policy, Industry Support, and Regulation

Australian Film Commission. *Australian Film and Television Finance and Investment Guide.* Sydney: Australian Film Commission, 1985.

———. *Film Assistance: Future Options.* Sydney: Allen & Unwin, 1986.

Bertrand, Ina, and Diane Collins. *Government and Film in Australia.* Sydney: Currency Press; Melbourne: Australian Film Institute, 1981.

Bishop, Rod, Dominic Case, Stela Axarlis, Johanna Plante, and Derek Allsop. "Innovation in the Australian Film Industry." Prime Minister's Science, Engineering and Innovation Council, 2000.

Cultural Activities Policy for the Creative Development Branch. North Sydney: Australian Film Commission, 1984.

Cultural Activities Review: Draft Papers, prepared with the assistance of consultant, Frank Maloney, North Sydney: Australian Film Commission, 1984.

Dusevic, Tom. "Nothing but True Blue Skies: Kiwis Are the Last Thing Australia's Film and Television Industry Should Fear." *Time International* 153, no. 15 (1999): 17.

Ferguson, Karen L. "State Intervention and the Contemporary Australian Film Industry." Thesis (BA Honours), Griffith University, 1984.

Harper-Nelson, John. *Government and the Arts (Critical Issues no. 9).* Perth: Australian Institute for Public Policy, 1987.

Horrocks, Roger. "New Zealand Cinema: Cultures, Policies, Films." 129–37 in *Twin Peeks: Australian and New Zealand Feature Films*, edited by Deb Verhoeven. Melbourne: Damned Publishing, 1999.

Jones, Ross. *Cut! Protection of Australia's Film and Television Industries.* Sydney, NSW: Centre for Independent Studies, 1991.

Macdonnel, Justin. *Government Policy and the Arts.* Sydney: Currency Press, 1992.

McClinchy, Aimee. "Kiwis Share in Production Bonanza Down Under." *The National Business Review*, 30 April 1999.

Ministry of Culture and Heritage. *Cultural Policy in New Zealand*, 1998.

Puttnam, David. "Film Industry Will Need Helping Hand." *New Zealand Herald*, 27 November 1996.

Rowse, Tim. *Arguing the Arts: The Funding of the Arts in Australia.* Ringwood, Vic.: Penguin Books, 1985,

Schou, Kirsten. *Policies for the Australian Film Industry: Part A, Rationale for Assistance and Direct Government Subsidy.* North Ryde, NSW: Australian Film and Television School, 1982.

Sherran, Garry. "Cinema Industry Brings Home Bacon." *Sunday Star-Times*, 21 January 1996.

Stevens, R.J. *Public Policy and the New Zealand Feature Film Industry: An Economic Appraisal.* Wellington: New Zealand Film Commission, 1984.

Stockbridge, S. "The State and the Moving Picture Industry, 1901–46." Thesis (BA Honours), University of New South Wales, 1979.

Wasson, L. "The Quota Question in the Film Industry in N.S.W. 1920–1940." Thesis (BA Honours), Australian National University, 1969.

Committee/Commission of Inquiry Reports

Australia, Senate. "Select Committee on the Encouragement of Australian Productions for Television, Report (and Minutes of Evidence)." *Parliamentary Papers 1962–63* vol. IV, pp. 69–948 (papers 304 and 304A). (The Vincent Report.)

Australia, Tariff Board. "Motion Picture Films and Television Programs, Tariff Revision Report." AGPS, Canberra, 1973. Also issued as Parliamentary Paper 181 of 1973.

Australian Council for the Arts, Film Committee. "Interim Report of the Film Committee to the Australian Council," 1969.

Australian Film Commission. "Interim Board, Report," 1973.

House of Representatives Standing Committee on Environment, Recreation and the Arts. "Report of the Moving Pictures Inquiry." Canberra: Australian Government Publishing Service, 1992.

"Inquiry into the Film Industry in New South Wales, Report." NSW Government Printer, Sydney, 1934. (*NSW Parliamentary Papers 1934–35*, vol. 3, pp. 905–75, 977–1007, 1009–94.)

John Giles Consulting. "Film Opportunities for the Gold Coast Albert Region." Brisbane: Gold Coast Albert Regional Development Committee and the Department of Business Industry and Regional Development, 1992.

Maddox, Garry. "Independent Film and Television Producers: Who's Making What and How They're Surviving." A Report for The Australian Film Commission, 1992.

Ministry of Culture and Heritage. Review of Government Screen Funding Arrangements, Discussion Paper, 2004.

National Film and Sound Archive (Australia), Advisory Committee. "Time in our Hands: Report of the National Film and Sound Archive Advisory Committee." Canberra, 1985.

Royal Commission on the Moving Picture Industry in Australia, (W. M. Marks, chairman), "Report," Government Printer, Canberra, 1928. *Parliamentary Papers 1926–28*, vol. IV, pp. 1371–409.)

Tariff Board. "Tariff Board Report: Motion Picture Films and Television Programs." Canberra: Australian Government Publishing Service, 1973.

Theatres and Public Halls Investigation Committee. "Report . . . together with Memorandum Submitted by the Combined Australian and British Film Industry." NSW Government Printer, 1938. (*New South Wales Parliamentary Papers 1938–40*, vol. 8, pp. 1495–1518.)

Studies of Government Film Organizations

Barnden, Richard Alan. "To Inform, Instruct and Enlighten: The State Film Centre (Victoria): 1945–1950." Thesis (MEd), La Trobe University, 1982.

Berryman, Ken. "Allowing Young Filmmakers to Spread Their Wings: The Educational Role of the Experimental Film and Television Fund." Thesis (MEd), La Trobe University, 1985.

Bourke, D. A. "The Department of Information and Censorship in Australia during World War II." Thesis (BA Honours), University of Newcastle, 1976.

Cox, Eva, and Laura Sharon. "'What Do I Wear for a Hurricane?' Women in Australian Film, Television, Video and Radio Industries: A Report." Woolloomooloo, NSW: Australian Film Commission, 1992.

"Film Finance Corporation: How It Works." *Filmnews* 18, no. 8 (September 1988): 14.

Film Finance Corporation Review Committee. "Review of Film Financing through the Australian Film Finance Corporation (FFC). Review of the Australian Film Commission's Special Production Fund." North Sydney: Film Finance Corporation, Australian Film Commission, 1992.

Jacka, Elizabeth. "The Government Film Organisations." 38–49 in *The Imaginary Industry: Australian Film in the Late '80s*, edited by Susan Dermody and Elizabeth Jacka. North Ryde, NSW: Australian Film, Television and Radio School, 1988.

Knopman, Catherine, ed. "Low Means Low: The Collective Papers from the Low Budget Feature Seminar." Sydney, NSW: Australian Film Commission, 1996.

New South Wales. "Independent Commission Against Corruption: Report on Investigation into the New South Wales Film Corporation and Pepper Distribution." March 1992. Sydney: The Commission: iv, 25

Peat, Marwick. "Mitchell Services, Towards a More Effective Commission: The AFC in the '80s." Sydney: Australian Film Commission, 1979.

Senate Standing Committee on the Environment, Recreation and the Arts. "Report on the Moving Pictures Inquiry." Canberra: Australian Government Publishing Service, 1992.

Shirley, Graham, and Judy Adamson. "Proposal for a History of Film Australia: Report to Tim Read by Graham Shirley and Judy Adamson on What Would be Involved in Writing a History of Film Australia." Typescript, 1980.

Te Manu Aute. "Te Manu Aute" *OnFilm* 4 no. 1 (1986).

Victoria. Parliament, Public Bodies Review Committee. "Report on Film Victoria." Melbourne: Government Printer, 1991. (Thirtieth Report to Parliament).

"Will the Film Finance Corporation Save the Industry?" *Filmnews* 18 no. 5 (June 1988): 3.

Willis, H. "New Zealand Report." *Cinema Papers* 14 (October 1977).

Zielinski, Andrew Michael. "The Establishment of the Australian National Film Board." Thesis (MA), Flinders University, 1978.

Censorship

Adams, Phillip. "The Faces on the Cutting Room Floor." *Bulletin* 100, 4 September 1979: 46.

Australia. Office of Film and Literature Classification. "What to See Before You See a Movie: Guidelines for the Classification of Films and Videotapes." Sydney: The Office, 1992: 7.

Australia. Parliament. Senate. Select Committee on Community Standards Relevant to the Supply of Services Utilising Electronic Technologies. "Report on Video and Computer Games and Classification Issues." Canberra: The Parliament of the Commonwealth of Australia, 1993: xv, 67, Chair M. Reynolds).

Bertrand, Ina. "Censorship and National Image: Melba and Evensong." 76–88 in *Nellie Melba, Ginger Meggs and Friends: Essays in Australian Cultural History*, edited by Susan Dermody, John Docker, and Drusilla Modjeska. Malmsbury, Vic.: Kibble Books, 1982.

———. *Film Censorship in Australia.* St. Lucia, Qld.: University of Queensland Press, 1978.

———. *Film Censorship in Australia.* North Ryde, NSW: Australian Film and Television School, 1981.

"Censorship in the 1990s: New Limits to Freedom?" Papers from a Seminar Hosted by the Free Speech Committee and the Communications and Media Law Association, August 1992. Sydney: Free Speech Committee, Communications and Media Law Association, 1992.

Christoffel, P. *Censored: A Short History of Censorship in New Zealand.* Wellington: Department of Internal Affairs, 1989.

Fricker, Maria, Linda Toshner, and Dimity Clarke. "Survey of the Attitudes of Cinema-Goers to Censorship." Melbourne: Australian Broadcasing Tribunal, Research Branch, 1983.

Melbourne Film Festival Censorship Symposium, Melbourne, 1969, Proceedings, Federation of Victorian Film Societies, Canterbury, Vic., 1969.

Mills, Jane. *The Money Shot: Cinema, Sin and Censorship.* Annandale, NSW: Pluto Press Australia, 2001.

National Research Bureau. Office of Film and Literature Classification New Zealand. "Public and Professional Views Concerning the Classification and Rating of Films and Videos: Qualitative Research Report." Auckland, 2000.

Phelps, G. *Film Censorship*. London: Victor Gallancz, 1975.

"The Sad End of James Bond." *Bulletin* 84, 16 June 1962: 3.

Small, Frank & Associates for OFLC and ABT. "Exploring Attitudes Towards Film, TV and Video Classifications: A Marketing Research Report." Sydney: Office of Film and Literature Classification, 1992.

Watson, Chris, and Roy Shuker. *In the Public Good? Censorship in New Zealand.* Palmerston North: Dunmore Press, 1998.

Westwood, John, and Paul Christoffel. "Public Attitudes to Film Censorship: An Analysis of Questionnaires Completed at Public Relations Screenings Run by the New Zealand Film Censor." Wellington: Dept. of Internal Affairs, 1992.

Williams, Eric. "Cultural Despotism—Film Censorship." 52–76 in *Australia's Censorship Crisis*, edited by Geoffrey Dutton and Max Harris. Melbourne: Sun Books, 1970.

Taxation

Australia. Senate, Standing Committee on Finance and Government Operations. "The Circumstances Surrounding the Various Court Actions Relating to the Film *The Return of Captain Invincible*." Canberra, 1987.

Australian Film Commission, Australia Council. "Tax Reform and the Arts." Sydney: Australian Film Commission, 1985.

Bowie, John. "The Taxation of the Feature Film Industry in New Zealand." Research paper (LL.M.), Victoria University of Wellington, 1984.

Court, David. "Life after 10BA." *Media Information Australia*, no. 43 (February 1987): 13–14.

Jacka, Elizabeth. "Financing Australian Films." 7–21 in *The Imaginary Industry: Australian Films in the Late '80s*, edited by Susan Dermody and Elizabeth Jacka. North Ryde, NSW: Australian Film, Television and Radio School, 1988.

Mannix, E. F. "Tax and the Australian Film Industry: Being a Commentary on Division 10BA of the Income Tax Assessment Act 1936 together with Text of the Legislation." Sydney: Butterworths, 1981.

Martin, Peter G. *Tax Incentives for the Australian Film Industry: Part One*. (Video recording: sd; col; 23 min.) North Ryde, NSW: Australian Film and Television School, 1981.

McDonald, Hamish. "*Mad Max* Could Be Last Refuge of Tax Dodgers." *Far Eastern Economic Review* 129, no. 36 (12 September 1985): 50–51.

Quinby, Rohan G.H. "Parallel Worlds: New Zealand and Film Incentives." *Scoop Media* (July 2003).

Saunders, Evelyn. "Government Assistance to the Performing Arts: A Case Study of Taxation Concessions to the Australian Film Industry." Thesis (BAdmin Honours), Griffith University, 1986.

"Tax Concessions for the Australian Film Industry." 63 in *Reform of the Australian Taxation System / Statement by the Treasurer The Hon. Paul Keating, MP*. Canberra: Australian Government Publishing Service, 1985.

"Tax Incentives and the Australian Film Industry Guide." Sydney: G & S Management Services, 1980.

DOCUMENTARY

Allender, Robert. "Disordered Cinema." *Landfall* V, no. 4 (December 1951).

———. "The National Film Unit." *Landfall* II, no. 4 (December 1948).

Alternative Cinema. "Interview with Geoff Steven (on Gung Ho: Rewi Alley of China and The Humble Force)." *Alternative Cinema* (December 1980).

Andrews, E.S. "Movie-Making in the Public Service." *Journal of Public Administration* 9, no. 2 (March 1947).

———. "Shadow Catching: Some Thoughts on Documentary Films in New Zealand." In *Year Book of the Arts in New Zealand 4*, edited by Howard Wadman. Wellington: Wingfield Press, 1948.

Australian National Documentary Conference. "The Big Picture: Documentary Film-Making in Australia." Papers from the 2nd Australian Documentary Conference, 29 November–2 December 1991. Clayton, Vic.: National Centre for Australian Studies, Monash University, 1993.

———. Collected Papers, 15–18 October, McLaren Vale, South Australia, 1987. Hendon, SA.

Auty, M. "*Patu!*" *Monthly Film Bulletin* 606 (July 1984).

Barden, Richard, and Ken Berryman. "A Symphony for Busy Clapperboards 1957–1975." 252–54 in *Cinema in Australia: A Documentary History*, edited by Ina Bertrand. Kensington, NSW: New South Wales University Press, 1989.

Benjamin, Julie. "Film Pioneers [Margaret Thomson & Kathleen O'Brien]." *OnFilm* 7, no. 4 (1990).

———. "Film Pioneer [Stanhope Andrews]." *OnFilm* 7, no. 3 (1990).

Bertrand, Ina, ed. *Cinema in Australia: A Documentary History*. Sydney: New South Wales University Press, 1989.

Beth, Stephanie. "Stephanie Beth." *Alternative Cinema* (Summer 1983–1984).

Bilbrough, Miro. "In Spring One Plants Alone: Telling the Story." *Illusions* 7 (1988).

Campbell, Russell. "The Discourse of Documentary: Narrational Strategies in *Bastion Point Day 507*, *Wildcat*, *The Bridge* and *Patu!*" *Illusions* 4 (1987).

———. "Plain Hard Hazardous Work: Cecil Holmes at the NFU." *Illusions* 7 (1988).

———. "The New Right and Documentrary Film in New Zealand: Someone Else's Country & Revolution." *Illusions* 29 (1999).

Chen Chui-Lee. "An Offshore Producer's Adventures in Maoriland." *Alternative Cinema* (Winter/Spring 1983).

Currie, Cathy. "Hidden Treasures: Documenting an Exhibition of Prisoners' Art." *Illusions* 13 (1990).

Davis, Catherine. "Tainui Stephens—Four Documentaries: The Challenge of Biculturalism." Thesis (MA English), University of Auckland, 1997.

Dawson, Jonathan. "After Grierson, Media Workshop." Griffith University, 1987.

Dennis, Jonathan, and Clive Sowry. *The Tin Shed: The Origins of the National Film Unit*. Wellington: New Zealand Film Archive, 1981.

"The Documentary Film." *Current Affairs Bulletin* 5, no. 2 (10 October 1949): 18–31.

Downey, P.J. "Documentary Film in New Zealand." *Landfall* IX, no. 4 (December 1955).

Edwards, S.R. "Docudrama from the Twenties: Rudall Hayward, Whakatane, and the *Te Kooti Trail*." *Whakatane Historical Review* 41, no. 2 (1993).

Henry, Ella. "Mana Waka." *OnFilm* 7, no. 2 (1990).

Hight, Craig, and Jane Roscoe. "Forgotten Silver: An Exercise in Deconstructing Documentaries." *Metro* 112, 1997.

Holmes, Cecil. "Unmade Australian Films (from Overland, April 1957)." 33–34 in *Cinema in Australia: A Documentary History*, edited by Ina Bertrand. Kensington, NSW: New South Wales University Press, 1989.

Horrocks, Roger. "New Zealand Documentary: Aims and Styles." *Alternative Cinema* (December 1976–January 1977).

———. "*Patu!*: Interview with Merata Mita." *Alternative Cinema* (Winter/Spring 1983).

Horrocks, Roger, and Karl Mutch. "Political Films in New Zealand: From 'Liberal' to 'Radical'." *Alternative Cinema* (Autumn/Winter 1982).

Jesson, Bruce. "*Patu!*: A Review." *Alternative Cinema* (Winter/Spring 1983).

Joseph, M.K. "Documentary Film in New Zealand." In *Arts Year Book 6* edited by Eric Lee-Johnson. Wellington: Wingfield Press, 1950.

King, Michael. "Tangata Whenua: Origins and Conclusions." *Landfall* 121 (March 1977).

Lang, Rachel. "Making History (Niuklia Fri Pasifik)." *OnFilm* 6, no. 2 (1989).

Lansell, Ross, and Peter Beilby, eds. *The Documentary Film in Australia.* North Melbourne: Cinema Papers in association with Film Victoria, 1982.

Lightman, H.A. "The New Zealand National Film Unit." *American Cinematographer* LX (March 1979).

Loizos, Peter. *Innovation in Ethnographic Film: From Innocence to Self-Consciousness 1955–1985.* Manchester: Manchester University Press, 1993.

Long, Martin. "Whose Voice Is It Anyway?—Six Films About Trade Unions." *Sites* 16 (Autumn 1988).

Maclean, Alison, et al. "Irene 59 (Interview with Shereen Maloney)." *Alternative Cinema* (Summer 1983–1984).

Maloney, Shereen. "Doc." *Alternative Cinema* (Autumn/Winter 1984).

Martin, Helen. "In Spring One Plants Alone: 'A Matter of Seeing It.'" *Alternative Cinema* (Spring/Summer 1984–1985).

Maunder, Paul. "Time of Transition (The Widows and the Generals, Street Rights, No Spy Waihopai, Standing Together, Kanaky au Pouvoir)." *Illusions* 9 (1988).

McDonald, Lawrence. "A Road to Erewhon: A Consideration of Cinema of Unease." *Illusions* 25 (1996).

McKinolty, Chips, and Duffy, Michael. "Guess Who's Coming to Dinner in Arnhem Land?" *Filmnews* 17, no. 10 (November 1987): 6 & 11.

Moran, Albert. "Nation Building. The Post War Documentary in Australia (1945–53)." *Continuum: An Australian Journal of the Media* 1, no. 1 (1987): 57–79.

Mustafa, Aysen. "AFI Screen Bibliographies. Documenting Australia." South Melbourne, Vic.: Australian Film Institute, 2002.

Noonan, Lisa, ed. "The Documentary Conference 1993: Reflecting the Future—Conference Papers." Lindfield, 1993.

O'Shea, John. "Documentary and National Identity." Auckland: Centre for Film, Television and Media Studies, University of Auckland, 1997.

———. Don't Let It Get You: *Memories-Documents*. Wellington: Victoria University Press, 2001.

———. "Ethnographic Films Made on the Maori Minority in New Zealand (a Report to UNESCO, 1966)." In *Don't Let It Get You*, 2001.

Parker, Dean. "Scoundrel Times at the Film Unit." *Illusions* 7 (1988).

Roscoe, Jane, and Craig Hight. "Silver Magic: Generic Transformation and Forgotten Silver." *Illusions* 25 (1996).

Samu, Lina-Jodie Vaine. "Framed in Reference: Tangata Whenua Represented in Documentary Film from 1971 to 1983." Thesis (MA English), University of Auckland, 1995.

Sanderson, Martyn. "Some Notes Struck by *Patu!*" *Alternative Cinema* (Winter/Spring 1983).

Selwyn, Gabrielle. "Evoking Memory, Truth and Testimony in the New Documentary." Thesis (MA), University of Auckland, 2002.

Sluka, Jeff. "Punitive Damage." *Illusions* 29 (1999).

Turner, Graeme. "Mixing Fact and Fiction." In *Back of Beyond: Discovering Australian Film and Television*, edited by Scott Murray. North Sydney: Australian Film Commission, 1988.

Turner, Stephen. "Cinema of Justice: The Feathers of Peace." *Illusions* 33 (Autumn 2002).

Wakefield, Philip. "Strangely Normal" (Opera in the Outback). *OnFilm* 6, no. 3 (1989).

Webb-Pullman, Julie. "People to People: The Widows and the Generals and Kanaky au Pouvoir." *Illusions* 6 (1987).

Wells, Peter. "Documentary Cinema in the Making." *Art New Zealand* 32 (1984).

Zwartz, Sally. "Getting an Idea Off the Ground: Flight of Fancy." *OnFilm* 4, no. 2 (1987).

———. "Making of The Mighty Civic." *OnFilm* 5, no. 6 (1988).

AVANT-GARDE AND EXPERIMENTAL FILM

Alternative Cinema. "Interview with Geoff Steven (on Gung Ho: Rewi Alley of China and The Humble Force)." *Alternative Cinema* (December 1980).

Australian Screen Studies Association Conference (1st), Melbourne, 1982. "Papers and Forums on Independent Film and Asian Cinema," edited by Barbara Creed, et al., Carlton South, Vic.: Australian Screen Studies Association (Victoria); North Ryde, NSW: Australian Film and Television School, 1983.

"Experimenta: A Major Survey of Film and Video Art: Melbourne, Nov. 20–Dec. 4, 1990." Melbourne, Modern Image Makers Association, 1990.

Herd, Nick. "Independent Filmmaking in Australia 1960–1980." North Ryde, NSW: Australian Film and Television School, 1983.

Horrocks, Roger. *Composing Motion: Len Lye and Experimental Filmmaking.* Wellington: National Art Gallery, 1991.

———. *New Zealand Film Makers at the Auckland City Art Gallery.* Auckland: Auckland City Art Gallery, 1985.

Horrocks, Roger, and W. Curnow, eds. *Composing Motion: Len Lye and Experimental Film-Making.* Auckland: Auckland University Press, 1984.

Martin, Adrian. "Exile." *Filmnews* 15, no. 7 (September 1985): 4 & 8.

Perry, Dave. *Australian Experimental Cinema.* (Video recording: sd; col; 37 min.) North Ryde, NSW: Australian Film and Television School, 1979.

Rohdie, Sam. "Avant-garde." 182–199 in *The New Australian Cinema*, edited by Scott Murray. Melbourne: Nelson, 1980.

Treole, Victoria, comp. and ed. *Australian Independent Film.* Sydney: Creative Development Branch of the Australian Film Commission, 1982.

Williams, Deane. "Mapping the Imaginary: Ross Gibson's *Camera Natura* with *Camera Natura* Shooting Script by Ross Gibson and John Cruthers." *The Moving Image* no. 4. Melbourne: Australian Teachers of Media, Australian Film Institute, Deakin University, 1996.

LITERATURE AND FILM

General Theory

"Cinema and Australian Literature." 157–158 in *The Oxford Companion to Australian Literature*, edited by William Wilde, Joy Hooten, and Barry Andrews. Melbourne: Oxford University Press, 1985.

Dowse, Sara. "The Impact of Film and Television on the Novel." *Island Magazine* no. 22 (Autumn 1985): 12–17.

Edwards, Denis. "Get It in Writing." *Quote Unquote* (April 1996).

Lennox, B. *Film and Fiction: Studies of New Zealand Fiction and Film Adaptations.* Auckland: Longman Paul, 1985.

Levy, Wayne. *The Book of the Film and the Film of the Book: A Bibliography of Australian Cinema and TV, 1895–1995.* Melbourne: Academia Press, 1995.

McFarlane, Brian. *Words and Images: Australian Novels into Film.* Richmond, Vic.: Heinemann Publishers Australia in association with Cinema Papers, 1983.

Rice, Cecilia. "David Williamson: Plays into Films." *Cinema Papers* no. 32 (May–June 1981): 122–127.

Turner, Graeme. *National Fictions: Literature, Film and the Construction of Australian Narrative (Australian Cultural Studies).* Sydney: Allen & Unwin, 1986.

Wales, Angela. "Book into Film: Advice for New Players." *Australian Author* 17, no. 1 (March 1985): 7–8.

Scripts

"*Bliss*: The Screenplay." *Metro* no. 71 (Spring 1986): 54–55.

Bowers, Denis. "Wake in Fright." *Metro* no. 51 (Autumn 1980): 54–55.

Carey, Peter, and Ray Lawrence. Bliss–*The Film: Based on the Novel by Peter Carey.* London: Faber and Faber, 1986.

———. Bliss: *The Screenplay.* St. Lucia, Qld.: University of Queensland Press, 1986.

Clancy, Jack. "Bringing Franklin Up-To-Date: The Film of *My Brilliant Career.*" *Australian Literary Studies* 9, no. 3 (May 1980): 363–367.

Dingwall, John. Sunday Too Far Away *(Australian Theatre Workshop series, 18).* Heinemann Educational, Richmond, Vic., 1978.

Drouyn, Carol. *Big Screen, Small Screen: A Practical Guide for Writing for Film and Television in Australia.* St. Leonards, NSW: Allen & Unwin, 1994.

Edwards, Denis. "Get It in Writing." *Quote Unquote* (April 1996).

Gammage, Bill, David Williamson, and Peter Weir. *The Story Of* Gallipoli. Ringwood, Vic.: Penguin, 1981.

Garner, Helen. The Last Days of Chez Nous *and* Two Friends. Ringwood, Vic., McPhee Gribble, 1992.

Green, Cliff. *Four Scripts.* Melbourne: Hyland House, 1978.

———. Picnic at Hanging Rock: *A Film, From the Novel by Joan Lindsay.* Photographs by David Kynoch. Melbourne: Cheshire, 1975.

Hamilton, Peter. "From the Dark Night: Thos. Kenneally on Jimmie Blacksmith." *Metro* no. 44 (Winter 1978): 22–27.

Humphries, Barry, and Bruce Beresford. Barry McKenzie Holds His Own, *an Original Photoplay by Barry Humphries, Written in Collaboration with Bruce Beresford.* Melbourne: Sun Books, 1974.

Lee, Gerard, and Jane Campion. Sweetie: *The Screenplay.* St. Lucia, Qld.: University of Queensland Press, 1991.

McFarlane, Peter, comp. *The Projected Muse: Extracts from Six Australian Film Scripts*. Adelaide: Rigby, 1977.

Mune, Ian. *Big Brother, Little Sister*. Wellington [N.Z.]: Dept. of Education, 1977.

Murray, Les. "*The Sentimental Bloke*: Filming a Poem." *Metro* no. 74/75 (Spring/Summer 1987): 8–15.

Olsen, Christine. Rabbit Proof Fence: *The Screenplay*. Sydney: Currency Press, 2002.

Parker, Dean. "Trying Not to Get Pickled." *Sites* 16 (Autumn 1988).

Wakefield, Philip. "Writing from Lessons." *OnFilm* 7, no. 4 (1990).

White, Patrick. The Night the Prowler: *Short Story and Screenplay*. Ringwood, Vic.: Penguin, 1977 (also Jonathan Cape: London, 1977).

Witcombe, Eleanor. The Getting of Wisdom: *Screenplay from the Novel by Henry Handel Richardson (Australian Theatre Workshop Series, 17)*. Richmond, Vic.: Heinemann Educational, 1978.

Books of the Films

Anobile, J., ed. *The Official* Rocky Horror Picture Show *Movie Novel; Screenplay by Jim Sharman and Richard O'Brien*. New York: A&W Visual Library, c.1980.

Bennett, Jack. *Gallipoli*. Sydney: Angus & Robertson, 1981.

Birtles, Dora. The Overlanders: *The Book of the Film*. Adapted from the Ealing Studios film written and directed by Harry Watt and produced and directed by Michael Balcon. World Film Publications Limited, London, 1946.

Burstall, Tim and Patrick Ryan. *Two Thousand Weeks*. Melbourne: Sun Books, 1968.

Burstall, T., and Gerard Vandenberg. *The Prize*. Based on the film written and directed by Tim Burstall and photographed by Gerard Vandenberg. London: Michael Joseph, 1962.

Chauvel, Charles. *Heritage*. Sydney: Angus & Robertson, 1935.

———. *Uncivilised*. Sydney: N.S.W. Bookstall Co., 1936.

Elliott, Stephan. *The Adventures of Priscilla, Queen of the Desert*. Sydney: Currency Press, 1994.

Ellis, Bob, and Anne Brooksbank. *Mad Dog Morgan*. Blackburn, Vic.: Corgi, 1976.

Green, Cliff. *Break of Day*. Sydney: Hodder & Stoughton, 1976.

Hayes, Terry, George Miller, and Brian Hannant. *Mad Max 1*. Sydney: QB Books, 1985.

———. *Max Max 2*. Cammeray, NSW: Horwitz, 1981.

Heer, Rolf de. *Bad Boy Bubby*. Sydney: Currency Press, 1996.

Hopgood, Alan. *Alvin Purple*. Scripts. Sydney, 1973.

Hume, Marion. "The Long Walk Home: Taken from Her Family, Molly Craig, 14, Walked 1,500 Miles across the Vast Australian Outback to Find Her Mother." *Reader's Digest* 161, no. 963 (2002): 150.

Johnston, Tony. The Man from Snowy River II: *The Story of the Film*. Sydney: William Collins, 1988.

Kaye, Terry, (pseudonym for Terry Hayes). *Mad Max*. Melbourne: Circus Books, 1979.

Lennox, B. *Film and Fiction: Studies of New Zealand Fiction and Film Adaptations*. Auckland: Longman Paul, 1985.

Lindsay, Joan. *Picnic at Hanging Rock*. Melbourne: Cheshire, 1967.

——. *The Secret of Hanging Rock*. North Ryde, NSW: Angus & Robertson, 1987.

Macklin, Robert. *Newsfront*. Melbourne: Sun Books, 1978.

McDonnell, Brian. "The Translation of New Zealand Fiction into Film." Thesis (PhD), University of Auckland, 1986.

Palmer, John. *Yoram Gross Presents Blinky Bill, the Mischievous Koala*. Melbourne: Budget Books Ltd in association with Yoram Gross Film Studios Pty. Ltd., c1992.

Popescu, Petru. *The Last Wave*. Sydney: Angus & Robertson, 1977.

Powers, John. *The Last of the Knucklemen*. Melbourne: Sun Books, 1979.

Ruhen, Carl. *Little Boy Lost*. Cammeray, NSW: Horwitz, 1978.

Shute, Nevil. *A Town Like Alice*. London: William Heinemann, 1950.

Smart, Ralph, and Mary Cathcart Borer. *Bush Christmas*. Melbourne: Pitman, 1947.

Thiele, Colin. *Storm Boy Picture Book*. Adelaide: Rigby, 1977.

Townsend, Helen. Phar Lap: *A Pictorial History*. Adapted from the screenplay by David Williamson; Photography by David Parker. Sydney: Landsdowne, 1983.

Vinge, Joan D. *Mad Max: Beyond Thunderdome*. Sydney: QB Books, 1985.

HISTORY AND FILM

Benson, John, Ken Berryman, and Wayne Levy, eds. "Screening the Past: The Sixth Australian History and Film Conference Papers." Melbourne: Latrobe University Media Centre, 1994.

Churchman, Geoffrey B., ed. *Celluloid Dreams: A Century of Film in New Zealand*. Wellington: IPL Books, 1997.

Clarke McKenna, N. *Angel in God's Office: My Wartime Diaries*. Birkenhead, N.Z.: Tandem Press, 1996.

Cunningham, Stuart. "The Text in Film History." *Australian Journal of Screen Theory* no. 17/18 (1984): 34–48.

Day, P. *The Radio Years: A History of Broadcasting in New Zealand*. Auckland: Auckland University Press, 1994.

Dennis, Jonathan, ed. *The Tin Shed: The Origins of the National Film Unit*. Wellington: The New Zealand Film Archive, 1981.

Doyle, Jeff, Bill van der Heide, and Susan Cowan, eds. "On Our Selection: Writings on Cinema's Histories." The 7th Australian History and Film Conference, 30 Nov.–2 Dec., 1995.

Heung, Marina. "Breaker Morant and the Melodramatic Treatment of History." *Film Criticism* 8, no. 2 (Winter 1984): 3–13.

Hutton, Anne. "Film and History: The Representation of History in Recent Film." Thesis (MA), University of Melbourne, 1982.

———, ed. "Papers of the First Australian History and Film Conference (Canberra, 1982)." North Ryde, NSW: Australian Film and Television School, 1982.

King, M. *New Zealanders at War*. Auckland: Heinemann Reed, 1981.

Lawson, Sylvia. "Towards Decolonization: Film History in Australia." 19–32 in *Nellie Melba, Ginger Meggs and Friends: Essays in Australian Cultural History*, edited by Susan Dermody, John Docker, and Drusilla Modjeska. Malmsbury, Vic.: Kibble Books, 1982.

Levy, Wayne, Graeme Cutts, and Sally Stockbridge, eds. "Papers of the Second Australian History and Film Conference (La Trobe University, 1983)." North Ryde, NSW: Australian Film and Television School, 1984.

Martin, Helen, and Sam Edwards. *New Zealand Film 1912–1996*. Auckland: Oxford University Press, 1997.

Murray, Scott. "A Short History of New Zealand Film: 1977–1994." *Cinema Papers* 97/8 (January 1994). New Zealand Supplement.

Neill, Sam. "Cinema of Unease: A Personal Journey." Documentary film in the series *Celebrating the Moving Image*, edited by Sam Neill and Judy Rymer, 1995.

New Zealand Film Commission. *1987–1988, 48 Feature Films, New Zealand*. Wellington: New Zealand Film Commission, 1987.

O'Regan, Tom and Brian Shoesmith, eds. *History on and/in Film*. Perth: History and Film Association of Australia (WA), 1987.

O'Shea, John. *Don't Let It Get You: Memories–Documents*. Wellington: Victoria University Press, 2001.

Roberts, Hugh. "Standing Upright Here." *New Zealand Books* 5, no. 4 (October 1995).

Ryan, Tom. "Historical films." 112–131 in *The New Australian Cinema*, edited by Scott Murray. Melbourne: Nelson, 1980.

Shepard, Deborah. *Reframing Women: A History of New Zealand Film*. Auckland: HarperCollins, 2001.

——. "Reframing Women: A History of Women and Film in New Zealand." Thesis (PhD), University of Auckland, 1999.

Sowry, Clive. *Film Making in New Zealand: A Brief Historical Survey*. Wellington: New Zealand Film Archive, 1984.

WOMEN AND FILM

Allard, Andrea C. "The Representation of Women in the 1930s: Australian Feature Films of Cinesound Studios." Thesis (MEd), La Trobe University, 1985.

Appleton, Gil. "Image and Reality: Women and Australian Film." Caroline Chisholm Lecture. Bundoora, Vic.: La Trobe University, 1983.

Bailey, Julie James. *Reel Women: Working in Film and Television*. Sydney: Australian Film, Television and Radio School, 1999.

Barton, Christina, and Deborah Lawler–Dormer, eds. *After/Image: Feminism and Representation in New Zealand Art 1973–1993*. Wellington: City Gallery, 1993.

Blonski, Annette, Barbara Creed, and Freda Freiberg, eds. *Don't Shoot Darling! Women's Independent Filmmaking in Australia*. Melbourne: Greenhouse Publications, 1987.

Bruzi, Stella. "Tempestuous Petticoats: Costume and Desire in *The Piano*." *Screen* 36, no. 3, Autumn 1995.

"A Catalogue of Independent Women's Films." Sydney: Sydney Women's Film Group, 1979.

Davis, Susan, Alison Maclean, and Helen Todd. "She Through He: Images of Women in New Zealand Feature Films." *Alternative Cinema* (Summer 1983–1984).

Delamoir, Jeannette. "Louise Lovely, Porno Stars and the AFI Awards." *Australian Screen Education* 25, (2000): 50-54.

——. "Louise Lovely: The Construction of a Star." Thesis (PhD), La Trobe University, 2002.

——. "Marie Bjelke Petersen's 'Virile Story': *Jewelled Nights,* Gender Instability and the Bush." *Hecate* 29, no. 1 (2003): 115–131.

Don't Call Me Girlie. Directed by Stewart Young and Andree Wright. (Motion picture: sd; col with b&w; 69 min.) Sydney: A Double L Films Production, 1985.

Dyson, Linda. "The Return of the Repressed? Whiteness, Femininity and Colonialism in *The Piano*." *Screen* 36, no. 3 (Autumn 1995).

"Films from the Women's Film Fund." Women's Film Fund of the Australian Film Commission, North Sydney, 1984.

Francke, Lizzie. "What Are You Girls Going to Do?" *Sight and Sound* 5, no. 4 (1995): 28.

Goldson, Annie. "Getting the Picture." *Women's Studies Journal* 11, no. 1–2 (August 1995).

Hardy, Ann. "Tales of Ordinary Goodness." *Illusions* 12 (1989).

Harwood, Elizabeth H. "A Brick in a Stocking: Abject Desires in *Heavenly Creatures*." Thesis (MA), University of Auckland, 1995.

Marno, Larissa. "Stubborn Passions: An Interrogation of the Gender Imbalance in the New Zealand Film Industry." Thesis (MA), University of Auckland, 1997.

Marsh, Marion, and Chris Pip, eds. *Women in Australian Film, Video and Television Production*. Sydney: Australian Film Commission and the Australian Film and Television School, 1987.

The Media as a Profession for Women: Problems and Perspectives. Sydney: Australian Film and Television School, 1976.

National SWIFT Directory: Source of Women Working in Film, Television and Video. Surry Hills, NSW: Women in Film and Television, 1992.

Pip, Chris, and Marion Marsh. "Women in Australian Film, Video and Television Production: 1987 Report." Australian Film Commission, North Sydney, 1987.

Robinson, Jocelyn, and Beverley Zalcock. *Girls' Own Stories: Australian and New Zealand Women's Films*. London: Scarlet Press, 1997.

Ryan, Penny, Margaret Eliot, and Gail Appleton. "Women in Australian Film Production." Women's Film Fund of the Australian Film Commission and the Research and Survey Unit, Australian Film and Television School, Sydney, 1983.

Schmidt, Johanna. "Mother, Monster or Mate: The Representation of Women in the Films of Four New Zealand Directors." Thesis (MA), University of Auckland, 1997.

Selected Case Studies of Women Working in the Australian Mass Media, background paper to the Unesco "Women in the Media" seminar and the "Women Media Workers" seminar, North Ryde, NSW: Australian Film and Television School, 1976.

Sheppard, Deborah. *Reframing Women: A History of New Zealand Film*. Auckland: HarperCollins, 2001.

———. "Reframing Women: A History of Women and Film in New Zealand." Thesis (PhD), University of Auckland, 1999.

———. "Writing a Woman Film-maker's Life and Work: A Bio-Filmography of Gaylene Preston." Thesis (MA), University of Auckland, 1992.

Smith, Jane. "Knocked About in New Zealand: Postcolonialism Goes to the Movies." In *Mythologies of Violence in Postmodern Media*, edited by Christopher Sharrett. Detroit: Wayne State University Press, 1999.

Wright, Andre. *Brilliant Careers: Women in Australian Cinema*. Sydney: Pan Books, 1986.

ABORIGINES AND FILM

Bail, Kathy. "Fringe Benefits." *Cinema Papers* no. 58 (July 1986): 14–17.
Barclay, Barry. *Our Own Image*. Auckland: Longman Paul, 1990.
Bickford, Anne. "The Last Tasmanian: Superb Documentary or Racist Fantasy?" *Filmnews* (January 1979): 11–14.
Blythe, Martin. "From Maoriland to Aotearoa: Images of the Maori in New Zealand Film and Television." Thesis (PhD), UCLA, 1988.
———. *Naming the Other: Images of the Maori in New Zealand Film and Television*. Metuchen, NJ: Scarecrow Press, 1994.
Bostock, Lester. "From the Dark Side: Survey of the Portrayal of Aborigines and Torres Strait Islanders on Commercial Television." North Sydney: Australian Broadcasting Authority, 1993.
———. "The Greater Perspective: Guidelines for the Production of Television and Film about Aborigines and Torres Strait Islanders." Sydney: Special Broadcasting Service, 1990.
Boyle, Anthony. "Two Images of the Aboriginal: *Walkabout*—the Novel and the Film." *Literature/Film Quarterly* 7, no. 1 (1979): 67–76.
Brown, Kevin. "Racial Referents: Images of European/Aboriginal Relations in Australian Feature Films, 1955–1984." *Sociological Review* 36, no. 3 (August 1988): 474–502.
Cleave, Peter. "Old New Zealand/New New Zealand: Representation of Pakeha-Maori in *The Piano*." *Illusions* 24 (1995).
Collins, Felicity, and Therese Davis. *Australian Cinema After Mabo*. Sydney: Cambridge University Press, 2004.
Davis, Catherine. "Tainui Stephens—Four Documentaries: The Challenge of Biculturalism." Thesis (MA), University of Auckland, 1997.
Dennis, Jonathan, ed. *Te Maori Film Season. He Pito Whakaatu a Nga Iwi Maori: Films of the Tangata Whenua*. Auckland: New Zealand Film Archive, 1987.
Dennis, Jonathan, and Sergio Toffetti, eds. *Te Ao Marama: Il Mondo Della Luce*. Torino: Le Nuove Muse, 1989.
Donnan, Shawn. "Australian Film Confronts Treatment of Aborigines." *Christian Science Monitor* (2002): 7.
Edwards, Sam. "Cinematic Imperialism and Maori Cultural Identity." *Illusions* 10 (1989).
———. "Docudrama from the Twenties: Rudall Hayward, Whakatane, and the *Te Kooti Trail*." *Whakatane Historical Review* 41, no. 2 (1993).

Eggleton, David. "Grimm Fairytale of the South Seas: *The Piano*." *Illusions* 23 (1994).

Elsaessar, Thomas. "An Anthropologist's Eye: *Where the Green Ants Dream*." 132–156 in *The Films of Werner Herzog: Between Mirage and History*, edited by Timothy Corrigan. New York & London: Methuen, 1986.

Hodge, Bob, and Mishra, Vijay. "Aborigines and Film." 64–70 in *Dark Side of the Stream: Australian Literature and the Postcolonial Mind*, edited by Bob Hodge and Vijay Mishra. Sydney: Allen & Unwin, 1991.

Jennings, Karen. *Sites of Difference: Cinematic Representations of Aboriginality and Gender*. Melbourne: Australian Film Institute, 1993.

———. "Ways of Seeing and Speaking about Aboriginal Women. Part 1: Black Women and Documentary Film." *Hecate* 13, no. 2 (1987–1988): 113–128.

Kael, Pauline. "The Current Cinema: Australians." *New Yorker*, 15 September 1980: 148–158.

Langton, Marcia. "Well I Heard It on the Radio and I Saw It on the Television . . ." an Essay for the Australian Film Commission on the Politics and Aesthetics of Filmmaking by and about Aboriginal People and Things. Sydney: Australian Film Commission, 1993.

Malone, Peter. "In Black and White and Colour: Aborigines in Australian Feature Films—A Survey." Jabiru, N.T.: Nelen Yubu Missiological Unit, 1987.

McDonald, Lawrence. "Film as a Battleground: The Construction of Social Space, Gender Conflict and Other Issues in *Once Were Warriors*." *Illusions* 24 (1995).

Muecke, Stephen. *Textual Spaces: Aboriginality and Cultural Studies*. Sydney: University of New South Wales Press, 1992.

Murphy, Kathleen. "Totems and Taboos: Civilization and Its Discontents According to Lee Tamahori." *Film Comment* (Sept/Oct 1997).

New Zealand Film Archive. *He Pito Whakaatu a Nga Iwi Maori: Films of the Tangata Whenua*. (Catalogue, 1987).

———. *Maori & Pacific Films from New Zealand/Des Films Maoris & Pacifiques de la Nouvelle-Zélande, 1901–1984*.

O'Shea, John. "Ethnographic Films Made on the Maori Minority in New Zealand (a Report to UNESCO, 1966)." in *Don't Let It Get You*, 2001.

Probets, Bryan R. "White Fantasies and Black Dreams: The Representation of Aborigines in Australian Feature Films since 1970." Thesis (BA Honours), Griffith University, 1992.

Turner, Graeme. "Breaking the Frame: The Representation of Aborigines in Australian Film." 135–145 in *Aboriginal Culture Today*, edited by Anna Rutherford. Sydney: Dangaroo Press, 1988.

Turner, Stephen. "Cinema of Justice: The Feathers of Peace." *Illusions* 33 (Autumn 2002).

Samu, Lina-Jodie Vaine. "Framed in Reference: Tangata Whenua Represented in Documentary Film from 1971 to 1983." Thesis (MA), University of Auckland, 1995.

Sklar, Robert. "Social Realism with Style: An Interview with Lee Tamahori." *Cineaste* 21, no. 3 (1995).

Spark, C. "Rethinking Emplacement, Displacement and Indigenity: Radiance, Auntie Rita and *Don't Take Your Love to Town.*" *Journal of Aboriginal Studies* 75 (2002): 95–103.

EXHIBITION AND VIEWING

Exhibition Venues and Practice

Allison, Sheila. "Let's Hear It for the Independents!" *Metro* 74/75 (Spring/Summer 1987): 56.

Bowley, Michelle. "Drive-in Theatres in Western Australia." *Media Information Australia* 47 (February 1988): 12–16.

Brand, Simon. *Picture Palaces and Flea Pits: Eighty Years of Australians at the Pictures*. Sydney: Dreamweaver Books, 1983.

Broatch, Mark. "Moviegoing." *Quote Unquote* (December 1995).

Cork, Kevin J. "An Awkward Site: The Hurlstone Park Theatre" (Cinema Heritage series no. 1). Sydney: K. J. Cork, 1987.

——. "The Flicks: A History of the Cinemas from Parramatta to the Nepean." Seven Hills, NSW: K. J. Cork, 1982.

——. "A History of the Cinemas of Ashfield Municipality" (Cinema Heritage series no. 6). 1986.

——. "A History of the Cinemas of Auburn, Concord and Strathfield Municipalities" (Cinema Heritage series no. 5). Sydney: K. J. Cork, 1986.

——. "A History of the Cinemas of Bankstown City" (Cinema Heritage series no. 4). Sydney: K. J. Cork, 1985.

——. "A History of the Cinemas of the Former Municipality of Granville" (Cinema Heritage series no. 7). Sydney: K. J. Cork, 1987.

——. "A History of the Cinemas of Hurstville Municipality" (Cinema Heritage series no. 1). Endeavour Printing, 1985.

Hayward, B.W., and S.P. Hayward. *Cinemas of Auckland: 1896–1979*. Auckland: Auckland Lodestar Press, 1979.

Ingham, G. *Everyone's Gone to the Movies: The Sixty Cinemas of Auckland . . . And Some Others*. Auckland: Cyclostyle, 1973.

Jenkin, Shelley. "Multiplexes in New Zealand." Research project (B Prop), University of Auckland, 1993.

Knewstubb Theatres. *CINEMAS: Dunedin and Districts*. Dunedin: c1974.

Lascelles, David. *Eighty Turbulent Years: The Paramount Theatre Wellington 1917–1997*. Wellington: Millwood Press, 1997.

Mann, Maria. *Reflections of the Sun: A Short History of the Sun Pictures Gardens: For the People of Broome Past and Present*. Broome, WA: Sun Pictures, 1991.

McGill, David. *Full Circle: The History of the St. James Theatre*. Wellington: Phantom House, 1998.

Richardson, John. "Movies Under the Stars: Drive-ins and Modernity." *Continuum: An Australian Journal of the Media* 1, no. 1 (1987): 111–115.

Smith, V. S. "Moving Pictures in Bygone Days." *Kino* (Australian Theatre Historical Society) 15 (March 1986): 14–18.

Thorne, Ross. *Cinemas of Australia Via USA*. Sydney: University of Sydney, 1981.

Theater Architecture and Decoration

Anderson, Judith. *Australian Posters 1906–1960*. Sydney: Currency Press, 1978.

Bartlett, P.J. "His Majesty's Theatre and Arcade." Auckland: University of Auckland, School of Architecture, 1980.

Bell, Max D. *Perth: A Cinema History*. Lewes, Sussex: The Book Guild Limited, 1986.

Brand, Simon. *Picture Palaces and Flea-Pits: Eighty Years of Australians at the Pictures*. Sydney: Dreamweaver Books, 1983.

Cardone, Maria. "A Study of Picture Interiors." Thesis (BA), South Australian Institute of Technology, 1984.

Cochran, Christoper. "St. James Theatre, Courtenay Place, Wellington: Cultural Heritage Assessment." New Zealand Historic Places Trust/Pouhere Taonga [Wellington]: The Trust, [1993]

Collins, Diane. "The 1920s Picture Palace." 60–75 in *Nellie Melba, Ginger Meggs and Friends: Essays in Australian Cultural History*, edited by Susan Dermody, John Docker, and Drusilla Modjeska. Malmsbury, Vic.: Kibble Books, 1982.

Geneve, Vyonne. "Deco: Early 20th Century Preservation in America: Comparisons with Western Australia." *The Architect* (Perth) 28, no. 1 (Autumn 1988): 30–32.

———. "William Leighton, Architect." *Kino* (Australian Theatre Historical Society) no. 25 (September 1988): 5–17.

Griggs, Ian C. *Arcadia, the Story of Sydney's Ace Suburban Theatre, 1915–1961*. Willoughby, NSW: Mockridge, Bulmer Pty. Ltd., under the auspices of Willoughby Municipal Council, 1971.

Middleton, P., and E. Bjelke-Petersen. "The Picture Palace: With Particular Reference to the Conservation of One of the Remaining Few—'The State,' Sydney." Thesis (BArch), University of Sydney, 1974.

Sharp, Barry. "A Pictorial History of Cinemas in New South Wales" (Showcases of the Past, vol. 2). Strawberry Hills, NSW: B. Sharp, 1983.

——. "A Pictorial History of Sydney's Prince Edward, Theatre Beautiful" (Showcases of the Past, vol. 3). Strawberry Hills, NSW: B Sharp, 1984.

Thorne, Ross. *Picture Palace Architecture in Australia and New Zealand.* Melbourne: Sun Books, 1976.

——. *Theatre Buildings in Australia to 1905: From the Time of the First Settlement to the Arrival of Cinema.* 2 vols. Architectural Research Foundation, University of Sydney, 1979.

Tod, Les. "Australian Cinemas." *Historic Environment* 6, no. 1, 1987: 28–32.

——. "Researching Theatre History." *Kino* (Australian Theatre Historical Society) 7 (March 1984): 18–19.

Zwartz, Sally. "Making of The Mighty Civic." *OnFilm* 5, no. 6 (1988).

Social Aspects of Viewing

Adams, Phillip. "A Cultural Revolution." In *Australian Cinema*, edited by Scott Murray. St. Leonards, NSW: Allen & Unwin in association with Australian Film Commission, 1994.

——. "Horror of Horrors—We're at the Violent Vanguard." *Bulletin* 100, 25 September 1979: 56.

The Best Remaining Seats. [Video recording; sd; col; 30mins]. Filmstruck series, Part 9. Writer/Presenter: John Baxter; Director: Ivor Bowen. Sydney, Kookaburra Productions for Mediacast, 1986.

Blythe, Martin. *Naming the Other: Images of the Maori in New Zealand Film and Television.* Metuchen, NJ: Scarecrow Press, 1994.

Broatch, Mark. "Moviegoing." *Quote Unquote* (December 1995).

Campbell, Russell. "Dismembering the Kiwi Bloke: Representation of Masculinity in *Braindead, Desperate Remedies* and *The Piano*." *Illusions* 24 (1995).

——. "Smith & Co.: The Cinematic Redefinition of Pakeha Male Identity." *Illusions* 7 (1988).

Edwards, Sam. "Cinematic Imperialism and Maori Cultural Identity." *Illusions* 10 (1989).

Hardy, Ann. "Tales of Ordinary Goodness." *Illusions* 12 (1989).

Menary, Bill. "The Moving Image: Australian Cinema and Society." Adelaide: English Department, Adelaide College of the Arts and Education, 1979.

Neill, Sam. "Cinema of Unease: A Personal Journey." Documentary film in the series *Celebrating the Moving Image*, edited by Sam Neill and Judy Rymer, 1995.

Norgrove, Aaron. "But Is It Music? The Crisis of Identity in *The Piano*." *Race & Class* 40, no. 1 (1998).

Samu, Lina-Jodie Vaine. "Framed in Reference: Tangata Whenua Represented in Documentary Film from 1971 to 1983." Thesis (MA), University of Auckland, 1995.

Seton, Jo. "We're Taking This Car to Invercargill or The Male Must Get Through." *Alternative Cinema* (Summer 1983–1984).

Sklar, Robert. "Social Realism with Style: An Interview with Lee Tamahori." *Cineaste* 21, no. 3 (1995).

Watson, Chris. "Sex, Angst and Deviance: Adolescent Film — A Genre — and New Zealand." *Illusions* 13 (1990).

ANNUAL REPORTS OF KEY FILM ORGANIZATIONS

Annual Report (Australian Film and Television School). [Canberra, Australian Government Publishing Service], 1975–1976 to 1984–1985.

Annual Report (Australian Film Commission). Canberra, Australian Government Publishing Service, 1975/1976–.

Annual Report (Australian Film Finance Corporation). [North Sydney], 1988/1989–.

Annual Review (National Film and Sound Archive (Australia)). Canberra, Australian Government Publishing Service, 1988–1989.

"Financial Statements for year ended December 31 . . ." (Australian Film Institute and AFI Distribution Limited). Melbourne, The Institute, 1988–.

New Zealand Film Commission. "Focus on expansion: New Zealand Film and Television Conference 1992." Wellington: *OnFilm*, 1992

———. *1987–1988, 48 feature films, New Zealand*. Wellington: New Zealand Film Commission, 1987.

Report on Activities (Office of Film and Literature Classification and Films Board of Review). Canberra, Australian Government Publishing Service, 1988–1989.

FILM PERIODICALS

Alternative Cinema Magazine.

Australasian Cinema: Forum of the Motion Picture Industry of Australia 1, no. 1 (November 1972) — 14, no. 12 (July/August 1985).

Australasian Exhibitor. 15 September 1938–October 1972.

Australian Film Review. Sydney, 1, no. 1 (February 17–March 2, 1983) 2, no. 8 (June 7–June 20, 1984).

Australian Journal of Screen Theory, Sydney, 1976–1985.

Cantrill's Filmnotes. Melbourne, 1971–.

Cinema Papers. Melbourne, 24 October 1969–13 April 1970; January 1974–January 2004.

Cinema Papers: History of Filmmaking in New Zealand 1970–1994. 20th Anniversary Issue 97–98 (April 1994).

Continuum: An Australian Journal of the Media. Perth, Department of Media Studies, WACAE, 1987–.

Film Archive Newsletter. New Zealand Film Archive, Wellington.

Film Weekly. Sydney, 2 September 1926–February 1973.

Filmnews, Sydney Filmmakers Co-op, 1970–.

Filmviews, Federation of Victorian Film Societies, 1980–.

Illusions. Wellington: Illusions Co-operative: Drama Studies, Victoria University of Wellington], 1986–.

Lumiere, Melbourne, June 1971–May/June 1974.

Media Information Australia. Sydney, 1976–.

Metro. Melbourne, Association of Teachers of Media, 1974–.

National Film & Sound Archive Newsletter. Canberra, ACT, No. 1, December 1984–.

Newsletter (Australian Commonwealth Film Unit). Lindfield, NSW, 1, no. 1 (January 1968) 4, no. 2 (April 1973). (Continued by Newsletter (Film Australia)).

Newsletter (Film Australia), Lindfield, NSW, 4, no. 3 (June 1973–).

New Zealand Film, New Zealand Film Commission Journal.

New Zealand Journal of Media Studies, Massey University, Palmerston North.

Onfilm.

Photoplayer. Sydney, 1923.

Real to Reel: The Film Australia Newsletter. March 1987–SCJ, *Sydney Cinemajournal*, no. 1 (Autumn 1966) – no. 4 (1968).

Show Business. Sydney, no. 1–21 (1973).

WEBSITES

Academy of Film and Television Arts of New Zealand: http://www.lonely.geek.nz/nzawardsindex.html

Australian Centre for the Moving Image: www.acmi.net.au

Australian Centre for the Moving Image Lending Collection: www.acmi.net.au/lending.htm

Australian Children's Television Foundation: www.actf.com.au
Australian Film Commission: www.afc.gov.au/
Australian Film Institute: www.afi.org.au
Australian Film in the Reading Room: wwwmcc.murdoch.edu.au/Reading
  Room/film/OzFilm.html
Australian Film Television and Radio School: www.aftrs.edu.au
Australia Now—Film in Australia: www.dfat.gov.au/facts/film_australia.html
Australian Screen Directors Association: www.asdafilm.org.au
Australian Writers' Guild: www.awg.com.au
Continuum: wwwmcc.murdoch.edu.au/ReadingRoom/continuum2.html
Enhance: www.enhancetv.com.au
Film Australia: www.filmaust.com.au
Film Finance Corporation of Australia: www.ffc.gov.au
Film New Zealand: www.filmnz.com/home/index.html
Film South New Zealand: www.filmsouth.com
Film Victoria: www.film.vic.gov.au
Fox Studios: www.foxstudios.com.au
Greater Union Birch Carroll & Coyle: www.greaterunion.com.au
Hoyts Theater Chain: hoyts.ninemsn.com.au
Inside Film: www.if.com.au
Internet Movie Database: www.imdb.com
Movie Express: http://worldfilm.about.com/gi/dynamic/offsitehtm?site=http
  %3A%2F%2Fmoviexpress.tripod.com%2Findex.htm
New South Wales Film and Television Office: www.ftosyd.nsw.gov.au/about.asp
New Zealand Film: www.zeroland.co.nz/new_zealand_film.html
New Zealand Film Archive: www.filmarchive.org.nz
New Zealand Film Commission: www.nzfilm.co.nz
New Zealand International Film Festivals: www.enzedff.co.nz
New Zealand Television Archive: www.nztvarchive.co.nz
Office of Film and Literature Classification (Australia): www.oflc.gov.au/
  splash.html
Office of Film and Literature Classification (New Zealand): www.censorship
  .govt.nz
Pacific Film and Television Commission: www.pftc.com.au
Screen Directors Guild of New Zealand: www.sdgnz.co.nz
Screening the Past: www.latrobe.edu.au/screeningthepast
Screen Producers Association of Australia: www.spaa.org.au
Screenrights: www.screen.org
Screensound Australia—National Screen and Sound Archive: www.screensound
  .gov.au/screensound/screenso.nsf
Screen Tasmania: www.screen.tas.gov.au

Senses of Cinema: www.sensesofcinema.com
South Australian Film Corporation: www.safilm.com.au
Urban Cinefile: www.urbancinefile.com.au
Warner Bros. Movie World—Gold Coast: www.movieworld.com.au/home/homepage.cfm
Western Australia Film and Television Corporation: www.screenwest.com.au

About the Authors

Errol Vieth was born in Brisbane, Australia. He obtained his BA from the University of Queensland and various education degrees from Flinders University (DipEd), Queensland University of Technology (GradDipMulticultEd) and Deakin University (MEd). He then changed his discipline area and completed a PhD in film at Griffith University in Brisbane, Queensland. He has taught in public and private secondary schools in Victoria, South Australia, and Queensland and in the Friedrich Harkort Gymnasium in Herdecke, Germany. Journal articles from the time attest to his interest in language and semiotics, an interest he carried into his university career. In 1989, he was appointed to Central Queensland University, where he has taught film and communication, and is currently associate dean for research in the Faculty of Informatics and Communication. His first book, *Screening Science: Contexts, Texts and Science in Fifties Science Fiction Films,* was published by Scarecrow Press in 2001. He is writing another historical dictionary for Scarecrow Press on science fiction cinema.

Albert Moran was born in Ireland and completed high school and university in Sydney, Australia. He has a master's from the University of Sydney and a bachelor of education in media studies from La Trobe University in Melbourne. His PhD was gained at Griffith University in Brisbane, Australia. He has held an appointment at Murdoch University and is now senior lecturer at Griffith. Visiting appointments have been held at Macquarie University in Sydney and Queens University in Canada. Australian film and television (as well as media in other places) constitute his principal areas of research interest. He has published extensively on these including over a dozen books as well as numerous book chapters and refereed journal articles. Among his recent publications are *Film Policy: International, National and Regional Levels*

(Routledge, 1995), *Copycat TV: Globalisation, Program Formats and Cultural Identity* (University of Luton Press), and *Television across Asia: Television Industries, Globalisation and Format Flow* (Curzon). Currently, he is completing another historical dictionary for Scarecrow Press concerning radio and television in Australia and, with Errol Vieth, a book on Australian film genres for Cambridge University Press.